# THE AMERICAN UNIVERSITY

# THE AMERICAN UNIVERSITY

TALCOTT PARSONS AND GERALD M. PLATT

with the collaboration of Neil J. Smelser
Editorial Associate: Jackson Toby

Harvard University Press   Cambridge, Massachusetts   1973

# PREFACE

In the fall of 1969 Martin Meyerson and Stephen Graubard asked me to undertake a monographic study of the American university system. Meyerson was the chairman of the Assembly on University Goals and Governance, which had been recently established by the American Academy of Arts and Sciences; Graubard was its Director of Research. My monograph was to be a part of the work of the Assembly. Though it was understood that I would concentrate on the American university, Meyerson and Graubard left it entirely up to me as to what kind of study I would undertake.

This was to me a highly congenial proposal. I had decided some years previously to devote special attention to the sociology of higher education and was at the time engaged, in collaboration with Gerald Platt, in a rather large study, by the method of sample survey, of members of American college and university faculties. From the knowledge we had already gained about the American academic world, the highly strategic role in it of the "full" universities of relatively high academic prestige had become clear. It was natural immediately to enlist Platt's collaboration and in consultation together and with our sponsors, we decided to center our monograph on this sector of the larger system of higher education and to treat it by a kind of "ideal type" method. The present book is the result.

For Platt and myself this work has constituted a long detour, delaying as it has the completion of our empirical study of faculty members. We have, however, continually drawn on the experience gained from that study, and now that we can turn to its completion, it should in turn be substantially enriched by our work on the present book.

The Assembly was also interested in securing the collaboration of Neil Smelser in its work in some form. This suggestion especially interested me because of my high regard for and long association with Smelser. After considerable consultation among us, Smelser decided that he would like to put his major effort into an independent study of the State of California's system of public higher education which was sponsored both by the Academy's Western

Center and by the Assembly. Smelser, however, agreed to undertake a limited collaboration in our enterprise as well. This took the principal form of his serving as a kind of "house critic" of our enterprise. Pursuant to this agreement we have sent him draft manuscripts, chapter by chapter, and he has responded by writing extensive critical commentaries, leaving it to Platt and myself what use we would make of them. They add up to a small volume in themselves and have been invaluable to us, having been extensively taken into account in our revisions. After considerable experience with this arrangement, however, the three of us agreed that the most appropriate form for Smelser's "visible" contribution to this book should be a wholly independent chapter. This is included as Chapter 9, the Epilogue. It might be noted that Platt and I reciprocated Smelser's critical services to us by giving him rather extensive critical comments on his first draft of the Epilogue.

We conceive this to be, at the same time, *both* an empirical *and* a theoretical work. We have presented and discussed a great deal of factual information about the type of American university which is our object of study, about its setting in the larger system of higher education and its place in the society as a whole. But, more than that, I had long decided that higher education, including the research complex, had become the most critical single feature of the developing structure of modern societies. It was indeed this conviction which led me in the first place into intensive concern with its study. From this point of view the book can be understood, not only as a monographic study of a particular organizational phenomenon in American society but as a contribution to the understanding of the modern world in a larger sense.

As a theoretical study it is a study in "sociology" but by no means only that. If, by a sociological study, without further subtleties, we mean one concentrated on the analysis of a social system or type of such system, the essential point is that we have come to realize with steadily increasing clarity that, certainly for this subject matter, the social system cannot be treated in isolation, but must be fitted, in complex and intricate ways, into what, in our technical terminology, we call the general system of action. In that setting the most critical "nonsocial" reference has been that of the *cultural* system, relative to which the "cognitive complex," which is so central a theoretical reference point of the study, must in the first instance be understood.

After the experience of writing this book we agree all the more with Edward Shils's statement that "the growth of knowledge is a disorderly movement."* For those who are skeptical of this view we suggest comparison of the formal analytical framework articulating the theory of the social system with that of the general system of action, on the one hand as presented in the relevant parts of the present volume, especially Chapter 2 and the Technical Appendix and, on the other hand, as presented in the article "Some Problems of General Theory in Sociology,"† which was written in the summer of 1969. The differences, which we believe to constitute a process of theoretical advance, could not have developed without detailed, problem-for-problem, and topic-for-topic confrontation with the *empirical* features, structures, conflicts, and dynamic processes of universities. This theoretical advance, if it is to be judged to be such, is by no means the product of neatly logical deductive procedures in isolation from empirical considerations.

Especially since there has been so much concern over the years with the difficulty of simply reading my work intelligibly, especially on more abstractly theoretical themes, we owe an enormous debt to Professor Jackson Toby of Rutgers University who has undertaken a thoroughgoing and meticulous editing of the whole manuscript in the interest of readability, clarity, and stylistic improvement. We are happy to name him as our "Editorial Associate."

Another important debt is owed to Mrs. Rachel Javetz who, in her more general capacity as my research assistant, has performed many services in accomplishing this work. Specifically, she has handled the whole problem of footnote referencing and a large share of the working out of diagrams. Most important, perhaps, she has been a highly intelligent participant in the discussion of many substantive problems. Finally, my secretary for the most decisive final period of the gestation of this book, Mrs. Peggy Polinsky, has performed heroic services in processing manuscripts and maintaining communications among the members of the team (Platt, Smelser, Toby, Javetz, and myself). She has earned our eternal gratitude.

The study has been conducted under the auspices of the Assembly

* Edward Shils, "Primordial, Personal, Sacred and Civil Ties," *Selected Essays by Edward Shils* (Chicago, Ill., Center for Social Organization Studies, Department of Sociology, University of Chicago Press, 1970), p. 51.

† Talcott Parsons, "Some Problems of General Theory in Sociology," *Theoretical Sociology: Perspectives and Developments*, ed. John C. McKinney and Edward A. Tiryakian (New York, Appleton-Century-Crofts, 1970).

on University Goals and Governance, a project of the American Academy of Arts and Sciences.

The research project on Faculty Roles referred to above, which has been so helpful to both Platt and myself in the present book, has been supported by the National Science Foundation (grants GS1479 and GS2425). We are very grateful for this help.

Talcott Parsons

Cambridge, Massachusetts
June 1972

# CONTENTS

# FIGURES

# FIGURES

# THE AMERICAN UNIVERSITY

# 1

## INTRODUCTION

This book is conceived not as a broad survey of the American academic system but as a specialized analysis of certain aspects of it. Such a conception necessitates concentrating attention on one sector of a diverse system. It is ultimately motivated by concern with trends of development in Western society and of the place of higher education in it.

What is thought of as *modern* society took shape in the seventeenth century in the northwest corner of the European system of societies, in Great Britain, Holland, and France. The subsequent development of modern society included three processes of revolutionary structural change: the Industrial Revolution, the Democratic Revolution, and the Educational Revolution. The three did not uniformly involve concomitant political violence.

These three revolutions have had features in common. Although they have all been fraught with tension, they have on balance advanced the level of the human condition as their impact has been diffused. To use a currently unfashionable term, they brought about "progressive" changes in an evolutionary sense. For both society and the individual, they contributed to freedoms from previously constricting limitations and to opportunities for previously impossible achievements. This occurred within a framework of *institutionalized individualism*. Institutionalized individualism means a mode of organization of the components of human action which, on balance, enhanced the capacity of the average individual and of collectivities to which he belongs to implement the values to which he and they are committed. This enhanced capacity at the individual level has developed concomitantly with that of social and cultural frameworks of organization and institutional norms, which form the framework of order for the realization of individual and collective unit goals and values. This institutional order is possible only if there is some consensus on the relevant

1

values and the basic patterns of cultural orientation with which these are associated.

*The Industrial Revolution.* The industrial revolution alleviated the constrictions of human welfare traditionally associated with the conception of "want." Thus the recent salience of the problem of poverty is an indication of the new faith that mass poverty is no longer necessary. One meaning of economic progress is the increase of generalized material facilities available for a broad range of uses. There is concern currently with the costs involved in the comparative affluence that has been achieved: such costs as the acceptance of labor and other organizational discipline, the development of technologies which can be put to destructive uses, pollution of the environment which is difficult to reverse, and some aspects of what is vaguely called "alienation." Nevertheless, few seriously advocate return to the level of the relatively primitive agrarian economy which prevailed prior to the last two centuries. Among the consequences would have to be a drastic reduction of population and indeed of life expectancy.

*The Democratic Revolution.* The democratic revolution has reduced coercive control over human individuals and subcollectivities by other human agencies, notably by governments. It placed authority more fully under the control of those who must act under it, especially the authority of those in elective office. Limitations exist on the effectiveness of these new freedoms, but on balance greater freedom has been gained. Bear in mind, though, that these democratic developments depend on facilitating circumstances, such as a regime of institutionalized law. It is difficult to realize that developments which have restricted previously arbitrary power have also led to an increase of the power potential of systems of collective action. For example, the freedom of economic enterprise means greater scope for organized entrepreneurship, including relatively modest firms. And the effectiveness with which democratic governments are capable of conducting destructive wars is evidence for their increased effectiveness in mobilizing larger resources, in maintaining a political order over large populations and territories, and in other spheres. For this reason, even totalitarian dictatorships have sought mass popular support; they have not been content to rely on the "divine right" of the dictators to rule. Perhaps it is not an accident that the Communist regimes call themselves *Peoples'* Democracies. Such considerations suggest that the average individual has greater political freedom than before (including freedom within nongovernmental associational contexts) and that concurrently capacity for effective collective action within modern societies has been enhanced. This means also enhanced collective freedom to implement values. Despite the instabilities and frustrations that the democratic revolution has entailed, few would advocate returning, if that were possible, to the political absolutism of the seventeenth and early eighteenth centuries in Europe or to feudal conditions.

*The Educational Revolution.* We must describe the educational revolution more fully. It has reduced ignorance and developed the capacity both of individuals and of societies to utilize knowledge in the interest of human goals and value-implementation. At the cultural level, knowledge is parallel to economic resources at the level of societal organization. Knowledge enhances capacity for *rational* action. Despite current preoccupation with the costs of these advances, such as the alleged damage to the nonrational or expressive aspects of human concern, we shall contend that the net impact of the educational revolution is constructive. The modern university, especially in its American version, is the current culmination of the educational revolution. It has become the lead component of an extensive process of change permeating modern society at many levels. Because of this lead status of the university, we have elected to concentrate on it.

Education, in the sense of institutional formalization of learning processes, may be regarded in terms of quantitative extension in populations and of levels of qualitative attainment within its relevant spheres. On the quantitative side, universalization of formal education for the masses has been achieved, at least to the point of general literacy. Before the nineteenth century, this had hardly been advocated, much less attempted, for the population as a whole. It had existed for small groups such as the male citizens of the leading Greek poleis, certain Diaspora Jewish groups, and certain religious sectarian groups, such as Protestants especially oriented to the Bible. The innovation was the policy of mass universal education for large societies This development, originating in Western Europe and North America, occurred in conjunction with the institutionalization of citizenship through the democratic revolution.

Once the process started, it spread to larger proportions of age cohorts. Moreover, upgrading of levels of educational attainment occurred so that increasing proportions of a cohort advanced to high levels of accomplishment, measured, for example, by years of formal schooling. In the United States, universal elementary education was largely realized by the turn of the twentieth century, and a marked increase in the proportions beginning secondary education was under way. This trend continued during the first third of the century. By the 1930's the universalization of secondary education, measured by completion of high school, was approximated. The next third of the century, especially the period immediately following the end of World War II, saw a swift upsurge in participation in the system of *higher* education. By the later 1960's, the proportion of the age cohort going on from high school graduation to some kind of higher education was more than 50 percent, a situation historically unprecedented.

Current discussion of the universalizing of *higher* education, the next logical step, leaves open the question of precise level to be sought. Most often advocated is the universalization of the four-year undergraduate college program. Minimal though this would seem from the point of view of graduate and professional levels, nothing like it has previously been dreamed of for mass populations. Note that the process of educational upgrading has not developed evenly for all population groups. Some groups surged ahead and others lagged behind. This has been especially characteristic of the United States with its local control of public school systems and its pattern of private and parochial schools. At the college level, the American system has been more diversified, with a large number of private colleges of many different types and quality, many originally founded under religious auspices.[1] American public institutions have been rapidly growing, although not at the federal level. State universities and colleges began first; more recently municipal institutions developed; and most recently community junior colleges. Higher education in the United States has never resembled the French system in which a central ministry administers for the entire country.

*The Development of the University System.* At the beginning of the Civil War there was no such thing as an American university in the European sense; there were only colleges, a large number of them. Shortly after the war, an innovative process began. This process centered in private institutions, first with development toward university status of existing private colleges

1. Everett C. Hughes, *The Sociological Eye: Selected Papers* (Chicago and New York, Aldine-Atherton, 1971), chaps. iv and v, pp. 29–51.

like Columbia and Harvard and, a little later, Yale and Princeton. Then new private universities were established: The Johns Hopkins, Cornell, and Clark, and later the University of Chicago and Stanford. A few state universities also emerged: Michigan, Wisconsin, and California at Berkeley. In this process, the undergraduate college was not superseded but incorporated. Indeed, among colleges that developed into universities, a correlation existed between level of success and continuity with their older traditions, as Columbia, Yale, and Harvard illustrated. One factor in the failure of The Johns Hopkins and Clark to maintain their early promise may have been their inability to upgrade their undergraduate colleges to the same degree as their graduate and professional schools.

The distinctive contribution of the American development compared with, say, German universities was graduate schools of arts and sciences and, within such schools and undergraduate colleges, the establishment of departments rather than "chairs." The undergraduate colleges have remained the channel through which the company of educated men and women necessarily passed in the acquisition of a general education and were complemented (for those being more highly trained) by graduate study in schools of arts and sciences and in professional schools. As *graduate* schools of arts and sciences grew more closely integrated into the university, both the relative quantity and the prestige of *undergraduate* professional training, for example, in engineering, declined. Concomitantly, professionalization of the research function developed rapidly, with contributions to the advancement of knowledge becoming an expectation for the higher prestige levels of academic faculties. The graduate schools supported this expectation because their functions came to be conceived not only as equipping their students with current knowledge but also with capacity for contributing to its advancement, including command of the procedures for making such contributions.

An intriguing analogy can be drawn between the educational and industrial revolutions: the distinct functions that developed within the system of higher education are somewhat comparable to distinct industries. At least four such industries (or functions) comprise the higher education complex. One is the general education industry, which formed the base line from which the others have differentiated. A second is the research industry, which is concerned with enhancing the cognitive capacity of society through adding to the cultural base on which it operates. A third is graduate training of the personnel who will be the successors of current academicians. A fourth industry is training in capacity to apply knowledge to areas where members of the society encounter practical problems, the handling of which can be improved by the use of expert competence grounded in systematic knowledge. The professions of medicine and law are the prototypes of this function; they are taught in special schools for the training of practitioners in the applied professions.

Another function which has not become so formally institutionalized in organizational divisions of the university system is that of contributing to the general cultural definition of the situation as distinguished from more particularized knowledge either in one of the intellectual disciplines or in knowledge relevant to applied practical problems. Cultural definition has historically been performed by the theological faculties of universities, which were not only training schools for the clergy but also centers of intellectual probing into problems of religious orientation. In the more secularized university system of today, this function is more ideological than religious. Some continuity exists between philosophical concerns of members of the university who operate at high levels of generality in discussing the human condition and intellectuals outside the university who are more explicitly ideological. The respects in which academic competence can contribute to the definition of these orientation problems and the nature of the balances between these cognitive contributions and other relevant components remain problematical.

In all these respects, the university has spearheaded the educational revolution, perhaps in ways comparable to those in which highly efficient firms spearheaded the mature phases of the industrial revolution. One feature of the process has been differentiation of the primary function from others (academic functions from generalized social-status complexes) as well as differentiation within the new sector in levels of attainment under the relevant subvalues. Thus the new university is no longer identified with a diffuse upper class, as were the elite institutions in this country, or Oxford and Cambridge in England, or the *grandes Écoles* in France.

*The Rise of the Professions.* What has emerged in place of quasi-aristocratic elitism is professionalism. Intellectual command of the requisite cultural components through training rather than status independent of exposure to such training has become the criterion of membership in academic communities. Not considerations of ascribed status but individual achievement in meeting standards of universalistically defined qualification have guided selection. *Competence* in some intellectual subject matter has become the ticket of admission to faculty membership and to the opportunity for research. Furthermore, for those who do not aspire to professional status in these senses, the criteria of successful study of cognitive culture are couched in terms of the same set of standards.[2] Professionalism is currently a subject of controversy. One view holds that it is an evil which must be extirpated if the academic system is to regain its health. We will discuss this problem at some length. For the present we wish only to point out the trend of professional development in the universities, our special concern.

Professionalism, which has advanced farthest in the lead sector of the academic system, the universities, is central to the general educational analysis of the present volume. In carrying out this analysis, we must pay attention to the internal complexity of American universities. We must bear in mind their interdependence with the rest of the academic system. Finally, we must relate the academic system to the nonacademic sectors of the society as a whole as well as particular parts of it: the political system, the economy, and aspects of the class system and of the societal community.[3]

2. Parallel statements can be made for other contexts. In the industrial field, despite the specific role still played by property rights in private enterprise or by political considerations in socialized enterprises, managerial competence plays a paramount role in the conduct of productive organizations. In the case of political organization, the situation is less clear, although it is common to speak of skill as a politician independent of prestigeful status in other respects.

3. We were aware of these facts about the special importance of universities in the educational revolution before the wave of campus crises emphasized the existence of basic problems in the academic system. The Berkeley disturbance of 1964 was considered an isolated campus aberration until the crescendo of confrontations in 1967–1969, especially the crisis at Columbia. Nonetheless, we did not anticipate such serious disturbances as in fact occurred. Such obliviousness might be interpreted as incapacity to undertake the present study, although we were certainly not alone in underestimating the disruptive potentialities of the underlying forces. Events of the past six or seven years have forced us to reassess these forces: the institutional structure of the academic system, as well as sources of conflict and instability, both internal to universities and in relation to other sectors of the society. The problem of stability-instability will be more fully discussed in Chapter 7, but this perspective permeates the study as a whole. It is hoped that this is a better book than it would have been had it gone to press in 1964, partly because it has sought to understand the crises of the academic system, partly because an analysis of structural base lines and of the pattern of development relatively independent of the crises may prove to be advantageous. A study focused on dramatic events without a solid background orientation acquired independently of the impact of those events is likely to suffer from the myopia dictated by preoccupation with the events themselves.

*Action Systems: Cultural Systems, Social Systems,*
*Personalities, and Behavioral Organisms*

The study will attempt to be accurate with respect to relevant matters of fact, but it will also select facts by the use of a complicated theoretical scheme. The present section will present an outline of the scheme. One task is to analyze relations among the subsystems of the cultural tradition of central concern here, the cognitive complex, and the fiduciary subsystem of the society.[4] In addition, it will be necessary to deal with the individual personality, especially in considering socialization. We shall treat both of these issues in the framework of the general theory of action. "Action" (in our conception) means human behavior insofar as it is symbolically oriented. Symbolic systems are organized in terms of codes similar to linguistic codes in that they constitute sets of norms regulating processes of communication. Action within the code can be diverse in the same sense that using a particular language does not commit a speaker to saying specific things, but enables him to adapt the content of his communications through linguistic utterance to a variety of exigencies and intentions. The concept of action assumes a linguistic level of symbolization, of codification of meanings. It assumes also that attempts to analyze the ordering of behavior must take into account the nature of systems of action and their component parts, the nature of their environments and their component parts, and the relation of systems and environments to each other.

Action is a kind of behavior, and behavior necessarily implies the existence of a living organism as the behaving entity. It follows therefore that action systems contain a plurality of living human organisms. When, however, behavior is oriented and given meaning in symbolic terms, there exists also a *cultural* system. Culture consists in codified systems of meaningful symbols and those aspects of action directly oriented to problems of the meaningfulness of such symbols. Thus, culture includes belief systems, sets of propositions of cognitive significance as well as expressive symbols, and the codes giving them meaning.

Analysis of behavior which has attained the action level must

---

4. The fiduciary subsystem of a society acts as a trustee of some interests in the society. E.g., conservation groups belong to the fiduciary subsystem insofar as they protect the societal interest in the natural environment. We shall be dealing in this volume with that portion of the fiduciary subsystem concerned with trusteeship of the cognitive cultural tradition.

have a dual reference: to the living organism behaving in its environments and to cultural meaning-systems. The articulation of these two ultimate reference points with each other necessitates the identification of two further action systems: social systems and personalities. Cultural systems are organized about meaning-complexes abstractable from particular acting units, individual or collective. Thus classical Greek culture persists many centuries after classical Greek society has ceased to exist. A cultural system of any considerable complexity is typically attached to several interactive systems, say, two or more societies. A social system always involves a plurality of concrete living human beings interacting with each other. Aspects of their interaction may, however, be analyzed for particular purposes without dealing with the constituent human organisms in their full concreteness. A social system is thus a special category of action system analytically distinguishable from the cultural systems of which it is the bearer and which order the interaction processes which occur in it.

A distinction should also be made between the individual personality and the social system, although we must guard against the ancient fallacy that every social system is composed of concrete individuals. In any particular interaction system only a part of the participating personality comes to be engaged. The concept of membership makes the proper distinction. As member of a given family, one is involved in certain interactions with other family members, but the same person may be a member of a number of other interaction systems, for example, the organization in which he is employed, that have little to do with his family roles. Another distinction is that between the aspect of the total living organism engaged in nonsymbolic behavior like breathing and the psychological aspect of the individual organism, the personality. This distinction hinges on the organic side on hereditary aspects of the organism, its anatomical structures, and patterns of physiological process, and on the psychological side on those aspects of the concrete living individual which relate to the processes of learning and the content of what he has learned. At the human level, crucial learning occurs in the social and cultural spheres, namely, at symbolic levels. What Freud called the "reality principle" referred to orientation to the context of "object relations," that is, to social interaction with other human beings. Similarly, command of language is necessary for truly human behavior. Though the capacity for linguistic performance is organically

9

inherited, there is no evidence that the specific language learned is a function of the genes.

*Four Subsystems of Action.* The distinctions among the four subsystems of action (behavioral organism, personality, social system, and cultural system) are not arbitrary. They constitute application of a general four-function paradigm for the analysis of living systems. This paradigm is so central to the analysis of the whole book and will be used so constantly that a somewhat fuller explanation at the present juncture should save the reader trouble later on. We will start with the two axes of the paradigm and then discuss the four categories of function which are derived from their cross-classification.

### The Two Axes

The first axis, by diagramming convention displayed as vertical, is called *internal-external*. This concerns the relation of a system of action to its environment(s). It is assumed that the system of reference is characterized by a *pattern* of functioning by virtue of which its internal states are at any given time different from those of the environment in significant respects. The direction of these differences is toward greater stability and a higher level of organization than that of the environment in the respects relevant to the system of reference. A larger component of randomness exists in the environing systems than internally in the system of reference: In short, the environment displays a greater degree of positive entropy, the system of negative entropy.

Systems of action, like other living systems, are *open* systems engaged in continual interchange of inputs and outputs with their environments. The categories of input required by the systems are not unitary but various. Moreover, the various categories of potential input available to an action system vary independently of each other. Thus for a social system both motivational inputs from individuals and cultural standards are essential, but the psychological states of individuals and the norms of a culture are not directly connected; social disorganization by alienation and by anomie need to be distinguished. *Pari passu*, the same can be said of the outputs of a system; they are various, not inherently bound together and have differential impacts on the environment.

# INTRODUCTION

Some matching exists between the differentiation of the system's relations to inputs from and outputs to the environment and its own internal structure. Thus what we will call "telic" systems with socialization functions and legal systems concerned with normative order are differentiated from each other in the more complex societies. Differentiation of input-output relations to the environment(s) and the related differentiation in the internal structure and processes of the system of reference itself create special problems for the system itself, *if* it is assumed that a pattern is maintained which is different from the environmental state of affairs. One problem concerns the maintenance of *boundaries* between system and environment and *pari passu* between subsystems within the system. If internal and external states are different, there cannot be continuous variation from some defined center of the system to zones which are nonsystem, but there must be points at which transitions are marked and interchange is selective rather than nearly random. This does not preclude boundary-zones rather than lines, but it does preclude the conception of continuity of transition over the whole range.

The second axis, which relates to process in time, we have labeled *instrumental-consummatory*. This is a somewhat narrow designation but in the right direction. A pattern does not in the real world actualize itself. The system for which it is a template must meet conditions and utilize environmentally available resources. Meeting conditions and utilization are possible only through processes which are inherently time-extended. Time is *one* aspect of processes which include energy input and utilization, organization or combination of components, and evaluation of stages. These processes are combinations of the logic of cybernetic theory with its conception of the implementation of a program and of economic theory with its logic of combination of factors evaluated by value-added criteria.

One functional problem involved here concerns the balances between input of resources, their processing to the point of being utilizable, and their actual consumption. These categories designate *stages* in a sequence of temporal succession. Resources cannot be processed before they are available through input to the system, and they cannot later be consumed until the process of production through combination has made them useful, that is, in the economic case endowed them with utility. Presumably, consumption

11

—the economic term is used here to designate all consummatory end-states—is the most highly valued of the states of affairs along the above sequence. But it is ineluctable that the level of consumables is a function of nonconsumption at earlier stages of resources which might be devoted to later stages. In the *time* perspective, the level of future consumption must be a function of abstention from possible current consumption—the idea of delayed gratification.

A second problem internal to the system is *integration*. If its interchange relations with its environment are differentiated and these differentiations involve differentiated structures and processes within the system, continued functioning requires meshing of these differentiated components so that, from the perspective of implementation of the system-pattern, they minimally interfere with each other and perhaps reinforce each other.

This is the basis for dichotomizing the variable defined by this axis as instrumental-consummatory. It is a distinction between processes which build up resources for future utilization and those which actually put them to use, thereby destroying them through consumption. This distinction can be conceived as defining the nature of system-processes over time rather than simply a point on a continuum. Cross-classification of the two axes, conceived as defining dichotomous variables then yields the four categories of function as shown in Figure 1.1.

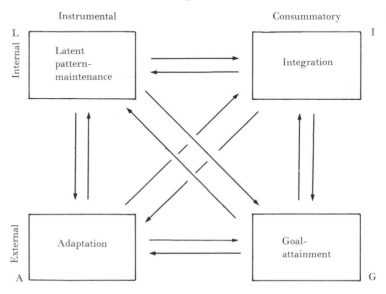

Figure 1.1. The Four-Function Paradigm

# INTRODUCTION

## The Four Functions

*Latent Pattern-Maintenance.* On both primary axes the pattern-maintenance function attempts to formulate the basis of the distinctiveness of the system of reference. It is the pattern which defines the distinctive nature of the system as contrasted with its environments. In the other axis it is the focus of the maintenance of *continuity*—including that of developmental pattern—over time. Thus our conception of a distinctive action system has much in common with that of Ernst Mayr[5] of an organic species. If that analogy holds up, the pattern-maintenance function should be thought of as equivalent to that of maintaining the integrity of the species' gene pool.

Conceptualization in this area has undergone development influenced by concepts from linguistics and from the area of cybernetic control and information theory, such as codes, templates, and programs. The newer concepts of genetics and of linguistics seem in some respects to converge.

The concept pattern is a conveniently imprecise term to designate a defining and controlling component of an action system, which is latent with respect to the operative functions of the system, especially those involving the action-equivalents of energy in the physical sense. This means it should be conceived to be at the same time controlling and insulated. Its features antedate the specific system-operations of interest and will survive them. In action terms, this is the culture concept; culture in certain senses transcends particular social and psychological systems. There is an analogy to the gene pool of a species which transcends any phenotypic individual or aggregate of them.

*Adaptation.* The function of adaptation, taken from biological theory, concerns the interface between system and environment with special reference to the longer-run interests of the system, not only in maintenance but in potentials of development from an evolutionary perspective. It involves not only the pattern, but the system's capacities for realistic functioning which at the same time maintains the integrity of the pattern and meets the environmental exigencies of its actualization. A dimension of adaptation is the generalization of adaptive capacity. By this we mean the development of modes of adaptation not specific to particular en-

5. Ernst Mayr, *Populations, Species, and Evolution* (Cambridge, Mass., Belknap Press of the Harvard University Press, 1970), chap. i.

13

vironmental exigencies but useful in coping with increasingly wide ranges of exigencies. Thus in action terms cognitive capacity is highly generalized in its adaptive significance. Knowing how to cope with mosquitoes as an annoyance to human beings but not with any other species of insects is a low level of adaptive capacity. Adaptation not only is passive adjustment to environmental conditions so as to avoid extinction but includes various modes of capacity to cope with environmental conditions and to utilize environmentally available resources in the interest of system functioning.

*Goal-Attainment.* The goal-attainment function refers to the needs of action systems to establish relatively specific system-environment relationships and the structures and processes which facilitate capacities of the system to do this. Thus, for a mobile animal, food-search is a function which is effectively performed if the animal, when hungry, can usually establish contact with appropriate food-sources and gain control of the food-objects. Goal-attainment is to be distinguished by its specificity from adaptation. This concerns specificity with respect to the relevance of the pattern of matching between system-need and environmental object and also temporally with respect to the specificity of occasions to activate goal-oriented behavior of specific types, as distinguished from the longer-run and more generalized adaptation to a total environment.

In proportion as a living system develops capacities to cope with a differentiated and varying environment, it must generalize capacities to do so rather than merely reacting to the ad hoc stimuli of the environment as these impinge on the system. This is the basis of the differentiation between goal-attainment and adaptation as functional categories.

*Integration.* Integration is the internal counterpart of adaptation to the environment. For reasons suggested above, a system comes to be internally differentiated and to be exposed to differentiated relations to its environment involving both inputs and outputs. These (as well as internal processes) activate internal units differentially in type of functioning and in time. Direct impact of these variable processes on the core of a system without any mediating mechanisms, which help mitigate potential conflicts and facilitate mutual reinforcement, would be disorganizing as seen from the point of view of pattern-maintenance and implementation. Here the factor of generalization is important, matching its importance for adaptive function. The functional needs of the system can, by integrative organization, be generalized so that they can be dealt with on a basis transcending their ad hoc impingement in particular circumstances. The conception of a relatively stable internal environment as developed for physiology by the French physiologist Claude Bernard and his Harvard successor, Walter B. Cannon, and for sociology by Emile Durkheim the French sociologist, whose name will recur frequently in this book, is an aspect of the organization of systems with respect to integrative functions.

The first use to which we put the general functional paradigm is its application to the general system of action as such which we conceive, as diagrammed in Figure 1.2, to be differentiated into four primary subsystems along functional lines. These, as designated, we shall call the cultural system (L), the social system (I), the personality system (G), and the behavioral organism (A), respectively. These subsystems, it should be clearly understood, are not conceived as classes of concrete entities but as analytically defined abstract entities, all abstracted from the mass of known and knowable "data" about human action and behavior.

This paradigm is of especially crucial importance for the present study because, as we shall have occasion to emphasize many times, its design necessitates dealing with two or more of these subsystems as explicitly distinguished from each other but at the same time specifically interdependent with each other. This cannot in a simple sense be a "sociological" study of the university, nor can it be a "cultural" study; it must be *both* in a very specific way and also a psychological and an organic study. The para-

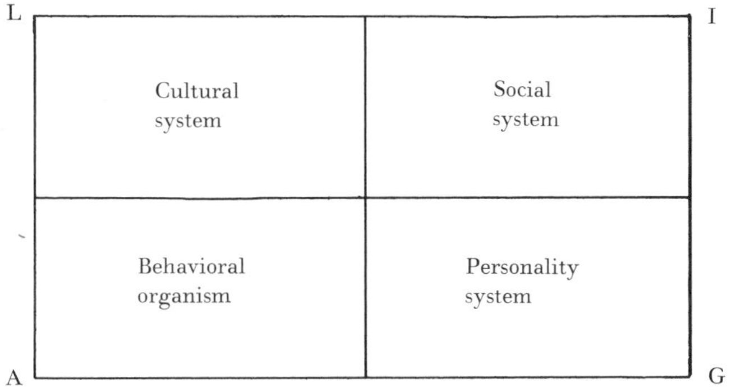

| L | | I |
|---|---|---|
| Cultural system | Social system | |
| Behavioral organism | Personality system | |
| A | | G |

Figure 1.2. Structure of the General Action System

digm presented in Figure 1.2 we consider an indispensable aid to orderly thinking in this inherently complex field.[6]

*Cultural Systems: Analogues of Genes.* Just as the genes in the higher species transcend the life cycle of a particular organism and are transmitted from generation to generation, changing more slowly and by different processes than does the individual organism, so do culture traits transcend the viability of their host society. A cultural system can die out through the extinction of the personalities and societies which are its bearers, but it can also survive its bearers. Culture is not only transmitted from generation to generation through teaching and learning; it can be embodied in externalized symbols, for example, works of art, the printed page, or storage devices such as computer tapes. Though there are differences between hearing Plato philosophize in the Academy at Athens and reading *The Republic*, especially in a language other than classical Greek, there is a sense in which the meaning of the cultural object is *the same.* Hence persons living in the twentieth century can share with Plato's contemporaries parts of the culture of Athens in the fourth century B.C. This is temporal continuity that no person can approach. Thus, a cultural system can be stable over time and relatively insulated from the effect of its environments, which include not only the physico-organic world but social, psychological, and organic subsystems of action. This stability enables a cultural system to serve as the prototype of an autonomous action system.

The core of a cultural system is its "code" component, which is more stable than are the concrete symbolic uses of the code in the course of communication.[7] Knowing a language in the code sense does not commit the one who knows it to communicating a particular idea on a particular occasion. Speech is an action process the content of which is a function of social and psychological developments and of changes in the state of the organism, of the physical environment, or of other aspects of culture than the linguistic code itself.

6. In what follows in this introductory chapter, however, we shall not attempt to present a general review of the theoretical scheme as a whole, but will confine our attention to selected aspects which will be of special importance for purposes of the present study. For the reader who has more general theoretical interests, however, we are including a technical appendix at the end of the book which will present a more comprehensive set of formal paradigms and a brief explication of them.

7. The word "code" is not used here in a specifically technical sense, e.g., as in the expression the "genetic code," but roughly in the sense in which Jacobson and Halle, for language, distinguish "code" from "message." See Roman Jacobson and Morris Halle, *Fundamentals of Language* (The Hague, Mouton, 1956).

# INTRODUCTION

Our main interest is with the *cognitive* subdivision of the culture of modern society. The cultural objects which comprise a cognitive system, abstracted from particular noncognitive action context, we will call *knowledge*. One test is the capacity of embodiment of such cultural objects in nonhuman symbolic form, for instance, the printed page. Knowledge is only one of the four categories in which we classify cultural objects. The other three are constitutive symbolization, moral-evaluative symbolization, and expressive symbolization. We will not at this point define them. However, we must point out that moral-evaluative symbolization has a special relation to the values institutionalized in social systems and will have therefore special significance for the subsequent discussion.

*The Difference between Cultural Objects and a Cultural System.* A body of knowledge, though a cultural object, is more specifically a complex of meanings symbolized within a code. A cultural system as a system of action, however, consists not only of cultural objects but, as a system, of *all* the components of action insofar as they are oriented in terms of cultural objects. Thus, the cognitive subsystem of action consists of action-components oriented to cognitive objects, those currently available in the situation of action and those potentially created by such action, for example, through research. It also includes actions oriented to the understanding of cognitive objects, that is, of knowledge, and to the dissemination of such understanding through teaching.

This conception of an action system with cultural primacy is an abstraction. The concrete actions are those of organism-personality units which typically engage in *social* relations with one another. We are interested in distinguishing between the cultural action systems of the American academic milieu and the social

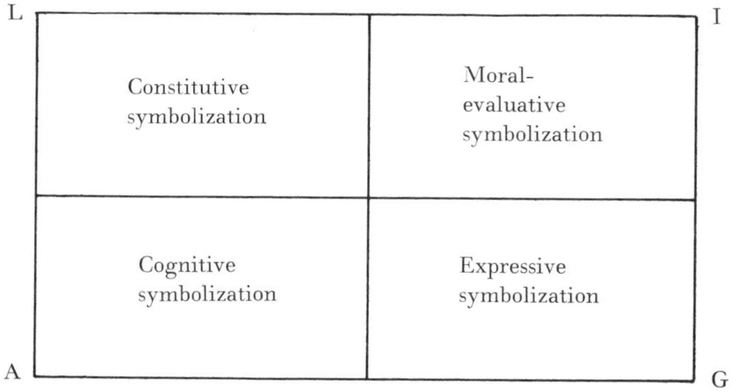

Figure 1.3. Structure of the Cultural System

17

systems in which these cultural systems are embedded. A social system is also an abstraction. It is concerned with symbolic behavior organized about the processes of social interaction among acting units, that is, with actions mutually oriented to other actors in a system of interaction. Although individuals are ultimately the participating members of social systems, collectivities can be the acting units of more inclusive social systems, for example, a society. Just as every concrete social system must involve the action of individuals—though not as total personalities—so every interactive system has a culture, though this does not mean that it *is* a cultural system. If it were scientifically legitimate to assume such an identity, the task of this book would be simple which, as the reader will discover in due course, it is not.

*The Fiduciary Subsystem.* Beyond this distinction between social and cultural systems, we wish to point out that an academic social system is a type of social system having a special relation to culture, special in that its primary societal function is to act as a trustee of cognitive culture and the interests associated with it. It is part of the *fiduciary* subsystem of a society, that subsystem involving closer articulation with cultural references than the three other subsystems. The other three subsystems of a society are, first, the *economy*, conceived as social organization in the interest of the production and allocation of generally disposable resources, especially in relation to the physical environment, second, the *polity*, concerned with the organization of social units for the society as a whole or its subsystems in the interest of collective goal-attainment, third, the *societal community* which has integrative functions on behalf of the society as a whole. It is also necessary for our purposes to subclassify the fiduciary subsystem of a society. The fiduciary system lies in the zone of interpenetration between cultural system and society. It includes action structures and processes where cultural meaning systems articulate with special function in the societal system. These special functions are the foci of institutionalization of relevant cultural patterns in the society. Hence there must be at least rough matching between the meaning-patterns at the cultural level and the social-functional references at the societal level.

*The Cognitive Subsystem.* A fiduciary subsystem with adaptive function at both cultural and societal levels we call the *cognitive* or rationality subsystem and consider that it is governed by theoretical codes. Its primary societal function is the *rationaliza-*

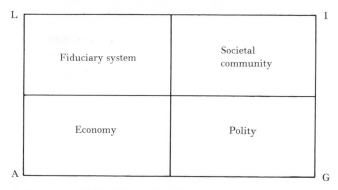

Figure 1.4. Structure of the Social System

*tion* of action. (Rationality may be used to designate a *type* of action, but it is also a component of action when the latter is not predominantly rational.) Thus, the adaptive subsystem of the fiduciary system is concerned with the maintenance of standards of rationality. Obviously, the rationality system is concerned with education and indeed with learning in general.

*The Moral Community.* A second subsystem of the fiduciary system involves on the cultural side moral-evaluative symbolization and on the societal side the function of ordering societal relationships by contributing to a sense of community. Both moral-evaluative symbolization and the societal community have integrative functions for their respective cultural and social subsystems of action, and their interpenetration has integrative significance for action generally. The moral-evaluative function integrates normative components of culture with the possibility of a normative definition of meaningful orientation of actors toward their ultimate concerns as well as toward the practical exigencies of their lives. The concept of moral community refers to collective organizations of acting units which can embody meaningful common orientations and at the same time command the loyalty of participants at the level of practical action. This combination reflects the institutionalization of systems of values common to the members of societal groupings.

These two subsystems are the most relevant subsystems of the fiduciary system for the university, since the latter is concerned with cognitive culture and its integrative significance for society and its individual members. At the same time the university must have a community structure differentiated into subcommunities and articulated with many other communities outside itself, both

19

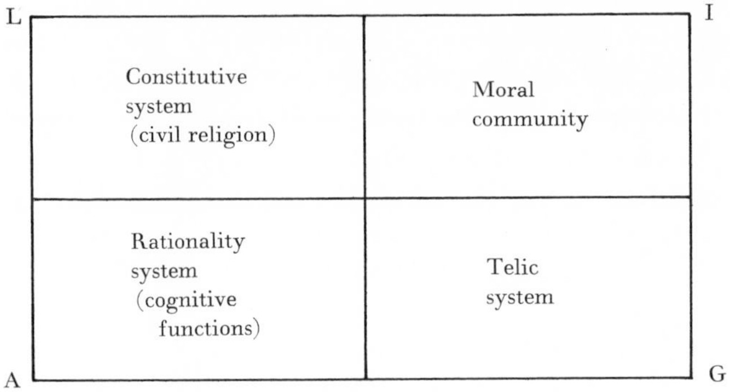

Figure 1.5. The Fiduciary System

in the academic world and in the nonacademic sectors of the society, and this differentiated community structure has relationships to the third and fourth subsystem of the fiduciary system.

*The Telic Subsystem.* The third subsystem of the fiduciary system, the telic subsystem, involves on the cultural side an expressive mode of symbolization. Whereas value-patterns are *conceptions* or "patterns" of the desirable, that is, they have normative significance for social action, the expressive sphere involves *desires* of individual personalities and organisms and also of collectivities. These desires are directed toward objects of and in the cultural, the social, the psychological and organic, the nonhuman, and the physical worlds and to the relations of acting humans to them. Like all symbolization, the expressive category involves negative as well as positive meanings, that is, what is feared as well as what is desired.

The fiduciary subsystem of society we conceived, as noted, as the primary zone of interpenetration between the social and the cultural systems with institutionalized values as the primary cultural component involved. Within the fiduciary system, however, the subsystem we are calling telic is the one which places the strongest emphasis on further integration with the personality of the individual. This further integration focuses on the function of goal-attainment which we conceive to be the *primary* function of the personality at the general action level. At that of the social system which is our present primary concern, however, goal-attainment is conceived to be in the first instance a *collective* process.

It is our view that values constitute the primary legitimizing framework for bringing about this synthesis because, first, they define what is conceived to be desirable, not only at the general level of action but within the context of social interaction and as a basis for the individual participant to discriminate between what he desires and what on a more general level can be considered to be desirable.

We must, however, be concerned not only with the way in which cultural values are institutionalized in the social system but also with the theoretical specifics of the articulation of the social system with the personality. To deal with this we have adopted the Freudian concept of *cathexis* as the "emotionally" underpinned commitment of an individual to a context of what Freud in his later work called "object relations."[8] We conceive cathexis in this sense to be the basis of individuals' capacity to participate in institutionalized collective goal-oriented processes, such as the "enterprise" of higher education. This "performance" of the individual in committing himself to meaningful but also costly "choices" can be said to be broadly "rewarded" by societal contributions to his own "affective economy," on the assumption, which we will develop and analyze in Chapter 2, that affect is the generalized medium anchored in the social system at the level of general action. The theoretical problem will be introduced in the latter part of Chapter 2, but its empirical relevance to the present study will be developed at some length in the analysis of undergraduate student socialization in Chapter 4.

The primordial focus of telic function in societies has been kinship systems, which provide a connection with the motivation of individuals. Thus, sociologists commonly think that a primary function of kinship, especially of the modern nuclear family, is to order the motivations of individuals in relation to their social roles. For adults this means especially the management of emotional tensions that might otherwise jeopardize role performance. For children, in addition to this, there is the central function of socialization in the social-psychological sense of learning the roles that are being taught to them. Kinship is also the sector of a broader telic system closer to the motivational balances of individuals at unconscious levels. This broader telic system involves extensive collective references culminating in political commitments of the societal community as a whole. We will also class solidary groups

8. Cf. Talcott Parsons, *Social Structure and Personality* (New York, The Free Press, 1964), chap. iv.

of peers at adolescent and studentry levels as belonging primarily to the telic subsystem.

*The Constitutive Subsystem.* The symbolic forms, which presumptively embody a nonempirical boundary reference so far as they become integral to the action system through cultural definition, are its *constitutive* symbolism—symbolism which is not referential relative to a specifiable empirical reality, but is essential to the understanding of the action system of reference as meaningfully coherent. Within the fiduciary subsystem of the society, this is collective organization with predominantly religious reference, such as a church or, at a different level, a "civil" religious complex.

*The Environments of Action Systems.* One consequence of an evolutionary point of view needs to be made explicit. The concept of "environment" must be regarded as relative. With the development of organic life, the environment is modified—pollution is one possibility—and new environments are created. In a population of unicellular organisms, the environment of any individual organism may consist of a nonorganic environment and the other unicellular organisms with which the organism of reference comes into contact. (With the emergence of multicellular organisms, a particular cell has an environment internal to the organism of which it is a part. A major theoretical advance in physiology was the introduction of the concept of the internal environment by Claude Bernard.) An organism then is increasingly exposed to an environment constituted by other members of its own species and, beyond this, by its membership in ecosystems consisting of many species interdependent with each other.

The development of new environments occurs also on the level of action systems. For Freud, the salient environment of the individual personality was the reality constituted by other persons interacting with the individual. Freud called this the field of "object relations." Durkheim extended this concept, independently of Freud, through his concept of the *milieu social.* Durkheim considered the social system in which the individual participated to be the crucial environment to which the action of a socialized individual had to adapt. In short, the individual human being has had to adapt to physical environments, organic environments, including his own organism viewed from the perspective of the self, his personality system as object rather than motivator, the personality systems of significant others, his social environment, his cultural environment, and finally his constitutive environment. Although these are a lot of environments, there is no way to reduce their number without oversimplifying a complex world. The physical environment is only a small part of the total environment of a human being.

*Integration.* A further aspect of our theoretical scheme ought to be discussed in this introduction: the place of integration in the evolution of living systems. If differentiated subsystems are to cohere in an overall system which maintains its adaptive capacity, there must be integrating mechanisms. The articulation of the bones of a skeleton through joints and ligaments constitutes one mode of integration, but on advanced evolutionary levels there emerge mechanisms which operate through communication of information. Such mechanisms at organic levels are enzymes, hormones, and neural processes. Biologists agree that the central nervous system, especially the mammalian brain, is primarily an information-processing system, not a source of energy like the alimentary system nor an energy-utilization system like the musculature. Its functions concern *control* of these other processes, not substantive contribution to them.

At the level of action, mechanisms have developed comparable to organic information processing. We refer to such mechanisms as "symbolic media of interchange." The one that is best understood (and therefore can serve as a model for understanding the genus) is money. Money, like all symbolic media, is a kind of language. A symbolic medium operates in terms of a cultural code, in the case of money that of rights of possession ("property"). Money transcends existing rights in concrete objects of utility by creating a basis for negotiating new rights when needed and desired—subject to mutual consent. The essence of money in its pure form is that it is symbolic. Dollars may be symbolized by coins, by paper-money bills, by checks, or by entries on account books; they have no reality except as a category of meaning of a cultural object. In short, money has, in the economist's term, no "value in use" but only "value in exchange." This does not mean it is not useful, but that its use consists of controlling access to objects of "intrinsic" usefulness: goods, services, and various forms of monetary assets. Money also functions as a measure of economic value, or utility, and, because its expenditure is optional in direction and in time, as a storehouse of value. For a unit in a system of social interaction to have money in specifiable amounts is to have been the recipient of special communications in the past and to be the potential agent of outward communications called "spending." To spend money is *only* to communicate a message to specified others.

Money is anchored in the economy, a functionally differentiated subsystem of a society, and is involved not only in mediating relations internal to it among economic actors but in mediating relations between the economy and the other subsystems of the society: the polity, the fiduciary system, and the societal community. Money should not be treated as a unique phenomenon but as one member of a family of media of interchange (political power, influence, and value-commitments) which, like money, are purely symbolic. Though the concept of power common in the social science literature has stressed distributive aspects rather than the interchange aspects stressed here, the societal impact of both money and power is generally recognized—as is the impact of influence and value-commitments, albeit vaguely. Money and power are certainly involved in university affairs, but influence and value-commitments are, though less recognized, at least as important, if not more so in linking the academic world to the larger society.

*Symbolic Media of Action.* In the course of substantive analysis of the American academic system we shall have to deal not only with the four symbolic media at the level of the social system, but also with corresponding media at the level of the general system of action, internally to each subsystem and externally linking each with the other three. Thus *intelligence* is such a medium anchored in the behavioral organism; *performance-capacity* is a medium anchored in the personality system; *affect* is a medium anchored in the social system; and *definition of the situation* is a medium anchored in the cultural system. Each of these media will be discussed at the point where its understanding becomes necessary to the analysis.

Two additional characteristics of the generalized media should be kept in mind. One effect of developing a symbolic medium is to introduce new degrees of freedom in the action-potentials of individual or collective units in the system and consequently greater flexibility in its functioning. For example, the development of monetary market exchange provided greater flexibility than barter. If money is acceptable in the relevant market system, the holder and receiver are free to choose the items on which to spend

24

instead of being dependent on what specific barter-partners have and are willing to part with. They can shop around among competing sources of supply for the same items, being freer to bargain over terms and not bound by time constraints imposed by the perishability, storage costs, or other inconveniences of holding concrete objects of possession.

A second characteristic of generalized media is that at a sufficient level of development, they possess mechanisms by which their volume can be expanded. Thus, the money supply can be expanded by the operation of credit creation carried out by banks and other financial institutions. This possibility is an extension of the increasing degrees of freedom which develop beyond the level of barter as markets widen, for example, from finished-product exchange to marketability of the factors of production and various forms of financial assets. The analogue of credit creation is found for the other symbolic media when they and the systems in which they operate have become sufficiently differentiated and integrated. We will eventually analyze "intelligence banking" in relation to the system of cognitive culture and its societal frameworks.

The evolutionary process of increasing degrees of freedom with a widening range of alternatives open to unit-action introduces not only flexibility but also potentiality of instability into action systems. In any exchange system, there are various potentialities for instability at a variety of locations in the system. The presence of symbolic media funnels tensions generated at particular points in the system into the functioning of the medium itself, notably into confidence or lack of confidence in its stability, an attitude on which its general acceptability is dependent. Where there is substantial freedom for credit creation, this potential of instability centering in the medium is accentuated. Cumulative escalations of self-accentuating motion occur, either toward excessive commitments expressed in terms of the medium or toward devaluation of such commitments and an increasing tendency to avoid them.

Economic fluctuations centering on the monetary system provide a ready illustration of these cumulative processes. The economic term for cumulative excess in monetary commitments is *inflation* and that for cumulative decreases is *deflation*. We shall adopt these terms for more general use; inflation or deflation will refer not only to monetary phenomena but to parallel processes involving any of the four symbolic media on the social system level or the four on the general action level. We shall ultimately (in Chapter 7) attempt to analyze some of the interrelations of inflationary and deflationary processes between two or more of the eight media which occur either simultaneously or in non-random succession.

These analytical problems are intricate and will not permit much more than hypothesis statement and crude empirical generalizations. Since theoretical analysis of academic systems has rarely been attempted in the action frame of reference, what little we will be able to accomplish should be better than not attempting it at all.

The chapter following this theoretical introduction (Chapter 2) will attempt to elucidate the components of the cognitive complex in human action systems, their relations to each other and to non-cognitive aspects of action generally and of the social system in particular. We shall deal with the concepts of cognition and learning, with knowledge as a system of cultural objects with cognitive primacy, and with competence as a cognitively grounded capacity of actors, individual and collective. We shall emphasize that sector of the institutionalized value pattern at the societal level encompassing cognitive rationality, since this value connects the cultural components of the cognitive complex with social organization, including the university. We shall, finally, pay attention to rationality as a component of action involving the relevance of cognitive standards of evaluation of its effectiveness.

The core value of the university is cognitive rationality. We shall devote Chapter 3 to its analysis and to its embodiment in the recently developed modern university. The institutional focus of this core value lies in the organization of research and of graduate training. We shall use this analysis of the cognitive complex to define points of articulation with subsystems of the society in which the values of cognitive rationality do not have primacy but must give way to some extent to other categories of societally relevant evaluation.

In Chapter 4 we shall turn to a context in which the primacy of cognitive rationality must be shared with another set of values, namely, those involved in the socialization of educated citizens as distinguished from the training of future academic professionals.

26

This function is carried out mainly through the general education aspects of undergraduate colleges. We are particularly interested in the more demanding programs of general education in the colleges of highest academic quality, many of them integral parts of universities with graduate schools and large research programs.

Chapter 5 will deal with a second context in which the cognitive complex is combined with other complexes of interests and values in the society that are not primarily cognitive. The first of these is the applied professions, such as medicine and law and, in another grouping, education and social work. Such schools of professional training have commonly become integral parts of the university structure. The practical goals such as maintenance of health or effective organization of the educational process must share prominence in the evaluative context with the standards of cognitive rationality of action in the pursuit of these goals.

Chapter 6 will concern the relevance of cognitive standards to the formulation of definitions of the situation for the individual, the society, and the culture as these are discussed by intellectuals within and outside the academic system. Broadly speaking, they are interested in ideology, thought of in a nonpejorative sense. Cognitive standards are relevant to ideological pursuits, but the problems of ideological orientation transcend the cognitive complex in directions of value-commitment, of expressive symbolism, and indeed of religion.

Chapter 7 will deal with certain dynamic processes in the university system and in the relations of the university to its social environment. This chapter will be concerned with the nature of the crisis which the system has encountered in recent years. We shall deal with its background in secular trends of change, in pathological processes associated with rapid growth, and in shifts of balance which have produced structural strains, for example, rapid growth of the research complex and of graduate training. The crisis itself we shall interpret as centering in the undergraduate sector of the institutions of high academic quality, connected with changes in the general social environment, including the war in Vietnam and economic recession with its cutbacks of financial support for academic functions. These circumstances have produced a state analogous to an economic depression; hence we must deal in Chapter 8 with the problem of the prospects for recovery.

Shorter-run processes have been proceeding in a context of possibilities of larger structural change. The remainder of Chapter 8 will be devoted to an analysis of these trends in order to arrive at some tentative prognosis of the main developments in prospect beyond mere recovery from the recent crisis.

Chapter 9 will consist of commentary on the first eight chapters written by Neil J. Smelser. Smelser has consulted extensively with the authors throughout the project. In particular he has given us detailed commentaries on the first draft of the manuscript, chapter by chapter. Many of the points he has made have been taken into account in revision. Nevertheless, it seemed desirable for him to undertake an independent statement of his views.

Finally, the book will end with a technical appendix, which, for the reader interested in the analytical scheme, will attempt a diagrammatic presentation of the elements used in the discursive analysis contained in the book.

To conclude this introduction with a few words about the nature of our enterprise: As sociologists, we consider it at the same time a study of the American university as an object of observation and a study in the sociology of knowledge in the sense that we, in our differing roles, have been active participants in the system we are trying to describe as objectively as possible. This illustrates a methodological dilemma of the social sciences in that, in a sense different from that of the natural sciences, investigators are necessarily part of the phenomena they investigate, if not of the specific case, then of the category of cases. Chapter 2, as part of its discussion of cognitive rationality, will analyze the problem of the objectivity of knowledge in all the intellectual disciplines, including our own social sciences. This concern has a double significance for us and for other students of this sector of modern action systems and societies. On the one hand, objectivity of cognition as a sociocultural *phenomenon* is a theoretical assumption of our study, namely, that some men in some settings do in fact act in approximate conformity to the standards of cognitive rationality. On the other hand, we, as participants in the academic community, sharing its dominant values, ask readers to believe that our own behavior accords with those values. This comes perilously close to setting ourselves up as judges in our own case.

The resolution of the difficulty may lie in the conception of an intellectual community which has developed as a result of the evolution of both culture and society. We are not the only judges in our case: we expose ourselves to the judgment of peers in an intellectual community, who, though fallible like us, will strive to implement these values in criticizing our use of empirical evidence and the cogency of our theoretical reasoning. In one sense, only professionally qualified academics can do valid research concerning the academic world, but not particular academics, since any particular ones are exposed, not only to criticism but to competition. This study is intended as a contribution to the self-conscious understanding of the academic community and through it of the society and culture of which it is a part. As in all intellectual endeavor, perfection is beyond our reach. But this does not mean that a claim to relative objectivity should be rejected a priori.[9]

9. François Bourricaud, *Universités à la dérive: France, Etat-Unis, Amérique du Sud* (Paris, Stock, 1971).

# APPENDIX TO CHAPTER 1
## ENVIRONMENTS OF ACTION SYSTEMS

The system of action is anchored in two distinct orientations. One direction is toward the physical-organic environment conditional to action (see Figure 1.6). Nature comprises the environment of action when the objects in that environment do not interact with actors at symbolically meaningful levels, as is often true of the physical environment and of concrete organisms, including the body of another person or of the acting individual himself. Of course, the body can also be meaningfully symbolic; an example would be the erotic significance of women's breasts.

There is ultimately a conditional component of the acting individual's organism, the core of which is his hereditary constitution. Meaningful interaction with the genes of one's own organism is not possible, although they in part determine what we are. Human access to the physical world, both the environment of the individual and his own body, occurs *only* through facilities provided by the organism. For coping with the external environment there are the senses, vision and hearing, and for coping with the internal world, proprioceptive capacities. Man's capacity to perceive has been extended by instrumentation. Defects of vision are corrected by glasses; long-base interferometry gains information about distant celestial bodies; and in the micro direction, the electron microscope provides data about very small objects. Such information-producing devices must be adapted to organic perception mechanisms; otherwise they cannot contribute to *human* knowledge about the physical-organic world. The same consideration applies to externalized *symbols*. To perceive and understand what is printed on a page, it is necessary to observe the marks on the page correctly and in their order through the mechanisms of vision. A blind person must have some alternative channel of perception.

The second direction of orientation of meaningful action systems (other than the conditional one just discussed) is toward a nonempirical realm. Contact with the nonempirical realm, whether it be a formulation of cognitive propositions or the expression of emotions must be mediated through human personalities and cultures, including capacities of the organism, and must articulate with the relevant systems of social interaction. In every human culture beliefs about the universe exist not identified with the conditional aspects of nature but conceived to be teleologically superordinate to nature. Such beliefs in Western culture include conceptions of the super-natural and of the desirable. These reference points for the orientation of human action may be symbolized in noncognitive ways, although noncognitive symbolization cannot be entirely independent of cognitively meaningful beliefs.

Empirical considerations help to justify the inclusion of the nonempirical realm in a theory of action which, after all, purports to be a part of the organon of empirical knowledge. One consideration is that the analysis of the organism as a living system requires that attention be paid to its teleological character. This point of view, as distinguished from the older mechanistic biology and behavioristic psychology is generally accepted in the life sciences and involves (1) a distinction between the conditions to which an organism must become adapted and the goals, the attainment of which it is conceived to be seeking within the conditions to which it is subject, both genetic and environmental and (2) the notion that the teleological system is in some sense open-ended, that is to say, that its goal-seeking is not wholly determined by some factor operating *on* the organism from outside. The second point is particularly relevant for human behavior. A second empirical consideration is the evolution of living systems, not

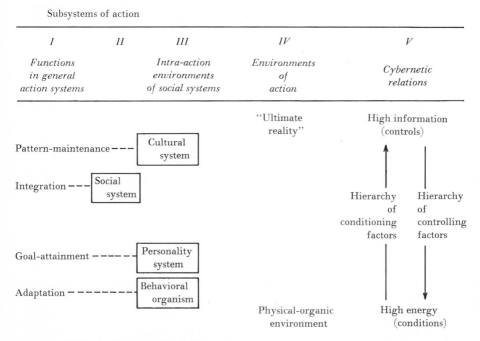

Figure 1.6. Action and Its Subsystems

*Note*: Figure 1.6 and text adapted from Talcott Parsons, *Societies: Evolutionary and Comparative Perspectives*, © 1966, p. 28, Table 1. By permission of Prentice-Hall, Inc., Englewood Cliffs, N.J.

only on organic levels, but also on the level of action. This evolutionary process, which includes social and cultural systems, does not occur by random variation but proceeds in a direction of increasing adaptive capacity. This is true despite the waste of organic resources through false starts, dead ends, and the pathologies of evolution. To assert directionality is not to assert predetermination of the outcomes of particular phases or of the evolution of terrestrial life as a whole.

The modern concept of adaptation is not confined to capacity of the living system to survive in the conditions of its environment, but includes the capacity to behave, within limits, independently of its environment and on occasion to *control* its environment in its own interests. ("Living system" refers to individual organisms but also to larger living systems of which the individual organism is a part, such as a species.)

The concept of a nonempirical environment to an action system is relevant to the process of adaptation. The nonempirical realm is the source of inputs to the system of action which give directionality to its functioning. Of course directionality may be conceived as internal to the system of reference, as has been assumed in several versions of the idea of emergent evolution. However, at the action level what is more prevalent are attempts to legitimate selections among alternative paths by invoking some source of authority outside the system of action as currently conceived by the acting units.

# 2

## THE COGNITIVE COMPLEX:
## KNOWLEDGE, RATIONALITY, LEARNING,
## COMPETENCE, INTELLIGENCE

The primary focus of the university is the cognitive complex, which is grounded in the cultural system and institutionalized in the structure of modern society. Higher education in general and the university in particular represent institutionalized concerns with cognitive matters. On the cultural side, it is concern with the cognitive subsystem of the cultural system; on the social side, it is with the fiduciary subsystem.

The functions of the fiduciary subsystem of the, society are largely latent (in Robert K. Merton's meaning of the term).[1] Concern with knowledge and its advancement is analytically independent of its practical uses. Similarly, art is not primarily concerned with furthering societal interests, nor is religion primarily an instrument of enhancing economic productivity.

Two concepts, institutionalization and interpenetration, illuminate the relations between culture and society. When a cultural pattern is institutionalized, it has *normative* meaning for social action and socialization. It tends to bring concrete action into proximate conformity with a desired or desirable state of affairs but which may not occur without the intervention of actors to bring it about or to safeguard an emerging outcome. In short, institutionalization organizes the principal social forces so that their combined pressure operates in the direction of promoting the attainment of a normatively defined state of affairs and/or its maintenance.

The key to the nature of institutionalized cultural patterns is the information-energy relationship developed in cybernetic

1. Robert K. Merton, *Social Theory and Social Structure*, rev. ed. (Glencoe, Ill., The Free Press, 1957), chap. i, "Manifest and Latent Functions," pp. 21–81.

theory.[2] Cultural patterns are informational. They do not determine concrete action processes, to say nothing of those of behavior.[3] This requires inputs of energy more than sufficient to counterbalance the energy committed to conflicting action patterns.

In societies, energy consists in the operation of interests at individual and collective levels; these interests are both economic and political. In relation to the conception of a cultural pattern, the criterion of institutionalization is the engagement of the interests of acting units, individual and/or collective, in the implementation of the normatively defined pattern. The main criterion of institutionalization is that, ideally, the goal-interest of the unit coincides with the functional significance of its contribution from the point of view of the subsystem. Short of this limiting case are instances where it is to the interest of the unit to act within the boundaries of the system, which means neither to move outside by emigration or resignation nor to orient action in such a way as to disorganize the social system.

Whatever the range of variation that typically exists within these limits, institutionalization contributes a range of further variation. This further variation concerns discriminating among, ordering, and analyzing of the directions in which institutionalization takes place. In one direction only a code without substantive content is institutionalized. Knowing a language will serve as an example—if there are no obligations involved other than to use the language intelligibly, which means correctly. Closer to our subject matter, an analogue would be knowing the cognitive code well enough to use it correctly, where cognitive matters are at stake, in order to avoid logical fallacies and allegations of fact (1) known to be false or (2) put forward in contravention of accepted standards of referential validity.

In neither the linguistic nor the cognitive case does correctness impose further constraints, granting that in the first case intelligibility of communication and in the second knowing something conceived to be worth knowing are desirable. A further stage has

2. Talcott Parsons, *The System of Modern Societies* (Englewood Cliffs, N.J., Prentice-Hall, Inc., 1971), chap. ii, "Theoretical Orientations," pp. 4–28.

3. Robin M. Williams, Jr., "Change and Stability in Values and Value Systems," in *Stability and Social Change*, ed. Bernard Barber and Alex Inkeles (Boston, Little, Brown, and Co., 1972), pp. 123–159. See also Florence Kluckhohn and F. L. Strodbeck, *Variations in Value-Orientations* (Evanston, Ill., Row Peterson, 1961).

been reached, however, when language is institutionalized in a "speech community" or a set of cognitive standards in a social system devoted to cognitive learning, such as a school. It is not merely whether a given speaker wants to be understood or whether a specific seeker after knowledge wants to believe that he authentically knows something. Institutionalization involves identification of the conditions under which a considerable group of persons can have confidence that they can intelligibly communicate with each other by the use of a common language—or, in the cognitive case, the conditions under which members of the relevant community can have confidence that they can mutually confirm each others' convictions that they authentically know certain things. Whatever the pitfalls of the idea of consensual validation, the norm of the communality of science[4] asserts that under social conditions individual subjective convictions of knowing are not sufficient unless they can be reinforced by the judgments of others, guided by common cultural standards.

The last paragraph moves from the cultural system level to that of the social system. Institutionalization of cultural patterns occurs when, beyond the user's interest in being understood, the pattern is built into a system of interactive sanctioning in such a way that *mutuality* of the corresponding interests of plural units becomes paramount. This is the case where the *generalization* of the normative pattern to a *population* has occurred. A shift from the cultural system level proceeds to other subsystems of action besides the social system. We will discuss the personality system, for example. But for the social system the shift involves not only the question of *levels of specification of the cultural pattern* but also the differentiation of types of substantive context to which it is relevant.

For the linguistic pattern, it makes a difference whether the language is used to write poetry, to describe the ordinary events of a working day, or to analyze an abstruse problem of scientific theory. Despite the tendency to distinguish a language of poetry and a language of science, this usage is metaphorical; both can intelligibly be discussed in the English language. Similar considerations apply in cognitive contexts.

The normative constraints imposed by institutionalization are

4. Merton, *Social Theory*, chap. xii, "Science and Democratic Social Structure," pp. 307–317.

not uniform throughout a social system. Thus the subvalues and norms institutionalized in a differentiated economy with regard to property and contract are different from those relevant to the fiduciary system, say, with regard to civil rights and freedom of religion. We are mainly concerned with subvalues and norms embodied in the rationality subsystem of the fiduciary system, but they relate in systematic ways to other parts of the society.

Institutionalization gives rise to a zone of interpenetration between the cultural and the social systems, the two components of which, though composed of parts of both systems, crosscut one another and constitute one subsystem. Thus, the parts of two interpenetrating systems are more intimately related to each other than the parts of the two primary systems which do not interpenetrate. For example, the *moral-evaluative* subsystem of the culture interpenetrates primarily with the *fiduciary* subsystem of the society. Interpenetration means that the cognate subsystems at each of the four-system levels constitute zones of "overlap" and thus affect each other across these boundaries.[5]

Interpenetration facilitates processes of interchange among all of the units involved in the zone of interpenetration, in our case both cultural and societal. Media of interchange such as influence and value-commitments on the social side, cognitive interest and moral authority on the cultural, operate across the boundaries of the interpenetrating systems. The cognitive complex is a zone of interpenetration involving not only the cultural and social systems but also personalities and behavioral-organic systems. In the social-cultural case, the focus of interpenetrating structure lies in common value-patterns institutionalized in both systems. The *same* value-pattern must have normative status in *both* interpenetrating systems. Such institutionalized values define the nature of the interpenetrating zone, the kinds of action positively and negatively sanctioned within it, and its boundaries.

Since the concept of value-patterns is fundamental to the discussion, we shall define it carefully. As Clyde Kluckhohn put it, "A value is a conception, explicit or implicit, distinctive of an individual or characteristic of a group, of the desirable, which influences the selection from available modes, means and ends of

---

5. These effects are through channels other than the formal interchanges specified in the Theory of Action; see Talcott Parsons and Neil J. Smelser, *Economy and Society* (London, Routledge and Kegan Paul; and New York, The Free Press, 1956), and the technical appendix of this book.

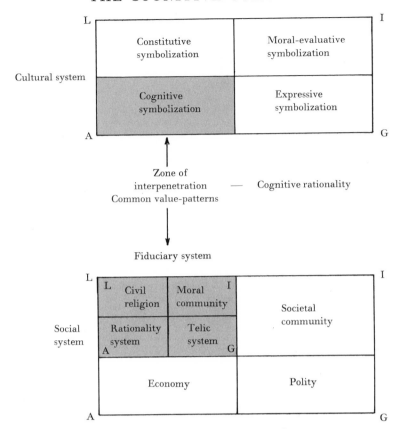

Figure 2.1. Interpenetration of Cultural and Social Systems

*Note:* The shaded areas show the respective interpenetrating systems. The A-sub-system of the fiduciary system is the *main linking subsystem* in this interpenetration on the societal side, as is the system of cognitive symbolization on the cultural side.

action."[6] In order to clarify the role of the cognitive component, we specify Kluckhohn's reference to "conception" as a "pattern of orientation," that is, relating an actor, individual or collective, to a manifold of objects in his situation of action. Commitment to this pattern of orientation on the part of one or more actors presumably has a *selective* effect on the relation, through action, of actors to their situation of action. This selectivity is preferential; some things may be *desirable* as distinguished from only desired though what is *desired* may also be desirable. Unlike some alterna-

6. "Values and Value-Orientations in the Theory of Action: An Explanation in Definition and Classification," in *Toward a General Theory of Action,* ed. Talcott Parsons and Edward A. Shils (Cambridge, Mass., Harvard University Press, 1951), p. 395.

tive conceptions of value, we do not treat it as a property of objects but as a component of the patterning of *action* that *relates* one or more orienting actors *to* one or more objects.

Either as a "conception" or as a "pattern of orientation," a value is a *cultural* object which, through internalization, can become a characteristic of an individual or, through institutionalization, of a group. A value is by definition normative in its significance for action by defining what is desirable; it is also a factor in the *organization* of a system of action, notably a social system, because it favors the development of some possibilities and discourages others. In their relation to the other components of action, value-patterns are informational rather than, like wealth or political power, factors of social energy. Only when institutionalized as parts of complexes which *combine* informational with high-energy components can values constitute major determinants of social processes. Even then, the institutionalized complex rather than the value-components alone is the determinant, but without the value-components the mode of determination would be different.

The cognitive complex, the subject of this chapter, is such an institutionalized complex. It embodies the value-component of *cognitive rationality*. The term "cognitive" has a cultural reference whereas that of the term "rational" is primarily social. Cognitive rationality is a value-pattern linking the cultural and the social levels which are not reducible to one another. This value-pattern is only part of the cognitive complex. Taken separately it would not constitute a major social force.

No value-pattern exists in isolation, only as part of a larger value-*system*. The value-patterns of a total society must constitute a highly differentiated system. Such a societal value-system is differentiated in at least two ways. In the first place, there will be values in it focused at differing levels of generality. Thus the humane treatment of domesticated animals may be a value, the acceptance of which is held to be desirable, but it is so restricted in its relevance that it is insufficient to order the selective preferences of an entire society. On the other hand, the "instrumental activism" formula with which we characterize the value-system of American society at the most general level[7] is devoid of concrete

---

7. See Talcott Parsons and Winston White, "The Link between Character and Society," in *Cultural and Social Structure*, ed. S. M. Lipset and L. Lowenthal (New York, The Free Press, 1961), pp. 89–135.

content; by itself it is not of much help in solving problems of selection by normative preference. The hierarchy of levels of generality of normative patterns is well illustrated in the legal system where the settlement of cases may turn on concrete legal rules as well as on such abstract principles as "equal protection of the laws."

The second basis of differentiation concerns object-categories relative to which judgments of normative desirability have to be made. Cognitive rationality addresses intellectual problems which are different from questions of the desirable patterns of behavior such as between parents and their adolescent children. This second basis of differentiation of a value system essentially defines the spheres within which given value-patterns are relevant and the differences which arise as concern is shifted from one sphere to another. The more highly differentiated and pluralistic the society, the more important differentiations in both these respects become.

In addition to these two axes of differentiation of a value system, two others may be mentioned. Beyond the differences among situational objects relative to which evaluative judgments have to be made, it is also possible to differentiate according to *who* is the actor, individual or collective, making the judgment, for instance, according to what status in the social system he occupies. The modern trend has been to play down the "personality of law,"[8] but various kinds of relativity conceptions from time to time assert claims to consideration, such as the allegation that the accepted truth of social science propositions is a function of the social status of the people who enunciate them. Second, the conception of institutionalized values should take account of the relation between stability and change, for example, distinguishing elements of instability (and hence openness of social systems to change) that derive from meager development of a system of institutionalized values and the associated norms from values that themselves define change as desirable. The cognitive complex places a premium on certain types of change since the advancement of knowledge is highly valued. Thus a field of science in which the state of knowledge was unchanged at the end of a generation would be evaluated

8. Charles H. McIlwain, *The Growth of Political Thought in the West* (New York, Macmillan, 1964).

as having failed. Here, however, the value-pattern can remain unchanged, whereas the evaluated state of the object-system changes profoundly. In many other areas, institutionalized values not only stabilize social systems but institutionalize incentives for change. This makes it important to distinguish between institutionalization or noninstitutionalization of values and openness or closedness toward change. These two variables do not constitute a single dichotomy; they define a fourfold table.

### The General American Value-System

The importance of the value-pattern of cognitive rationality for American society can be better understood by placing it in the context of the value-system of the society as a whole. We do hold that there is and has been a single, relatively well-integrated value-system institutionalized in the society which has "evolved" but has not been drastically changed. As such it must be considered at a high level of generality.[9]

The value-patterns which are part of the structure of a society are those values which implicitly or explicitly define the desirable type of society or its subsystems. In the nature of the case, a

9. In the social-system use of the term "value," there has been a tendency to regard it as essentially a description of a type of concrete action. In a society where many changes take place, almost any change is therefore regarded as a change of values. Whether this is the case is an open question, but the question must be attacked analytically and not prejudged.

|  | Relative | |
|---|---|---|
|  | Openness | Closedness |
|  | Toward change | |
| Institutionalization | Substantive knowledge, etc. | Value-pattern |
| Noninstitutionalization | "Fluidity" | Interlocking of interests |

Figure 2.2. Cognition and Problems of Stability and Change

40

value-system does not describe the concrete state of affairs of the system in which it is institutionalized: it is always a source of normative tension between the actual state of affairs and that conceived, in value terms, to be desirable.

Subject to these considerations, the phrase "instrumental activism" is an appropriate characterization, at a high level of generality, of the main value-pattern institutionalized in American society. Instrumental activism characterizes the desirable type of society, not other classes of objects which Americans regard as desirable.[10] The society as a system tends to be evaluated, not as an end in itself but as *instrumental* to bases of value outside itself. Its desirability is to be judged in terms of its contribution to these *extra*societal grounds of value. The value orientation is *activistic* in the sense that, in the relation between the society and its environments, what is valued is not passive adjustment to the exigencies of the environment but increasing the sphere of freedom of action within the environment and ultimately control over the environment. Of course, the environments of a society are not only the physical world, the biosphere, and other societies but also the organisms and personalities of the constituent individual members and the cultural system. Normative tensions are inherent in this type of value-system. The activistic component exerts pressure in the direction of treating the society as a goal-oriented system, as is suggested by the discussion of national goals and the soul-searching over the apparent prevalence of apathy instead of commitment to collective goals. If the instrumental component could be led back, as it was in the earlier religious phase, to an explicitly transcendent goal (namely the mandate of God to establish His Kingdom on Earth), then instrumental and activistic considerations would coincide. The main evolutionary trend, however, has been in an individualistic direction; hence the goals to which the instrumental component applies have become those distributively allocated to individual citizens and to subcollectivities. Individualistic normative pressure operates against the types of centralization and hierarchy characteristic of societies oriented predominantly to collective goals. In Herbert Spencer's phrase, the tendency has been more to the "industrial" type of society rather than to the

10. Clyde Kluckhohn, "Have There Been Discernible Shifts in American Values during the Past Generation?" in *The American Style*, ed. Elting Morison (New York, Harper and Bros., 1958).

"militant."[11] This trend explains our evaluative concerns with equality and freedom, concerns that have persisted in varying forms from the days of the founding fathers. Concern with freedom and equality contrast with the collective discipline of the Calvinistic movements and, what in some respects is a cultural revival and extension of them, Communist versions of socialism.

The emerging pattern in modern societies is *institutionalized individualism*. An early delineator of this pattern was Durkheim in connection with his conception of organic solidarity. Organic solidarity referred to a differentiated society in which different individuals and groups performed different functions. Its members are at the same time integrated through common ties of loyalty to the society and to each other as fellow citizens. This carries with it the complication that the differentiated functions are the source of valued *contributions* to the welfare and implementation of the values of the society. On such grounds a normative justification both of certain freedoms and of certain inequalities can be accepted.[12] This pattern of institutionalized individualism requires a balance of solidarity on a basis of pluralistic differentiatedness and high valuation of the freedom and dignity of the individual, what Durkheim called the "cult of the individual,"[13] as well as commitment to standards of *justice* in balancing the treatment, rewards, and access to facilities of different individuals and subgroups of them.

The normative pressure of the institutionalized individualism pattern has encouraged active achievement for the society as a whole and for its various subunits. Nevertheless, a social structure has emerged which does not emphasize hierarchy in the interest of collective effectiveness but incorporates an associational emphasis: it provides freedom of action for numerous differentiated subgroups and individuals. Higher education is one important field of institutionalization of institutionalized individualism, a field in which the associational emphasis is particularly strong.

The general value-pattern of instrumental activism has underlain the development of Western civilization through its Christian

11. *The Principles of Sociology* (New York and London, D. Appleton and Co., 1924), vol. II (in three vols.), pt. 5, chap. xvii, "The Militant Type of Society," and chap. xviii, "The Industrial Type of Society."

12. Talcott Parsons, "Equality and Inequality in Modern Society; or, Social Stratification Revisited," *Sociological Inquiry*, 40 (Spring 1970), 13–72.

13. Robert N. Bellah, ed., "Introduction" to *Emile Durkheim*, Heritage of Sociology Series (Chicago, Ill., University of Chicago Press, 1973).

heritage.[14] Though science, industry, and commerce have not been confined to Protestant societies, Max Weber's insight about the facilitating influence of ascetic Protestantism has been generally supported by later research.[15]

The United States constituted a Puritan version of Protestantism which had time to become consolidated before the large-scale Catholic immigration took place.[16] Moreover, the form of the Puritan heritage which came to predominate was the individualistic one that crystallized in the eighteenth century[17] before the Independence movement and the settlement of the American constitutional framework. Bear in mind that separation of church and state and nearly complete religious freedom as well as denominational pluralism were thereby achieved for the first time in Christian history. Within the Christian framework two selective choices characterized liberal Protestantism: (1) the concern for "this world," for the quality of life in secular society, as contrasted with withdrawal into devotional spirituality, and (2) the individualistic trend, the centering of religio-moral sanctions on the conduct and role of the individual, not the collective achievements of a "church militant."

We are not concerned here to go into the many subtle problems about the status of this inherited value-pattern.[18] Privatization of religion and other aspects of secularization may suggest that *any* religiously grounded values have ceased to have implications for American society. A basis for this view is the alleged decline of the Protestant ethic. We believe that this allegation rests on misinter-

14. Talcott Parsons, "Christianity," *International Encyclopedia of the Social Sciences,* ed. David L. Sills (New York, The Macmillan Co. and The Free Press, 1968), II, 425–447; Talcott Parsons, "Some Problems of General Theory in Sociology," in *Theoretical Sociology, Perspectives and Developments,* ed. John C. McKinney and Edward A. Tiryakian (New York, Appleton-Century-Crofts, Educational Division, Meredith Corporation, 1970), pp. 27–68; Parsons, *System of Modern Societies.*

15. Robert K. Merton, *Science, Technology and Society in Seventeenth Century England* (New York, H. Fertig, 1970); Joseph Ben-David, *The Scientist's Role in Society: A Comparative Study* (Englewood Cliffs, N.J., Prentice-Hall, Inc., 1971).

16. Perry Miller, *Errand into the Wilderness* (Cambridge, Mass., Harvard University Press, 1964).

17. Johannes J. Loubser, "Puritanism and Religious Liberty: A Study of Normative Change in Massachusetts, 1630–1850," unpub. diss., Harvard University, 1964.

18. The controversies over Weber's Protestant ethic thesis have recently been summarized in three works: *The Protestant Ethic and Modernization: A Comparative View,* ed. S. N. Eisenstadt (New York, Basic Books, 1968), Introduction, pp. 3–45; David Little, *Religion, Order and Law* (New York, Harper Torch Books, 1969), "Bibliographical Essays: (A) Representative Literature Critical of the Protestant Ethic"; and Benjamin Nelson, "Weber's Protestant Ethic: Its Origins, Wanderings, and Foreseeable Futures," in *The Scientific Study of Religion: Beyond the Classics,* ed. Charles Y. Glock and Phillip E. Hammond (Harper & Row, 1973).

pretation of the nature of societal value-systems and of their role in actual societal structure and process.[19]

In terms of our paradigm of functional analysis, the value-pattern of instrumental activism should exert normative pressure on the society to stress adaptive functions, that is, orientation to the environment as distinguished from orientation to internal pattern-maintenance or integrative functions. As between the two types of environment-oriented functions, the adaptive emphasis is primarily economic as distinguished from goal-attainment. (At the societal level goal attainment is *collective* goal attainment leading to political organization with a hierarchical flavor.)

Weber had the insight to see that, at the period of development he was considering, a special affinity existed between the ethic of Protestantism and a high valuation of economic productivity. This high valuation had something to do with the fact that Americans followed the British example as pioneers of the industrial revolution and, with their greater population and resources, became the world's premier industrial nation. It was not the profit motive in its blatantly hedonistic meaning that Weber stressed, but the *valuation* of contribution to production as a "calling." Monetary earnings were a *measure* of that contribution, not its ultimate motivation.

Productive and profitable economic activity depends on rationality of action. Relatively high levels of rationality were attainable in the economic field especially because, unlike politics, production dealt with problems of the management of physical objects rather than with human relations. Weber was aware of these connections; he repeatedly called attention to the concept of economic rationality.

Only within recent decades has a technology grounded in science rather than empirical know-how begun to play a dominant role in economic production. However, the pattern of rationality has contributed to a pattern-congruence between economic and cognitive rationality rather than direct causal influence of one factor on the other—for example, an economic pay-off of knowledge.[20] As opportunities opened up, the normative pressure of the value-system worked to encourage concern with rationality, not

19. Parsons, *System of Modern Societies*, esp. chap. vi, "The New Lead Society and Contemporary Modernity," pp. 86–121, and "Conclusion: The Main Pattern," pp. 138–143.

20. This, and the remainder of the discussion in the paragraph, is one example of interpenetration.

only in the economic direction but also in the cognitive and in certain others. The link lies in the adaptive function which at the societal level is exemplified by economic production, at the cultural level by cognitive symbolization, the cultural focus of which is knowledge. Cognitive standards must provide the criteria to distinguish between rational and nonrational or irrational modes of behavior.

In our view the primary impetus to the development of the cognitive complex within the last century of American history did not lie in its function as an investment in enhanced economic productivity, though in its later phases it has had that consequence. Whatever the impetus, however, *the same* value-system that favored economic development also favored cognitive development. If, by whatever combination of forces, the process of development of a society follows the *direction* of the normative pressure exerted by its value-system, then a process of *upgrading* generally takes place. An immense economic development did in fact take place in the United States. This provided resources some of which were made available for the support of education and research. However, once successfully attained, the goals of production became relatively less urgent, and some people turned to alternative goals, goals congenial from the point of view of values that were already institutionalized. Both the rapid development of the academic profession and the commitment of large numbers to higher education in the role of students seem understandable in these terms. In short, the cognitive complex is in the same position—primarily adaptive—in the cultural system as the economic complex is in the society. If an upgrading process takes place within the framework of the paramount American value-pattern, the successful attainment of economic goals should be followed by an increase of concern with cognitive matters. This perspective will be central to much of the discussion that follows.

## Institutionalization in the Fiduciary System

Chapter 1 included an outline of the fiduciary system of the society. The fiduciary system is the social locus of institutionalization of the cognitive complex because it is that aspect of the society in which the zone of interpenetration with the cultural system primarily is located. Since the focus of the cognitive complex is first of all cultural, its main societal involvement can be expected to appear in the fiduciary subsystem and within the fiduciary subsystem in the *rationality* system.

Within this formal framework, we wish to outline some consequences of the thesis that, at both the cultural and the social system levels, the cognitive system as institutionalized in the academic world has become a *differentiated* system with substantial autonomy vis-à-vis other subsystems but also interdependent with them in new ways. On the cultural level, the three boundaries whose differentiation had to be worked out and boundary-patterns redefined are those relative to religion, to the expressive-aesthetic sphere, and to moral-evaluative symbolization.

In the past religion has been a focus of strain, but the main structural problem was resolved in the nineteenth century in the period during the early phases of development of the American university system. The accepted formula is that the universities were secularized in a respect parallel to secularization of the state, though the university system was divided between private and public sectors. With the exception of the Catholic system of higher education, by the turn of the century there were no longer religious tests for faculty appointment or student enrollment; and officially sponsored denominational religious exercises with a claim on the university community for participation had become much less common. Denominationalism has lingered in colleges, although not to an appreciable extent in universities. Until recently, it also characterized Catholic institutions, though in the last generation they have undergone rapid change in the direction of integration with the rest of the system. Interestingly enough, the religious issue in its traditional form has been absent from recent controversies that have shaken the American system of higher education.

Differentiation of the cognitive complex from religion has been a focus of tension, although not recently. The expressive-aesthetic case has followed a different pattern. Noncontroversial in the past, it has recently experienced an upsurge of concern, not only in the society at large but especially in the academic community. Extremists have advocated virtual equal status in the university of the creative and performing arts with the intellectual disciplines and even tipping the balance in favor of the former on the ground that the intellect is not truly creative. A long, complicated history lies behind this tension which dates from the tension between rationalism and romanticism during the Enlightenment in

France.[21] The American academic system, especially in its socialization functions, has to a degree neglected expressive-aesthetic interests, and this may account for the compensatory pendulum swing that has been taking place. We shall consider this question in Chapters 4 and 6.

The form of differentiation between cognitive and moral-evaluative cultural orientations lies in the foreground of controversy at present. Part of the differentiation of the moral and cognitive components of culture occurred concomitantly with the differentiation between religious and cognitive orientations. This differentiation of cognitive from moral-evaluative orientations does not mean that the modern university has become morally indifferent but rather that guardianship of the moral heritage of the society is not defined as a *primary* function. This point will become clear later in this chapter when we analyze the cognitive complex in relation to values in general and that of cognitive rationality in particular.

The central core of the normative system of the university, which is embodied in its social organization, is the valuation of cognitive rationality. Cognitive rationality is not the general value-system of the society but a differentiated sector of it. The autonomy of the university with respect to cognitive rationality is paralleled by the autonomy of the economy with respect to economic rationality and of the legal system with respect to constitutional freedoms, justice, and equity. In our view, the nearest thing in American society to a fiduciary subsystem primarily concerned with general moral-evaluative questions is the legal system grounded as it has come to be in Constitutional principles. As trustee of the principal societal moralities, the legal system is subject to continual critical interaction with other cultural realms, especially the religious and the intellectual, which are also concerned about moral values, and on the societal side with political entities that channel interests and grievances into bases of moral evaluation. The complexity of these interrelationships prevents the university from pretending to be the moral arbiter of the society; such a role would presuppose a premodern level of differentiation such as occurred in the early Lutheran tradition when the *theological faculty* of the university was expected to function as the

21. Priscilla P. Clark and Terry N. Clark, "Writers, Literature, and Student Movements in France," *Sociology of Education*, 42 (Fall 1969), 293–314.

Prince's Conscience (in a moral-evaluative as well as in a primarily theological sense).

Differentiatedness implies autonomy in one context but enhanced interdependence in others. Given the fact of secularization, the normative basis of the cognitive complex and hence the moral justification of the university tends to relate to the moral-evaluative complex. One relevant aspect of the moral-evaluative complex, derived from differentiated autonomy, concerns the university's right to exist and to do the kinds of things it is committed to doing. Another relevant aspect concerns the *contributions* the university may be expected to make toward the welfare and value-implementation of the society. At the moral-evaluative level, some balancing of inputs in the form of protection of rights with outputs in the form of valued contributions is a condition of the stable functioning of a university system. The university cannot enjoy the autonomy it has gained and still be fully self-legitimized. In various contexts it is subject to moral pressures to justify itself in terms of the general moral culture of the society; there is an expectation that its privileges will be matched by contributions as evaluated by moral rather than cognitive standards.

The parallel problem of interdependence exists between the

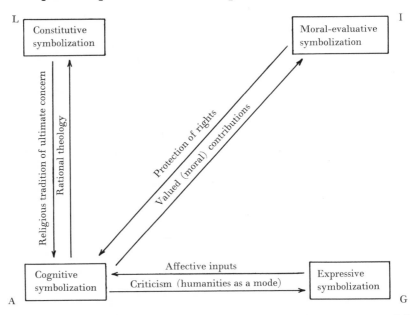

Figure 2.3. Interchanges between the Cognitive Complex and the Other Subsystems at the Cultural Level

cognitive and expressive complexes of modern culture; the increased emphasis on cognitive concerns, especially among faculty and students, requires grounding of the affective base of their participation in cognitive culture and the articulation of affectivity with academic functions. The arts, like the family of orientation and the student peer complex at social system levels, are a source of affective inputs to the university system. In short, the university has come to need the arts. At the same time, just as there is a danger of overmoralizing the university and of overreligionizing it, the danger exists of overaestheticizing it. Knowledge and art are culturally distinct categories; they should be interdependent but not confused, one should not overwhelm the other. The primary contribution of the university to the arts is *criticism*, which is essential to the arts themselves.[22] The interchange point of aesthetic and cognitive interests lies in the humanities as intellectual disciplines in the university setting; the humanities should cultivate close relations with the arts.[23]

As for interdependence between the cognitive and the religious contexts of culture, the contribution of the university to religious thought has long been prominent because rational theology has been basic to Western religious functioning. The contribution of the great religious traditions to the university is more likely to be overlooked; there is a tendency for the cognitive enterprise to succumb to the illusion of total self-sufficiency, sometimes formulated as "positivism" or "scientism," and to be unaware of its connections with the religious traditions of ultimate concern.

It is not easy to distinguish neatly the input-output relations of interpenetrating systems at both the cultural and the social system levels. Whereas at the cultural level religion focuses on belief, symbolization, and ritual patterning, at the societal level religion in our tradition is organized in churches and denominations. The secularization of the university has usually meant its organizational autonomy vis-à-vis religious organizations, but lurking in the background has been the cultural autonomy of cognitive symbolization. Similarly with the interchanges. One area of interpenetration of the religious and the rational subsystems of the fiduciary system has been the ancient tradition of university

22. Northrop Frye, "The Critical Path: An Essay on the Social Context of Literary Criticism," *Daedalus*, The Journal of the American Academy of Arts and Sciences (Spring 1970), pp. 268–342.
23. Talcott Parsons, "Theory in the Humanities and Sociology," *Daedalus* (Spring 1970), pp. 495–523.

schools of theology. On current and probable future levels of differentiation, such schools would not make sense if the cognitive *output* to religion in theology, religious history, the sociology of religion, and the rational organization of pastoral functions were not needed by contemporary organized religion. Religious *inputs* to academia constitute the obverse interchange. Within the fiduciary system, the rationality subsystem is integrated with both religion and the moral community. The most necessary input to the university system from religion is that of legitimation—not primarily of authority, though this plays a part, but of the prestige accorded to the academic world generally at the social level and more specifically to cognitive concerns, both culturally and psychologically. The locus of questioning of such legitimation has lain in the moral community—for example, about the morality of connections with economic and political interests. Morality, however, is so deeply intertwined with religion that it would be distorting to attempt to isolate it too drastically. A considerable portion of the clergy of all denominations, including the Catholic, have joined radical critics of many features of contemporary society; and their stance extends into the university community partly through divinity faculties. Moreover, the university has been one target of this religio-moral criticism.

Profound as is the university system's need for moral legitimation with a religious background, including what Robert Bellah calls the civil religion,[24] it must maintain its autonomy relative to the moral community in society at large. To be an authentic moral community in its own right, the university must maintain a primary commitment to its own moral values rather than attempt to be a microcosm of the morality of society as a whole. Vis-à-vis the larger society, its contribution is cognitive criticism of values in the society—including its own—but without pretending to be a general moral arbiter. It receives in exchange the moral component of the legitimation to which we have just referred. The accessibility of such legitimation depends on adequate appreciation in nonacademic sectors of the legitimacy of academic criticism of nonacademic attempts at value-implementation. Legitimation depends on a widespread conviction that the academic world preserves the integrity of its own values which are, after all, part of the general societal value-system.

24. Robert N. Bellah, "Civil Religion in America," *Daedalus* (Winter 1967), pp. 1–21.

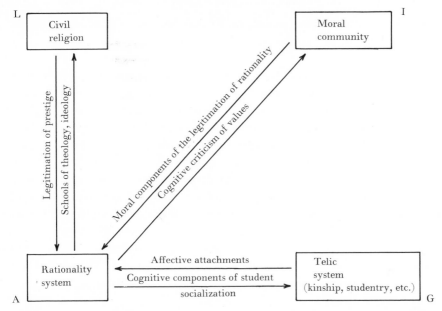

Figure 2.4. Interchanges between the Cognitive Complex and the Other Subsystems of the Fiduciary System (at the Social-System Level)

The *telic* system institutionalizes at the social level the expressive interests which are symbolized at the cultural level; these interests in turn interpenetrate with the motivational needs of personalities on the expressive-affective side in a manner parallel to that of the articulation of economic and of cognitive interests with the needs of personalities. All three are goal-oriented at cultural, societal-fiduciary, and psychological levels, respectively.

In the zone of interpenetration between the telic subsystem of the fiduciary system and the personality of the individual are anchored the two particularly important structures of kinship systems, on the one hand, and, on the other, of the adolescent and postadolescent (studentry) peer solidarities with which we shall have to be concerned. One process of differentiation giving rise to modern society has been differentiation of family household as a solidary unit from the occupational organization; the household has lost most of its role as an economic producer to the occupational organization. Although the typical student has been brought up in such a differentiated family household, enrollment at college usually separates him from it; in a substantial proportion of cases he lives apart from his family at college. At the same time he has not yet usually established a family of procreation and is still depen-

51

dent economically and emotionally on his family of orientation and on some kind of student aid and academic community solidarity.

Chapter 4 analyzes the psychodynamic relations of family background to peer solidarity and the bearing of both family background and peer solidarity on academic communities. To note one point here, however, a structural difference between undergraduate students and faculty members is that the faculty typically live in family households scattered through the general residential community among families·with a similar style of life, whereas students are often concentrated in student housing without regard to their family backgrounds. This circumstance creates an opportunity to develop distinctive student styles of life, that is, expressive symbolism that emphasizes the autonomy of student status and sometimes its antagonism to the "square" style of life of parents and of college teachers, each of whom belong to about the same generation.

This is another instance of the differentiated autonomy of the academic system, in this case a fostering of age-graded solidary groupings with primarily expressive-aesthetic rather than cognitive functions, groupings differentiated from their nonacademic counterparts. At fiduciary levels a contribution of the university in this direction is the cognitive components of the newly important student socialization. In return the college needs inputs of affective attachments, not only from students but also from other telic solidarities.

How are fiduciary subsystems differentiated from the non-fiduciary subsystems of the society and what are the principal modes of interdependence between them? The academic, as part of the rationality subsystem of the fiduciary system, shares certain problems with the other fiduciary systems; its autonomy is grounded in a differentiated subset of the more general societal value-system centering on cognitive rationality. One aspect of differentiation is the autonomy of the fiduciary system and the status of the university as part of the fiduciary system. We have already touched on the autonomy problem in the context of moral legitimation. Beyond legitimation, it arises again because of the relation of the fiduciary system to the societal community and to the two principal types of interests at the societal level: in political power and in wealth.

The university must be organized as a concrete associational structure. This structure must at the same time be integrated with the larger structure of the societal community at many different levels. The principal grounding of its autonomy must lie in the value of cognitive rationality to which it is committed internally but which is also shared in the wider community, though not usually at the same levels of intensity.

The university can provide many outputs of service to the community where the functions involve values other than cognitive rationality. Three important ones are contributions to the socialization of an educated citizenry (to be discussed in Chapter 4), to practical goals through the applied professions (to be discussed in Chapter 5), and to the definition of the situation at ideological levels (to be discussed in Chapter 6).

Two main categories of inputs are dependent on these categories of service. One is reinforcement of the values of cognitive rationality, especially on the part of various publics outside the academic system, but including reinforcement of confidence in them by its own members through a sense that the paths they have chosen to be useful are also worthwhile. The other is the input of loyalty.

When we come to the interest complex, although business firms have performed some of the functions which universities perform, such as research, no university has been set up as a commercial enterprise subject to the imperative of profit or perish. In other words, the academic enterprise has typically been economically subsidized on a considerable scale. Indeed, tuition fees have been regarded more as contributions to a valued enterprise than as the price of a service. Of course, the American university system is financially dependent on both private and public sources, with the latter growing in relative importance recently.

This financial dependence creates tension with respect to the autonomy of the university. It is not literally true that "whoever pays the piper, calls the tune" in this case, but the piper must come to terms with those who pay him. The university must share values at some level with private donors or with state or federal legislators and their constituencies.

What kind of outputs can offset the financial deficits involved in the operations of the typical university? At the societal level, one is the implementation of the obligations of service to the societal community, namely, in student socialization, in applied professional service, and in ideological services. Another output is contribution to a style of life which operates through the educated citizenry but also through intellectuals. This concerns primarily the intellectual component of the shaping of consumption patterns: matters of taste falling outside academic disciplines but which have permeated the field of consumption. There are subtle interrelationships between strictly intellectual fare, as in highbrow periodicals, a broader permeation of the mass media, tastes in the arts, and tastes in household furnishings and other matters.

On cruder levels, the economic interest problem was fought out in controversies over academic freedom and tenure which led to the founding of the AAUP and marked its early history. A recent focus has been the seductive effect of the availability of large Federal funds for academic research. Doubts have been expressed both inside and outside the universities about the compatibility of the terms on which research grants were available with the integrity of academic values.

This economic aspect of the problem of complicity shades into a political aspect and indeed into the general problem of the relation of academia to the political system. Even more than in relation to economic production, the university is a deficit operation with respect to political power. Economic and political aspects overlap with respect to the governmental role in university finance. But the political problem goes beyond financial support; it affects the support of the academic enterprise in such fields as the protection of academic freedom and the utilization of academic expertise in public affairs. Such support must be implemented through power which cannot be reciprocated by the academic community. Academic autonomy therefore depends on the academic system generating outputs which are valued from relevant political points of view. One contributory output is a component of *interest demands,* which means that, parallel to the intellectual component of consumers' tastes that is valued, there is also an intellectual component of the interest demands of constituencies, and these constitute a factor in the generation of political power.[25] One focus of the intellectual component of interest demand of constituencies is the question of rationality. The relation between valuation of political and of cognitive rationality provides the context in which the university may close the "power gap."

The goal-attainment boundary problems of the cognitive

25. Talcott Parsons, "On the Concept of Political Power," in *Politics and Social Structure,* ed. Talcott Parsóns (New York, The Free Press, 1969), pp. 352–404 (reprinted from *Proceedings of the American Philosophical Society,* 107 [June 1963], 232–262).

complex constitute sources of vulnerability to disturbing influences when under pressure. At the cybernetic top, the cultural level, a series of boundary problems starts with concern for the expressive-aesthetic complex as distinguished from the cognitive. At the level of the fiduciary subsystem of the society, it focuses on the telic complex, which articulates the societal with the personality systems and in an academic context with the function of socialization. At the more general societal level, it focuses on the political problem.

In a parallel sense to that of the affinity of the cognitive and the economic which we have outlined, there is, in potential conflict with the cognitive, an alliance between expressive and political interests in the university in preferring telic interests of the peer group over cognitive concerns. We shall discuss the nature and conditions of this alliance at length in Chapter 7.

## Outline of the Cognitive Complex

Within the setting we have outlined, we now come to the cognitive complex itself. Subject to the values of cognitive rationality, the cognitive complex involves four classes of phenomena in which cognitive functions are salient and cognitive standards have normative primacy. On its boundaries this primacy is shared with standards supported by values other than cognitive rationality. These four categories are *knowledge*, the relevant category of cultural object, *rational action*, the type of social action in which cognitive standards have primacy as guides to action, *competence*, a form or component of performance capacity grounded in the individual personality, a capacity to utilize relevant standards of rationality in action, and, finally, *intelligence*, a medium of interchange at the level of the general system of action anchored in the behavioral organism and thereby utilizing capacities of the central nervous system.

We are placing Figure 2.5, as a rather crude diagrammatic representation of the cognitive complex, at the beginning of our explication of that central concept. We do not expect the reader to comprehend it fully here before reading the following text discussion, but we hope it will prove to be a useful reference focus. It should, of course, be thought of in relation to the diagrams already presented in Chapter 1 and in the earlier part of the present chapter and also in relation to the technical appendix.

The paradigm starts with the consideration of knowledge as a type of cultural object. As such it is placed in the adaptive subsystem, in the lower-left corner of the representation of the cultural system. (Compare Figure 1.3, Chapter 1.) Here we use the term knowledge, rather than "cognitive symbolization," in order to emphasize at this point the importance of the class of cultural objects to which we are referring as distinguished from the cultural system in the perspective of "action" which stresses more "cognizing" as type of action process.

As will be developed more fully in the following exposition, we then conceive knowledge to be, as internalized in the personality system, a primary ingredient of what we call the *competence* of individual persons, a capacity for effective performance which we understand to be acquired through processes of learning, only minimally to be inherited genetically, in anything like a specific action-pattern sense, though of course genetic components "underlie" competence.

The competent performance of individuals we then conceive to operate predominantly within a matrix of social interaction, sensitive to the sanctioning—positive or negative—significance of the reactions of actors other than the performer. This matrix of interaction in the normative regulation of which cognitive standards play a central, though by no means always primary role, has seemed to us to be the proper place to focus the much discussed concept of the *rationality* of action. Our grounds for this focusing will be stated in the text later in the present chapter. We conceive rationality to be institutionalized in social systems in a sense parallel to that in which competence is internalized in personality systems.

The relation of intelligence, which we here treat as a generalized symbolic medium of interaction, to the behavioral organism is perhaps a little more complicated. We attempt to explicate it more fully below. For the present, suffice it to say that the "capacity" for intelligent action is assumed to be grounded in the human central nervous system, especially, of course, in the brain. This capacity, however, can only become operative for action in that it articulates with a complex of "meaning" of its "problems" and outputs at the cultural level. In the cognitive context, which is our current concern, we find the grounds of this meaning in the cultural category of knowledge. *Intelligent* action is then action oriented in terms of the search for knowledge, the evaluation of cultural objects by the cognitive standards appropriate to knowledge, and the utilization of knowledge for the satisfaction of interests, whether or not they are primarily cognitive.

Besides labeling the four primary components of the cognitive complex and locating them in our functional paradigm, we have included in Figure 2.5 highly schematic characterizations of the six interchange relations among these four functional reference-categories. These do not attempt a "breakdown" into formal double-interchange sets, but only to give a broad idea of what each of the six interchange sets is "all about."

The cognitive process, defined functionally and at the general level of action, is an aspect of adaptation to the environment. The cognitive process attempts to understand. Among adaptive modes the cognitive is for *our*[26] purposes that which is cybernetically controlled by culturally articulated symbols, organized and

26. Many levels of presymbolic cognitive processes have figured in comparative psychology. What we are dealing with here is the cognitive aspect of action, not cognition in general.

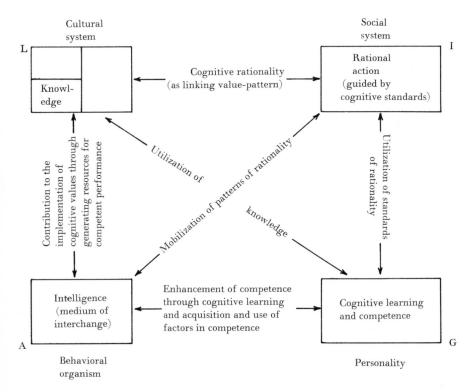

Figure 2.5. The Cognitive Complex

given meaning by *codes*. The dominant symbol-type is what Charles Morris has called "designative"[27] symbols, which are oriented to understandable properties of the objects of orientation. By contrast, expressive symbols have meanings oriented to the states of actors or classes of them, individual or collective; and moral-evaluative symbols have meanings relating actors to objects in terms of the systemic-integrative function of the actor-object relationship. Finally, constitutive symbols have meanings oriented to the nature of the relevant action system as a whole, independent of its subparts either as actors or as objects or of the special actors and objects in which they are interested.

Thus interpreted, the cognitive category refers to one aspect of action at symbolic levels, although action in which cognitive components play a part always involves *the other* components. Therefore, to speak with clarity about the cognitive aspect necessitates relating it to noncognitive components involved in various types of action. This involves relative *primacies* among cognitive and various noncognitive components.

### Knowledge

Knowledge is the type of cultural object with respect to which the cognitive-designative meanings of symbols and codes have primacy. Knowledge, though a product of action, is, as a cultural object-type, independent of any particular actor. This is indicated by the fact that not only is knowledge internalized in personalities but it is also externalized, as in written or recorded form. Whether incorporated in a book or in someone's head, it can still be *the same* knowledge.

Knowledge shares with other cultural objects another feature: The meanings of cultural objects cannot be appropriated by particular actors except by erecting barriers to communication. Since the cognitive complex at the cultural level is parallel to the economic complex at the societal level, there is a relation here to objects of utility, that is, of economic value. The term for rights in objects of utility is "possession"; the term for the institution defining those rights is "property." Particular symbols of cogni-

---

27. The classification of types of symbols worked out by Morris fits our purposes admirably. Designative symbols are for cognitive-adaptive function, prescriptive for goal-attainment functions, appraisive for integrative functions, and formative for constitutive pattern-maintenance functions. See Charles Morris, *Signification and Significance* (Cambridge, Mass., The MIT Press, 1964).

tive meaning may be possessed in the property sense; for instance, a person may own a copy of a book and thus the symbols impressed on its pages are his. But since all copies of the same book are alike, he does not thereby acquire exclusive *rights* in the meanings of the symbols; these are in the "public domain." The same principle applies to all cultural objects. A particular work of art, a painting, may be possessed by a particular individual or a museum. But the meaning of its symbolic content is not confined to this case of externalization, but can be communicated in a variety of ways. The absence of exclusive rights of possession of meanings implies a further property of cultural objects: that their transmission to others by communication, though it may lead to gain by the recipient, does not result in a corresponding loss by the communicator. The director of a museum, by opening the museum to the public, does not lose the meanings valued by him and transfer them to visitors; he still retains them, though they have been imparted to others by communication. The central aspect of these communicable meanings is pattern abstractable from concrete symbols and indeed often expressed in a variety of symbolic media.

Knowledge, then, is a class of cultural object. In the ideal type case it will meet the standards of cognitive validity and cognitive significance. Knowledge is a case of Weber's treatment of the ideal type as incorporating an ideal in the normative sense of fully meeting certain standards. The distinction between cognitive validity and cognitive significance is crosscut by the distinction between the logical and the referential components of a body of knowledge.[28] In order to make these distinctions, it is necessary for the cultural symbols to be arranged in propositional form. (Of course, a painting is only in a metaphorical sense a set of propositions, although it contains symbolic meanings.) Criteria of cognitive validity are used to evaluate the *truth* of a proposition. The logical part of the validity standard concerns the cogency of statement of what the utterer of the proposition *means*. Are the terms he uses precise or ambiguous? In making inferences from premise to conclusion, is the statement free of logical fallacy? Error, unclarity, and inconsistency constitute grounds for questioning the cognitive adequacy of the proposition.

28. Max Weber, "Objectivity in Social Science and Social Policy," in *Max Weber on the Methodology of the Social Sciences*, trans. and ed. Edward A. Shils and Henry A. Finch (Glencoe, Ill., The Free Press, 1949), chap. ii, pp. 50–112.

Propositions thus embody a logical code. The basic units of propositions are concepts—generalized symbols which can be used referentially to designate a subset of otherwise varying particular entities. A proposition relates two or more concepts to each other in such terms as a subject-object relation or a cause-effect relationship. Logic is the normative reference of the cognitive code because it formulates the symbolic conditions for asserting the validity of a proposition and of inference from one part of a propositional system to others. It demands clarity (unambiguousness) of conceptualization and inference according to definite rules. Certain formal disciplines, notably logic itself and mathematics, concern the structure of propositional systems in abstraction from specific referential content. On such levels we may speak of the logical validity of propositions and sets of them.

On the referential side, cognitive interest lies in the properties of objects not reckoned as part of the actor, the putatively knowing subject, or of the logical cognitive code itself. For example, the symbol "dog" designates an animal species so that the proposition, "Look, there goes a dog," may be declared to be referentially valid in the sense that the presence of a dog within the range of vision can be empirically verified by "looking." Validity in this sense depends on knowledge of the code, in this case both the language and the logic it embodies, so that the word dog is understood as referring to a canine animal and not, for example, to a star.

Knowledge, to which the canons of cognitive validity apply, is inherently bound to the subject-object relationship; hence knowledge is referentially knowledge *of* objects which are not analytically part either of the knowing subject or of the cognitive code. This is the basis of the distinction between cognitive and expressive symbolization; in expressive symbolization the referential component does not concern an object, or category, or system of them, but expresses some meaning pertaining to the subject of the process of symbolization, that is, an actor. This view does not deny that, in the case of knowledge, the knowing subject contributes; it does not conceive the subject as an unexposed photographic plate. Nor does it deny that concrete expressive symbolization can be treated as a set of objects and hence as the data source of a body of knowledge.

We have used the term "referential" rather than the term "empirical" because we do not intend to foreclose the existence, as object-systems, of entities beyond what, in the appendix to the introduction, was called the second boundary of the system of action. The term "empirical" designates objects presumed to constitute part of the conditional environment of the knower. Such entities as "God" and presumptively possible future events, may be treated as cognitively meaningful objects, even though they are not empirically observable. The cultural structure of knowledge of such entities is essentially the same as that of empirical objects.

Normatively, propositions which purport to constitute knowledge are subject to canons of validity or truth. Negation of validity at the logical level is contained in such conceptions as ambiguity or fallacy. The canon of validity includes the cognitive meaningfulness of the major premises on which inference is based. On the referential side, for the empirical case the usual formulation concerns validation by a process of observation, which involves sense impressions. The concept *fact*,[29] as the referential component of empirical knowledge, should be defined as a proposition that is observationally verifiable but at the same time couched "in terms of a conceptual scheme."[30] A fact is *not* part of the phenomenal object but of the cultural structure which purports to have the status of valid knowledge about the phenomenon. Where the referential component is regarded as nonempirical, the parallel concept to a fact is a category of cognitively meaningful content not reducible to terms of the logical code alone, but purporting to characterize objects external to it. Of course, the mode of experiencing such objects would have to be different from that of empirical observation.

In this connection Smelser[31] points out that since facts and the referential component of nonempirical knowledge are propositions therefore the *integration* between the more general code level of knowledge and the more particular level involved in facts and other referential components involves *conceptual* levels of symbolization. Both code and referential components of a body of knowledge must be "bound together" at this level. This consideration raises the problem of significance. If knowledge consisted in

29. Talcott Parsons, *The Structure of Social Action* (Glencoe, Ill., The Free Press, 1949), chap. i, pp. 41–42.
30. Cf. *L. J. Henderson on the Social System*, ed. Bernard Barber (Chicago, Ill., University of Chicago Press, 1970), chap. iii.
31. Neil J. Smelser, *Essays in Sociological Explanation* (Englewood Cliffs, N.J., Prentice-Hall, Inc., 1968), with special reference to the essay, "The Optimum Scope of Sociology," pp. 58–59.

discrete, isolated propositions, the definition of knowledge as an ideal type could be confined to criteria of validity. The issue, however, arises of the relationship between any one proposition and its context in larger systems of propositions, including those at various levels of generality. *Cognitive significance* refers to the significance of one set of propositions for other sets within a body of knowledge or for the body of knowledge as a whole. As opposed to particular statements of fact and problem-solutions, higher-order cognitive significance generally involves theory and frames of reference. Generality at the level of theory is tested by the capacity for inference from one part of a body of knowledge to others so that the implications of a fact or solution of a particular problem can be traced throughout the system. The cognitive significance of a particular propositional item is thus a function of the range of implications within a wider cognitive system, knowledge of which enables a knowing subject to trace such implications.

A second aspect of the significance of knowledge is for *noncognitive* aspects of the cultural system. Thus, systems of expressive symbolization can be treated as objects for cognitive study, and the knowledge gained by this study may contribute to the appreciation of such symbol-systems, say, as works of art. They may also become components in the competence of artists so that knowing the traditions and techniques of an art may make for "better" artistic output.[32]

There is also a cognitive component in systems of moral-evaluative symbolization. Although we do not subscribe to the possibility of a scientific ethic, as many in the positivistic tradition have done, we believe in the possibility of a rational ethic. An ethic can be relatively rational in so far as the moral commitments which it engenders are articulated with belief systems, empirical and nonempirical, which conform in significant respects to standards of cognitive validity. Max Weber, in his comparative studies in the sociology of religion, stressed the importance of such belief systems, especially at nonempirical levels, for ethical orientations grounded in religion.

Finally, knowledge has significance for systems of constitutive symbolism, certainly in relation to rational theology, which shades off into aspects of philosophy. In the latter case, however,

---

32. This cognitive concern with expressive symbolization seems close to what Northrop Frye has meant by *criticism*, primarily in the context of literature. Cf. Frye, "The Critical Path."

the cognitive factor tends to have a primacy which does not hold for most theology.

Cultural objects which cannot be described in the pattern-form of a set of propositions should not be called knowledge. Thus, to use a previous example, as art criticism or art history, propositions may be stated about a painting, and these propositions may constitute valid knowledge. But the painting itself does not consist of propositions and is not knowledge, though the painter's knowledge was a factor in its production.

Our ideal of valid and significant knowledge at the systemic level suggests the desirability of closure. Closure has been not only aimed for but claimed again and again in the course of intellectual history. As concrete reality, however, closure seems to be illusory. There always are questionable assumptions, problems of levels of generality, internal contradictions, ambiguities of meaning, and referential uncertainties so that no body of knowledge is impervious to justified criticism and ultimately to change.[33] It does not follow from this that cognitive validity is a mirage, that all propositions are arbitrary.

Our ideal of valid and significant knowledge assumes a high level of differentiation between knowledge and other categories of cultural object. Since the process of rationalization, as Weber called it, has proceeded farther in the modern Western world than in other civilizations, approaches to this ideal type are particularly important at this time—especially to the Western university system. We do not claim complete differentiation between knowledge and other cultural objects, but the existence of phenomena which deviate from an ideal type does not mean that the type is analytically useless.

Durkheim, in a classic manner, showed the sense in which primitive religion was the cultural matrix from which the principal branches of culture have been differentiated.[34] What is usually called "belief systems" involve noncognitive elements, both in their assumptions and in other ways: these noncognitive elements are frequently mixed up with the cognitive. Not always, however, are they accountable for cognitive imperfections; they may simply not be distinguished from essentially valid cognitive compo-

33. Alfred N. Whitehead, *Science and the Modern World* (New York, Macmillan, 1967 [originally published in 1925]).

34. Emile Durkheim, *The Elementary Forms of the Religious Life*, trans. Joseph Ward Swain (Glencoe, Ill., The Free Press, 1954). Original French edition, 1912.

nents. Moreover, different cultures will weight their cognitive components differently relative to noncognitive elements. Thus the classical Greeks were more cognitively oriented than were the Romans of the same period.

In this sense, allowance must be made for cultural variability, both in historical and in comparative terms, although this does not mean that logic is only one of a family of alternative ways of organizing knowledge. Thus, the mode of symbolic integration in the ancient Chinese cosmological world view (centering on what Durkheim, Marcel Mauss, and Marcel Granet called the emblems of Tao, Yang, and Yin[35]) constitutes a case of cultural symbolization but not a philosophy in the sense of a branch of knowledge.

In order to present the conceptual structure which has just been reviewed diagrammatically, it has been necessary, as shown in Figure 2.6, to distinguish two different levels, both of which are essential to our analysis. The first, the upper part of the diagram (a), concerns the components of the structure of knowledge itself, considered as cultural objects which are identifiable as sets of propositions, in the sense outlined above. The second level, shown in the lower paradigm (b), concerns the modes of involvement of knowledge as cognitive objects in action.

The first, the upper paradigm, simply orders very familiar modes of categorization of the components of knowledge in terms of our functional scheme. It makes distinctions, however, which are by no means always clearly stated or consistently held to. The pattern-maintenance position is occupied by what we call the "frame of reference" within which substantive cognitive propositions are formulated. This is not as such substantive knowledge at all, but a form of code or template which "organizes" knowledge. Two examples may be given; thus the frame of reference of the classical mechanics[36] included the conceptions of Euclidean three-dimensional space, process in time (motion) as fitting on a linear continuum, physical bodies as "particles," located at any given moment at a mathematical point in space, characterized by the property of mass, and conceived as moving from location to location, motion being analyzable in terms of the concepts of velocity, and of direction, which in turn is broken down into the three

35. Emile Durkheim and Marcel Mauss, "De quelques formes primitives de classification," *L'Année Sociologique*, 6 (1901–02), 1–72; Marcel Granet, *La Pensée chinoise* (Paris, A. Michel, 1950).

36. Alfred N. Whitehead, *Science and the Modern World* (New York, Macmillan [1925], 1967).

# THE COGNITIVE COMPLEX

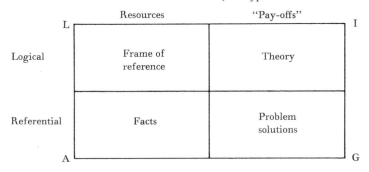

Components of Knowledge
as Cultural Object-Type

| | Resources | "Pay-offs" | |
|---|---|---|---|
| **L** | | | **I** |
| Logical | Frame of reference | Theory | |
| Referential | Facts | Problem solutions | |
| **A** | | | **G** |

Part (b)

Status of Cognitive Objects
in Action System

| | Cognitive primacy | Noncognitive relevance | |
|---|---|---|---|
| **L** | | | **I** |
| Cognitive significance | Position in corpus of knowledge | Integration in general culture | |
| Cognitive validity | Levels of cognitive certainty | Modes and levels of noncultural relevance (including concern with cognitive validity) | |
| **A** | | | **G** |

Figure 2.6. The Structure of Knowledge and of Its Involvement in Action

Euclidean dimensions. In classical mechanics no "fact" can be stated except in terms of this frame of reference nor can any theoretical generalization such as Newton's famous four "laws of motion."

The second example is the "action frame of reference" as it is used in the present study. The analogue of space is the manifold of possible meaning-references of action undertaken by actors—the latter are analogous to particles—which have certain properties such as "motives" and "capacities." Actors then are conceived as "acting," in interdependence with other actors in social systems, through processes which result in "changes of state" of the position of the actor, of his relations to other actors, and of the system comprised by a plurality of actors. The vectors of Euclidean motion in classical mechanics are paralleled by the "directions" in which actors bring about this change of state. We conceive the four-function paradigm to formulate a manifold of differentiable directions in this sense. There must, finally, be some kind of "energy" concept, comparable to velocity in mechanics, which formulates the magnitude of the pressures toward change of state relative to the "resistances" to such changes.

"Facts," then, we conceive to be referential statements about objects external to the actor—conceived here as knowing subject—and to the cognitive code, which is what we mean by the frame of reference. The logical and referential components then can be combinatorily organized in two primary modes. Theory in the present sense we conceive to be analytically generalized propositions stating relationships between variables and units in systems defined by the relevant frame of reference, but which do not include any specific statements of fact. Problem solutions, on the other hand, we think of as the result of the mobilization of both facts and theory within the frame of reference to "solve" a cognitive problem with referential relevance. For the purposes of this paradigm, however, it should be clearly kept in mind that we are thinking of *cognitive* problems, the solutions of which constitute valid knowledge, not of other kinds of problems where the cognitive components are combined with others as in the case of "how to" save the life of a person stricken with an acute and dangerous disease—an example we shall refer to several times below.

In the second, the lower (b), paradigm, the pattern-maintenance position is a matter of the position of the cognitive object(s) of reference in the corpus of knowledge itself. In this setting it must be accorded some order of cognitive *significance*, as that conception has been set forth above. Thus from a cognitive point of view interest is never *only* in the question of whether, in what respects and within what limits, a proposition or set of them is or is not *true*, but always also, at some level, with the question in a cognitive sense, "What of it?" Completely valid propositions can be completely trivial in the light of any larger cognitive context.

While still within the context of cognitive primacy of interest, then, there is always the question of the modes and levels of validity, not only of simple propositions but above all of those of high levels of generality and of the different parts of complex sets of propositions. In other words the question, "Is it true?" admits of simple answers only in limiting cases. Thus this question addressed to the status of Newtonian mechanics as a theoretical system, in the light of the subsequent development of physics, is neither a simple yes nor a no, but a complex pattern of evaluation with different answers according to the context of cognitive relevance. Similarly there can be no simple yes or no answer to the question whether Marx's "theory of capitalistic development" is true or false or whether Durkheim's theory of the relations between mechanical and organic solidarity is "true."

These problems of the nature and levels of cognitive validity and significance, however, must be systematically articulated with the questions of the *relevance* of the answers to the above questions to the variety of noncognitive concerns in culture and society with which we shall have to deal. The two right-hand boxes of the lower (b) paradigm attempt to formulate two crucial reference points for considering these questions of relevance. Since we consider knowledge to constitute a category of cultural objects, it is logical to raise the question of the relation of knowledge to other, noncognitive, categories of culture, as a special question not analytically mixed up with problems of social systems, personalities, or organisms. On the other hand, the latter problems are also highly relevant to our analysis and will be particularly important in Chapters 4 and 5 below.

It should be noted that our formulation is couched in terms which make the validity of cognitively relevant propositions problematical. In noncognitive contexts the propositions in which actors show interest may or may not be valid cognitively, and the answers to the questions of validity may be highly complex. However these considerations may be, they are always combined, in the box we are talking about, with noncognitive components of meaning and interest, the significance of which cannot be evaluated in terms of cognitive standards alone.

## Knowledge and the Other Cognitive Components

Knowledge is the primary adaptive resource for action generally. Concern with adaptive function creates a built-in interest in knowledge, in the validity of what purports to be knowledge, in the cognitive significance of items composing it, and in its generality and boundaries of relevance. On the methodological level there is an inherent interest in the feasibility and the costs of advancing knowledge and in the uses to which knowledge can be put, especially the implementation of values not themselves primarily cognitive. The adaptive consequences of such an interest structure depend not only on the nature of knowledge and on its available quantity and quality but on other features of the action system. In this light let us consider the relevance of the three components of the cognitive complex other than knowledge itself.

At a general action level the *implementation* of action-interests focuses in the personality subsystem. Therefore the first question about personalities is directed toward features with significance for the implementation of cognitive interests: in acquiring, advancing, or utilizing knowledge. A parallel question arises on the social system level of analysis. On the personality and social-system levels, the question is not only the conditions of facilitating the effectiveness of adaptive processes operating through cognitive channels but also the integrative problems involved in adjustment of the relations between these cognitive interests and various noncognitive concerns.

At the level of the social system, the problem can be formulated in terms of rationality. All three concepts are very familiar concepts prominent in intellectual history. If they are to serve our purposes with precision, we must select among historically common usages. We shall do so in each case by focusing on the *cognitive* reference of the concept.

With respect to competence, we distinguish between competence and effectiveness. We use the term "competence" to designate the capacity of an individual personality to achieve a goal by processes of choice in which valid and significant knowledge play a focal part, if not in commitment to the values or even the goals in question, in choosing and implementing the procedures by which goal-attainment processes operate. Effectiveness is conceived more broadly to designate any capacity of the personality to achieve desired goals regardless of the mode of involvement of cognitive components in the grounds of commitment or in the process of implementation.[37]

With respect to the concept of cognitive learning, general agree-

---

37. E.g., a parent's response to a temper tantrum of a child may be anger expressed by speaking harshly to the child or perhaps by spanking him. This response is sometimes effective in ending the tantrum, but this effectiveness is not necessarily due to the competence of the parent to handle irrational behavior on the part of his children. If, however, there is a chronic tendency for the child to stage frequent and escalating tantrums, the parent may enlist the services of a child psychiatrist. Presumably the main ground of selection of the psychiatrist is belief in his competence to deal with such problems.

ment exists that learning refers to the class of processes by which acting persons acquire capacity to comprehend and use elements of their cultural environment, as, for example, learning a language. A question that arises is whether the concept of learning should be applied to the continuing relation to the personality of *any* aspect of the environment in *any* context of its potential significance for the personality or should be restricted in some way. Thus, some would say that a child may learn to handle his parents by staging temper tantrums and provoking them to angry responses, whereas others would question the sense in which the child knows what he is doing and in which he is competent to bring about this effect when he wishes to do so. This is a case where cognitive components may be involved but are minimally differentiated from others. The sense in which the cognitive capacity has been learned is remote from the sense in which learning is a central category in understanding formal subjects, as in processes of higher education and research. For this reason, in speaking of learning as part of the differentiated cognitive complex, we will focus on the ideal type where the outcome of the learning process can be evaluated in terms of cognitive rationality and its derivatives: enhanced understanding of bodies of knowledge, enhanced capacity to solve cognitive problems, and enhanced capacity to utilize knowledge effectively in the interests of action-concerns that are not primarily cognitive.

As Jean Piaget's work suggests, cognitive aspects are vital in virtually all learning. We wish, however, to avoid unnecessary begging of questions. Therefore, we will speak of *cognitive* learning without prejudice to the question of how far and in what ways the learning concept is relevant to processes of acquisition by personalities of command over noncognitive components of the environment, especially of the cultural environment.

Competence could be understood merely as the capacity to act rationally. This would put the focus of the concept of rationality at the level of the individual personality. We wish to introduce a further constraint into the conception of rational action: that it should be treated as a category of *social* action rather than as action of the individual. Seen in this way, rational action is the effective implementation of the values of cognitive rationality in contexts of social interaction. It is the ideal type of conformity with a *socially* defined and *institutionalized* standard of desirable action typically implemented in interactive situations, whereas competence is capacity to conform with and implement an *internalized* standard at the level of the personality.

Although questions may be raised about the choice of these terms, they make it possible, without resorting to ad hoc definitions for every context, to distinguish between involvements of the cognitive complex at the cultural, the psychological-personality, and the social system levels. In each reference the relative significance of the cognitive component is differentially variable. Thus in some sectors of the social system, notably the economy and the educational system, rationality is at a premium, in others, such as the system of religious symbolization and ritual expression, it is less so. But this variability should not be confused with that between fields of competence and areas of noncognitive sentiment at the level of the personality or between economic rationality and symbolic reinforcement of kinship solidarity at the societal level. The social and the psychological levels can be distinguished by the role of interactive comparison and sanctioning, both positive and negative, of cognitively involved proposals and overtures. The hypothetical protoscientist in the state of nature may have some knowledge and competence, but he has only experiential successes or failures of his cognitive ventures to rely on for guidance. A prototype is Dr. Johnson's retort to Bishop Berkeley, that stubbing one's toe against a stone compels belief that the stone exists independently of the mind of the knower, who is sufficiently indiscreet to venture into an only partially known physical environment.

Consensual validation is not a criterion of the cognitive validity of propositions. But looked at from the point of view of developing the potential of the cognitive complex for enhancing the adaptiveness of human action systems, the institutionalization of cognitive values in social systems increases the adaptive capacity of the action system. The rationality complex, defined as focusing at the social level, contributes to a major function of the university as an agency of *rational* action.

The three components of knowledge, competence, and rationality may be conceived as bound together by common but differentiated relations to the medium of *intelligence*. We shall treat intelligence *not* primarily as a trait of the individual but as a generalized symbolic medium of interchange operating at the level of the general system of action. Intelligence is a generalized *capacity* controlled by any acting unit to contribute to the implementation of cognitive values through knowledge, through the process of cognitive learning, through the acquisition and use of competence, and through the pattern of rationality. Because intelligence is a generalized medium in the cognitive context (at the level of the general system of action), intelligence has functional parallels to money at the level of the social system.

Just as money is grounded in the economy and its resources, intelligence is grounded in the behavioral organism, the source of the facilities of the human central nervous system. The central nervous system provides the organic basis of the human capacity for symbolization, that is, for action as distinguished from metabolic function. *Land* in the sense of given physical resources for economic production has significance for the economy similar to that of the central nervous system for the behavioral organism.[38] The central nervous system is a basic resource; it contributes to capacity and limits capabilities in accordance with its biological characteristics.

Every symbolic medium must link an organic, environmental, or other resource base with a cultural level of code and symbolic structure. In the case of money, this linkage is between physical resources and the institutionalization of rights of possession in physical objects (property). Money is a generalized form of these rights and implies the capacity to acquire, dispose of, and legitimate the utilization of rights of possession *without reference* to *any* specificities of the concrete objects involved.

The prototype of objects of intelligent action, parallel to objects of possession, is knowledge as a category of cultural objects, which cannot be exclusively possessed but can be, in a different mode of access, acquired, used, and transmitted, that is, commanded. Intelligence, like money, can perform these functions at a level of generalization independent of *any* particulars of content of knowledge. That is to say, intelligence is the capacity to mobilize whatever cognitively relevant resources are available for the solution of cognitive problems, whether these are pure problems of the advancement of knowledge or problems involving the relation of cognitive considerations to use, transmission, and so on.[39]

38. John Maynard Keynes, *The General Theory of Employment, Interest, and Money* (London, Macmillan & Co., 1951), p. 343.

39. These considerations underlie our skepticism of the adequacy of treating intelligence as a trait of the individual, however much of the individual's command of intelligence characterizes his potential in a system of action. This command is a function of various traits of the individual in question, such as his genes and his educational attainments, which may enhance his capacity to acquire and use intelligence. But this is not the same thing as to say that intelligence *is* a trait of the individual.

The link, in the economic case, between the command of resources necessary for economic functioning and the rationale of their productive use lies in the connection between land, the ultimate unproduced resource, and the codified symbolic meanings of resources from the point of view of the societal interest in production. Property is the code or program implemented in productive economic action, and money is the generalized mode of institutionalizing that code.[40]

Similarly, brain capacity is the ultimate cognitive resource for human action, though not able to function without combination with other resources. To constitute this resource, it must be linked with codes and their programmatic implementation at the *cultural*, not the organic level. Knowledge is the *primary* output of cognitive processes and is received and evaluated primarily at *cultural* levels. The highest level of codification, which is also an instrumentality in concrete action, is intelligence. Command of specific knowledge lies on a scale of declining levels of generality relative to the contentless status of intelligence. Thus, *theoretical* knowledge is parallel to the level of institutionalization of rights of possession that are alienable. In short, at the level of generalized theory, theoretical knowledge is transferable among many empirical contexts, just as property rights may be transferable among many owners.

At the next lower level of generality, problem solutions are bodies of knowledge relative to any generalized body of theory, which still mobilizes plural considerations of fact. Parallel to specific rights of possession are rights of control—meaning rights to decide who shall use an object of possession for what purposes. Finally, the lowest level of generality is that of knowledge of fact, considered independently of relevance to the solution of particular cognitive problems or to the validation of particular theoretical propositions. Knowledge of fact is parallel to rights of use in an object of possession, such as a renting tenant's rights to use residential premises.

---

40. This attribution to land of the status of the ultimate economic resource in comparison with money may seem to conflict with the conception that monetary metal is the security base of money. Our suggestion is that gold is a displacement from land because of the closeness of its properties to those of land, but at the same time its potential of involvement in exchange systems is superior to land in the concrete physical sense.

### Further Considerations about Intelligence

If intelligence is a generalized symbolic medium it must circulate. As a circulating medium, intelligence operates differently from knowledge, which, as a cultural object, is in the public domain. Unless impeded by barriers to communication, knowledge is a free good for an acting unit in the culture of reference. To function as a circulating medium, however, intelligence must be *scarce*.

Intelligence is scarce because all three of the cognitive functions, the acquisition, transmission, and use of knowledge entail *costs* as processes of action. Intelligence is a mechanism by which it is possible to regulate and mediate cost-benefit relations and balances. To act intelligently is to "spend" intelligence; it is to commit a variety of resources besides knowledge to the enhancement of cognitive benefits in action. Such commitment of resources necessarily entails the sacrifice of alternative uses. Thus, an investigator, in committing his time and energy to the solution of a cognitive problem, foregoes whatever alternative benefits other uses of this time and energy might have brought, for example, enjoyment of leisure. The question whether such a choice was intelligent concerns the balance between the significance in his action system of his chosen modes of advancing knowledge and the significance of various other interests, including nonrational ones, that are meaningful to him.

The cost of commitment to such a decision and its consequences is a sacrifice of the benefits which might have accrued from alternative uses of the same scarce resources. This is a type of opportunity cost, as that conception is used in economics. Intelligence is expended in the sense that it is the reference-standard which makes reasonable the preference of one way of using resources over others, a preference which is generally irrevocable in terms of concrete choice.

If intelligence can be expended, as money is expended, through processes of communication, then it can also be acquired by communication. In the economic system the ideal type of producing unit both produces goods and makes money, when economic production is the outcome of appropriate rational combinations of the factors of production, and when the economic value of output, utility, is a function of the way in which consumers' wants are satisfied. The parallel to economic goods in the general action

73

system is *knowledge* seen in terms of its *cultural* significance to those acting units interested in it. Cognitive processes produce knowledge, not merely facts previously unknown but also the transmission and adaptation of knowledge to use. Cognitive processes, which produce increments of knowledge can, in a sufficiently differentiated cognitive system, *also* produce intelligence. This should be understood to mean that the producers of knowledge acquire enhanced capacity to make intelligent decisions, both in the further production of knowledge and in other respects.

The analogues of economic consumers in the general action system are role players with an interest in knowledge—of many sorts and at many different levels. They supply factors in cognitive process, analogous to labor, and are also the source of demand for cognitive outputs. In order to allocate their command of factors, they require an input of intelligence—analogous to money wages—and this income of intelligence becomes available to function as demand for various types of cognitive output and is spent in their acquisition.

Intelligence, like money, is thus a circulating medium. Intelligence occupies a status intermediate between the underlying cognitive code and knowledge, which is the cognitive significance of particular objects and classes of them. Intelligence is a way of mediating both acquisition and transfer of such objects in the sense of knowing them. Thus intelligence functions as a measure of (cognitive) value because by combining judgments of cognitive validity and significance it serves as the primary reference-point for evaluation at the societal level of the rationality of action. It also provides standards for evaluating the outcome of processes of learning, hence of competence.

In measuring cognitive value, intelligence performs another function, cognate with solvency in the case of money as a regulator of the functioning of the firm. For firms in a market economy, an imperative is solvency; a firm is institutionally expected, over appropriate time periods, to cover its money expenses from its money receipts. Without solvency there is pressure for liquidation. The imperative of solvency serves to control costs in the internal operation of the firm. Where the function of the organization is not primarily economic production, as is the case for universities, the imperative of solvency is relaxed; universities are financially subsidized; still, total expenses are expected not to exceed total income. A university which ran continuing financial deficits without provision for covering them would soon be in trouble. These relationships are diagrammatically represented in Figure 2.7.

In the case of social units with primacy of cognitive function, the analogue of solvency is the standard of *cognitive* significance. In the circulation of intelligence into and out of the unit, the imperative is to balance inputs and outputs of intelligence in the course of operations. The primary market for cognitive output constitutes the demand for *knowledge*, the secondary market the demand for *competence*. Intelligence functions internally as a mechanism of cost control in that the competent and rational use of intelligence ensures that cognitive standards will be observed. The value-pattern of cognitive rationality is the legitimating base for the functioning of intelligence in this way.

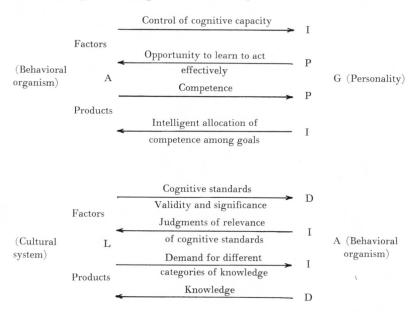

Media: I. Intelligence
P. Performance capacity
D. Definitions of the situation

(Part of Figure A.7 of technical appendix)

Figure 2.7. Interchanges between the Behavioral Organism and the Personality and Cultural Systems (General Action Level)

In many concrete cases where cognitive functions and hence intelligence are involved, there is less than full cognitive primacy. In such cases where criteria of the significance of knowledge and competence other than the cognitive are treated as legitimate, the unit must receive an intelligence subsidy from sources other than its own operations. If such subsidies are to facilitate outputs which meet cognitive standards, these subsidies must consist in genuine intelligence. Intelligence functions in this way in the three contexts of university activities where the cognitive complex shares its legitimacy with other societal interests; intelligence persists as a mechanism of cost control.

A cultural commitment to meeting of cognitive standards may extend beyond cases where cognitive interests have clear primacy. Thus, in the applied professions, for example, medicine, though the goal is not the promotion of learning and the advancement of knowledge, there is a conviction that the cognitive basis of diagnoses and therapeutic measures should be sound by cognitive standards. This may be regarded as an intelligence subsidy to the system of medical practice and research, say, on the part of those as much or more interested in health as in cognitive concerns.

Where the focus is not primarily cultural but personal, there may be expenditure of intelligence for the acquisition of competence, motivated not by interest in competence for its own sake, but interest in its instrumental significance, as, for example, interest in the improvement of the health of the population. The former type of subsidy is especially important for medical science and the latter for the training of medical practitioners. Finally, there may be special inputs of intelligence out of concern for the intelligent allocation of affective commitments; we shall discuss this issue in the socialization context (Chapter 4). The psychoanalytic interpretation is an instance of this kind of subsidy. The analysand's interest is not in self-knowledge for its own sake but for enhancement of his capacity to cope with the complexities of the moral and affective aspects of his life.[41] But intelligence is an essential ingredient of such coping, and intelligence must be generated in the competent analysand by a subsidy for the psychoanalytic enterprise.

41. Marshall Edelson, "Toward a Study of Interpretation in Psychoanalysis: An Essay on Symbolic Process in Psychoanalysis and the Theory of Action," in *Exploration in General Theory in Social Science*, ed. Johannes J. Loubser, Rainer Baum, Andrew Effrat, and Victor Lidz (New York, The Free Press, 1973).

One further point about intelligence must be made here, although it will be further developed in the next chapter. As became evident first in the case of money, in operations involving the circulation of the symbolic medium, circumstances arise in which a zero-sum condition does not obtain. That is to say, there is the possibility of credit-creation through banking; this produces a net increase in the amount of money in circulation. Similar possibilities of medium-creation exist for the other social system media, notably power and influence,[42] and it is more than likely that medium creation occurs in the general system of action as well. The intelligence medium seems to operate in this way; the university functions as an intelligence bank the operations of which, under favorable conditions, result in net increases in the amount of intelligence circulating in the system of action. We shall postpone a detailed analysis of these processes until the structural background of the modern university has been set forth.

## Competence and Cognitive Learning Again

What is the link between intelligence as a symbolic regulator of cognitive processes and competence in the personality system? Despite differences, competence parallels to an extent the role of intelligence in the production and utilization of knowledge. Distinct from knowledge, but nevertheless an output of cognitive production, competence is an internalized component of the personality structure (developed through learning). This means that, guided by intelligence, competence is capacity to handle cognitive problems at a detailed and hence relevant level. A person may be very intelligent—as parallel to being very rich—without specification of the inventory of his competences. When we speak of his competence, we must be able to specify competence with respect to what. He may be competent in the methods of survey research or in psychotherapy or in the management of investments, but omnicompetence is an illusion because competence, like knowledge, is particularized. Competence can only be acquired at the cost of expending scarce resources and hence at the sacrifice of competence in alternative fields.

Competence then is one of the resource-categories underlying the capacity of persons to achieve their goals effectively. This is

42. Parsons, "On the Concept of Political Power," and Talcott Parsons, "On the Concept of Influence," in *Politics and Social Structure*, pp. 405–438 (reprinted from *Public Opinion Quarterly* [Spring 1963], pp. 37–62).

important to action generally because the personality is the executive agent of action. The most generalized form of goal-achievement capacity, corresponding to intelligence at the general action level and to money and political power at the social system level, we call *performance-capacity*. Like intelligence, performance-capacity is not primarily a trait of the individual person, although he may *have* little or a great deal of it. Performance capacity is anchored in the personality, but circulates through the general action system as intelligence does.[43] The basis for considering performance-capacity a scarce medium that circulates is essentially the same as that just outlined for intelligence. From the consumers' side, expending performance-capacity is giving recognition[44] which is used in the societal community to attract identifications. This is parallel to the expenditure of intelligence, which occurs by the intelligent ordering of cognitive interests, that is, as a means of acquiring particularized significant knowledge. Parallel to the compensating income of intelligence from the maintenance of the cognitive standards that guide the intelligent use of cognitive resources, for performance-capacity, the compensating income category is cathexis of objects—motivational commitment to act appropriately in relation to them. The personality system is not, however, the *consumer* of personality functioning but its *producer*. The primary outputs of the personality system are identification and intelligent combinations of cognitive resources. These are the sources of an income of performance-capacity, analogous to the firm's making money and the organism's income of intelligence. Scarcity and cost are due to the fact that identification is not possible in all potential associative relationships nor can any one person command indefinite cognitive resources.

The equivalent of physical resources (land) for economic production and of the brain for intelligent action is for the personality system *character structure* (that is, identity). Character structure provides a combination of potentialities and constraints for the individual's performance. The anchorage of character structure lies in the adequacy aspect of what Erik Erikson calls personal identity. In short, the potentialities of character structure are processed in combination with other essential ingredients of adequate performance to produce capacity to perform. Adequacy is evalu-

43. Such circulation is a function of the level of differentiation of the action system.
44. William I. Thomas, *The Unadjusted Girl* (Boston, Little, Brown & Co., 1931).

ated in terms of the medium of reference, not only within the personality but also in the form of demand for its performances.

The relevance of performance capacity is not confined to cognitive contexts, but is also concerned with both affective and moral and "existential" involvements of the personality. Like other generalized media, performance-capacity operates as a cost control mechanism. It is concerned not only with balancing various alternatives of the acquisition and use of competence against each other but also with the value of competence as distinguished from other directions of utilization of resources available to the personality and hence of different modes of adequacy.

The intrapersonal counterpart of performance-capacity is ego-strength (in the sense used in recent psychoanalytic thinking). The ego, performing executive functions in the personality, is the source of operative decision-making and of the mobilization of psychologically significant resources in the interest of personal goal-attainment. Thus, capacity to act competently does not stand alone among the potentially valued capacities of a personality system to perform. Both acceptance of moral obligations and concern with the responses of others in social identification are foci of alternative concerns with adequacy and its components. This is one reason why we make a distinction between competence and effectiveness.

All these types of adequacy can be learned in the course of the individual's life history. Cognitive learning consists of the process of acquisition of the various forms of command of knowledge and of various forms of competence. But clearly, learning in the more general sense goes beyond cognitive components and types. Among the combinations of cognitive and noncognitive components especially important to our analysis is that of cognitive and affective components as we shall discuss them under the heading of student socialization in Chapter 4.[45]

45. Following Piaget and his associates we attribute greater significance to cognitive learning (including maturation) than has been customary in the last generation of developmental theorizing. We do not consider this to be contradictory to our emphasis on the tradition of Freud on the side of socialization and on the involvement of affective-expressive considerations in the development of personality. Piaget's scheme of developmental stages should not be ascribed to the factors of organic maturation alone but be put explicitly in terms of the interaction of the behaving organism with its environment. For a recent presentation of the stages, see Lawrence Kohlberg and Carol Gilligan, "The Adolescent as a Philosopher: The Discovery of the Self in a Post-conventional World," *Daedalus* (Fall 1971), pp. 1051–1086; for more general background, see Jean Piaget, *Structuralism*, trans. and ed. Chaninah Maschler (New York, Basic Books, 1970), and Jean Piaget, *Biologie et connaissance* (Paris, Gallimard, 1967).

## *Rationality as Mode of Social Action*

Having treated competence as a form of cognitive capacity internalized in the personality of the individual, we now turn to its counterpart, rationality as a mode of action institutionalized in social systems. Rationality is characterized by conformity with cognitive norms and values wherever such conformity is relevant. The individual is conceived to act rationally *in social roles* where expectations are structured in favor of cognitive criteria and where conformity with such expectations will be rewarded. For the individual to act rationally presupposes the requisite levels of competence and the functioning of an interactive sanction system. Such a sanction system requires certain levels of knowledge as part of the cultural environment, knowledge which may be either internalized or institutionalized or both.

This perspective on rationality avoids certain psychological complications. That action should be rational can rest on limited psychological assumptions. In cybernetic terms, rational action must be programmed so as to be guided by the values of cognitive rationality, but may also include specification of possibly noncognitive goals. A course of action deviating from the pattern laid down in the program will produce negative feedback which ought to activate corrective mechanisms, which in turn operate to bring the course back to the track of rationality. The social dimension acts as an amplifier of the feedback-corrective process on both positive and negative sides It thus becomes a powerful regulator, but subject to oscillations if the interactive sanctions fail to mesh with each other or with the requirements of the program. This conception of rationality of action does not depend on a special set of psychological mechanisms, so much as on special normative controls over action.

As in all cases of institutionalized action, there are limits to the effectiveness of cybernetic controls. They may generate resistances that become cumulative and lead to chronic deviation from rational norms. Deviations from rationality fall into two categories: irrationality and nonrationality. Irrational action is action oriented toward rational patterns, but which deviates from such patterns. The sources of such deviation may lie in psychological compulsions, in social conflicts, or in cultural factors. The deviation is referable to the failure of feedback and other corrective mechanisms to operate effectively. Nonrational action covers any component of action structure and processes not part of the cognitive complex. As cultural objects, such components do not constitute knowledge; as part of personality structure, they are not aspects of competence; as media of interchange, they are not forms of intelligence; and as patterns of social action, they are not as such rational. It follows from this view that the category, irrationality, applies only to types of action, not to components of action. Irrational action is the resultant of a combination of components. Since all concrete types of action involve in some way all components of an action system, rational as well as irrational types are codetermined by nonrational factors, though for the type to be rational these components must be organized so as to be effectively controlled in the interest of rational norms and values. Empirically, cases of irrationality are familiar; we are seeking now to clarify what irrationality *means*.

At least as significant as the *sources* of nonrational or irrational behavior in areas where rationality is institutionalized is clarification of the *relevance* of norms and values of rationality. Where extended courses of action are involved, rational components are not uniformly relevant. At one extreme is the case where cognitive interests have primacy, for example, in the advancement or effective transmission of knowledge, although noncognitive and nonrational components of action may have to be mobilized for such courses of action. Where values of cognitive rationality define the goals and choices of means and where individual actors are committed to the primacy of cognitive interests, noncognitive and nonrational components will be organized so as to maximize these interests.

From this case, there are various directions of departure short of the total irrelevance of cognitive standards; one such direction is the situation where goals are defined by primarily noncognitive interests (for example, the case of health-improvement as the primary goal of medical practice), but where the choice of means is preferably rational. Thus, in the health case, the cognitive interest in rational procedure requires some integration with the noncognitive interest in health. This case is comparable to that of economic rationality and is an example of Max Weber's category of instrumental rationality (*Zweckrationalität*).[46] Another direc-

---

46. Max Weber, *The Theory of Social and Economic Organization*, trans. A. M. Henderson and Talcott Parsons (Glencoe, Ill., The Free Press, 1947), chap. i, sec. 2, pp. 115–118.

tion of departure from pure cognitive rationality occurs when values are grounded not cognitively but in constitutive symbolism and moral-evaluative commitments developed in the religious tradition and in other aspects of our culture. Cognitive interests, values, and standards may still be partially relevant. Constitutive symbolism and moral evaluative commitments must be associated with beliefs which are cognitive with respect to the consistency of the components of a system of orientations and commitments as well as their implications for implementive action. This is approximately Weber's other type of rational action, value rationality (*Wertrationalität*).[47]

Still a third departure from pure cognitive rationality deserves some extended clarification. This third departure concerns the component of rational action in the academic community itself, especially with reference to the function of undergraduate education and the articulation of undergraduate education with the larger societal community. Integrative rationality concerns the socialization function of higher education generally and at undergraduate levels in particular and involves special modes of integration between cognitive and noncognitive components in the educational process. One type of integrative rationality is based on the idea that the modern societal community embodies "institutionalized individualism," a concept derived from Durkheim. The societal community is now more fully institutionalized, and a form of rationality is one feature of its institutionalization. This is the rationality expected of an educated citizenry who develop capacities not only, in the passive sense, for adapting to their social environments but for supporting its maintenance and further development. This is rationality oriented to the obligations of citizens to implement the central societal values in a variety of different circumstances.

To elucidate the relationship of integrative rationality to cognitive considerations it is necessary to discuss some highlights of the affective complex of action. The cognitive focus is on the relation of an actor, a knowing subject, to one or more objects; the ideal type of a stable relation is that of valid knowledge. This relational state can be symbolically expressed and the meanings either internalized or externalized. The affective mode is the obverse: an actor, a feeling rather than a knowing object, identifies with other actors in

47. Ibid.

such a way as to minimize their cognitive significance to each other as objects, but emphasizes instead their feelings of associatedness or its obverse.

There is no such thing as knowledge in general but only particular knowledge of particular objects. Intelligence is a contentless generalized medium; in a sense parallel to that in which money has no value in use, intelligence has no cognitive value in itself, but only as a medium for implementing cognitive values. In an analogous way *affect* is a generalized action medium mediating relations of actor to actor in the affective mode. Just as cognitive function structures the relation of action to its external environment, affective function, as a mode of integration, structures the relation of the actor to the *internal environment* of action.[48]

Affect is contentless in a sense parallel to that in which intelligence is contentless. Similarly, just as knowledge must be considered particularized, so there is no stable interpersonal relation that is purely affective. To constitute genuine identification, the relationship must be particularized by both the participating individuals and the functional categories in terms of which they are related. Thus identification cannot be only a state of being but must involve reciprocities of performance with reward-deprivation meanings. Furthermore, the relationship nexus must have identifiable characteristics; the mode of relatedness as objects must somehow enter in.

Parallel to the problem on the cognitive level of the relative instability of particularities of knowledge not fitted by criteria of cognitive significance into larger bodies of knowledge is the problem for affective identification of fitting particular associations into a larger network of associations. This seems to be the focus of Durkheimian *solidarity*.[49] Solidarity is the *institutional* stabilization of affectively toned relations of association and identification. The distinction between influence as a generalized medium at the social system level and affect at the general action level is that the use of influence *presumes* institutionalized solidarity, whereas the use of affect does not.

Treating affect as a generalized symbolic medium dissociates it from exclusive involvement in personality and establishes it as a

48. Claude Bernard, *An Introduction to the Study of Experimental Medicine*, trans. Henry Copley Greene (New York, Dover Publications, 1957).

49. Talcott Parsons, "Durkheim's Contribution to the Theory of Integration of Social Systems," in *Sociological Theory and Modern Society* (New York, The Free Press, 1967), pp. 3–34.

mediator of communication between persons as well as between culture and the organism. In this sense its *social* focusing seems meaningful. Bear in mind the parallel with intelligence, which has been defined in this book, not as a trait of the individual as psychology usually does but as a circulating symbolic medium. Underlying our definition of affect is the conviction that emotional meanings are not expressed raw any more than sense data enter into knowledge raw. They are not just events but acquire meanings which come to be symbolically organized: at the cultural level in systems of expressive symbolism, at the personal level in systems of motivation, and at the social level in patternings of solidarity. Solidarity is affectively grounded, that is, has properties of affective validity (authenticity) parallel to properties of cognitive validity.

We draw a further parallel. Action, including action in the pursuit of cognitive goals, may be intelligent without being rational, because intelligence does not imply social institutionalization. Similarly, action which expresses identification may be affectively authentic without implying solidarity—the institutionalization of affective attachments to constitute bonds of solidarity.

The cultural grounding of intelligence lies in the criteria of cognitive validity of knowledge, just as that of money lies in the value of the utility of commodities. In the case of affect, it lies in the moral-evaluative sector of the cultural system. This is the basis of Durkheim's insight that in order to have stable solidarity a social system must constitute a moral community. This means that the normative structure which mediates between affective attachments and the ordinary level of functioning of a social system must be grounded in values and norms having moral authority. Recall that Durkheim recognized that these values and norms came typically to be internalized in the personality of the individual.

Such a moral order of social relationships, as institutionalized, becomes for its participating individual members empirically given as an *object*. This is the milieu social of Durkheim, the internal environment of action. Its factual basis is part of reality for those participating in social life. As Peter Berger[50] has emphasized, there was in the nineteenth century an increasing realization that the human social order is, in a sense not true of the

50. *The Sacred Canopy* (Garden City, N.Y., Doubleday and Co., 1967), pp. 81–101.

physical world or of the human organism, not given in nature but "constructed" in the course of human action. Berger's conception of the nature of alienation as the feeling of loss of affective attachment to a humanly constructed entity, namely, this factually given social order, is compatible with our analysis.[51] It may be interpreted as a withdrawal of affect from identification, not from other persons but from the institutional order.

If the central meaning of the affective complex lies in the moral-evaluative sector of the culture, the ultimate resource base, which presumably has interindividual integrative significance, lies at the level of the proto-action bases of togetherness of two or more human beings, paralleling the sense in which land is the ultimate resource base of the economy and the central nervous system the resource base of the cognitive complex. The primordial aspect of this base is *blood* relationship, the symbolic significance of which has been worked out by David Schneider.[52] Human kinship systems are rooted in the mammalian extension of infantile dependency. Bisexual reproduction, socially organized through the incest taboo to include associational relations between potential parents who are not ascribed kin to each other, broadens this base to approximate the kinship nexus independently of institutionalization. Erotic attraction, including the mutual attraction of children and parents, especially the maternal parent, as well as adult heterosexual eroticism that leads to reproduction constitutes the core of this resource base. Eroticism is not as such affectively organized any more than physical land is by itself economically productive or the unaided human brain a cognitive machine.

To return to institutionalized individualism, the modern social order is a normative order in two senses: It claims moral authority and also exists as a social fact which must be intelligently understood and, within limits, adapted to. In addition to this underlying duality of meaning, it is both an individualistic and a pluralistic order to its participants. It is individualistic in the sense of Durkheim's cult of the individual—the placing of high value on individual autonomy and welfare. It is pluralistic in the sense of extensive division of labor: highly differentiated with respect to different groups and subgroups which perform different functions in the society while concomitantly each individual member plays

51. Ibid., chap. iv.
52. *American Kinship: A Cultural Account* (Englewood Cliffs, N.J., Prentice-Hall, Inc., 1968).

plural roles in various group activities among which he must allocate affective attachments and loyalties.

Such a society becomes dependent for its functioning on high levels not only of affective integration and solidarity among its members but of cognitive capacity and intelligence. These two ingredients of institutionalized individualism are analytically distinct. In recent phases of development, both within and outside the academic world, the affective complex has been somewhat played down in favor of the cognitive. Nevertheless, as we shall try to demonstrate, stability cannot be achieved by radical anti-intellectualism which denies the value in a modern society of high development of cognitive concerns.

## The Problem of the Value-Neutrality of Science

The foregoing survey of the cognitive complex in human action systems provides a basis for a tenable position on the controversial problem of the value-neutrality of social science. Max Weber serves as a reference point, including an initial ambiguity in the meaning of "science."[53] One meaning of science is knowledge, a cultural object-class claiming cognitive validity and significance. The other meaning of science is a process of *action*, for example, investigation, teaching, learning, or an application of these processes, as in such expressions as "medical science." Our main point is that the cognitive validity of propositions which purport to have the status of knowledge is not a function of the values of the investigator or other actors with an interest in such propositions. Judgments of scientific validity concern the relevance of cognitive standards and the ways in which the propositional set in question measures up in terms of those standards. This was Weber's concern in his early essay (1904) on the *objectivity* of knowledge in the social sciences.

Weber, reinforced later by Alexander von Schelting,[54] main-

53. Weber used the term *Wissenschaft* which is better rendered in English as "intellectual discipline" than as science, since *Wissenschaft* includes the humanities and involves no ambiguity about social science, as much English discussion does, e.g., such expressions as "the sciences and the social science." Weber's interest was in the social sciences. Weber, "Objectivity in Social Science," and Weber, "Science as a Vocation," in *From Max Weber: Essays in Sociology*, ed H. H. Gerth and C. Wright Mills (New York, Oxford University Press, 1946), pp. 129–156.

54. Alexander von Schelting, *Max Weber's Wissenschaftlehre* (Tübingen, J. C. B. Mohr [P. Siebeck], 1934). A useful recent discussion is W. G. Runciman, *A Critique of Max Weber's Philosophy of Social Science* (Cambridge, Eng., Cambridge University Press, 1972).

tained that the epistemological problem of the grounding of the claim to objectivity was not essentially different in the natural and the social sciences. With respect to content and to specific procedures of empirical validation, there are differences between classes of disciplines, but this does not alter the issue of whether propositions in the different fields can be objective in the same sense. Weber argued that all disciplines in the scientific realm had in principle the same potentialities for objectivity, and we agree with him.

Objectivity is grounded in the rules of logic as well as in the factual basis of knowledge; logic and facts should be regarded not in isolation from each other but in combination. Logic and facts and their combinations are oriented to the standard of truth and are not dependent on the other action-values of investigators and users of knowledge. Knowledge, as part of culture, is man-made, but it is in a status similar to that of the structure of a language used in a speech community; it is there and can only be changed by particular users in marginal ways.

Knowledge has a double relation to action. It is a way of orienting to aspects of the situations and/or environments of action, of making this orientation into a knowable cultural object. When this cognitive action-process succeeds, knowledge becomes a category of object which can be known. In other words, there can be knowledge of knowledge as well as knowledge of phenomena. "Doing science," on the other hand, is not a category of cultural object but a mode of human action. Like other modes of action, it involves values to which relevant actors are committed. For the role of scientist, the relevant value-pattern is that of cognitive rationality.[55]

Scientific action should be regarded as a special case of value-relevance. Among the values which might be decisive in scientific action, the positive valuation of cognitive interests takes precedence: interests in acquiring knowledge, transmitting it, or utilizing it. Because cognitive interests rank high in the scale of value-preference, the validity of the propositional systems which lay claim to the status of knowledge becomes a major concern; it is

55. This is the context of Weber's other main statement about science, his essay "Wissenschaft als Beruf" (translated as "Science as a Vocation"), where he spoke of the role of investigator dedicated to the implementation of cognitive values. Weber insisted on the distinction between such values and those underlying roles of political effectiveness. This essay was written at least fifteen years later than the one on objectivity. Weber, "Science as a Vocation," *From Max Weber*.

scarcely possible psychologically to be committed to the solution of a complex cognitive problem and not to care whether the solution arrived at is valid.

Cognitive values, however, never stand alone in a value-system but must somehow be integrated with those of noncognitive significance. These other values, for example, in effective attainment of predominantly noncognitive goals like health or economic production or in effective socialization into the role of educated citizen should be as fully cognitively grounded as possible but should not neglect noncognitive concerns. Noncognitive concerns are at cultural levels more expressive, more moral-evaluative, or more constitutive and can be combined with the cognitive in complex value-structures. These define types of *rational* action. In short, rationality includes an orientation where cognitive concerns have primacy and orientations where cognitive concerns can be successfully synthesized with noncognitive components of the value system. Weber's concept of value-relevance covers both cases. In the case of pure cognitive rationality, the cognitive value-component has primacy; the interest in the relevant parts of the system of knowledge is likely to be in the extensiveness of its informational content and the modes of its organization in theoretical terms. Where other value-concerns are predominant, the basis of interest in knowledge may shift away from cognitive validity. Thus there has long been a category of knowledge called medical science which is not organized mainly in terms of its intrinsic cognitive structure but in terms of its relevance to practical problems of health.

These concerns for noncognitive relevance do more than affect the selection of items of knowledge to be used for certain purposes. They enter into the statement of problems for the solution of which knowledge is valued, hence they affect the structure of knowledge itself. In particular, politically significant ideologies have had this impact on knowledge. Weber pointed out that the standards of cognitive validity and significance are basically *independent* of these considerations. Although noncognitive values influence what people want to know and what knowledge they want to use, the *cognitive* validity or invalidity of the propositional system itself is not determined by these noncognitive values. This is the meaning of the contention that the standards of knowledge should be considered "value-neutral" or "value-free." It does *not* mean that seekers after knowledge are or should be dehumanized creatures whose action is not guided by any values.

This claim to independent standards of objectivity is grounded in the factual basis of the environments of action, including not only the physical environment but the social and cultural environments. Knowledge is not only a function of the intrinsic nature of the phenomena but also of the action conditions and processes of knowing. But the primary action-*meaning* of cognitive endeavors is to maximize the potential of available cognitive resources for the implementation of cognitive values. In ideal type, objectivity is the primary norm. Not everything that purports to be knowledge is fully objective, but it is more objective than the extreme relativist view would maintain. Relativists say that the cognitive enterprise is worthless either because its goals are intrinsically impossible of attainment or because it has been all too successful in destroying the "really" important meanings of human life.

The factual basis of objectivity is not a special case confined to the cognitive function. The teleological propensity of the human condition, as manifested in the drive of human personalities to valued achievement, is also grounded in the evolutionary potential of the world of living things. The directionality of the evolutionary process (mentioned in the Introduction) tends to confirm this propensity.

Indeed, even in the context of the affective complex the frame of reference must include something more than the arbitrary level of spontaneous feelings. The potentialities of individual and collective achievement and the potentialities for human expression and attachment belong in a framework of human action which is necessarily constraining partly because constraints define the opportunities that make the human adventure meaningful. We repudiate the view that *only* the cognitive conditions impose constraints and that everything else manifests self-actualization. In this respect, *all* of the essential ingredients of the human condition are on the same footing.

# APPENDIX TO CHAPTER 2
## THE ARTICULATION OF THE COGNITIVE
## COMPLEX IN SOCIETY

As an appendix to Chapter 1, we presented a schematic diagram of the system of action in relation to its environments. We follow the same strategy here by presenting in the present appendix a series of four schematic diagrams which are meant to delineate the main rationale of the plan of the book for the next four chapters, Chapters 3, 4, 5, and 6, which essentially deal with the principal functions of the university in relation to each other and to its environments. It seems better to concentrate presentation of the series in this one appendix so they can be readily compared with each other, rather than to scatter the four diagrams in each of the subsequent chapters where the reader would be less likely to compare them systematically.

The formal background of the series has been presented in Figures 2.5 and 2.6 of Chapter 2. These deal, respectively, with the formal structure of the cognitive complex and with knowledge, the primary cultural component of the cognitive complex, in its internal constitution and its position in the action system.

On the background of these considerations, Figure 2.8, the first of the present series, deals with the theoretical rationale of the principal functions of the university as a whole. Here we have reduced the fourfold complexity of the general action system to the two subsystem references which are of primary significance for our analysis, namely, that to the cultural and the social systems. This is a self-conscious measure of simplification, and in a discursive way we attempt to deal with some of the involvements of personality and the behavioral organism in our later discussions. The complexities of the level of formalization we are attempting here, however, are such that we thought it better to confine ourselves to the two primary references. Each of the four figures, then, is divided into two subparadigms, the first of which focuses at either the general action or the cultural level, the second at the social system level. We designate these as part (a) and part (b), respectively.

We do not consider Figures 2.8–2.11 of this appendix, with the exception perhaps of Figure 2.8, especially part (b), to constitute a strictly deductive formulation. The designations placed inside the cells have been chosen to correspond as closely as seemed feasible with clusters of empirical phenomena which we have found it important to try to analyze and relate to each other in the course of our exposition. We think that, at this level, the correspondence is relatively gratifying, especially perhaps in Figure 2.8 and Figure 2.10. We would like especially to stress, in part (a) of Figure 2.8 the logic of the placing, on the one hand, of the standards of cognitive validity and significance, and, on the other hand, of the values of cognitive rationality, relative to other aspects of the general action system. In part (b) of Figure 2.8, then, we think the rationale of the division of subject matter of the succeeding four chapters is relatively clear on a formal basis.

In the case of Figure 2.10 we were struck by the fit of seven categories of profession, once the differentiation of the (a) and (b) clusters and the fact of involvement of the academic profession at both levels with different emphases were seen. This seems to us to come close to being an empirical classification which can claim analytical generality of significance.

When it comes to the rubrics which define the axes on which the four-fold tables are organized there seems to be somewhat more tentativeness, as is also the case for some, at least, of the cell designations in Figures 2.9 and 2.11. As we note toward the end of our final Technical Appendix, we think deductive clarity in these areas will require a great deal more work than we have been able to put into it for purposes of this book. This includes the fact that, whereas the present set is organized about the cognitive complex, eventually it will have to be systematically related to the other complexes of the action system, and each of these adequately analyzed.

We faced the choice, as authors, of remaining wholly or mainly at the discursive level, or presenting to the interested reader our crude and tentative attempts at formalization in the hope that they will prove stimulating to him. Placing these materials in appendices, however, is meant to underline our opinion that the reader who is not interested in following out the technical intricacies in which we have become involved in composing this book, can quite justifiably skip them. Diagrams which we have included in the text, however, we have thought of primarily as aids to following the analysis, which at times becomes relatively complicated.

We think Shils's characterization of the advancement of knowledge, quoted in the preface, as a "disorderly movement," clearly applies to the present kind of attempt at formalization, provided Shils's own meaning of that characterization is properly interpreted. To judge this one should have read the whole article from which the quotation is drawn.

*The Principal Functions of the University.* Part (a) of Figure 2.8 is adapted by rearrangement in the familiar fourfold cell diagram form of the essential content of Figure A.8 in the technical appendix, which deals with the more general theoretical framework of the book. As we have tried to make clear in Chapter 2, there are two primary foci of the cultural grounding of the cognitive complex, not one. The first of these concerns the cognitive standards which embody the grounds of cognitive validity and

Grounding of cognitive rationality in the general system of action

| | Meanings | | Values | |
|---|---|---|---|---|
| L | | | | I |
| Foci of cultural grounding | l Constitutive grounds of meaning in the human condition | Institution-alization of socially relevant meanings  i | l Value-rationality grounded in moral authority | Harmonization of identities grounded in social imperatives  i |
| | Grounds of cognitive validity and signif-icance  a | Internali-zation of personally relevant meanings  g | Cognitive rationality grounded in cognitive standards  a | Instrumental rationality grounded in practicality  g |
| Modes of articula-tion in operative action | Factor interchange categories of meaningful action | | Product interchange categories of value-implementation | |
| A | | | | G |

Institutionalization of Cognitive Rationality in the Structure
of the University

| | Knowledge "for its own sake" | Knowledge for "problem-solving" |
|---|---|---|
| L | | I |
| Institution-alization of cognitive complex | The core of cognitive primacy (research and graduate training by and of "specialists") | Contributions to societal definitions of the situation (by "intellectuals" as "generalists") |
| Utilization of cognitive resources | General education of "citizenry" (especially under-graduates as "generalists") | Training of professional practitioners (as "specialists") |
| A | | G |

(Adapted from Figure A.8 in the technical appendix)

## Figure 2.8. The Theoretical Rationale of the Principal Functions of the University

*Note:* This diagram [Part (b)] will be reproduced at the beginning of each of the following four chapters to help the reader locate its subject matter on the "map" of the theoretical organization of our analysis.

significance, whereas the second concerns the values of cognitive rationality as culturally grounded in the aforementioned cognitive standards. The L and I cells of part (a) of Figure 2.8 serve to place these two basic components in their setting, on the one hand, in the meaning structure of the cultural system and, on the other hand, in the value structure of the involvement of cultural meanings in action. Since we think of values as a primarily social category, the concept rationality appears in three of the four cells of the integrative complex and could well be adapted to the fourth, though there we thought it slightly more appropriate to use the term "harmonization of identities." The A and G cells of part (a) are such that it did not seem necessary to spell each of them out at the fourfold level of further differentiation. We have labeled these two cells "modes of articulation in operative action." It is here that we would place in the A cell the relevant factor interchange categories as spelled out in Figures A.7 and A.8 of the technical appendix and in the G cell, the corresponding product interchange categories. These products we conceive to be the principal categories of value implementation at the action level.

Part (b), then, presents the rationale of the modes of institutionalization of these components in a highly differentiated social system. Among other subsystems of the modern type of societal system, we consider that of higher education and more specifically the university to be the one which has been differentiated with respect to the primacy of cognitive functions. In this respect it differs profoundly from the economy, the polity, many aspects of the societal community, and, for example, religious systems. This primacy, however, is not absolute but must be seen in relation to its articulation with other primary functions of the society.

We, therefore, conceive that what we shall treat in Chapter 3 as the core of the university functional system, the institutionalization of the primary functions of "pure" research and of graduate training for membership in the academic profession, to be only one of four primary functional subsystems of the university. This we place in the pattern-maintenance position. We think of it as approximating the treatment, as we have headed the column, of "Knowledge for its own sake" and to be a primary locus of the institutionalization of the cognitive complex. In the structure of the ideal type of American university it has been "differentiated out," above all, in faculties of arts and sciences and for them with respect of their combined functions of professional level research and the training of graduate students for primarily academic functions.

The second of the four primary functions is that of general education, which we will treat in some detail in Chapter 4. We will analyze this around the conception of the role of what we call an "educated citizenry" in a society the primary community structure of which is characterized by the pattern which we call "institutionalized individualism," a concept which we will discuss at a number of points further along in the book. We consider this to be another instance where "knowledge for its own sake" is paramount because the educated citizen in our sense is not conceived to be a specialist, and the cognitive component of his socialization is not primarily characterized by any particular form of competence. He or she should be a person capable of a higher level of the mobilization and utilization of cognitive resources in the solving of both private and public problems of the society than would characterize persons with a lower level of education. General education, however, we think of as a mode of utilizing the cognitive resources which have more than anywhere else been generated in the L aspect of the university system, though this of course, as in the case of other functionally differentiated subsystems, is by no means exclusive.

Chapter 5, then, will deal with what is here formally portrayed as the G cell of part (b), namely, the utilization of cognitive resources in the applied professions. As distinguished from the faculties of arts and sciences, the professional faculties in their position in the university structure are conceived to be engaged in the training of practitioners who will be primarily "client oriented." They are to produce services which are needed and to a problematical degree "wanted" by persons who are not primary participants in the cognitive complex itself, such as municipalities needing engineering services to design and build an underpass for traffic facilitation, sick people needing medical services, or government agencies worried about the constitutional status of certain of the procedures they are engaged in needing legal services, in this case particularly of the higher order courts. This we conceive to be another case of the utilization of cognitive resources. But this time it is for relatively specific problem-solving purposes, not for the development of capacities to deal with an indefinitely wide range of problems as they arise.

The fourth cell, the integrative one, depicts the subject matter of Chapter 6, the contribution of the university to the role of the somewhat indefinite category we have called "the intellectuals" with reference to the definition of the situation for the society. We presume that intellectuals who in the current situation operate, above all, at the level of ideology are concerned primarily with "problem-solving." They are not primarily concerned with knowledge or "theory" as such, but, to use a famous phrase, with the relations and, most of them hope, "unity" of "theory and practice."

Of these four categories we think it legitimate to suggest that the academic professionals whose primary locus is the core functions and the applied professionals are more than otherwise "specialists." On the other hand, the intellectuals and the educated citizens can, in a certain relevant sense, be called "generalists."

In Chapter 3, then, notably in Figure 3.1, we try to spell out in a very schematic way the primary components of the core functions of "pure" research and graduate training and the specific institutional agencies of performance of these functions.

# APPENDIX TO CHAPTER 2

*The General Education Function.* In Figure 2.9 of the present series we take up the subject matter of Chapter 4 on the components of the general education function. Again, this is dealt with on two levels. At that of the general system of action we attempt to present the primary relations, on the one hand, between the cognitive components of the general education-socialization complex and, on the other hand, the noncognitive components which can be treated as in the first instance a combination and balance of the moral and the affective. The two levels, that is, as between the L-I and the A-G rows, we think of as concerning relations between the primary patterns of institutionalization of this complex and the primary modes of articulation of actor-object relationships, that is, in the action of individuals in their social environments and context of cultural meaning. In the first context it almost goes without saying, on the basis of the preceding analysis in Chapter 2, that we attribute great importance to the internalization of cognitive standards and standards defining their relevance in contexts of action other than the pursuit of knowledge itself. The I cell then simply states the place of the moral and affective structuring which should be enhanced by the general education process, again primarily at the level of internalization. We think it particularly appropriate to mention "rational social responsibility" in this context because of the special place we have accorded to the concept of rationality at the social level of general action.

It then seems to us particularly important to recognize a place for what we call individual self-realization, namely, in the G cell of the part (a) paradigm. We will show in the early part of Chapter 6 that it is essential to recognize a particularly intimate relation between expressive standards at the cultural level and the concerns of the personality of the individual, both looked at in general action terms. We suggest then that "self-realization," about which there is so much discussion these days, should be looked at in the context of its interdependence with the other action foci of general education, with its special concern for the "whole person." It will be a major purport of our analysis in Chapter 4 that the synthesis of cognitive and noncognitive components is fundamental both for the functioning of mature personalities in terms of their role as responsible educated citizens and for higher levels of personal self-realization than would be on the average attainable without having been through the process of higher education, at least at the college level. Finally, in the A cell we stress in particular the relevance of the cognitive complex components of general education to the facilitation of satisfactory performance of the role of an educated citizen.

Part (b) then attempts to present schematically the main components of the social context of higher general education, the college community, as we shall attempt to develop in some detail in Chapter 4. We conceive this community as a framework within which both the process of cognitive

Part (a)

Action foci of general education

|  | Cognitive components of capacities for rational action | Moral-affective components of capacities for rational action |
|---|---|---|
| Code-templates for culture of the educated | Internalization of cognitive standards | Moral-affective structuring of rational social responsibility |
| Articulation in actor-object relations | Standards of relevance of cognitive resources | Individual "self-realization" |

Part (b)

Social functions of the college community

|  | Commitments to rationality | Framework of socialization |
|---|---|---|
| Balances between freedom and constraint | Trusteeship of values of rationality— cognitive and moral | Provisions of moral authority and affective support |
| | Learning of cognitive content | Provision of protected environment through academic freedom |

Figure 2.9. Components of the General Education Function

learning and the internalization by the individual student of the noncognitive components of socialization can be facilitated. The L cell we conceive as particularly concerned with the trusteeship of the values of rationality. We have stressed cognitive rationality in Chapter 2 and shall continue to do so, but we hope to have already made clear that we do not wish to confine the category of rationality to the cognitive level. Following Weber, we in particular want to stress its relevance to the moral level. In the socialization function, then, we conceive the combination of cognitive and moral rationality to become synthesized with the affective component, as we have outlined this in Chapter 2. This is the primary focus of the I cell. It is suggested that successful internalization of these components cannot be achieved except in a social environment of the individual where moral authority is securely institutionalized and where cognitive values are highly regarded,

96

but where also there is a strong disposition to affective support in the face of the difficulties of becoming socialized.

In Chapter 4 we shall also stress the importance of the protective environment in which all members of the academic community live, which is a function of the differentiation of the academic community from the rest of the society. Students on the whole enjoy more immunities from outside pressures than do the senior members of the community, but this protection is, we shall argue, a feature of the whole academic system and has a great deal to do with the conception of academic freedom. Finally, not least of the important functions of general education is facilitation of the learning of cognitive content. This may well have been overstressed relative to the other functions in the recent history of universities, but this fact should not be allowed to obscure its central importance. Perhaps we can leave it at the statement that anyone who in the technically cognitive sense does not "know anything"—meaning the phrase as signifying knowing something beyond the common sense of the people as a whole—can scarcely claim to belong to the "company of educated men and women."

The distinction between the rows of part (b) is difficult to characterize, but we think of it as involving balances between freedom and constraint with, however, allowance for the fact that the constraints of an earlier phase of a learning and socialization process, for example, through cognitive discipline and morally grounded authority, may lay the groundwork for later capacities to implement opportunities for freedom, for instance, through competent performance and responsible action.

*Training for the Applied Professions.* Figure 2.10 concerns the rationale of the classification of the professions which will be presented in Chapter 5. Part (a) is concerned with the general action level and part (b), that of social-system function. It was a primary insight gained in the course of writing Chapter 5 that the principal applied professions could be classified in two distinct clusters. The first group, which are located in the diagram of part (a), are the more or less "classical" liberal professions, including the academic. The academic has been placed in the pattern-maintenance cell and its characterization there formulated to emphasize cognitive primacy, hence the "pure" concern with the intellectual disciplines. The legal profession seems to be appropriately placed in the I cell because of its concern with the normative structure of social order. Medicine as the focus of the health cluster of professions belong in the G cell because of its special concern with the personality of the individual. Finally, we have placed engineering in the A cell because of its concern with relations to the physical environment as mediated through the behavioral organism.

The formal designations of the two primary axes in Figure 2.10 we have suggested are particularly tentative, but it seemed better to include them. It seems broadly correct to treat the left-hand column as having a special concern with what might be called the "trusteeship" of adaptive resources, in one case the cultural resources of the cognitive complex, in the other case the rational handling of relations to environmental resources. The right-hand column then seems to have to do with problems more internal to action at the social and personality levels, respectively. We think that, in the American type of society and the highly differentiated and integrated university type which is the subject of this book, it is proper to treat this as concerned with the utilization of cognitive resources within the framework of institutionalized individualism—a concept which we have already introduced and will elaborate considerably in the course of subsequent chapters; it might well be different for other types of society.

The distinction between the two horizontal rows is somewhat more difficult to state. The upper, the L-I row, as in the other cases, concerns the framework with respect to cognitive culture and social order, respectively, within which the functions of the applied professions are grounded. It is at least tempting to associate this with Durkheim's concept of the relation of action to the social environment if we give the social environment a definitely cultural interpenetrating framework. We have discussed this concept earlier in Chapter 2. The lower row, then, has to do with the environmental conditions themselves, on the one hand, and the capacities of individual participants in the action system as acting units, on the other, as conditions of value-implementation. Control of the physical environment is a necessary condition of relatively rational action as is health of the individual, at least from the point of view of developing his capacities so he can take advantage of available opportunities.

The paradigm omits two important groups which have sometimes been treated as professional. The first of these is the clergy. Their role certainly comprises a cognitive component, but one the significance of which lies in the "direction" opposite to that of application as we shall treat it in Chapter 5. It concerns the constitutive "grounding" of human *orientations* in action, in which, as we have argued at various points, a cognitive component is essential, but never alone sufficient.

The second group whose role is omitted are the "intellectuals," as these will be discussed in Chapter 6 below. We consider their role to be defined as that of a kind of societal rather than general action "clergy" whose concern is primarily with the most general diagnosis and prognosis of the societal situation, not purely cognitively but in Northrup Frye's sense of "concern" (see reference to Frye in Chapter 6).

Part (b) then presents patterns of articulation of the cognitive culture in the facilitation of the performance of certain societal functions. We again place the academic profession in the pattern-maintenance cell, but this time with an emphasis on the organization of cognitive resources, notably knowledge, as adapted to what in Chapter 5 we shall call the "clinical focus," which is necessary for effective utilization. This aspect of the academic profession is centered in the faculties of professional schools

Part (a)

Articulation of cognitive culture with general action interests

| | Trusteeship of adaptive resources | Trusteeship of framework of institutionalized individualism | |
|---|---|---|---|
| **L** | | | **I** |
| Patterning of cultural-societal order—the *milieu social* | Academic profession as concerned with "pure" cognitive resources | Legal profession as concerned with normative structure of societal order | |
| Control of environmental conditions and the states of acting units | Engineering profession as concerned with adaptation to the physical environment | Medical profession as concerned with the health of individuals | |
| **A** | | | **G** |

Part (b)

Articulation of cognitive culture with societal functions

| | Trusteeship of adaptive resources | Trusteeship of framework of institutionalized individualism | |
|---|---|---|---|
| **L** | | | **I** |
| Foci of the *institutionalization* of rational social responsibility | Academic profession (especially in professional school faculties) as focus of "clinical" responsibility for societal functions | Profession of education as concerned with capacities for citizenship in societal community | |
| Foci of the *implementation* of rational social responsibility | Cluster of welfare professions as concerned with conditional prerequisites of citizenship | Professions of administration as concerned with rational implementation of collective goals | |
| **A** | | | **G** |

Figure 2.10. Rationale for the Classification of the Professions

rather than in those of arts and sciences but not confined to them. The other three professions included here are all relatively new in having attained the status of university-level training. In the integrative cell we have placed the profession of education as that has come to be trained for in university schools of education. We conceive this as concerned with training professionals who are qualified in turn to help develop the capacities of the population for citizenship in the societal community. In one sense it is the extension outside the university of the basic functions of general education within it, but carried out mainly at the primary and secondary school levels. In the G cell we have placed training for the profession of administration, both public and private, the latter above all in the field of business. The administrative function in this sense depends on what might be called the technology of the rational implementation of collective goals, whether the collectivity of reference be the society as a whole, or one of its segmental territorial or functionally differentiated units, as in the case of government, or of private collectivities, as in the case of business. Finally, in the A cell we have placed the cluster of welfare professions, notably social work. We think of these as concerned with helping to provide certain of the conditional prerequisites of citizenship as distinct from the personal capacities to perform citizenship roles. We think that the two columns can be looked at as having essentially the same significance in part (b) as we attributed to them in part (a), namely, the trusteeship of adaptive resources and of the framework necessary for a system of institutionalized individualism. The two rows, finally, may be interpreted as having to do, respectively, with the foci of institutionalization and of implementation of rational societal responsibility in each of the two relevant classes of functional contexts.

We shall also, in the text of Chapter 5, briefly discuss two other professions: accounting and architecture. Accounting it seems to us may reasonably be considered as an auxiliary of administration, dealing with one special but very important function of the latter. The relation is a little like that of dentistry to medicine. Architecture, on the other hand, seems to combine two main aspects of the Adaptive Resources complex, represented in part (b) and part (a), respectively, namely, the welfare complex as especially concerned with housing and urban design and engineering. The higher order aesthetic aspects of architecture then bring it into the circle of the arts, the full professionalization of which, in the present sense, is problematical. As we point out a number of times, at any rate the arts should not be simply "merged into" the category of applied cognitive resources which is the focus of our discussion in the present chapter.

*The University and the Intellectuals.* Finally, Figure 2.11 presents the main paradigmatic framework of the analysis which will be developed in Chapter 6, namely, it concerns the action structure of the functions of intellectuals. In part (a) we have not delineated the relevance of these functions to the action system as a whole but have confined it to the *cultural* concerns of intellectuals, since we think of intellectuals as particularly involved with the cultural level of definitions of the situation. Here the problem of the relevance of knowledge is a special aspect of its relevance to ideological concerns, as we shall put this, since, for a variety of reasons, we are not treating the religious level as paramount for purposes of the analysis of this book. In the pattern-maintenance cell we refer to the grounding and relevance of cognitive standards for ideological purposes. This concerns the sense in and degree to which the ideologically oriented intellectual feels bound by these standards. In the integrative cell we have included a comparable relation to moral standards. The G cell then has particular reference to expressive standards, whereas the A cell, rather than dealing with cognitive standards, concerns the relevance of various types of actual cognitive resources.

As between the columns, the primary problem concerns the definition of the cognitive factors or components of ideologies, on the one hand, and the relevance of noncognitive components, on the other, and, of course, the balance and modes of integration between them. The upper row, however, concerns more the general code-template type of framework within which

Part (a)

Foci of the Cultural Concerns of Intellectuals

|  | Cognitive components of ideologies | Noncognitive components of ideologies |
|---|---|---|
| Code-template components of ideologies | Grounding and relevance of cognitive standards | Relevance and cognitive classification of moral standards |
| Articulation with the empirical action system | Relevance of cognitive resources | Relevance and cognitive classification of expressive standards |

Part (b)

Foci of Social Concern of Intellectuals

|  | Components of ideological rationality | Noncognitive emphases of concern |
|---|---|---|
| Articulation of normative orientations | Concern for normative validity of societal values | Critical appraisal of societal norms |
| Empirical evaluations | Diagnosis and prognosis of societal states and trends | Definitions of societal goals |

Figure 2.11. Action-Structure of the Functions of Intellectuals

101

ideologies are formulated and the lower row the articulation with the more empirical considerations involved in the action system.

As in Figures 2.8, 2.9, and 2.10, part (b) moves to the social level of concern and with it to the special relevance of societal values. In the L cell we have placed ideological concern for the normative validity of societal values and, of course, in our context this would place special emphasis on the role of cognitive rationality relative to other value components. In the I cell we move from values to the level of norms. In both respects we may consider the ideological intellectual to be a "social critic," though we do not mean to imply by this that his criticism must necessarily be negative. To be an intellectual, however, he must be critical in the sense of applying critical analysis to the relevant problems.

The G cell, we think, appropriately refers to the definitions of societal goals, or the goals of subsystems of the society, and the A cell to the kind of empirical generalization which is appropriate in the context of the role of intellectuals, which we have formulated as the diagnosis and prognosis of societal states and trends. The axes of organization seem to have essentially the same meaning here that they did in Figure 2.10. The left-hand column is more concerned with the role of cognitive considerations in the structuring of ideologies and in the right-hand with the noncognitive emphases. The upper row, then, is concerned particularly with the normative aspect of the orientations of intellectuals, whereas the lower row is concerned with the "application" of these normative orientations in relatively empirical contexts. We assume throughout, however, that the primary role of the intellectual is always evaluative. He should have concern for pure cognitive considerations, but essentially in terms of their relevance in his evaluative interests.

# 3

## THE CORE SECTOR OF THE UNIVERSITY:
## GRADUATE TRAINING AND RESEARCH

The foregoing chapter attempted to provide background neces-sary to understand two principal features of the American univer-sity: (1) that it, and with it the institutionalized cognitive complex, has become a differentiated part of a complex society and (2) that it has become upgraded in prestige and influence within the society to the point that some commentators describe it as the central institution in the society.[1] In order to elucidate these processes of change and some of their probable consequences, it has been necessary to review the structure of the cognitive complex, its grounding in the place of knowledge in the cultural system, its role in the nature of rationality as a mode of social action, and its relation to learning and competence in the personality of the individual and to intelligence as a generalized symbolic medium of action.

Though differentiated from other institutions and focusing in the cognitive complex, the university does not have one but a plurality of functions. The distinction among these functions is emphasized in this book; it is between functions where the value of cognitive rationality has clear primacy over others and functions where this primacy is shared with other value-sectors of the gen-eral value-system. A prototype of the primacy of cognitive rationality is the graduate school of arts and sciences and the asso-ciated institutionalization of research. This prototype will be singled out for special treatment in the present chapter.

In terms of formal organization, two principal cases exist where other values share primacy with cognitive rationality, namely, undergraduate colleges within universities and professional schools, which are concerned with the training of practitioners in the

1. Daniel Bell, *Reforming of General Education: The Columbia College Experience in Its National Setting* (New York, Columbia University Press, 1966), p. 301.

applied professions. These two cases are organizationally distinct entities relative both to the graduate schools and to each other, despite overlap and interpenetration. Thus, the same faculty members often teach both graduates and undergraduates, though in varying patterns in different universities, and research is institutionalized in many professional faculties. The undergraduate college especially attempts to synthesize the cognitive learning function with the function of socialization. Thus the college constitutes an extension to older age levels of patterns of the integration of the social system and of personality which have been found in studies of family socialization; this extension will be treated in Chapter 4. The function of training in the applied professions will be discussed in Chapter 5.

We use the concept of "relevance" to designate *any* context in which the cognitive complex is a source of potential value and value-implementation. This usage is in accord with Max Weber's use of the concept of the "value relevance" (*Wertbezogenheit*) of knowledge.[2] There remains a distinction between cases of clear primacy of cognitive considerations and cases where the cognitive component must share its focal position with other values, such as in the socialization of an oncoming age-cohort or with respect to the practical benefits to be gained from the utilization of knowledge and related modes of involvement of rationality, learning, and intelligence.

Another context of the relevance of the cognitive complex has not come to be organized in as specific institutional terms as the university, the undergraduate college within the university, and the professional school. In one perspective, this is a modification of the traditional religious functions of the university, where, for example, especially in the Lutheran pattern, the theological faculty was treated as the "keeper of the Prince's conscience." In contemporary terms, this has become an ideological function: the responsibility of a class of persons commonly called intellectuals whose formal status-locations are both inside and outside the academic world. Most of the nonacademics among them are at least college graduates; hence considerable two-way communication occurs between academic and nonacademic intellectuals. The very term, intellectuals, suggests a two-way interchange involving the

2. "Objectivity in Social Science and Social Policy," in *Max Weber on the Methodology of the Social Sciences*, trans. and ed. Edward A. Shils and Henry A. Finch (Glencoe, Ill., The Free Press, 1949), chap. ii, pp. 50–112.

relevance of knowledge and the other components of the cognitive complex to noncognitive concerns as well as vice versa.

As suggested in the previous chapter, on the cultural level there tends to be a bifurcation on whether the emphasis in modifying cognitive primacies should lean in the expressive-aesthetic or the moral-evaluative direction, with explicitly religious concerns standing somewhat in the background. On the social level, however, there is a tendency, favored by the activistic component of the value system, to emphasize *political* concerns.

Ideological movements are almost by definition sentencious. Hence it is to be expected that the role of intellectuals will chronically raise questions about the proper differentiation and autonomy of the university and about the boundaries of its institutional status generally and of its primary functions in particular. This problem area includes both ideological defenses of the academic status quo and ideological attempts to justify changes in it, sometimes radical changes. It also includes questions of the balance between the cultural and the collectively solidary character of the academic system and its individualistic components. Thus one wing tends to regard the educational framework as an opportunity for the individual student to express himself, to "do his thing," with only minimal reference to the intellectual discipline which has figured in academic tradition.

The inclusion of these four patterns of the relevance of the cognitive complex in the *same* institutionalized social organization is not to be taken for granted. The combination of the graduate school and the undergraduate college is relatively distinctive to the American pattern, but it seems rather firmly institutionalized.[3] Several other systems have gone further in the direction of separating the research function from teaching, notably in France and in the Communist world. Professional training has also been separated from the universities as, for example, in England and in the Soviet Union. Indeed, why have our faculties of arts and sciences continued to include the range of intellectual disciplines at both graduate and undergraduate levels and not split off into more specialized faculties of natural science or of humanities? We will not be able to analyze these questions fully, but they should be kept in mind as background questions for understanding the university as a social system. In particular, the problematical character

3. Joseph Ben-David, *The Scientist's Role in Society: A Comparative Study* (Englewood Cliffs, N.J., Prentice-Hall, Inc., 1971).

of the integration of all these functions in a single type of social organization may serve as an index of the severity of the tensions involved in the integration. There are two main classes of pressures tending to break down the pattern we have sketched. One is to weaken the boundary between the differentiated academic system and other sectors of the society, and the other is the centrifugal one of pressure to separate off parts integral to it, for example, teaching from research.

With regard to the prime importance of the cultural level, our main concern is with social organization in contexts which involve learning processes in the individual. Our analytical focus, there-fore, will be in the role structure of faculties, student bodies, and administrations and their articulation with processes of learning at the personality level. In the background, to be explicitly discussed from time to time, are the macroinstitutional structures, the type of collectivity which is the university and its various subcollectiv-ities, and the norms and values which define its characteristics and functions and which regulate performance on the part of its various units.

In this context the primarily academic role-types, those which carry with them "membership" in the university (or college), are concerned with the encouragement, facilitation, and discipli-

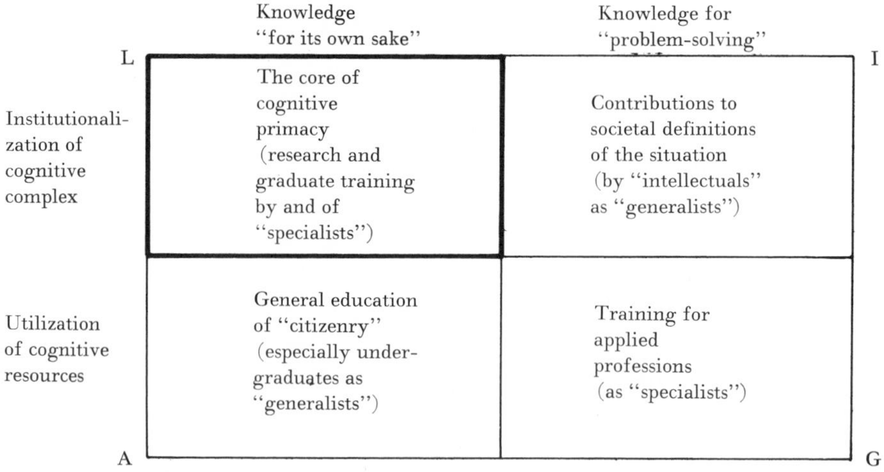

| | Knowledge "for its own sake" | Knowledge for "problem-solving" |
|---|---|---|
| L | | I |
| Institutionali-zation of cognitive complex | The core of cognitive primacy (research and graduate training by and of "specialists") | Contributions to societal definitions of the situation (by "intellectuals" as "generalists") |
| Utilization of cognitive resources | General education of "citizenry" (especially under-graduates as "generalists") | Training for applied professions (as "specialists") |
| A | | G |

Figure 3.1. Institutionalization of Cognitive Rationality in the Structure of the University

Note: The heavily outlined subsystem is the substantive focus of this chapter. For a more formal analysis of this figure and its relation to other subsystems, see the appendix to Chapter 2.

nary evaluation of processes of learning and their outcomes. More specifically, the distinctions between "teaching" and "research" and between "teaching" and "learning" in the narrower sense, referring to students, become secondary distinctions. In the more general perspective, they are all variants of learning. At the same time, sociologically considered, they are subject to the role-expectations of rational action which presuppose the relevance of cognitive standards, either as paramount for the whole learning-role combination or for specific parts of it. Thus the teacher of a specific medical diagnostic technique does not need to consider whether or not improvement of the health of the patients to which it might apply is legitimated by societal values, nor does the teacher of research techniques need to consider whether it is worth while to advance knowledge in the ways competent use of them may promise. He can still act rationally in both cases in imparting command of these techniques to his students.

Students are cast in the role of "learners." But so are researchers since it does not make sense to investigate if there is nothing to be learned in the process. The difference lies in the fact that the research investigator cannot rely on a human teacher who already has specific answers. Otherwise there is no research, only plagiarism. The researcher can rely on teachers as masters of the traditions relevant to his own problem-formulations, as masters of methods of investigation, and as models of what an investigator should be. But no previous physicist taught Max Planck the properties and theoretical significance of Planck's Constant since, before Planck's own investigative work, there was no such concept. The investigator is thus learner—even student—but not of any human teacher with superior specific knowledge, but from or of the phenomena which he studies. The meaning of such experience of phenomena depends on the nature and the sources of the feedback which exposure to them produces. One difference between the natural and the social sciences lies in the fact that for the physicist or chemist the object of his study, for instance, atoms or molecules, do not "talk back" to the investigator in the sense of a two-way *symbolic* process of communication, whereas the social subject does.

The case of classroom teaching is somewhat different. At one extreme it can be said that the teacher learns nothing in the process, that it is thus entirely a one-way process. This, however, is a limiting case. Overall, especially in the intellectually more sophisticated aspects of higher education, teaching involves a learning process for the teacher as well as the student.[4] More important than classification of the various possible balances in this respect is that all these academic functions are performed as part of relational systems of social interaction. Even the solitary scholar working alone in his study is, like the teacher preparing a lecture, oriented to an audience from whom he eventually expects feedback, and most academic functions are performed in some kind of setting of immediate social interaction. In short, learning is always a major function of any academic relational system. Process in such systems typically results in enhanced levels of knowledge, competence, and/or intelligence *in the system*, even though some participants in some systems do not share in this.[5] Indeed, even the teacher who does not learn anything in his teaching (the limiting case) may enhance his competence as a teacher through the experience of teaching. Addition to specifiable knowledge is not the only output of learning processes.

This perspective on the function of learning throws light on the concept of rationality. Recall the discussion in the last chapter of the role of cybernetic mechanisms in the implementation of standards of rationality. Given the necessary value-commitments specified to the acceptance of certain learning goals, the bearing of standards of rationality is in the *evaluation* of results—not only "end" results—though variations of concrete motivation on the part of learners may be compatible with attainment of the same standards of rationality. This explains the significance of evaluative institutions at all levels of the academic enterprise. Students are not alone in having their work subject to evaluative scrutiny. Faculty members in their capacity as research investigators are subject to the evaluation of their peers in the relevant sector of the intellectual community when they publish results. Fundamental as institutions of evaluation are, we shall argue that they need to be balanced by areas of protection from evaluative pressures. Indeed, providing such partial immunity is one of the functions of the institutions of academic tenure and academic freedom.

---

4. Even in the case of the type of lecture where no interruption is permitted, preparation requires marshaling new facts and organizing material in new ways. From this point of view, the students differ as audience only by degrees from the readership of a research report where the reader also cannot immediately talk back.

5. Professor James Olds, a leading authority on brain research, informs us that the mammalian brain is overwhelmingly specialized in *learning*—not simply knowing—functions (personal communication).

This delicate balance between evaluation and immunity from it is related to another feature of academic life. Not only is much of the knowledge and cognitive interest involved in the pure sector of the system esoteric and apparently remote from practical uses, but there is an element of uncertainty parallel to the uncertainties of many fields of practical action. Practitioners of the cognitive complex in its higher reaches are dealing with problems where frequently they do not know the answers. They are working on the frontiers of knowledge. Not only is there sheer ignorance which can gradually be reduced by research but there are grey areas where some people *believe* certain propositions to be true, but others contest these beliefs, and there seem to be no unambiguous procedures by which to settle the differences. Thus, schools of thought factionalize the academic world as a social system. Particularly in the social sciences, though many statements of fact can be unambiguously verified or disproved, empirical generalizations as well as more abstract theories often cannot be proved or disproved. Here science merges into ideology, especially since such unprovable belief always has functions other than the purely cognitive one in action.

These areas of ambiguity and contention are usually not wholly intra-academic; the academic participants in the disagreements are in communication with those outside the academic system. These familiar facts underscore the difficulty of firm institutionalization of cognitive standards and competence in many areas of knowledge. This difficulty is one reason why the differentiation of the academic system from others is so important. The handling of intellectual ambiguity can then be carried out in an atmosphere and in a relational system where cognitive values are paramount, where other considerations are not so likely to sway opinions. The treatment of problems of intellectual ambiguity is brought into a community setting in which bodies of knowledge and the people who teach and learn them not only have high prestige but are not to the same degree beset with problems of ambiguity. Less ambiguous fields can set cognitive standards to which those concerned with other fields are exposed and are thereby given incentives to live up to them so far as possible.

These are some of the considerations underlying the institutionalization of the university around a professional tradition, that of the academic profession itself. (The academic profession is that group *primarily* concerned with the cognitive complex: with the advancement, perpetuation, and transmission of knowledge and with the development of cognitively significant competence.) Although the cognitive complex is relevant to other realms within the academic system, especially through the function of teaching those not destined themselves to become academic professionals, academic professionalism constitutes the *core* of the modern academic system.

With the development of the full university, the center of gravity of academic professionalization has come to be located in the graduate schools of arts and sciences and in the research complex. In the American education system, research and graduate education are closely intertwined. Research, namely systematic devotion to the advancement of knowledge in particular fields, is, both in science and in humanistic scholarship quite old, but the modern era has witnessed an immense development of it, not only quantitative growth but its institutionalization in professional groups.

Where do such professionals come from? In earlier stages, the main contributions have been made by amateurs such as gentleman scholars and certain types of ingenious men curious about scientific matters (like Benjamin Franklin). Joseph Ben-David has pointed out that there must be enough of such people in a given location so that they can, through their mutual associations, form a critical mass of mutual communication and stimulation.[6] In the sciences, such a critical mass first occurred in Renaissance Italy and somewhat later in England and northern Europe more generally.

The full institutionalization of the research function at professional levels occurred mainly through the graduate schools of arts and sciences, which were committed to the training of persons in capacity to advance knowledge at professional levels. There were two precursors of the current graduate school: (1) the various academies in European countries which, however, were relatively weak on the training side and (2) the Institutes which grew up, in the nineteenth century especially in the German universities, centering about a professor, who at the same time held the *Lehrauftrag* and the directorship of a research institute. Such professors tended to recruit their students into the role of apprentices in research, in the humanities centering about the Seminar, in the natural sciences about the Laboratory.

6. *Scientist's Role in Society.*

The depersonalization of this pattern was, however, primarily the contribution of the American system.[7] The candidate for an academic career was no longer mainly under the patronage of a senior man in the field but the graduate of a systematic program administered by a department within the supervision and rules of a graduate faculty. Thus Ben-David maintains that, besides the graduate school itself, the department was the key American innovation, and the two were closely interconnected.[8] The department, relative to European university organization, replaced the ascendancy of *the* Chair. In the European university there was usually only one professor in a field, which enhanced the importance of patronage.[9]

The rise of departments tended to emphasize universalistic standards of performance and competence as distinguished from standards congenial to a single patron. It also encouraged the exposure of department members and their graduate students to critical evaluation of their work in a wider forum: in an intellectual marketplace. The particular department became one node in a wider network of centers in the field that communicated among themselves and also exchanged personnel. The new stress on universalistic standards was associated with the other components of the validity-significance complex which we outlined in the last chapter, namely, the stress on cognitive methods, on intellectual "productivity," and on "discipline."

"Discipline" is a particularly significant term, since, with reference to intellectual content in addition to that of control, the same period which saw the development of an academic profession also saw a provisional conceptual structure of the world of knowledge, namely, a rounding out of modern intellectual disciplines. The

---

7. Some personal experience of the senior author is relevant here. The German philosophical faculty of the pre-Nazi period, where he received his doctorate, was not a graduate school in the American sense, but mainly a training school for gymnasium teachers. A small elite group then went on to try for professorial academic careers beyond the German doctorate, at a level below that of the best American Ph.D.'s. There was, however, no systematic program and no basis of financial support of students until, in the natural sciences only, laboratory assistantships became available in considerable numbers.

8. *Scientist's Role in Society.*

9. The American departmental system, as compared to the European institution of the one chair, did not altogether eliminate the tendency of strong individuals to assume patronage roles, but it reduced it. A more recent trend in Europe has been in the American direction. On the difficulties of developing the institutionalization of a new discipline under French conditions at the turn of the century, see Terry N. Clark, *Prophets and Patrons: The French University and the Emergence of the Social Sciences* (Cambridge, Mass., Harvard University Press, 1973).

oldest branch of these disciplines derives from classical antiquity; it has come to be called the humanities. Another branch, the natural sciences, emerged since the Renaissance. And most recently the so-called social sciences developed.[10] Each of these categories is subdivided into familiar specialties, such as physics, chemistry, biology, or psychology, economics, political science, sociology.

This development is often perceived as a process of increasing specialization, which in some respects it has been. But an equally striking process has been a centripetal pressure, manifested in the insistence on representing all of the modern disciplines in the same faculty: at both the graduate school level and that of undergraduate colleges. It might have seemed more natural to establish separate faculties of humanities, natural science, and social science, as was sometimes done in Germany, or even to break down the universe of intellectual disciplines more finely so that whole schools were devoted to only one discipline. This centripetal process, though not recognized by most commentators on the academic scene, is at least as significant as specialization. Historically, the disciplines become organized *across* the divisions among employing institutions. The turn-of-the-century generation was the time of the establishment of the principal disciplinary associations which served national and international functions on two levels: (1) communication of knowledge and (2) mechanisms of evaluation. Evaluation implied, formally or informally, the setting of standards of performance and competence. Two mechanisms of evaluation were meetings at which members from a variety of institutions met with each other for presentation of papers and discussion of topics and new research results and new professional journals in which communication could take place. As soon as the output of manuscripts began to exceed the space available in the journals, and this happened very quickly for financial and other reasons, acceptance for publication became honorific; the editors of journals acquired an evaluative role, both helping to establish reputations—or diminish them—and setting evaluative standards.

This social process, once it had acquired momentum, tended to move the academic center of gravity away from undergraduate teaching toward increased concern over professional standing in the department—including prestige among students and their attraction to the graduate school. More attention was focused on cosmo-

10. Talcott Parsons, "Unity and Diversity in the Modern Intellectual Disciplines: The Role of the Social Sciences," *Daedalus* (Winter, 1965), pp. 39–65.

politan bases of standing and reputation beyond the individual's own department, own institution, and local community. In this context, publication had a salient position, for publication was the surest way for a rising young scholar or scientist to become known—apart from the informally communicated opinions of his teachers and fellow-students (peers). Among our four criteria, then, productivity became especially prominent, and the most tangible kind of productivity was in research communicated through publication.

Though foundations and academies have had importance, in the academic social system the key structure at the professional level has come to be the *dual* one of membership in a local faculty and membership in one or more associations devoted to subject matter fields. The department has been the structural node where the two have usually intersected.

The department-disciplinary association connection has been the focus of the *identity* of an academic professional; he may thus be a *biologist* at *Yale*, both identifications contributing roughly equally to defining his professional identity. Contribution to identity calls attention to features of departments and disciplinary associations which are not strictly part of the cognitive complex, but which serve as institutional mechanisms reinforcing solidarities. Thus, the annual university commencement and the annual meeting of a disciplinary association both reinforce solidarity. In both cases there is a ritual surfacing of a combination of individual and group achievement and an affirmation not only of its value through recognition but for the solidarity of those who share the same identification. For annual meetings, the communication of research findings may be less important than the symbolic aspects of the occasion—publication is by and large a more effective means of communication. "Giving a paper," however, symbolizes professional status and the significance attached to the subject of the paper and to the achievements, standing, or promise of its author. The culmination of the honorific-ritual aspect of such associations is the election annually of a member to the presidency and the ritual occasion on which he delivers his presidential address.

These two foci of professional identification must be balanced. An academic lives most of his professional life on his own campus, associating with his colleagues and teaching his students as well as carrying out his own research. His faculty appointment is a *job* status. For most academic men, association membership is more peripheral; indeed, a minority treat it as trivial. Even those who attain high office and accept responsibilities in disciplinary associations do so only part time and usually not intensively for long periods.

This imbalance with respect to participation commitment, however, is compensated by another consideration. It is with respect to the cognitive content of the discipline's interests, the knowledge achieved, and the competence involved that the primacy of cognitive values is brought to focus and symbolized. For the individual academic this is the principal social reference-group in which his professional standing can be struggled for and evaluated. For the discipline as social system, it is the organizational framework embodying, more than any other, his commitment to the "intellectual life." A biologist can teach and practice the profession of biology at Yale or any one of many other universities, but identification *only* as a "Yale professor" without regard to field of competence, is not a qualification for a wide range of useful functions. In this sense, disciplinary *identification*, partly because it certifies competence, stands cybernetically higher in the control system of the academic world than does faculty *membership*. The graduate department in which an individual was trained, independently of his later location, is an intermediate link between disciplinary identification and current membership. In a circular feedback process of mutual reinforcement, the greater the distinction achieved by its former graduate students, the greater the enhancement of the prestige of a graduate department and hence of the university of which it is a part. On the other hand, having been trained in a distinguished department is a component in the opportunity-structure within which a professional, especially at the beginning of his career, operates. There seems here to be involved an important example of what Merton has called the "Matthew Effect."[11]

The evolution of the discipline and its organization at the social as well as the cultural level has been the lever by which the university system has rendered the cognitive complex so salient. In the process, conflict with the parochial particularism of specific faculties was inevitable, especially in the case of faculties which were heavily engaged in undergraduate teaching and where the aspira-

11. Robert K. Merton, "The Matthew Effect in Science," *Science*, 159, no. 3810 (January 1968), 56–63.

tions of students are, for the most part, not strongly oriented toward cognitive achievement.

The discipline has been able to contribute to this process because it packages knowledge so as to make it intelligible (the cultural counterpart of "useful" in the economic sense) at the node of intersection between the cultural level of the cognitive complex and the imperatives of its social institutionalization. Specifically, the system of intellectual disciplines has come to be structured about the frame of reference of human social action itself. Thus the humanities, including intellectual history, have concerned themselves with cultural objects. The natural sciences have concerned themselves with the objects comprising the conditional environments of action, in the biological case interpenetrating with the core of action itself. In between, the social disciplines treat the action system as a system of objects of cognition. Within each of these three principal groupings of disciplines, there have emerged specific subjects, again according to distinctions related to the structure of social action. Thus, in the social science sector, economics, political science, and sociology are flanked on one side by psychology, which is concerned with personality, on the other by anthropology, which is especially concerned with culture. In the case of the humanities, the bases of subclassification seem to be (1) "cultures," especially those using different languages, (2) "media of expression," for example, literature, the visual arts and music, and (3) those discriminating historical periods of cultural creativity, such as Renaissance or Enlightenment. For the natural sciences the subdifferentiation seems to follow a gradient of increasingly close involvement in the phenomena of life. Thus physics, including astronomy, is the most remote because of the generality of its cosmological references; chemistry is intermediate; and biology is explicitly the life science. Finally there is the group of metadisciplines, such as philosophy, logic, and mathematics, which cannot be neatly classified in the threefold paradigm.

How can the relevance of this pattern of packaging knowledge be defined for the noncognitive *cultural* bases of interest in it? The more expressive-aesthetic concerns have been closer to the scholarly concerns of the humanities than to the concerns of either of the other two sectors. Presumably history has been a connecting thread, since if it is to have an impact on present and future, it must be cognitively understood. There is a similar relation of the social or action disciplines to the moral-evaluative aspect of culture. Thus Durkheim and his disciples were concerned with sociology as a *science des moeurs,* in a sense which included both William Graham Sumner's conception of the mores and a more normative conception of morality. Perhaps the term "cosmology" indicates the dual concern of the natural sciences with problems which are empirical with respect to specific realities but which also extend into concerns with the "secrets of the universe" in a sense bordering on theology.

These contexts of cultural relevance of knowledge constitute a background of the problem of the social level of relevance; it is the problem of the conditions under which concern develops over the *rationality* of action and hence over the resources necessary to enhance levels of rationality.

In this perspective the three sectors of noncognitive relevance of the cognitive complex discussed in the last chapter constitute a matrix from which a concern for the promotion of pure cognitive interests has been differentiated. One, the ideological concern, is a concern for the meaningfulness of the cultural definition of the situation within which people live, above all those of higher status. The second concern focuses on socialization and involves the problem of identity in a modified Eriksonian sense, namely, what it means to be an educated person, including contentions that it is better not to be educated. The third concern is the area of coincidence between the validity of knowledge and its practical usefulness (in a sense close to economic utility).

In *none* of these cases does the organization of knowledge in the framework of disciplines closely fit the demand requirements of relevance. In all of them knowledge, to be relevant, must involve a selective combination of elements derived from several disciplines; we shall illustrate this later by contrasting medical science with even such a subdiscipline as microbiology.

From such considerations we conclude that the principal pressures toward the disciplinary organization of knowledge have been cultural in reference, but cultural in the context of the imperatives of social institutionalization of a complex with cognitive primacy. Why such a complex is sufficiently important to be supported from outside itself, at both cultural and societal levels, is a further question.

*The Core System and Its Relation to Other Functional Fields.* At a level of definiteness not previously present, the social organization of the core system (the university) has come to focus on the framework of the cultural structure of knowledge, the academic disciplines. The reference-system channels action in such a way that, by and large, the values of *cognitive* rationality can maintain primacy. The conceptions of "contribution to knowledge" in a disciplinary sense and "competence" understood as command of the content and methods of a discipline have been a normative role definition for the core structure. Again the discipline has constituted the framework of the output-package which has made it possible to integrate supply and demand where cognitive interests are paramount. When we move to the other sectors of university function and modes of relevance, however, other patterns become necessary, which use the same components of the knowledge system, but in different combinations.

Although these patterns will be dealt with in later chapters, brief sketches of three patterns may prove useful. The simplest is the applied case, where knowledge is mobilized to contribute to the rationality of action in pursuit of a relatively nonproblematical type of extracognitive goal, of which health is a prototypical example. It is necessary to draw cognitive resources from a plurality of disciplines. The criteria of relevance concern their bearing on the pragmatic tasks in hand as evaluated by standards of instrumental rationality. The professionalization of engineering, connected as it is with industrial production is prototypical; medicine is a next step in a more humanistic direction, while law has to deal with problems integral to the ordering of the society itself. Even law, however, should not be regarded as an intellectual discipline, for example, in the same sense as economics, because of the applied orientation of the legal profession. Law, however, is near the borderline and begins to merge into other modes of uses of cognitive resources.

The ideological context of relevance is at the other extreme from the applied case. Its focal substantive concerns are with definitions of the situation at the general action level, with the balance between cultural, societal, and individual interests. There is a concern for problems of identity at the personality level and for problems of value-integrity at the societal. The focus of the problem of rationality here is *Wertrationalität* in Weber's sense, though not necessarily bound to direct implementation. Since, in its societal focus, ideology is especially relevant to fiduciary considerations, the system of education is closely involved. The contribution of cognitive resources is the use of knowledge and critical intelligence to order patterns of reasonable orientation, especially focusing on value problems and on their implementation.

The position of the socialization function is intermediate between the ideological and applied cases. Specific competences, though not unimportant, do not stand at the core; the main thrust of undergraduate education is less and less vocational, to say nothing of professional. Neither, however, does it approximate indoctrination; this would recall the educational philosophies of the era before the secularization of higher education. We shall argue in the next chapter that the focus is coming to be socialization for rational, autonomous, and responsible participation in a system of institutionalized individualism, which takes the form of a special mode of integration of a highly socialized personality type in a pluralized social system. The contribution of cognitive resources here is to the rational patterning of harmony and balance among the various components of such a pattern of integration. The goal for the individual is the development of optimal capacities for the intelligent ordering of his commitments, loyalties, and participations, having due regard for the public interest as well as interests private to himself. There is good reason to believe that capacity to deal with knowledge at theoretical levels is essential here.

Once institutionalized, and having due regard for the elements of vulnerability in its position, the university has the capacity to maintain its position and to grow in the modern type of society. The value of the outputs embodied in performance of these three relevance functions other than its own core professional membership constitutes the basis of the demand that makes this functioning possible. At the general action level, three outputs of the cognitive system are knowledge itself, cognitive capacity which may be controlled for other than cognitive functions, and capacity for the intelligent ordering of a pluralistic social order and participation in it. At the social-system level, the contribution is ingredients necessary to optimize the rationality of social action.

*History of the University Core.* An extensive historical analysis of the processes by which the core university system developed is beyond the scope of this book. There is, however, a presumption that either what has happened is just natural and scarcely needs explanation or that it is so improbable that it must be regarded as something of a miracle. A brief sketch of probable circumstances will help to avoid this Scylla-Charybdis dilemma. We must keep

118

in mind here both the motivation of direct participation and that of nonparticipatory support; such roles as that of trustee occupy an intermediate position.

The pragmatic common sense prevalent in our culture emphasizes one category of demand, namely, that based on appreciation of the practical utility of knowledge. On the other hand, much can be said for the view that support on the basis of instrumental usefulness has been mainly a secondary reinforcement of the development of the cognitive complex and has played a predominant role only recently, as in the massive practical pay-off of natural science for industrial, military, and medical technologies in our generation. It should not be forgotten that the technological component of the industrial revolution was not primarily applied science but the inventions of ingenious men. The growth of industry has increased sensitivity to the possibilities of practical payoff from knowledge, but it would be difficult to explain getting over the cultural barrier of the organization of knowledge around disciplines rather than around practical interests on the basis of a yen for practical pay-off. In addition, the populist anti-intellectualism expressed in the old saying "those who can, do; those who can't, teach" and the image of the absent-minded, unworldly college professor militate against this.

We have classified law as an applied profession, but it is a special case because of a social focus and its fiduciary position in society. In the United States some evidence exists that the gap created by the decline of the relative prestige position of the clergy was largely filled by lawyers.[12] Their calling related them to part of the intellectual world, though law as a discipline has remained aloof from the core cognitive structure, not so much with respect to its values as to its pattern of organization; changes are in process at present. The American constitutional system, with its institutionalization of judicial review, emphasized legal functions, and this emphasis was built upon by the great lawyers of the first half of the nineteenth century : Chief Justice John Marshall, Chancellor James Kent, and Justice Joseph Story, a founder of Harvard Law School.[13]

12. Perry Miller, *The Life of the Mind in America: From the Revolution to the Civil War* (New York, Harcourt, Brace & World, 1965).

13. Cf. Arthur E. Sutherland. The founding fathers of the American Republic were steeped in the rationalism of the Enlightenment, some of it with legal emphasis. Thus, Thomas Jefferson was a lawyer as well as a landed gentleman. Science was also part

In short, the ascendancy of lawyers was a symptom of the beginning secularization of not only American culture in the narrower sense but of social organizations which emphasized cultural concerns. Furthermore, the valuation of science was also in the picture, as shown by the receptivity to scientific medicine when it came along. Many young Americans went to Europe, especially Germany, to study arts and sciences subjects and also medicine in the founding generation of the American university system. Thus, there was a favorable cultural atmosphere, especially among the upper strata of the leading Eastern cities, New York, Boston, and Philadelphia, and also in Providence, New Haven, and Baltimore. It is not incongruous from a Protestant ethic point of view that there should be supportive values, *both* for economic enterprise and for things intellectual, especially on the part of groups who constituted an urban patriciate, with some attributes of an aristocracy. The American situation paralleled the intellectual interests of the gentries in England and Holland in the seventeenth century and the French aristocracy during the Enlightenment. If we are right about the general character of instrumental activism outlined in the last chapter, the affinity is close between economic and cognitive interests because of their adaptive significance at the social system and the cultural levels, respectively. Both of these two directions of concern are rooted in ascetic Protestantism, as Weber and Merton analyzed them, and continued to operate. A tendency to increased emphasis on the cognitive component was favored by relative affluence in high-status circles so that the pressure for economic achievement was eased, especially if business was not congenial to all of their sons.[14]

Economic success for these upper groups brought with it a quasi-aristocratic status. It meant that Europe provided reference-models on a new basis. Some Americans were in a position to emulate European intellectual life, as well as European culture generally.

of the rationalism of the founding fathers. Recall the figure of Benjamin Franklin. Franklin founded the American Philosophical Society "to promote useful knowledge," and his fellow-father of the republic, John Adams, founded the American Academy of Arts and Sciences in Boston. Both were men of affairs, but the two academies they founded have retained a leading position in the United States among private institutions of this character. Sutherland, *Law at Harvard: A History of Ideas and Men, 1817–1967* (Cambridge, Mass., Harvard University Press, 1967).

14. To take familiar Boston examples, the James family were well-to-do Bostonians, but in one generation they produced an unusual pair of intellectuals: William and Henry. Adamses also showed similar tendencies, as illustrated by the brothers Henry and Brooks. Charles W. Eliot was a son of a Boston merchant family; he first became a chemist and then a university president.

The same period that saw the rise of universities was also marked by the development of art collections, accompanied by a tendency to take community pride in them as well as lending prestige to their benefactors and collectors. The congeniality of cognitive values in this context fostered the development of the cognitive complex not primarily for practical reasons.[15]

Behind these circumstances lay secularization. The decline in the community status of ministers was associated with a marked diminution of theological concern and controversy in religious circles and a turn to Revivalism.[16] This, in turn, was associated with the increased importance of law. A strengthening of intellectual concerns, deriving partly from our own indigenous combination of Puritan and Enlightenment rationalism and partly from the prestige of European culture as reference-model, helped fill the gap.

The third main context of relevance is that of the socialization function with reference to general undergraduate education. As Ben-David shows, the older American college emphasized a combination of a rigidly defined classical curriculum, almost wholly prescribed, and a component of moral philosophy directly expressive of the denominational sponsorship of the institution.[17] This curriculum could cope neither with the implications of secularization nor with the diversification of the intellectual world, especially the rise of the sciences to prominence. The symbolic break was the elective system introduced by Charles Eliot at Harvard soon after his assumption of its presidency in 1869. Eliot's move created a furor, but in a short time was widely imitated.

A gap was created which could be filled by the intellectual disciplines. It was not filled in a rigidly prescribed format but as a manifold of choice open to the student. This was the path which, in curricular terms, undergraduate education took. In this decisive period, the leading colleges were overwhelmingly attended by the children, especially the sons, of upper-status groups; thus being

15. Similar considerations are revelant to the motivations of the founders of the two earliest large philanthropic foundations, John D. Rockefeller, Sr., and Andrew Carnegie. Both favored intellectual enterprises. The largest single benefaction was the gift of Rockefeller which made possible the founding of the University of Chicago. Rockefeller and Carnegie were, compared to the older upper-uppers, self-made men who wished to identify themselves with the cultural concerns of high-status members of American society.

16. Miller, *Life of the Mind in America.*

17. Joseph Ben-David, *American Higher Education: Directions Old and New* (New York, McGraw-Hill, 1972).

educated became a status requirement for members of these groups. This circumstance brought the world of the developing intellectual disciplines into a position of being helpful to the most influential groups in society. Had the bulk of college students of that time been upwardly mobile members of the lower middle class, the story might well have been different.

In getting the cognitive component of the university structure established, these two bases of relevance outweighed that of practical pay-off. Indeed, the case of legal education provides some confirmation; law had more prestige than engineering, and law schools compared more favorably in prestige with faculties of arts and sciences than any other professional school—both were rooted in the needs of the upper-status groups.

Though Eliot introduced the elective system at Harvard in 1869, a graduate school was not formally established at Harvard until 1895. This meant that the more professional functions of the faculty, including the training of their successors, were performed within the matrix of Harvard College. As Ben-David has shown, the development of the scientist role as a distinctively differentiated type of role depended on the development of a critical mass of persons with similar interests and competence who could directly communicate with each other.[18] This happened to large sectors of the teaching faculties of the higher-prestige colleges and was the main path by which both the graduate schools and the institutionalization of research as a professional function and not an amateur avocation developed.

Furthermore, this is the context in which the packaging of pure cognitive output, namely around disciplines, developed. This mode of packaging was developed by emerging professional academics for their own purposes, but under the conditions of the elective system academic disciplines proved saleable to undergraduates. Without the development of the critical mass of academic professionals, they could not have been institutionally developed at all—though much if not most of their cognitive structure could have been borrowed from Europe. However, without the undergraduate colleges and the elective system, they could not have become institutionalized in American universities.

There is one further aspect of the relation between the professionalized academics and the undergraduate colleges, which has been prominent in the United States and to a lesser degree in Great

18. *Scientist's Role in Society.*

Britain : Graduate schools first developed, at high levels of prestige, in a small number of institutions, especially differentiating from undergraduate colleges, though there were a few new institutions that did not bother with colleges. Their output soon exceeded the capacity of the training institutions, individually or as a group, to provide alumni with careers. This problem was met by the demand for well-trained academics to serve as teachers in the large number of existing colleges without graduate schools, so that in the end an extensive system of academically respectable undergraduate colleges came to be staffed by faculty trained in the graduate schools.

*The Professionalization of Academics.* The foregoing historical sketch offers a perspective not only on the nature but on the origins of the academic profession. Professionalization of the faculty role is a key aspect of the development not only of the university system but of the whole system of higher education.

The main institutional structure of the arts and sciences sector of the university community has come to be organized about the patterns of tenure and academic freedom, together constituting a pattern of institutionalized individualism. Furthermore the keystone of this structural arch is the core academic profession. The central definition of the roles of its members is that they are exercising a fiduciary responsibility on behalf of the other sectors of the society. Fiduciary responsibility must be grounded in commitment to values—in this case the value of cognitive rationality. The presumptive commitment of members of the academic profession, especially in its higher echelons, legitimizes the privileged status which academic tenure and academic freedom confer. Since tenure and academic freedom in different ways build in exemptions from pressures which operate in other organizational settings, there must be a presumption that the modal incumbent can be *trusted* to perform his expected functions without the detailed controls, for instance, through market competition, bureaucratic enforcement, or democratic accountability to a defined constituency, which operate in other sectors.

This is an example of the individualistic component of institutionalized individualism; in considerable part it is shared by other membership-categories of the academic community than the senior professional. At the same time there is an institutional as well as an individualistic component. The institutional component focuses on the pressures on members and subunits of the system to conform to certain criteria and standards, pressures reinforced by complex systems of rewards and, on occasion, deprivations. These operate at the thresholds of membership or change in it, as in the admission of students and the appointment of faculty members and their promotion or nonpromotion. Only exceptionally does it involve dismissals. But it operates conspicuously at various levels of evaluation of performance. Perhaps the greatest single difference between student membership status and that of faculty is that the faculty are exposed to formal evaluation by agencies *outside* their particular academic community.

Thus, commitment to the relevant values, exercise of competence, and use of resources necessary to act competently constitute *one* aspect of the functioning of an academic community as a social system. However, it is not a social system without mechanisms of social control, but one which institutionalizes special types of social control. The use of economic incentives and of authority and power is minimized, though not wholly absent. Appeal to the validity of value-commitments (at the other end of the societal sanction scale) is more prominent. The focus of the sanction system lies in the realm of prestige and influence; the effort is to be persuasive, but on levels of generality which preclude persuasion solely through letting the facts of a situation speak for themselves. More of this later.

### The Arts and Sciences Subsystem of the University

This chapter is concerned mainly with the institutionalization of graduate training and research. The historical sketch just presented suggests that there has been a common origin of the undergraduate college and graduate training and research and that, through the changes that have come about, a continuing *symbiosis* exists between these components. There has also been a symbiosis between arts and sciences and the professional schools, but one that is less close.

Two salient structural facts dominate this symbiotic relationship. First, though the graduate school differentiated from the undergraduate college, it did not displace it. Second, though graduate faculties exist, they are far from having become the dominant structural pattern. On the contrary, most faculties of arts and sciences are made institutionally responsible for teaching at both graduate and undergraduate levels; there is indeed overlap of specific personnel and courses. This is partly owing to the fact that the majority of those trained in graduate schools will teach under-graduates in colleges without graduate schools.[19]

The rest of this chapter treats the arts and sciences complex as a whole, including the faculty role of teaching undergraduates and the student status of undergraduates. Fuller treatment of under-graduate socialization will be reserved for Chapter 4.

In delineation of the structure of an arts and sciences system and the analysis of its functioning, three models of social organi-zation are not highly relevant to its organization because they do not confront adequately the nature of a fiduciary system. These three models are (1) that of an economic market—the faculty are producers, the students consumers; (2) that of bureaucratic orga-nization—the trustees and top administrators are the bosses, fac-ulty members are middle-level and lower executives, students are the workers who have to obey orders; and (3) that of the demo-cratic association where all involved are in principle equal partici-pants or citizens, including sometimes not only faculty and students but employees without any academic qualifications or goals. According to the model of the democratic association, the collectivity is a self-governing democratic community where those who assume special responsibilities are accountable to the whole membership as a constituency. These three alternative models to the main pattern, as we shall present it, are admittedly caricatures, but discussing them should help in clarifying the nature of the main pattern as well as the problems of the directions of change to which it may be subject.

Why, if an arts and sciences faculty is a producer of *services* to graduate and undergraduate students, should it *not* be treated as a kind of factory—related to its customers through a teaching ser-vices market? Why should its products *not* be turned over to and paid for by the customers without a special relation of solidarity maintained between producers and consumers? Bear in mind that there are different kinds of markets. The salient outputs of the process of economic production are the traditional economic cate-gories of goods and services. At the social level the outputs of the academic system are special kinds of goods and services. The goods

19. In the Continental European system of higher education, there has been no close equivalent either of the American undergraduate college or the graduate school. Thus, the German philosophical faculties have not been graduate schools in our sense. The German doctoral degree was roughly the equivalent of our M.A., and the further training of academic professionals was mainly on a private basis. Only gradually has a system resembling the American been developing in Great Britain.

in question are exemplified by knowledge embodied in impersonal form, such as the printed word. At least part of this output is marketed on at least quasi-commercial bases through publication of books by commercial publishers. Publication also takes place on a noncommercial basis through professional journals, and subsidized university presses, but these cases do not force the economist to deny the relevance of the market model.

The employment of persons after being educated in the academic system also fits the market model as services in the economic sense. Though most colleges and universities operate employment services, services of graduates are not usually marketed by the institution but constitute individual choices and arrangements. Institutional involvement is stronger at the graduate-school than at the college level, but even at the graduate-school level mainly through evaluative recommendations by faculty members. Academic employment has in common with other cases where the employment agency is a collectivity that employment carries with it a status of membership in the employing organization, though at faculty levels this membership status is different from the ordinary status of worker.

Where employment follows a preceding stage of the life course, it is usual that preceding solidarities should carry over from earlier stages, notably from the family of orientation, but also from school associations and those of home community if residential location has changed. New solidarities also are formed, notably in the family of procreation through marriage. Alumni status by virtue of having attended an undergraduate college is an accentuation of continuing solidarities through school association; it is in most cases stronger than those to secondary schools, but not in principle entirely different.

The most distinctive involvement of the academic man in solidarities concerns the solidarity of his profession. The strongest of these, except for that in the employing institution, is with his discipline and is customarily expressed through the disciplinary association, though his loyalty to it need not be exclusive; he may belong to more than one as well as to interdisciplinary associations. Moreover, a lawyer in a government agency or a business firm may be active in the Bar Association, so professional solidarity is not unique to the academic context. It is, however, a focus of occupational identity—the authors of this book are all sociologists and not *only* professors at Harvard, Berkeley, and the University of Massachusetts, respectively. We have noted that the usual point of articulation between professional and institutional identities is the academic department.

This cross-cutting of institution-oriented and disciplinary ties is a focus of fiduciary features of the academic professional role. The *single* line of differentiation which has stood at the center of economic analysis, namely, that between producers and consumers does not adequately characterize the relational structure of this system. (Nor does the bureaucratic conception of line authority.) There *is* a sense in which, vis-à-vis students of all categories, colleges and universities as collectivities are the producers of education and students the consumers, while faculty members act in representative roles on behalf of their institutions. But faculty involvement with their disciplines provides a certain autonomy vis-à-vis the employing institution and also their students. (The institution of academic tenure implicitly recognizes this by introducing a distinctive feature into the academic labor market.) Professional meetings and publications channel part of the output of the faculty member; this market is constituted by colleagues outside his own institution who for the most part are not students or at least not *his* students. The heart of this market is the discipline. Undergraduate students are not the primary consumers of disciplinary packages.

The fiduciary component enters because this outside context symoblizes responsibility to cognitive standards and their implementation through processes of critical evaluation. This evaluation is shared by the institution, as in the process of reaching decisions about appointment or promotion on the part of departments and administrations, but such decisions lean on outside reputation and evaluations. This rather than solidarity with the institution or responsibility to student-customers as judged by them is the main focus of professional status. One implication of the departure from a market structure is the fact that faculty, graduate students, and undergraduates are organized in a market which comprises *all* the cognitive "industries" (disciplines) instead of those differentiated by particular classes of consumer wants.

In recent controversies over academic organization, the charge has been made that universities have become huge bureaucracies in the pejorative sense of any large organization not fully democratic. In sociological usage, bureaucracy refers to a type of organization characterized by a hierarchy of offices from top levels of authority to the lower levels where roles have only implementive responsibilities. The main integrating institution is line authority, with each level controlled by and responsible to the one next above. Functionally, a defining characteristic of bureaucracy is centralized planning at the top of the organization to carry out top management's plans. Coordination is mainly by authority and power.

Empirically, many modifications of the pure bureaucratic pattern exist, especially those introduced by the involvement of professional and technical expertise and by organization at labor levels. A substantial bureaucratic component characterizes university organization, the more so the larger the university. Bureaucracy is concentrated in the administration and deals mainly with such nonacademic functions as buildings and grounds and the management of complex equipment. The core social structure, that of faculties, departments, and student bodies, is notably nonbureaucratic; they constitute a stratified collegial association. The delineation and analysis of this organizational type is the task of the rest of the present chapter.

Those who allege that bureaucratization is the main organizational trend of universities should consider the hard and stubborn fact of the *combination*, at faculty levels, of high competence with the differentiation of the fields of competence into a great variety of specialties. The realistic capacity of the bureaucratic executive to understand the problems involved at every level and in every part of the organization is a condition of the effective centralization of authority. But a university president or dean cannot understand more than a small part of the substantive intellectual problems confronted by the members of his faculty. Bureaucratization would necessitate confining the scope of a faculty to a small sector of the universe of knowledge, whereas the actual organizational tendency has been the reverse: the broadening of faculty responsibility as the range of knowledge has broadened.

If individual faculty members with similar competence are to function at high levels in the same organization, each must be autonomous in dealing with his own subject matter. This circumstance underlies the institution of academic freedom, which is the antithesis of bureaucratic subordination. Academic freedom is structurally bolstered by the extrainstitutional references of the faculty members' status, organized especially around disciplines. These loyalties cannot be controlled by the central administration of a faculty member's university. In a strict bureaucratic organization, such outside loyalties would be defined as a conflict of interest.

Critics of the university allege not only that the university has adopted undesirable bureaucratic patterns but has substituted them for desirable patterns of the democratic association. Their democratic ideal is (in Lincoln's phrase) government "of the people, by the people and for the people." The people are the citizen body defined as equals on the principle of "one citizen, one vote"; the only power over them held to be legitimate is that exercised by officeholders whom they themselves have elected. The argument in favor of participatory democracy goes even farther; it seeks to minimize reliance even on elected officers in favor of each member participating directly in collectively important decisions.

The attempt to redefine the university as a democratic association attacks its stratification and especially the status differences between faculty members and students. Sometimes the attempt seeks to include all employees in the academic community, whether their functions or qualifications are academic or not, as equal members. The obstacle to implementing this ideal pattern lies in the role of special knowledge and competence which comes from training and experience; a flat equalization of participatory rights means that newly entered freshmen and senior professors may not occupy different statuses in the governance of the institution. Differential competence and intelligence with respect to cognitive matters, if valued at all, would suggest that the democratic ideal cannot be literally used as the model for university organization.

### Tenure and Academic Freedom

The absence of fiduciary responsibility for the performance of a *differentiated* set of societal functions makes all three of the above structural types inappropriate to the academic case. Markets and bureaucracies do not have fiduciary responsibilities, and democratic government is not functionally specific enough for the academic system. On the other hand, the stratified collegial association is a type of social organization well suited to academic functions. The institutions of tenure and academic freedom are central to the stratified collegial association.

Among the various fiduciary complexes in modern society,[20]

20. Talcott Parsons, "Equality and Inequality in Modern Society; or, Social Stratification Revisited," *Sociological Inquiry*, 40 (Spring 1970), 13–72

the academic one carries with it responsibility for the integrity, development, and implementation of knowledge and other components of the cognitive complex. No given mode of knowledge or level of attainment in it is a general property of human beings; therefore such fiduciary responsibilities are differentiated by both kinds of knowledge and hierarchically by levels. In addition to the question of integrity in faithful discharge of fiduciary responsibilities, there must always be questions of competence in the specification of knowledge from general to particular kinds and in recognizing the contexts of its relevance.

The institutionalization of fiduciary responsibility at the social system level requires legitimation according to the relevant values —in this case cognitive rationality—of three other activity spheres. The first sphere is one within which members are institutionally encouraged and helped to make their contributions. This achievement complex must be governed, normatively speaking, by recognition of maximal achievement, which is bound to be differential in type and in qualitative level, and by norms of equality of opportunity. The second sphere concerns norms and practices dealing with the conduct of social relations where cognitive issues are involved, such as the mode of discussing controversial issues. This sphere is related to legal procedures and to the conduct of meetings through such codes as Robert's *Rules of Order*, but special aspects are involved where the content of actual and potential disagreement is primarily intellectual.

The third sphere concerns the solidarity which must obtain among the units cooperating within a system of institutionalized individualism. The individualistic component is manifested explicitly in the academic version of the achievement complex. In the preceding chapter theoretical reasons were given why individual autonomy should figure more prominently in this sphere than in others and which help to explain the resistance of academic systems to bureaucratization. The individualism of this complex, however, tends to operate within a matrix which contrasts with a market system. The evaluation of impersonal outputs (the equivalent of economic goods) is not left to the given preferences of those interested in them (the parallel to consumers' wants) but is subject to sharply defined and common evaluative standards. This applies not only to research output through publication but also to students' outputs: quizzes, course examinations, major papers, doctoral dissertations. In the other direction, the autonomy of academic production at all levels but especially at high levels of intellectual sophistication militates against bureaucratic organization within faculties and also in the teacher-student relationship.

Units do not relate to each other, either in terms of a market type of contractual relationship of the sort usual in the purchase and sale of commodities or in terms of the bureaucratic type of contract of employment. By contrast with both, they enter into mutual associations which are legitimized by commitment, in the relevant form and level, to implementation of cognitive values in a fiduciary role.

At the faculty level, the symbol of this status in a fiduciary associational collectivity is academic tenure. Tenure is relatively old in the history of European universities and has become widely established in America, though it is now under attack. Calling it a *symbol* of status in an academic community stresses the distinction of tenure from the status of ordinary contractual employment. Tenure is the badge of *full* membership in the local academic-collectivity. A tenured faculty member is thereby *trusted* on a higher level than are other members. Tenure implies that it is not necessary that his performances or other qualifications be repeatedly reviewed—and conversely it might be considered insulting to him to insist on a review. Tenure does not, however, imply freedom from *any* normative control. The tenured member is expected to fulfill high standards of fiduciary responsibility and is trusted to do so. In this context it is an institutional form of professional autonomy.[21] Thus, the main significance of tenure is not necessarily its protection of the faculty member's status security.

Critics have found this institution anomalous in the occupational sector of an achievement-oriented type of society and have suggested the assimilation of academic status to the contractual or democratic types with which we have contrasted it. Our typological placing of it points more outside than inside the principal contexts of rational instrumental orientation and relates it to others prominent in institutional history, namely kinship, religion, and national citizenhsip. Although secularization is conspicuous in the

21. It would be surprising if tenured faculty members never abused this privileged position and operated at less than the normatively ideal level. It does not follow, however, that more stringent controls, e.g., of a bureaucratic character, including the administration's right to dismiss for unsatisfactory performance, would improve average levels of performance in the academic world.

history of American higher education, the academic system has not, in becoming differentiated from the religious complex, moved into a predominantly economic, political, or even integrative sector of the society. The academic system remains predominantly part of the fiduciary sector with especially intimate relations to the integrative sector (the societal community).[22]

Similarly, the kinship system in modern societies has undergone a process of differentiation from a diffuser matrix and has developed into the isolated nuclear family. Placing academic organization in the structural company of religion and the family helps to establish certain continuities in terms of modes of participation and relations to the life cycle. From the point of view of the individual, we will emphasize socialization even more than we did with respect to the phenomena of studentry in an earlier paper[23] in which we applied the term to the undergraduate phase of higher education.

Classical analyses of the socialization process have had empirical reference to the family as the main socializing agency—and particularly the child's parents. At a later stage of the life cycle, the college becomes a socializing agent which, in the good biological usage of the term, is *analogous* to the family for earlier stages. In the next chapter we will have more to say about the socialization aspect of the undergraduate studentry phase. But we will also extend the concept of socialization to include the entire system of higher education—and of course of education before that stage— *including* the research function. Even at preoedipal familial levels, for the learning of cognitive content and the matrix within which such content has meaning, the value of cognitive rationality and the procedural standards of how to test validity and significance are involved in embryonic form. At the same time, the child has to learn to attach affective meaning to this content. This involves the *integration* of rational and nonrational components of the motivation of the individual and, concomitantly, of the social and cultural systems. The general principle is, *no* cognitive learning without noncognitive learning: the socialization of the personality

22. For a discussion of the relevance of the current academic situation to certain religious themes, see Walter P. Metzger, "The Crisis of Academic Authority," *Daedalus* (Summer 1970), pp. 568–608.
23. Talcott Parsons and Gerald M. Platt, "Age, Social Structure and Socialization in Higher Education," *Sociology of Education*, 43 (Winter 1970), 1–37.

of the learner in a wider action system in which cognitive knowledge and competence are not the only constituents.[24]

For reasons of this order, neither the market nor the bureaucratic model nor that of the democratic association is appropriate to the academic system, including its elements of status asymmetry. Within the fiduciary model, however, faculty tenure should not be regarded as a unique institution: in a sense *all* members of the academic community enjoy tenure. What is distinctive about faculty tenure is that, subject to retirement policies, it is, as the official Harvard phrase puts it, "without limit of time." All categories of students may also be regarded as having tenure which, however, is limited either to a specified time period, as are "term" teaching and research appointments, or to the time necessary to complete a program of study to which the student has been admitted. Once admitted and while in good standing the student becomes a member of the university and enjoys the privileges which pertain to that status so far as they are relevant to his program. He may pay tuition and various fees while faculty members are paid and receive various perquisites, but this is not the essential aspect of the status distinction.[25] Membership in fiduciary groups in the other three types of case also carries a status resembling academic tenure. Thus in the case of kinship, relationship by birth is indelibly ascriptive, but a son can be repudiated by his father for very "grave misconduct," for instance, in Orthodox Judaism for marrying a Gentile. Similarly, the marriage contract is not an ordinary contract, but divorce is traditionally "for cause." In the case of national citizenship something closely resembling tenure exists, as is broadly true of membership in religious bodies.

The categories of tenured faculty members, nontenured fac-

---

24. Cf. Jean Piaget, *The Moral Judgment of the Child* (New York, The Free Press, 1965); Lawrence Kohlberg, "Stage and Sequence: The Cognitive-Developmental Approach to Socialization," in *Handbook of Socialization Theory and Research,* ed. David A. Goslin (New York, Rand McNally & Co., 1969), pp. 347–480; and Jerome Kagan, "A Conception of Early Adolescence," *Daedalus* (Fall 1971), pp. 997–1012.

25. The concept "in good standing" means that students may lose their tenure for reasons of inadequate academic performance and faculty members on "term" appointments may fail to be promoted and thus forced to leave the institution—in both cases in part as a result of evaluative judgments on the part of faculty members and/or administrative officers. For all three categories, "good standing" has another aspect, namely, with respect to the ethical rules of professional conduct. Students may be suspended or dismissed on disciplinary grounds and even fully tenured faculty members may be dismissed on grounds of "grave misconduct," in the Harvard formula.

ulty members, graduate students, and undergraduate students resemble estates in earlier polities. They share common bases of membership, but these memberships at the same time are differentiated on *two* main bases, not one. One of these is the qualitative differentiation of fields or programs. Neither a full professor of sociology nor an undergraduate student in that field has the kind of access to the physics laboratory that both professors of physics and students concentrating in physics have. Many kinds of access, not only to physical facilities but to people, have to be allocated on that kind of basis—thus we have an obligation to see sociology students which does not extend on the same terms to students in other fields. The other basis is the hierarchical basis of differentiation. This hierarchy differs both from that of estates and from that of classes in the usual social stratification sense, in that the principle of hierarchization is primarily one of *stages* in a life course and of survival in processes of selection. The stage in a life course resembles the generation difference in the structure of the family and of wider kinship groupings. The basic difference from kinship, however, lies in the *selective* component of academic status. Membership in the family by birth is the classical case of ascription of status, but admission and appointment in the academic case mark a transition from a status of nonmembership, with no presumption of prior right to it, to that of inclusion. On both levels, standards of eligibility are taken for granted although among applicants for admission as students some criteria of relative academic desirability are used, including reference to probable level of academic performance, and among candidates for faculty appointment criteria of level of academic attainment and prospective future performance. Once admitted or appointed, however, status becomes ascriptive for the period of tenure in that only "for cause" may the individual be deprived of it, whereas in ordinary cases of employment the mere fact that the employer no longer needs or wants the employee's services is sufficient justification for dismissal (again subject to certain legal and union restrictions). For the student or junior faculty member the cause may include inadequate academic performance, but it is still cause; the burden of proof is on the dismissing or nonpromoting institution, not on the member.[26]

26. Student tenure in this respect has markedly grown. Thus a generation ago the Harvard Law School had a systematic policy of flunking out one-third of the entering class at the end of the first year, whereas now every effort is made, once a student

This general approach to the sociological character of academic organization has implications on both the axes of equality and inequality and of freedom and constraint, in particular with respect to the nature and limits of authority in such a system and of the freedoms and access to unequal facilities and rewards appropriate within it. With particular respect to the faculty-student relationship, difference of place in the stage of career cycle and the relation of this (1) to levels of competence and levels of commitment to the relevant values and (2) to the symbolic definition of the situation which underlies them constitute reference points for assessing the legitimacy of different modes of balance between equality and inequality and between freedoms and constraints. It seems best to deal with the two categories of students involved separately, graduate students in the present chapter, undergraduates in the next.

At this point a brief discussion of the status of the other main structural component of academic organization is needed, namely, the administration. The administration consists of suborganizations and the people who staff them; it mainly performs functions other than the core academic functions of processing knowledge through learning and teaching. These functions include financial transactions, health services, planning and care of physical facilities, managing of complicated technical equipment, including libraries, and many others.

Administrative organizations are stratified; their staffs fall into the categories of nonacademic employees and of officers of administration; the latter category has status comparable, making allowance for stage of career, to that of primarily academic members; a nonadministrative example would be physicians in a university health service. Nonacademic employees do not enjoy a membership comparable to academic personnel, essentially because they do not share the characteristics which underlie it. Some radical critics are attempting to define nonacademic employees and indeed even residents of the local community with no formal academic connections as having the full rights of membership, but this would shift the focus of academic organization in the direction of

---

is admitted, to carry him or her through the whole course, and only a small percentage leave for academic reasons. Policies similar to that of the Law School in flunking a specific proportion of the entering class used to be followed at the undergraduate level by many state universities which have been required by law to admit any resident of the state with a high school diploma.

the democratic association model. The fiduciary character of the university imposes an obligation on it to observe high ethical standards in its employment policies, but the full inclusion of nonacademic personnel would blur the boundaries of the distinctive academic community.

Officers of administration and some categories of professional personnel present a more complicated problem of membership. A not inconsiderable proportion of the former are drawn from faculties and some continue to perform faculty functions—as in the case of a dean who does some teaching. Others close to the corporate affairs of faculties, including the implementation of decisions, are given the status of faculty membership—though often the granting of such status to the incumbent of the office is subject to faculty action. Finally, many regular faculty members perform administrative functions, a salient case being the departmental chairmanship.

Clearly, a zone of interpenetration exists between faculties and administrations and other high-level technical functionaries. As in the case of other pairs of interpenetrating subsystems of a larger system, there is a problem of the proper lines of division of labor and the proper balances of power and influence. With the exception of a few at the top of the administrative subsystem, such as presidents and members of governing boards, generally speaking the tenured senior faculty has higher *prestige* (or influence) than the administration.[27] On the other hand, the administration has greater *power* in the making and implementation of binding decisions. This balance is a predictable consequence of faculty concentration in its fiduciary relation to knowledge combined with its interdependence with the rest of the society in its need for access to many facilities and many kinds of support. Generally speaking, the roles of administrations are facilitative of faculty and student functioning rather than managerial.[28] Recently, though, this has come into flux with administrators attempting to take more aggressive roles regarding institutional growth and change. However, in crisis situations, faculties attempt to take over increased shares of corporate decision-making power which in quieter times has been

27. Officers of administration are not usually accorded tenure in their positions. A dean of the Harvard Faculty of Arts and Sciences has no tenure, he serves "at the pleasure" of the Corporation, but as Professor of X, he has tenure.

28. Many student and other radical dissidents wrongly perceive the university mainly as a power structure and in the process tend to impute to the administration a managerial role relative both to faculty and to students.

left in administrative hands. This has happened at a number of universities in connection with the student disturbances of recent years.[29]

One reason why officers of administration are not structurally assimilated to the status of faculty members more than they are and nonacademic employees to student status is that neither category is undergoing a process of socialization in the same sense as academic personnel. In what sense are faculty members in process of being socialized? Didn't that process stop with their acquisition of the Ph.D.?

Both teaching and research are processes with a socialization component. Take the case of research. Research is a process of learning where the investigator combines the roles of teacher and of student, although some components of the teacher role seep into the subject role, especially if research subjects happen to be human beings, as is common in the social sciences and in medicine. For example, recall the account of the way in which patients on a research ward of the seriously ill came to cooperate at semiprofessional levels with members of the research team.[30] The contributions to the advancement of knowledge which are the goals of research activity constitute the visible criteria of success. But an investigator is not the same man after completion of a program of research as he was before. If what he has come to know is original in the sense that it has not previously been known by others, in the process he has had to reorganize the structure of his thinking and, as part of that process, the internalized cultural and normative components of his personality. He has not merely discovered new facts but has ordered them in terms of new and more generalized theory; thus he has achieved a new perspective on the relevant portions of his field. At the very highest levels of research creativity, this may be a phase of a "scientific revolution" in Thomas Kuhn's sense.[31]

Processes of intellectual as well as of artistic creation are accompanied by strong emotional reactions, at some moments pleasurable ones, but often anxious. These features would not be so

29. Gerald M. Platt and Talcott Parsons, "Decision Making in the Academic System: Influence and Power Exchange," in *The State of the University: Authority and Change*, ed. Carlos E. Kruytbosch and Sheldon Messinger (Beverly Hills, Calif., Sage Publications, 1970), pp. 133–180.

30. Renée C. Fox, *Experiment Perilous: Physicians and Patients Facing the Unknown* (Glencoe, Ill., The Free Press, 1959).

31. Thomas S. Kuhn, *The Structure of Scientific Revolutions* (Chicago, Ill., University of Chicago Press, 1962).

prominent were the process of research a mechanical following out of a routine plan where being industrious and observing rules of procedure were enough. Under the rubric of research, this kind of routine activity is included, but it is not what sets the tone for research in the knowledge system.

Risk and uncertainty play a part in the research process, for the simple reason that *if* it is research, the investigator cannot know in advance what his findings are going to be; even if he can clearly state a hypothesis, it may turn out to be wrong; and often findings turn up which could not have been anticipated even in the form of hypothesizing. In this as in other respects, research is similar to the experience of the child who cannot know on entering a phase of his socialization what it will be like to have completed it. Clearly no six-year-old, entering primary school, knows cognitively or emotionally what it will be like to be a college student.

In terms of the cognitive complex, research extends the frontier; such geographical metaphors, including exploration, are often used to characterize it. There are no parents who have already crossed the frontier of knowledge and can guide the investigator in penetrating it. This circumstance defines the limits of the sense in which the process can be treated as one of socialization. In three respects, though, a socialization situation can be approximated, and there is evidence that their presence greatly facilitates success. First, there is a process of social facilitation of the investigator's activities. Not only is much research conducted in situations of positive collaboration (team work), but there are looser settings where people are engaged in research with varying modes of connection with what other individuals or collaborative teams are doing.[32] At the level of concrete personal actors, these associations reinforce the will to overcome resistances and uncertainties. A formally structured audience for the communication of findings, for instance, the readership of published statements, is also important. Second, at the cultural level the great tradition yields answers not in terms of what is validly known but in terms of criteria of *significance* in the cognitive sense discussed in the preceding chapter. This defines aspirations of researchers on the basis that "*if* I—or we—could solve that problem or break through on this front," it would be a memorable achievement.[33]

32. Cf. Ben-David, *Scientist's Role in Society;* and Nicholas Creed Mullins, "Social Networks among Biological Scientists," unpub. diss., Harvard University, 1967.
33. An example is the case of Watson and Crick with respect to the chemical structure of DNA. They knew, in terms of the tradition which embodied the development

Mediating between the social and cultural levels are models of research virtuosity who can in a sense serve as parental figures. Children can no longer model themselves on their parents in the modern world in the literal sense of becoming like them because there has been so much social change since the parents were their age. When they attain that age, things will be unpredictably different. Hence in fields of socialization in the traditional senses, the socialization must, to be effective, be oriented to situations and roles the shape of which is only vaguely definable at the time when the socialization takes place. In this sense, even young children are being socialized to be researchers.

For the mature researcher, concrete role models may include his own teachers. To be sure, he is not trying to repeat what they did, but having some knowledge of what they started from and what they were able to achieve, he can more readily visualize what he himself *might* be able to achieve, given the state of knowledge and the other resources with which he is able to work. He uses his teachers' "quality of mind" to define standards for his own work. They need not be the investigator's own teachers, but other figures, perhaps in the remote past, such as the greats of intellectual history. One category consists of major figures in his own field of interest, whose contributions he becomes aware have been constitutive for the structure of problems and the theoretical frameworks within which he works.[34]

The mature academic man undergoes a process of socialization as teacher that is the obverse of his research role. The socialization of teachers by students parallels the reciprocal socialization of parents and children. Teachers are stimulated by their students just as, in the development of common law as a system, common law courts were stimulated by the obligation to adjudicate *any* case presented to them through procedurally correct channels. The process of adjudication does not consist only in arriving at a decision by the court but in publicly giving grounds for such decisions, which are subject to review in the appellate process and to

of microbiological genetics, that "it" was there to be discovered, and that great prizes awaited whoever first succeeded in "finding" it. See James D. Watson, *The Double Helix: A Personal Account of the Discovery of the Structure of DNA* (New York, Atheneum, 1968).

34. This last type of model was relevant to the development of the senior author of this book. Max Weber, Emile Durkheim, and Sigmund Freud, none of whom he encountered in person, critically influenced his thinking and the directions of his investigative work. See Talcott Parsons, "On Building Social System Theory: A Personal History," *Daedalus* (Fall 1970), pp. 826–881.

critical evaluation in the learned profession of the law. New cases and decisions concerning them continually raise questions of general significance for the cognitive structure of the law as a system of knowledge, which has been continually reorganized in the light of the handling of such questions.

Analogously, apart from the more direct intellectual contributions which they may make, students are inherently askers of questions. Their questions constitute cases with reference to which the teacher must render some kind of opinion to the best of his ability. His opinion is not final, but is subject to criticism in the light of the authorities in the field, some of which stand higher in the appellate hierarchy than he does, and of the procedures of intellectual discourse. Exposure to the questioning of intelligent and inquiring students may thus serve as stimulus to continual restructuring of the teacher's body of knowledge and opinion in his field. The teacher cannot control the flow of questions to which he is exposed any more than the researcher can control the data which his investigative operations will produce. In both cases he must react in cognitive terms to the best of his ability, in the one case to explain the data, in the other, to give answers to the questions. This example suggests how the mature academic in his role as teacher undergoes a process of socialization unless he is too rigid to change in any significant way. Such cases are familiar, but it seems fair to treat them as belonging to the pathology of the teaching profession rather than as its ideal type.

*Differentiation and the Research Complex.* There has been a process of differentiation of the cognitive complex from the rest of culture and from the social system. Insofar as this process of differentiation has taken place, the research function might be expected to assume a more prominent position; insofar as a type of action is valued in terms of cognitive rationality, the highest esteem in that area should go to achievements which are the most difficult and hence rare in terms of this value. This situation is not in principle different from that of the valuation of creativity in the arts. The status of a Newton in the history of science parallels that of a Michelangelo in the history of art.

Such considerations, within the general analytical framework used in this study, constitute our main explanation of the rise of the research complex to prominence and with it the special valuation of relatively pure research or that which produces knowledge at high levels of theoretical generality and significance. This in turn has much to do with the emergence of graduate schools into a salient place in the university structure as well as the prominence of training for research in the larger context of graduate training.

With due account for overlapping and interpenetration, the graduate student as distinguished from the student in a school of an applied profession typically is training to be an academic professional. This means, first, giving primacy to cognitive considerations relative to other bases of interest and, secondly, high levels of competence in the cognitive area. The first desideratum distinguishes the academic professional from both the applied type and the intellectual—a category which will be discussed further in Chapter 6. The second implies an order of specialization transcending the level of general education which we will discuss in the next chapter as appropriate for the cognitive emphasis of undergraduate study.

There is an apparent paradox in the concept of academic specialization. As used here, specialization does not refer to special knowledge of a concrete sector of the world of phenomena, although it may include that, but mastery of a sufficiently well-defined cognitive subject matter so that knowledge of it can attain a high *technical* level. Thus a philosopher can be a specialist in the theory of knowledge or a physicist in the theory of subatomic physical phenomena. Specialization should not be equated with "dry as dust" empiricism. In this broader sense the academic professional *must* be a specialist, a sense which does not preclude his being a specialist in some highly abstract area.

A complex process of cognitive learning is involved in attaining requisite levels of competence. This is the familiar aspect of the process of training. At the same time, there is also a necessary process of socialization. It requires internalization, on foundations laid down in earlier phases, of the value of cognitive rationality. It requires developing a capacity for intellectual detachment beyond common sense in everyday life[35] and also beyond the capacities of most members of the practicing professions as well as of less discipline-oriented intellectuals. Such internalization defines an ideal type, which is only approximated in the concrete action of academic professionals.

---

35. Cf. Harold Garfinkel and Harvey Sacks, "On Formal Structures of Practical Actions," in *Theoretical Sociology: Perspectives and Developments*, ed. John C. McKinney and Edward A. Tiryakian (New York, Appleton-Century-Crofts, Educational Division, Meredith Corp., 1970), pp. 337–366.

It is nevertheless a significant ideal type because the structure of knowledge as a cognitive cultural system does not correspond point by point with the structure of the empirical world. *Every* concrete empirical reality, physical, biological, or action itself, is from the point of view of cognitive understanding a node where many cognitive systems interpenetrate; each, taken separately, is abstract. Hence higher-level cognitive understanding cross-cuts the subdivisions of practical and empirical interest. A paradigmatic example is the expression: the science of medicine. In the disciplinary sense—meaning organized about theoretical systems—a science of medicine does not exist; there is merely a confluence of *many* sciences such as physics, chemistry, and branches of biology, psychology, sociology, and so forth. The attainment of intellectual detachment from practical and other interests, along with the attainment of requisite levels of competence, defines the problem of socialization for graduate study—and for continuing socialization after completion of the latter. Performance within the framework of such detachment must come to be felt to be meaningful, and the normative conditions of operating successfully in this definition of the situation must not only be cognitively understood but emotionally accepted.

As a preliminary to developing the conditions favoring this understanding and acceptance in Chapters 4 and 5, let us consider why the personality and role types socialized through the graduate school experience have positive functions in contexts other than the self-perpetuation and further development of the cognitive complex itself. The cognitive specialist is typically not only a researcher and a teacher of graduate students but a teacher of undergraduates. Ramifications also extend into training in the applied professions and into the more general cultural world of intellectuals. All three of these lines of extension will have to be dealt with later. In all three, the cognitive basis of interest and hence the relevance of the value of cognitive rationality must articulate with other bases of interest deriving from the cultural, social, and personality systems, but different interests articulate in different ways.

*Elaboration of the Core Sector and Selective Academic Processes.* The remainder of the present chapter will attempt to extend somewhat farther the analysis of the institutional structure of the core academic sector and some of the ways in which this structure relates to the cognitive upgrading of the system through the advancement of knowledge, both in the repository available in the cultural system and in its internalization and institutionalization in personalities and social systems.

The institution of tenure and the closely related one of academic freedom suggest two aspects of the institutional structure typical of the academic world. *Both* presume that the academic community is part of the fiduciary complex and that the commitments which go with this status are given. This is the basic reason why universities, like churches, families, and national communities, cannot be *primarily* market systems, bureaucratic organizations, or democratic associations, though concretely they may involve components of all three, though the national community comes closest.[36]

As a set of collectivities, the academic system should be regarded as a stratified set of collegial associations; they manifest principles of Chinese-box inclusion and principles of cross-cutting differentiation (and hence interpenetrations) because of these structural facts. The concept, "association," suggests the democratic principle of equality of status and, where binding collective decision-making is at issue, the principle that one member shall have one vote. Democratic decision-making typically implies that executive functions are performed by leader members who, when the principle of collective sovereignty is raised, have only one vote; the department chairman is a prototype. Such leaders may be either elected or appointed. That they need not be elected is related to the distinction between the fiduciary collegial association and the democratic association. In the fiduciary collegial association membership is not attained either by universalistic ascription or entirely by personal choice but by admission or appointment. The candidate may apply or let his availability be known and, conversely, he may refuse offers of admission or appointment or, once in, may withdraw or resign. These features of the membership structure are relevant to the nature of the academic system.

Democratic associations are different in these respects. National citizenship is, in most polities, available to all who meet the criteria of birth under the political jurisdiction of reference; in addition, opportunity exists for actively seeking membership by naturalization. In the case of voluntary associations, on the other hand, the

36. In the case of the American national community the most visible fiduciary component is that of "Constitutional principles" which cannot be altered by simple majority vote of the electorate or the action of elected officials.

decisive criterion is the decision to join. The academic association, like professional associations in some respects, is intermediate between ascribed and voluntary associations. One aspect of this intermediacy is that the candidates' peers do not have full responsibility for maintenance of standards, including qualifications for membership. Thus, the granting of Ph.D. degrees is not left exclusively to the judgment of graduate students in the field, nor the appointment of junior faculty members to tenure status to their peers on the junior level. This would convert membership status into elective office of the democratic association type and thereby destroy the autonomy of the full-tenure status as a distinctive component of the larger organizational system. The same principle applies at each transition between levels. Those eligible for graduate study, even if willing, are not selected by their undergraduate classmates by democratic vote. Nor are those, among doctoral candidates eligible for faculty appointment, selected by a vote of current graduate students in that field at that university.

The pattern of stratification of the system is built upon the life course through the four stages of tenure: undergraduate studentry, graduate studentry, junior professional, and senior professional with full tenure. This stratification pattern is articulated with another involving both fields and institutions. Admission and appointment procedures are mechanisms of allocation among levels during the life course; it is a selective system. Note, however, that students are not ordinarily admitted to an undergraduate college as candidates for a particular course of study. Such directions of specialization as they may undertake are usually chosen after admission, often at the end of the first year. Graduate students, on the other hand, are typically admitted to differentiated programs of study, though transfers are often possible. Both junior and senior appointments are to particular positions in particular fields, usually carrying with it membership in a department.

At each stage a selective process involves not only determination of attainment or nonattainment of a status but a level on which it is attained. Consequently the more elite undergraduate colleges are overapplied with candidates who meet their formal admission requirements, and their admission officers choose those applicants they consider the best. The majority of those rejected go to a college, but one of a lower order of choice. The same is true of graduate and professional schools after completion of the undergraduate program. Since in the graduate schools a choice of field has generally already been made by applicants, failure to secure admission to the school of first choice or an offer of favorable financial terms leads to admission to another graduate school of a lower order of desirability but in the same field. Of course, not all students agree on the order of their preferences at either under-graduate or graduate levels.

Between graduate school and junior appointments another selective process takes place with the candidate for faculty tenure generally taking more initiative to find the most promising position available to him. Finally, in most universities, especially elite universities, there is not room for the promotion of all junior faculty members to the full tenure level, and in addition some universities may prefer a candidate from outside or some junior faculty may prefer to go elsewhere.

These processes according to which colleges, schools, faculties, and departments select among candidates to become members determine and are determined by the prestige scale of institutions, faculties, departments, and individuals. Hence, the egalitarian tendency within the principal status units—a college class, the graduate students in a department, the junior faculty and the senior faculty in a university—is interwoven with a scale of stratification *between* such units.

As is true of stratification systems in liberal, pluralistic, mobile societies, this pattern is not formalized and not fully integrated, although its main outline is observable. Since graduate and professional schools and their research activities have high academic prestige, the highest statuses are occupied by universities with the most distinguished faculties in most of the important fields. Various rating studies have been made; they generally agree on ten to twelve "top" universities. This list is not only a recent consensus, it has been rather stable during the present century.

Not far below these "top" institutions, judged by level of distinction of faculties, are a group of elite liberal arts colleges. From there on down, there is an interlarding of universities and colleges of many different types. There is, however, a unifying thread with respect to staffing by products of the graduate schools: the larger the proportion trained at the graduate schools of higher prestige, the greater the prestige of the school in question.

Another structural fact is the inclusive tendency of universities and colleges with respect to disciplines and other categories of subject matter. Most faculties of arts and sciences comprise all of the major intellectual disciplines, and most universities with professional schools include most of the major professions, though there are exceptions. Moreover, a tendency exists to attempt to keep departments in a faculty at a level of roughly comparable distinction; this is to say, universities do not generally lead from strength and strengthen, say, an already strong chemistry department and let a weak English department become still weaker. Finally, institutions which have been specialized in earlier periods tend to broaden themselves. Thus engineering schools—M.I.T. is an example—have introduced both humanities and social sciences on a considerable scale.

This inclusive tendency has something to do with the egalitarian principle as it is applied to collegial academic bodies. Because of the centrality of achievement values, individuals cannot be equally distinguished in bodies as large as university faculties. But if departments approximate this situation, there is a certain leveling out. The faculty maintains a delicate balance between the equality of membership status and the differentiation of individuals by levels of achievement; it does so in a context of intellectual disciplines that differ immensely from each other in qualitative terms. If departments approximate equality of distinction, relative to others in the same field, then members of departments, as members of the faculty or indeed of the student body, can claim presumptive equality across disciplinary lines. A university which favored chemistry over English would make it difficult for *any* professor of English to hold up his head in the presence of one of chemistry.[37] Such considerations suggest that the pressures toward equality of collegial status within faculties are strong. These pressures work against the tendency for the university to become bureaucratized. If bureaucracy prevailed, not only individuals but the bases of their expertise would tend to be ranked by criteria of their usefulness to management. This does not explain why such diverse fields should be included in the first place. Why not a faculty of economics alone?

The explanation of the inclusive tendency, however, seems to be

37. The late Henry W. Holmes was the first Professor of Education at Harvard and was located in the Faculty of Arts and Sciences before the establishment of the Faculty of Education—he later became the latter's first Dean. He once told the senior author that on being received by the Faculty of Arts and Sciences a senior member said to him, "You are very welcome, Mr. Holmes, but I must make it clear to you that you bear the onus of your subject."

another aspect of egalitarianism but at a different organizational level. It concerns the egalitarian component in the status of *institutions* in comparison with each other. The stratification of the latter is not simply a continuous graduation but tends to constitute a set of tiers, so that sister institutions within a category have a rough equality of status—for example the "seven sister colleges" or the "Ivy League." From this point of view, including a discipline within their faculties of arts and sciences or having a law school or a medical school become status symbols of the standing of the institution. This relates to the likelihood of a member of the government department at X university feeling the peer of one from Y university or, if he communicates with members of the faculty of Y not in his own field, feeling emotionally supported by the fact that Y has recognized the field of government.[38]

The structural patterning we have been discussing calls attention to a criss-crossing between membership in a faculty and department (of graduate students and faculty) and anchorage in a discipline or other technical field, an anchorage transcending the particular employing institution. The outcome of simultaneous integration on *both* of these axes is the distinctive associational pattern of collegiality, which has become the pattern not of any one faculty or department but of a nationwide academic community.

If there is pressure toward egalitarianism within the units of the national academic community, there is equally strong pressure toward aspects of stratification which we have reviewed. The reference point for these aspects is in the system of values of cognitive rationality, in the central position of achievement, and in the bases of achievement in capacity and opportunity. Complete institutionalization of the egalitarian principle would be incompatible with the achievement component of the cognitive complex. The phases of transition from one principal maturational level to the next and the selective processes at each of these choice-points,

38. Such processes as the "acceptance" of new academic disciplines within the academic system are to a considerable degree understandable in these terms. Thus in the last generation, the acceptance of sociology has spread from being a Midwestern subject—with exceptions—to nationwide status; its establishment at Harvard (1931) and later at Berkeley (about 1950) were two landmarks of the new phase. The senior author was personally involved in the Harvard step and then at the University of Cambridge (1953–54), when the title "Visiting Professor of Sociology" could not be officially used (the term actually used was "Social Theory"), even though it was understood not only that the title at Harvard was Sociology but that the reason for the invitation to Cambridge was to help introduce sociology there.

involving as they do processes of evaluation, are ways in which the integrity of the achievement aspect of the system is protected. That this syndrome should produce a stratified system is sociologically obvious.

The egalitarianism of collegiality, through tenure and academic freedom, links egalitarianism with stratification based on accomplishment. On the opportunity side, collegiality facilitates achievement, initially in cognitive contribution, but also on the various levels of the socialization process which are involved. The academic system has built up a unique pattern of balance between these components which in certain respects oppose each other. Features of this balance may change, and perhaps should change, but this analysis calls attention to the need for balance and the components which must enter into such a balance.

One of the functional reasons why the structural character of the academic system has been fiduciary rather than political in either the bureaucratic or the democratic association sense lies in the fact that its members, students and faculty members alike, are not primarily concerned with arriving at corporate decisions of policy or in their implementation through administrative machinery. They are primarily concerned with learning and teaching. Within this context research is a process of learning, and the learning involved is primarily cognitive learning, though it contains nonrational socialization components.

The social structure in which these functions are performed must provide optimal conditions for their facilitation and minimization of interference with them. In discussing tenure and collegiality we have stressed *membership* status. One basis of its importance is maintenance of the *differentiation* between academic functions and those of other roles and collectivities in the society. Disciplinary identification serves to maintain the *internal* differentiation of the cognitive system and the social units organized around it. Both together are essential to maintaining the primacy of the cognitive enterprise at its structural core. The department, the primary collective unit within the faculty, serves as the point of articulation between a given faculty and other units of the national academic community.

Academic freedom may be interpreted as an aspect of the institutional framework of the complex of *opportunity* for academic achievement. The concept of opportunity for achievement should be interpreted in the light of the preceding discussion. It includes research achievement at faculty levels, contributions to the teaching function, and achievement of students. Of course, the tradition of the Ph.D. dissertation as a contribution of knowledge brings it into the research complex, and the same pattern has been extended to undergraduate theses. But this is only part of the larger complex of achievement in learning.

The main academic functions focus primarily at the cultural level. Cognitive learning is the learning of intellectual subject matters: of knowledge, no matter how much the process may be interwoven with nonrational components of action. Learning, however, is different from the utilization of fully institutionalized bodies of knowledge—whether in practical activity or ideologically, whether it be learning of such knowledge by the individual for the first time or utilization of the output of new knowledge from the cognitive system in other sectors of the society and culture.

Learning can most effectively take place in protected situations. Membership status, which defines boundaries of the academic system and reinforces its differentiation from other systems, specifies the range of this protectedness. Academic freedom defines conditions of opportunity *within* these boundaries that bear on the performance of these primary functions. Although academic freedom is internal to the academic system, it must be legitimized more generally since the academic system is a differentiated sector of a society, not itself a society or a microcosm of a society.

In this protected status academia does not stand alone either in modern or in other societies. A protected status is characteristic also of the three other fiduciary subsystems which have become differentiated from each other and from other subsystems of the society in the modern world. These are (1) religion, which has become differentiated through the differentiation of church and state, (2) the cultural aspect of nationality, which has become differentiated from the societal community, and (3) the kinship system.

The socialization function is involved in all four of these.[39] Socialization has traditionally been attributed to kinship, but it clearly extends well beyond kinship. Its relevance to religion springs from the cultural tradition, and education for citizenship has had a wide appeal. Where the present treatment provides a shift

---

39. Socialization always includes the internalization of a body of normative culture. In the academic case this centers on the "great tradition" of cognitive culture. Academic freedom implies commitment to the responsible trusteeship of this tradition.

of emphasis is in the notion that the socialization process extends all through the educational course, starting with the preschool stages in the family, through elementary and secondary education, undergraduate phases, graduate study, and even the faculty role-level both in teaching and in research.

The common functional reference of the four categories of protected sectors is provision of conditions under which resources of long-run significance to the society can have an opportunity to mature in some kind of insulation from the pressures toward immediate utilization to satisfy practical social exigencies. Eventually, unless something goes wrong, their outputs will prove *more* significant for the larger system than would have been the resources utilized in a less mature state of their protected development.

The transition from purely organic to sociocultural evolution might be considered to be the mammalian system of reproduction; the new generation is brought to some maturity within the uterus of the maternal organism as contrasted with fertilization and embryonic development in relatively open water as in the case of the fishes. In man this is accentuated by the fact that, though the period of gestation is relatively long, the new-born human infant is less mature than are other mammals, say a puppy or a colt. This immaturity necessitates a prolonged period of care and socialization by adult human agents before the child can become independent. In the spirit of this comparison, the growth of the educational complex in human societies is an extension of this evolutionary trend rooted at organic levels.

In this perspective, the tensions within higher education can be interpreted as arising from the transition from protected status to that of full independence within the wider society.[40] The problem of balance between what, with reference to the academic system, is belonging inside or belonging outside becomes acute. Perhaps the distinction itself is meaningless; perhaps there should be no boundaries. But here we have treated students and academic professionals as alike, in the fact that they both have status within this protected system.[41]

40. Erik H. Erikson, "Reflections on the Dissent of Contemporary Youth," *Daedalus* (Winter 1970), pp. 154–176.

41. The concept of the protected subsystem with the potential of contributing to the long-run future of the larger sociocultural system in question has more remote parallels besides that of economic investment. One parallel is that of the role of the "seed-bed" societies of Israel and Greece in laying cultural foundations for modern society (see

An apparent paradox illuminates the place of this system within the larger society. The progression from undergraduate status levels upward is from greater to lesser dependency in the sense of moving from nearly total involvement of the individual person in his academic role to the mature professional level where the incumbent normally participates in a family as well as in other occupational, political, and cultural activities outside of academia. Marriage, especially for men, does not usually take place during the undergraduate phase, but after it. The other side of the paradox is that the less fully involved full professionals enjoy higher prestige within the system and to some extent greater authority.

The resolution of the paradox lies in the fact that the academic system is not only protected but must also articulate with the nonprotected sectors. Capacity for such wider participations and rights to them are a function of the attainment of stages of maturation within the system. By analogy with the family, children will in due course become parents, though not in their own families of orientation. But one cannot become a parent without having served an adequate apprenticeship in the role of child to one's own parents. Leaving the role of dependent child symbolizes readiness to assume the role of parents. Similarly leaving the role of student symbolizes readiness to become a professional—academically or otherwise or to take on other mature roles in the society. Because of this structural situation, the academic freedom of the professional contingent is typically wider in scope than is that of the student.

What is this protected system protected against? At the social system level, the three inappropriate structural types discussed above, namely, the market, the bureaucratic system, and the democratic association, help provide the answer. Various concrete pressures can be identified by their tendency to redefine the collective structure by one or more of these three models. Thus challenges to the status-prestige of the professional component are

Talcott Parsons, *Societies, Evolutionary and Comparative Perspectives*, Foundations of Modern Sociology Series [Englewood Cliffs, N.J., Prentice-Hall, Inc., 1966], chap. vi, "The 'Seed-Bed' Societies: Israel and Greece," pp. 95–108). Another is Christianity itself, which went through many centuries of isolation before becoming culturally constitutive of the societies in which it gradually became institutionalized (cf. Talcott Parsons, "Christianity," *International Encyclopedia of the Social Sciences*, ed. David L. Sills [New York, The Macmillan Co. and The Free Press, 1968], II, 425–447). Finally there is the case of religious orders within Christianity—and in other ways, Buddhism —which preserved the religious tradition in the face of multifarious secular pressures and eventually influenced social development along the lines which Troeltsch called the emergence of "Christian societies" (see Parsons, "Christianity").

often expressed in demands to treat the academic system, including all status components, as a democratic association. Another challenge of disadvantaged elements is to insist that since tuition-paying students are paying the bills, faculty members should merely be providing services for them.

At the cultural level, a formidable pressure comes from commitment to expressive interests: the notion that academia should abandon or mitigate its traditional emphasis on cognitive concerns in favor of the self-expression of participants in artistic form. Not unrelated is the tendency to moralize the academic enterprise, to urge that the value commitments involved should give no special priority to cognitive rationality, but should become moralistic in a much more general sense, namely, should become commitments to see that "right" prevails in the human condition as a whole. This pattern of "dedifferentiation" is a syndrome we have described as "moral absolutism."[42] Finally, there is the demand to desecularize the academic system, to make it, as Robert Morison has suggested, the vehicle of a new path to salvation, even though the meaning of salvation is not obviously recognizable in terms of traditional religious positions.[43]

The pressures from the dynamics of personality will be taken up again in the next chapter. Academic norms emphasize "ego functions," but within a firm pattern of controls. There are two obvious ways of deviating from this. One, most prevalent in the more mature reaches of the system, concerns tendencies to give interests other than those germane to the academic complex priority over those that *are* germane; financial self-interest and personal ambition are examples of such nongermane interests. More prevalent in the student stages are tendencies to sacrifice ego-concerns in favor of id-drives, centering in themes of self-expression, not excluding propensities to violence. For purposes going beyond first approximation, this dichotomy is oversimple. It avoids reference to superego concerns relevant to tendencies to moralism—the very fact of protectedness favors a sense of moral superiority. Furthermore, there remains an underlying problem of relation to personal identity in the sense especially discussed by Erikson.

42. Talcott Parsons, "The Academic System: A Sociologist's View," *The Public Interest*, no. 13 (Special Issue, Fall 1968), pp. 173–197.
43. See Robert S. Morison, "Some Aspects of 'Policy-Making' in the American University," *Daedalus* (Summer 1970), pp. 609–644; see also, Metzger, "Crisis of Academic Authority."

*The Core Sector and Academic Freedom: Further Thoughts.* Let us now return to the content of academic freedom. It follows from our analysis that the pattern-maintenance component of this freedom is *freedom to learn,* with emphasis on the *cognitive* aspect of learning. The meaning of freedom to learn is clear for a conceptually isolated individual. It includes freedom of research (within one's own conceptions of probable validity, cognitive significance, and relevance in other respects) to investigate subject matters and problems which seem important to the investigator and choices among possible fields which run from undergraduate choice of courses and of concentration—if this concept survives—to graduate students' choice of disciplines, and to professionals' choice of research interests.

Such freedom, however, cannot be restricted narrowly to freedom to learn, but must include freedom to communicate and otherwise associate with others in the learning enterprise and in the use of its outputs. Given its fiduciary character, the academic community institutionalizes freedom to communicate findings to colleagues, students, or lay audiences and to solicit their reciprocal interests in such communications and their cooperation in the learning process itself.

In the context of the complementarity of the functions of learning and teaching lies the special role of teaching. From the point of view of the learner, the teacher facilitates the process of his learning, but in the process he typically also learns. Thus the teacher-learner *system* should, if the process is successful, gain in total knowledge. From this point of view, academic freedom includes a right to participate in the relevant modes of social interaction with other participants in the academic system and with significant others outside the system, such as lay audiences.

Another component of the complex of academic freedom is that of *freedom,* with minimal institutional hindrance, to maximize contributions, that is, to achieve the best of which the person or unit is capable in appropriate terms. This applies not only to the individual, in whichever of the role-levels we have outlined, but also to collectivities such as departments, faculties, and research teams. This component is likely to stand in the greatest tension with the pattern of collegial egalitarianism. However, its consequences are mitigated by the loopholes of stratification which interphase and interinstitutional relationships make possible. Purely egalitarian communalism would prove fatally suppressive of the impetus to improvement in the state of knowledge at many levels, from that of the freshman student to that of the mature research investigator.[44] Improvement as a goal is inseparable from the probability of differential outcomes of contributory endeavors.

Finally, as an aspect of equality of opportunity, academic freedom should include freedom of access to the facilities essential for academic achievement as well as the help of teachers and colleagues toward it. This category should comprise access to the current state of knowledge in the relevant fields embodied in books and journals through libraries, access to data banks and to the knowledge commanded by other members of the system, not only teachers but colleagues and fellow students. One feature of an academic community is that social interaction is encouraged and that there is a concentration of facilities available to aid in the learning process.[45]

Academic freedom, like the institutions in which it is socially embodied, is stratified. This is a consequence of the salience of the achievement component. Within limits, it is a case of what Merton has called the "Matthew Effect."[46] If high achievement is valued, it must, in an integrated social system, also be rewarded more highly than lesser achievements. Rewards cannot realistically be limited to specific prizes, but tend to diffuse out to include the larger milieu of those whose achievements are especially esteemed. Hence, if academic freedom can be thought of as a name for levels of opportunity for the effective performance of academic function, those who perform or promise to perform on higher levels than others tend to enjoy higher levels of such opportunity.

Every freedom has to be protected by constraints operating to control and counteract forces tending to undermine it. Such constraints operate at the boundaries of the academic system in relation to tendencies to distort its pattern. They must also operate at the boundaries between levels within it to maintain distinctions in appropriate ways—for example, the necessity to maintain such distinctions is a main reason for the inappropriateness of the model of the democratic association for an academic community. One set

44. Thus an academic community cannot take the sociological form of an Israeli kibbutz, especially of the "bund" type. See Yonina Talmon, *Family and Community in the Kibbutz* (Cambridge, Mass., Harvard University Press, 1972).

45. Ben-David, *American Higher Education.*

46. Merton, "The Matthew Effect."

of internal constraints from the point of view of the effective implementation of the pattern of academic freedom is the procedural norms for the conduct of intellectual discourse. These are related to the rules governing corporate decision-making in associational bodies, such as Robert's *Rules of Order,* and the quasi-legal procedures involved in the area of rights and responsibilities with respect to acceptable conduct within the academic community, yet they are different. The principle of ensuring equality of opportunity for the presentation of communication underlies academic freedom. In interactional communication situations generally, if they are face-to-face, there is one factor of scarcity, namely, time to speak. The most egalitarian case is perhaps a conference discussion where the participants are presumed to be peers. But those with experience of such situations are aware of the directive role of a good chairman in fairly rationing the opportunity to speak. There are also limits on acceptable things to say—for example, direct personal derogation of other participants, as distinguished from disagreement with their intellectual positions, is generally inadmissible. Maintaining a standard of relevance to the topic of discussion is also a problem. There is here a subtle interplay between the consensual atmosphere created by the participants and the explicit regulatory actions and rulings of a chairman.

The teaching function should also be looked at in this framework. The lecture, which is under considerable attack today, is a limiting case, especially in the form where no interruption is tolerated. Many cases of predominantly lecture teaching, however, permit audience participation through raising questions or making comments. If, however, the ostensible goal of communicating a complex description or analysis is to be achieved, these interventions on the part of participants other than the lecturer must be kept under some kind of control in terms of volume and hence time-consumption and of relevance to the subject in hand. Capacity to exercise this control constitutes one skill of a good teacher.

The lecture thus merges into the discussion class, of which a prototype is the seminar. Here the roles of teacher and of chairman tend to be fused, but in varying combinations, again involving subtle elements of skill; the leader is at the same time authoritative—not authoritarian—yet gives the fullest possible opportunity for the other participants to implement their rights of academic freedom and prevents a minority among them from monopolizing such opportunities.[47]

Another communication context is that of publication. Whatever exigencies authors have coped with in preparing a manuscript for consideration for publication, there remains an obvious scarcity problem with respect to any one channel of publication. The editors of the high prestige journal in a given field clearly cannot accept all the manuscripts submitted but must select among them. Selection implies evaluation—they want to publish what, by their standards and those of their constituency, are the best. In attempting to be fair in their selections, editors often resort to anonymity rules, that is, they seek to prevent referees to whom manuscripts are sent from knowing the identity of the author and/or the author from knowing the identity of the referee. Generally speaking the editorial responsibility is considered a high one, and editors are given wide discretion; there is little tendency to try to subject their editorial decisions to a popular vote of some allegedly relevant constituency. If there is dissatisfaction, the recourse is to a different kind of editor, not detailed control over whoever happens to be editor at the time.

The above examples are illustrative, not exhaustive. They should, however, make clear that the implementation of academic freedom is dependent on a complex network of procedural institutions, operating with respect to all levels and their interrelations and all components of academic function. Despite this diversity, two central reference points exist for this procedural complex. One is implementation of the imperative of equality of opportunity. There must be fairness with respect to access to channels of communication. This standard is related to that of fairness in decisions of admission and appointment. The second reference concerns evaluation. Only fair evaluation can legitimize the differentiations of academic prestige status other than those anchored in stages of the life-course itself. The two foci are also interdependent; promise of future achievement is often a criterion in the allocation of opportunity and its attendant freedoms. Attribution of high promise, however, is an evaluative judgment.

---

47. An experiment in maximizing the initiative of nonteacher participants has been the course Social Relations 120, given for some years at Harvard, for which the task has been the self-analysis of the group. Even here, however, as in the related cases of group therapy, the role of the teacher or leader has not proved to be superfluous.

The institutional complexes which we have analyzed in terms of the combination of the concepts of tenure and of academic freedom together constitute the legitimizing framework for the social structure of the academic system, particularly in the higher reaches of its prestige system. These institutional complexes contribute to the acceptability of the academic system, both to its members and to various publics outside the membership.

Given the paramount concern for knowledge in the system and hence commitment to the values of cognitive rationality, the basis of legitimacy of the system and of what Walter Metzger[48] calls the asymmetries which pervade it, namely, those of stage of life-course grading and those of prestige within each principal grade, depends on what is assumed to be fiduciary responsibility in relation to the cognitive system. This responsibility is to the values of cognitive rationality, to their importance in society and culture, and to the obligation to implement these commitments in the relevant modes of action.

This entails, given that an academic system is *socially* institutionalized, three further foci. The first is that differential achievement and promise of it—"excellence" in McGeorge Bundy's term[49]—is, according to the relevant standards, fundamental and must both be given the greatest opportunities and its achievements rewarded. The second is that the socially relevant pursuit of these values and goals must be institutionalized in the framework of a set of solidary collectivities, for which these values are paramount, and which, as solidary, claim major loyalties from their participants. The third is that the interactive relationships within which cognitive concerns are paramount must be governed by and adhere to a set of procedural institutions which guarantee, within the relevant limits, both fair equality of opportunity and fairness of evaluation. This framework is a prominent example of institutionalized individualism.

*Ideal-Type of the Core and Its Boundaries.* The analysis presented here implies that undergraduate education, especially where it is not explicitly vocational, is a boundary-structure of the main academic system, as are the professional schools, rather than a central constituent, as are the research and graduate-training functions. One reason for this is the fact that, although

48. Metzger, "Crisis of Academic Authority."
49. McGeorge Bundy, "Were Those the Days?" *Daedalus* (Summer 1970), pp. 531–567.

academic professionals will devote their careers to academic matters, the majority of undergraduates will not; and even those going on to professional schools will, after graduation, be as much nonacademic as academic. This means that the socialization component of the educational process, so far as prospective academics are not segregated out at the undergraduate level, is essentially different, because it is not necessary and would be undesirable for nonacademically oriented students to internalize academic values and role-expectations at the same level of primacy and motivational intensity as the academically oriented. For this reason we have chosen to deal more intensively with the academically oriented in a separate chapter.

What has been presented in the present chapter is an "ideal type" in the Weberian sense of that term. Such a type has both normative and explanatory significance, which derive from the assumption that values and norms formulated as part of it may influence the concrete action of participants in the system being analyzed. One further question is how far these values and norms are shared by the observer-analyst of this action system. He has certain degrees of freedom within which he can choose to advocate or to implement changes from the position which has been institutionalized in the system of reference. Another question is how far the ideal type used for analytical purposes in fact describes the actual behavior within the system of reference and in what principal respects is deviant from it.

We believe that the ideal type, especially for elite sectors of the system, constitutes an adequate first approximation. Explicit analysis of the various modes of deviance from it would require more space than this book can afford. In this connection, we recognize that as an empirical structure this ideal type emerged relatively recently to its present position of salience in the American academic system. Therefore, it is to be expected that it stands in some kind of tension with parts of the matrix from which it has developed. The undergraduate college is the center of this matrix, but a symbiosis between the new graduate-research sector and the undergraduate sector has persisted, a circumstance which constitutes one facet of the present situation.

That this core pattern of the university lends itself to delineation as an ideal type should not obscure the fact that, *as a social system*, it is permeated with tensions that have on occasion erupted into open conflict. A résumé of some important strains may lay the groundwork for the dynamic analysis to be undertaken later. Regarded as one type of community within a social system, the core arts-and-sciences academic community has its special versions of two types of tension fundamental to modern societies generally, namely, that over equality and inequality and that over freedom and constraint.[50] In both respects the institutional pattern we have outlined has embodied delicate balances. The pattern of collegial estates embodies the principle of *equality*. Indeed this may constitute a principal reference-point for the many demands to organize the system in purely egalitarian terms. At the same time it is a stratified system with inequalities deriving from several interrelated bases, notably, stage of the life cycle, survival in a series of selective processes involving admission, appointments, promotions, and so on, differential achievement, putatively evaluated by universalistic criteria, and differential levels of corporate responsibility and power.

These problems of equality and inequality arise *within* the particular institutional community in faculty ranks, in faculty-student differences, and in graduate school-college differences and *between* institutions. Such integration as has taken place results largely from the mechanisms of prestige and influence. This is to say that rank in the system of stratification and with it access to facilities, opportunities, and rewards is expected to be *justified* in terms of functional contributions, promise, opportunities, and so on, which are fairly evaluated by reference to the value of cognitive rationality and to its place in the more comprehensive general value-system. Not surprisingly, a substantial incidence of feelings of relative deprivation exists at many points in such a system, for example, of junior vis-à-vis senior faculty, of students vis-à-vis faculty, of undergraduates vis-à-vis the graduate school-research complex, of less prestigeful vis-à-vis more prestigeful institutions. Certain emergent groups, such as teaching assistants, have ambiguous status, part teachers but still students, which exacerbates the

50. A further grounding of the rationale of stress on the axes of strain of equality and inequality on the one hand, freedom and constraint on the other, will be found in Parsons, "Equality and Inequality in Modern Society," especially the Technical Note on pp. 56–69. Full realization of the close connection between the two dichotomies did not emerge until the draft article was being revised, so it is not as well worked out in the body of the article as in the Note. It now seems that these two axes constitute the main framework of organization of the societal community, i.e., the integrative subsystem of a differentiated society, and that the pattern of institutionalized individualism in the ideal type of case (where it is fully differentiated and integrated) is a pattern of optimal balances among these four components.

strain upon them. The current attack on the institution of tenure may be regarded as symptomatic of strains over inequality, especially since tenure suggests to some security in a sinecure.

There are other manifestations of strain and tension in this area. For example, among colleagues within an academic department, there tend to be conspicuous inhibitions on communication in technical matters. The life of most departments is not a continuing feast of mutual intellectual enlightenment. Balancing the ambitions of individuals for distinctive personal achievement with the imperatives of collegial equality is responsible for this. The institution of academic freedom helps to ease the tension through legitimizing the efforts of each faculty member to pursue his own interests independently of his colleagues. This situation is highlighted by contrast with the greater ease of communication among participants at conferences outside the home setting and within such enterprises as the Center for Advanced Study in the Behavioral Sciences.

The institutionalization of academic freedom constitutes one of the most developed complexes of freedom to be found in any society, but it is linked to functions of the cognitive complex. Thus traditionally it is not primarily an umbrella to cover freedom for political action to be organized on and from the campus; similarly, the question of how far members of the academic community, especially students, should be exempted from the obligation to conform with general community standards in matters such as the use of drugs and sex raises subtle boundary questions. Another problem is the linkage of levels of academic freedom with the stratification of the academic community, so that the occupants of the higher-tenure levels appear to enjoy greater freedoms; hence those on lower levels may feel relatively deprived. At issue here is the status of academic requirements imposed on students and of the traditional evaluative procedures applied to their performance. Is not "freedom" defined by exemption from such requirements?

Serious tensions result from the imposition of requirements and evaluation as well as from stratification, with the two closely linked. Furthermore, in addition to these tensions indigenous to the academic community itself, its vulnerability is increased by the presence in the larger society of a wave of pressure for greater equality as expressed in the questioning of many received forms of inequality and for greater freedom as expressed in the questioning of many received forms of constraint. Thus, dissidents within the academic community have been in a position to claim that their dissidence is "in tune with the times."

One further focus of strain on this core sector of the system is the massive fact of extremely rapid growth and development of the system. Two consequences are pressure on inherently scarce resources and the related pressure toward overcommitment of the system and its various constituent parts. Thus, at the levels both of students and faculty there has been an intensified competition for the "best." In both colleges and graduate schools in the elite sectors of the system, there has been a spectacular shift in the qualified application-admission ratio. In faculty appointments, the 1960's were characterized by a seller's market from the point of view of prospective appointees—one manifestation of which has been the "star system." In both contexts the consequence seems to have been to increase the steepness of the stratification slope and to increase the demands for performance on the part of those selected, the more so the more elite the selecting institution.

For students competition for admission has placed higher expectations of performance after admission on those who successfully cross that barrier. This has been compounded by the increase in the proportion of graduates of the more elite colleges wishing to undertake graduate study, which has in turn enhanced the competition for admission to the better graduate and professional schools, naturally placing higher premiums on good scholastic records for undergraduates. These circumstances have tended to shift the balance of undergraduate atmosphere toward greater competitive stress on scholastic achievement. The resulting strains constituted the setting for a good deal of student dissent.

At faculty levels similar increased pressures have operated with increased competition for the best products of the graduate departments. Sometimes this has meant that professional getting ahead has become easier, but in another context the pressures of the "rat race" have increased. Not only has there been pressure to greater academic achievement, especially through research, but the increasing complexity of the university and its increasing involvement outside have increased pressure on responsible faculty members to undertake administrative and committee responsibilities, to assume office in disciplinary associations, to accept membership in study councils of Federal granting agencies, and so forth. The successful homo academicus is not being encouraged to rest on his oars; he is a member of a heavily burdened occupational group.[51] Among the commitments which has had to be reduced under these pressures has been the level of attention of senior faculty members to undergraduate teaching.

51. As an example of reaction to such pressures, an unpublished study of the Harvard Faculty of Arts and Sciences by a Committee of which the senior author was a member found some 20 years ago that associate professors who had tenure "without limit of time" felt more anxiety about satisfactory professional performance than did assistant professors who did not. This anxiety focused both on research and on other functions such as "faculty citizenship." A check showed that it was the most recently appointed associate professors who expressed the highest levels of anxiety—although some would say that since they had already acquired tenure, "Why should they worry?"

# 4

## GENERAL EDUCATION AND
## STUDENTRY SOCIALIZATION:
## THE UNDERGRADUATE COLLEGE

The college experience, participated in by about half of the contemporary age cohort,[1] constitutes a new stage of socialization in the life course.[2] The mass impact of college on the young has created the stage, *studentry*.[3]

Every change in the social structure which introduces role differentiations necessitates new patterns of socialization for those passing through that stage. During the period in which such patterns are being institutionalized, strain and tension are the lot of *all* who are involved. We believe that *a* source of contemporary student disturbances and related faculty and administrative disturbances is the recent rapid development of mass higher education and the process of institutionalizing the studentry socialization phase. The contemporary situation resembles the situation which occurred during the latter part of the nineteenth century when the oedipal phase of socialization was the center of tension. The oedipal crisis owed some of its tension to changes in the family structure

1. According to conservative estimates, 40 percent of persons 18 to 21 were enrolled in degree credit institutions of higher learning in 1961. See American Council on Education, 1969: data for 1963, p. 93. For an article devoted to varying effects and problems engendered by universal higher education, see Martin Trow, "Reflections on the Transition from Mass to Universal Higher Education," *Daedalus* (Winter 1970), pp. 1–42.
2. We made this point in our previous paper, "Higher Education, Changing Socialization, and Contemporary Student Dissent," in *Aging and Society*, ed. Matilda White Riley, Marilyn E. Johnson, Anne Foner, and Associates (New York, The Russell Sage Foundation, 1972), III, 236–291. A substantial portion of this paper was published by us as "Age, Social Structure, and Socialization in Higher Education," *Sociology of Education*, 43 (Winter 1970), 1–37.
3. Ibid.

and to the development of generalized elementary education, both of which were associated with the industrial revolution.[4]

Similarly, the prominence of "youth culture" in the twentieth century and the attention given to adolescence were associated with the near-universalizing of secondary education between World Wars I and II.[5] Associated with this change was the upgrading of the occupational structure which made it problematic for those who had not completed high school to participate effectively in the occupational world.[6]

The phenomenon of contemporary studentry, including its disturbances, may be interpreted from the same perspective rather than as an extension of adolescent youth culture, although there are continuities between the two interpretations. Undergraduate education is a distinct socialization phase. Studentry is a process differentiated from adolescence on one side and from full maturity on the other.[7]

*The Character of Undergraduate Education.* Undergraduate general education is related to the core university functions embodying the value of cognitive rationality. General education is among those activities which must be combined with other values and in particular the values of the societal community. Although not in the political sense, undergraduate education focuses on the

4. On these issues, see Fred Weinstein and Gerald M. Platt, *The Wish to Be Free: Society, Psyche, and Value Change* (Berkeley and Los Angeles, Calif., University of California Press, 1969), especially chaps. v and vi; and Neil J. Smelser, "Sociological History: The Industrial Revolution and the British Working-Class Family," in his *Essays in Sociological Explanation* (Englewood Cliffs, N.J., Prentice-Hall, Inc., 1968), chap. iv.
We are suggesting an analogy between *two* periods of change that gave rise to similar responses on the part of those involved in these historical changes. We are *not* suggesting, as Lewis Feuer has, that contemporary student dissent is a product of unresolved oedipal responses upon the part of student dissenters. See Lewis S. Feuer, *The Conflict of Generations: The Character and Significance of Student Movements* (New York, Basic Books, 1969).

5. See Christopher Jencks and David Riesman, *The Academic Revolution* (New York, Doubleday and Co., 1968), pp. 75–90.

6. Social scientists during this era attempted to explain the tumultuous character of teenage life. Ruth Benedict, in a typical analysis, approached this issue from a cross-cultural perspective. Ruth Benedict, "Continuities and Discontinuities in Cultural Conditioning," *Psychiatry*, 1 (1938), 161–167. On the general topic of generation relations, see S. N. Eisenstadt, *From Generation to Generation: Age Groups and Social Structure* (Glencoe, Ill., The Free Press, 1956, second edition, 1971).

7. Kenneth Keniston, a social scientist who has been distinguishing adolescence from "youth," made this point in a talk on "History, Social Science, and Youth" at a conference at Clark University in 1971. Some of these points were also made in his "Youth: A 'New' Stage of Life," *The American Scholar* (Autumn 1970), pp. 631–654, and in his "You Have to Grow Up in Scarsdale to Know How Bad Things Really Are," the *New York Times Magazine*, April 27, 1969.

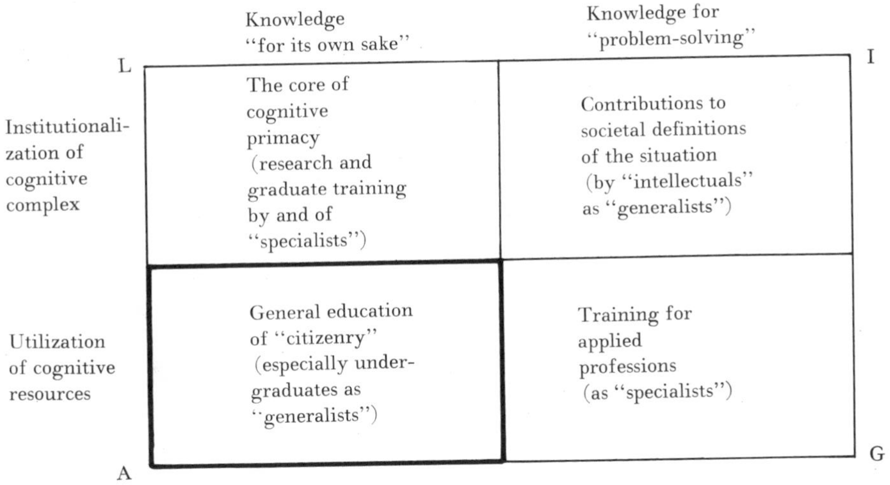

|  | Knowledge "for its own sake" | Knowledge for "problem-solving" |
|---|---|---|
| L | | I |
| Institutionalization of cognitive complex | The core of cognitive primacy (research and graduate training by and of "specialists") | Contributions to societal definitions of the situation (by "intellectuals" as "generalists") |
| Utilization of cognitive resources | General education of "citizenry" (especially undergraduates as "generalists") | Training for applied professions (as "specialists") |
| A | | G |

Figure 4.1. Institutionalization of Cognitive Rationality in the Structure of the University

*Note:* The heavily outlined subsystem is the substantive focus of this chapter. For a more formal analysis of this figure and its relation to other subsystems, see the appendix to Chapter 2.

development of an "educated citizenry." Citizenship means here the capacities for participation in the societal community with competence and intelligence. Such capacities are grounded at the moral levels of culture and the affective levels of personality.

Like undergraduate education, graduate training and the development of research capacities entails socialization as well as cognitive learning. There are qualitative differences, however. Most obviously, an undergraduate education universally precedes graduate or professional study. More significantly, graduate and professional training is oriented to the development of *special* competences. Even though preprofessional elements exist in undergraduate curricula, the main focus of such education is on generality.[8] The majority of American undergraduates do not go on to graduate or professional study, although the proportion who do go on has been increasing.

The increase in the number of those who pursue graduate and professional work does not invalidate our argument; indeed it lends some strength to it. Many postgraduates pursue a variety of graduate disciplines, frequently changing concentrations in mov-

8. Neil Smelser has emphasized that one stress upon contemporary students has been the infusion of intense cognitive standards more appropriate for graduate training and research than for undergraduate education.

ing from undergraduate to graduate education. It has also become less important for undergraduates to concentrate in a discipline specifically related to the graduate or professional career they intend to pursue. Thus, the problem remains: What general competencies does an undergraduate education develop?

In contrast to Clark Kerr,[9] we believe that undergraduate education is aimed at facilitating occupational effectiveness but cannot be interpreted as *training* for occupational participation. The term "educated citizenry" was used to imply the development of general rather than specific occupational capacities. An indication that this interpretation is correct is the fact that up until recently college-educated women have participated proportionately less in gainful employment than college-educated men, although there has been something approaching consensus in the middle class on the value of an educated female citizenry.

Societal growth in the West placed pressure on higher education for the development of an expanded undergraduate (nonprofessional) system. The trend of societal development has been toward increasing differentiation of both society and culture. Increased differentiation implies greater complexity but also greater instability. This instability is a result of the greater autonomy of decisions possible for units of action in the system. Differentiation, while presenting more opportunities, also imparts to the units a greater obligation to act and greater consequences of their actions for themselves and for the system as a whole. Sociologically, this is emancipation of social action from ascriptive ties and from traditionalism, which means higher average levels of responsibility for personal action and thus a greater need for knowledge, competence, and intelligence to guide action. This adaptive upgrading trend of modern societies is from the personality point of view the development of "personal morality."[10]

Cognitive upgrading in these respects, if not integrated with other components, can be disruptive. These cognitive components, therefore, must be integrated with value-commitments at the societal level and the moral component at the cultural level. In the moral context, the Durkheimian issue is the level of moral authority enjoyed by the normative order of a cultural or social sys-

9. Clark Kerr, *The Uses of the University* (Cambridge, Mass., Harvard University Press, 1963).

10. An important version of this conception is Durkheim's idea of the modern "cult of the individual." See Robert N. Bellah, ed., *Emile Durkheim*, Heritage of Sociology Series (Chicago, Ill., University of Chicago Press, 1973).

tem. Naturally this moral authority of institutions operates through internalization in the personality of individuals, that is, through their superegos. One objective of this chapter is to describe how this cognitively upgraded component is integrated with value-commitments and with moral authority and how they are internalized within the context of the undergraduate experience.

Another component in the undergraduate experience is the affective component, which is involved in the mutual attachment of persons to each other within collectivities and to the collectivities themselves. The total of such attachments on the part of its members constitutes the groundwork for the integrative base on which a collectivity can be stable and can perform effectively. Difficulties in this area contribute to the phenomenon called "alienation."[11]

Once a society has reached a high level of differentiation, affect becomes a generalized circulating medium in a manner similar to that of intelligence.[12] As a medium, it is available for exchange in a variety of more specific modes of expression, for example, identification, response, cathexis, and so on, among action units in the system. Ascriptive boundedness of affectivity to particular persons, collectivities, or institutions is an obstacle to its freedom of allocation. Thus, only in societies where action is relatively freed of its ascriptive base does affect constitute a generalized medium, acting as a mechanism integrating action units with each other rather than being mainly internal to the personality.

Early socialization in the family and student socialization share two structural features. One is the relative insulation of the individuals being socialized from systems external to the socializing

11. See Gerald M. Platt and Fred Weinstein, "Alienation and the Problem of Social Action," in *The Phenomenon of Sociology: A Reader in the Sociology of Sociology*, ed. Edward A. Tiryakian (New York, Appleton-Century-Crofts, 1971), pp. 284–310. Alienation has enjoyed many definitions. For reviews of some of them, see Melvin Seeman, "On the Meaning of Alienation," *American Sociological Review*, 24 (1959), 783–791; and for the point of view of a Soviet analyst, see Igor S. Kon, "The Concept of Alienation in Modern Sociology," *Social Research*, 34 (1967), 507–528.

12. Talcott Parsons, "Some Problems of General Theory in Sociology," in *Theoretical Sociology: Perspectives and Developments*, ed. John C. McKinney and Edward A. Tiryakian (New York, Appleton-Century-Crofts, 1970), pp. 27–68. See also Talcott Parsons, *Politics and Social Structure* (New York, The Free Press, 1969), chap. xiv, "On the Concept of Political Power," pp. 352–404, reprinted from *Proceedings of the American Philosophical Society*, 107 (June 1963), 232–262; chap. xv, "On the Concept of Influence," pp. 405–438, reprinted from *Public Opinion Quarterly* (Spring 1963), pp. 37–62; and chap. xvi, "On the Concept of Value-Commitments," pp. 439–472, reprinted from *Sociological Inquiry*, 38 (Spring 1968), 135–160. For Karl Marx's concept of alienation, see Anthony Giddens, *Capitalism and Modern Social Theory* (Cambridge, Eng., Cambridge University Press, 1971), chap. i.

unit. Referring to college students, Erikson called this condition a moratorium from engagement with life and with society.[13] A second is the relatively undifferentiated character of the individual being socialized. In early socialization this relates to the biopsychological levels of the infant which become differentiated through the vicissitudes of early instinctual and social life. In the college condition, undifferentiatedness (dedifferentiation) is created in the studentry stage by breaks with family and community ties.[14] The function of both early and college socialization is to increase differentiation and to reduce isolation, thereby producing a restructuring of commitments and a wider network of collective identifications.

The socialization process starts with a child in a simple social and cultural environment in which the earliest strata of internalized object systems and culture are minimally differentiated. In this context the primitive superego treats the difference between right and wrong as a simple dichotomy, and early familial attachments make only the distinction between "we" and all others.[15] Keep in mind that the studentry phase is analogous with the early socialization phase. Isolation and dedifferentiation are continuities generated out of adolescent peer-solidarities. Adolescent peers emphasize a diffuseness of belonging (analogous with the early "we") combined with fierce loyalty that overrides all others. Often such loyalty is achieved at the cost of repressing competing claims to solidarity, as in the rejection of parents and their values.

During the studentry phase there is on the commitment side a tendency to develop a moralism that is as undifferentiated as the diffuse "we" is on the solidarity side. This moralism is characterized by a clearly defined "right" associated with the "we" and opposed to all others; "they" are defined as "wrong." A normative prescription belongs unambiguously to one category or the other.

13. Erik H. Erikson, *Childhood and Society* (New York, W. W. Norton and Co., Inc., 1950).

14. Peter McHugh makes a similar point suggesting that some social structural and personality disintegration and some desacralization of previous values are a precondition for radical value change and socialization. See his "Social Disintegration as a Requisite to Resocialization," *Social Forces*, 44 (1966), 355–363; Edward A. Tiryakian makes a similar point for societal value change, see his "A Model of Societal Change and Its Lead Indicators," in *Theory and Method in the Study of Total Societies*, ed. Samuel Z. Klausner (Garden City, N.Y., Doubleday and Co., 1967), pp. 69–97.

15. Jean Piaget, *The Moral Judgment of the Child* (New York, The Free Press, 1965).

These conceptions of diffuse undifferentiated solidarity[16] and of moral absolutism constitute reference points from which to analyze student socialization. The end product of student socialization should be the differentiation of college peer-solidarity and student acceptance of participation in plural involvements. Concomitantly, the morally absolute position should be differentiated into a plurality of morally important positions; and commitments should be made to a limited number among these.[17]

*Societal and Personality Development.* The frame of reference for the analysis of student socialization and cognitive learning is adapted from one designed for the analysis of societal evolution.[18] The problems posed for the socialization of individuals have been generated from a larger context, namely, the educational revolution.[19] Our paradigm of evolutionary change starts with the process of differentiation. Differentiation becomes consolidated and built into a society when *adaptive upgrading, inclusion,* and *value-generalization* also occur. Parallel processes occur in personality development. In a society the principal meaning of *adaptive upgrading* is economic. In the personality it is increased cognitive capacity or competence. Personality differentiation (ontogenetically or historically) necessitates an upgraded cognitive component, which brings action under more intelligent and rational (conscious) control.[20]

16. Our analogy between the solidarity of the family and the structure of college peer-solidarity is based upon David M. Schneider's work on American kinship. See his *American Kinship: A Cultural Account* (Englewood Cliffs, N.J., Prentice-Hall, Inc., 1968).

17. One effect of college on students is to relativize their thought. See, e.g., William G. Perry, Jr., *Patterns of Development in Thought and Values of Students in a Liberal Arts College* (Washington, D.C., U.S. Department of Health, Education and Welfare, April 1968), and his *Forms of Intellectual and Ethical Development* (Cambridge, Mass., Harvard University Bureau of Study Counsel, 1968). In their review of the literature, Kenneth A. Feldman and Theodore A. Newcomb indicate that a strong influence of college on students is the decline in levels of authoritarianism. The F-Scale is as much an indicator of moral absolutism as it is of facism. See their *The Impact of College on Students: An Analysis of Four Decades of Research* (San Francisco, Calif., Jossey-Bass, Inc., Publishers, 1969), I. We have in mind a similar process; that is, the transformation of moral absolutism to moral pluralism and to ethical considerations in Erikson's terms.

18. A full exposition of the social-system developmental scheme and its rationale is in Talcott Parsons, "Comparative Studies and Evolutionary Change," in *Comparative Methods in Sociology: Essays on Trends and Applications*, ed. Ivan Vallier (Berkeley, Calif., University of California Press, 1971), pp. 97–139.

19. Jencks and Riesman, *Academic Revolution.*

20. Lawrence Kohlberg, "Stage and Sequence: The Cognitive-Developmental Approach to Socialization," *Handbook of Socialization Theory and Research*, ed. David A. Goslin (New York, Rand McNally and Co., 1969), pp. 347–480.

In the societal case, *inclusion* means the extension of collective solidarity over a wider range than before, incorporating previously excluded populations or including newly differentiated structures within the previous solidary framework. For the personality, inclusion refers to a sense of personal identity which develops the capacity to cope with its own increased differentiatedness and to deal with the inclusion of wider elements of interpenetrating subsystems of action. This occurs largely at the cognitive level because knowledge and competence are internalized as parts of the personality. But it must also involve interpenetration of the personality with social-system participations expressed as increasingly differentiated role-sets. Differentiated participation maximizes the use of upgraded cognitive capacities and lends support and moral grounding to differentiated personalities.[21]

The personality equivalent to social-system *value-generalization* presents a problem. One link between the evaluative subsystem of culture and other subsystems of action is through the personality; cultural moral standards are linked to definitions of personal moral standards (superego). However, consistency between standards internalized by different individuals is inherently related to the coherence of a cultural system; both are related to normative groundings of social order. Random variation of moral standards—as they approach independence of individual wants, they approximate the utilitarian formulation—are modified in the direction of integration at both cultural and social levels. Cognitive understanding of moral values is a resource for their ordering. In consistent moral systems cognitive competence plays an essential role. This competence should be distinguished from the cognitive capacity to attach, in retrospect, moral claims to unrelated impulsive needs.[22]

In adapting the developmental scheme from a version appropriate for evolutionary change in societies to the development of personality, the term "differentiation" seems equally appropriate to both cases, although personality differentiation clearly differs from societal differentiation. In the societal case, the reference of adaptive upgrading is economic, whereas in the case of the person-

21. Charles R. Wright and Hebert H. Hyman, "Voluntary Association Membership of American Adults," *American Sociological Review*, 23 (1958), 284–294, found voluntary associational membership more prevalent among the highly educated.

22. Harold Garfinkel, "Common Sense Knowledge of Social Structures: The Documentary Method of Interpretation in Lay and Professional Fact Finding," *Studies in Ethnomethodology* (Englewood Cliffs, N.J., Prentice-Hall, Inc., 1967), pp. 76–103.

ality the focus is cognitive but integrated with motivational resources at the personality level, that is, integrated with knowledge
and competence guided by intelligence.[23] Intelligence is a basis of
the organization of motivational resources. The equivalent of social
inclusion is the incorporation into the personality of interpenetrating boundary aspects of the other subsystems of action, including
the cognitive and motivational resources of the behavioral organism. Also incorporated are memberships in social-system interaction and the moral-evaluative standards of culture. All of these
taken together constitute the pluralization of participations and of
the resources and standards relevant to them. Finally, whereas in
the social-system case the focus of generalization of the base of
commitments is on value-patterns, in that of the personality it is
close to what Erikson means by identity.[24] The relevant direction
of change is enhancement of the "catholicity of identity" which
means identification in a differentiated plurality of values, interests, goals, and memberships which are integrated with each other
so that the personality is not torn by irresolvable conflicts.

In the course of the discussion, *both* of these versions of the
change paradigm and their relation to each other must be kept in
mind. Our concern is with certain *relations* between social system
and personality and not with either separate from the other.

*Differentiation-Diffuseness and Achievement-Equality.* Academic institutions have often been stratified on a scale of prestige.
This constitutes one dimension of differentiation among them. In
our empirical work, prestige has been a basis for analyzing variations in attitudes and behaviors among academic men.[25] Another
dimension of differentiation exists along the axis of intellectual
subjects and disciplines.

23. Compare the discussion of intelligence and affect in Chapter 2 of this book.
24. Erik Erikson, "Identity and the Life Cycle," *Psychological Issues,* 1 (1959).
See also his summary article, "Identity, Psychosocial," in the *International Encyclopedia of the Social Sciences,* ed. David L. Sills (The Macmillan Co. and The Free
Press, 1968), VII, 61–65.
25. In our work we have defined institutional prestige on a "scale of institution
differentiation." Although there is ambiguity between the theory of the scale and the
operations that derive it, the types of attitudinal responses associated with our scale
seem closer to differentiation than to prestige. See Talcott Parsons and Gerald M.
Platt, "The American Academic Profession: A Pilot Study," multilith MS, Harvard
University, March 1968. We have used this scale in analyzing a survey of a national
sample of academic men. These findings will soon be published. Institutional prestige
scales are also found in the works of Alexander Astin, *Who Goes Where to College?*
(Chicago, Ill., Source Research Associates, 1965); David G. Brown, *Academic Labor
Market,* A Report to the Office of Manpower, Automation, and Training (Washington,
D.C., U.S. Department of Labor, September 1965); Bernard Berelson, *Graduate Education in the United States* (New York, McGraw-Hill, 1960).

Although prestige differentiation is more closely associated with the specific social values academic institutions attempt to implement, for instance, emphasizing the development of an educated citizenry or going beyond that and preparing the young for postgraduate work,[26] the disciplinary dimension of differentiation is more closely articulated with cultural levels of implementation of the cognitive rationality value-pattern. Departmental social organization focuses on disciplinary concerns; from that organizational node academic men engage in the core activities of research and graduate teaching.

Although these analytic distinctions are important, there are many complexities in distinguishing them. For example, incorporation of the whole range of disciplines as departments in an arts and science faculty (such incorporation is the general developmental trend of American liberal arts colleges and universities)[27] is critical for undergraduate socialization. The range of disciplines exposes the undergraduate to the spectrum of cognitive values and standards and presents him with a complexly differentiated environment.

Another dimension upon which differentiation occurs on the social-system side is that of levels of membership. Membership is stratified into four classes: undergraduates, graduate students, junior faculty, and senior faculty. Movement through levels is according to a selective process which begins with acceptance into undergraduate school. A unique feature of this stratification system is its relation to the human life course rather than to wealth (in the economy), power (in the polity), or general prestige (in the societal community).[28] Faculty members are, on the average,

26. Talcott Parsons and Gerald M. Platt, "Considerations on the American Academic System," *Minerva*, 6 (1968), 497–523.

27. Eric Ashby, "The Future of the Nineteenth Century Idea of a University," *Minerva*, 6 (1967), 3–17; Joseph Ben-David, "Universities," *International Encyclopedia of the Social Sciences*, XVI, 191–199; also Joseph Ben-David and Abraham Zloczower, "Universities and Academic Systems in Modern Societies," *European Journal of Sociology*, 3 (1962), 43–84.

28. Parents' socioeconomic background and parents' educational achievements certainly have an effect on these selective membership processes, particularly going to college. However, the relation of *position* in the academic system is not as closely associated with parental wealth as parental wealth is with the socioeconomic position of offspring in the economy. And with changing policies concerning entry into college, e.g., "open admissions" policies as CUNY has recently established, the effects of parents' background upon the selective process through the academic system may diminish further. On the effects of background on going to college, see William Spady, "Educational Mobility and Access: Growth and Paradoxes," *American Journal of Sociology*, 7 (1967), 273–286.

about as old as the parents of their students; the average age of American faculty is forty-two; thus the generation difference is built into the structure of the higher educational system.[29] Indeed the slogan "never trust anyone over thirty" comes close to drawing the line between the two generations since graduate students usually have not completed their training before that age and few junior faculty and senior faculty are under thirty.

Differentiation of the academic system occurs first *among* institutions and then *within* institutions along lines of intellectual disciplines and membership tenure. These institutions have bases of community and possess solidarity. In spite of disciplinary differences, all faculty share a common concern with the implementation of cognitive rationality in teaching and research. And at each tenure stratum there are ties of collegial equality. Even across tenure levels there is the solidarity of involvement in a common enterprise and of membership in a single institution. Thus, the phrase is often heard in Cambridge, "the Harvard community," meaning all levels of membership.

The sharpest division, between faculty and students, occurs primarily because faculty membership is an occupational commitment from which faculty members receive their salaries and support their families. Studentry is a temporary status passed through on the way to graduation. Furthermore, students, particularly undergraduates, do not usually earn their own livings and, despite separation from their parents, are financially dependent upon parents. There are thus continuities and divisions, within and among these solidarities, along these lines of differentiation.

Within this pluralistically solidary environment, student socialization takes place. Socialization generally occurs in special settings because the conditions for successful socialization are precarious. For the person being socialized, he must participate in a social organization according to standards of conduct that are only partially known to that individual. The individual must internalize value standards and their use, and he must learn the attitudes and feelings toward these standards while not being fully aware of how they are communally held, used, and evaluated.[30]

29. John McBrearty, Gerald M. Platt, and Talcott Parsons, "Demographic Characteristics of Academic Faculties and Some Recent Trends," in "The American Academic System: A National Survey of Faculty," Gerald M. Platt and Talcott Parsons (forthcoming). Also see on this point, Jencks and Riesman, "The War Between the Generations," *Academic Revolution*, chap. ii, pp. 28–60.

30. Harold Garfinkel, "Passing and the Managed Achievement of Sex Status in an Intersexed Person, Part I," *Studies in Ethnomethodology*, pp. 116–185.

Such requirements of the socializee necessitate a special type of environment in which those responsible for socialization must make allowances for failures, sustain conditions of diffuse support, and exert pressure for the successful acceptance of the communal morality. In such an environment the tendency among the young is to idealize the supportive components and to resist the constraints imposed by the morality; among the socializers the opposite tendency may exist. Much contemporary conflict in student socialization can be explained along lines of the balance between freedoms engendered by diffuse support and constraint engendered by efforts to gain acceptance of a particular morality.[31] Thus, another source of precariousness in socialization situations exists in ideological and behavioral overemphasis on the freedom or the constraints by any of the parties involved.[32]

Let us make explicit how the college experience conforms to these conditions. Robert Dreeben has remarked that students carry with them from previous situations capacities that enable them to participate in new school environments.[33] But the college student is also engaged in discovering, exploring, and learning about new social organizations and about new and old values at deeper levels of intensity. The entering freshmen as well as the upperclassmen, even with forewarning and information, can have only partial familiarity with what they will encounter. In this context, the faculty have to socialize students to internalize the values of cognitive rationality and to more specific disciplines and institutional values.

In addition to the insulated and undifferentiated character of student life, the college environment is diffuse and supportive. In industrial societies three indices of adulthood are leaving one's family of procreation, marriage and the establishment of one's own family, and gainful employment. Although undergraduates accomplish the first by differentiating themselves from constant, intense familial support, they rarely are financially independent or married and employed full time. In colleges and in large state

31. Alex Inkeles, "A Note on Social Structure and the Socialization of Competence," *Harvard Educational Review*, 36 (Summer 1966), 265–283. Inkeles makes a point similar to the one made here.

32. Although the young tend to stress the freedom side and older persons to stress the constraint side, these emphases can occur in real situations in any combination. Thus, excessive parental or faculty permissiveness is a type of overemphasis on the freedom components in each of these socialization contexts.

33. Robert Dreeben, *On What Is Learned in School* (Reading, Mass.: Addison-Wesley, 1968), pp. 1–6.

and private universities, there is pressure for students to live on campus and to lead their academic and extracurricular, their personal and cultural lives, largely within the university community. Summers aside, undergraduates spend a large portion of their lives within the academic community.

Despite differences in scale and content, structural parallels between early socialization in the family and student socialization at college are substantial. Both family units and systems of higher education are stratified on the basis of stages in the life cycle, parents and teachers being the upper stratum, children and students the lower stratum. Moreover, children and students are immersed in an insulated "total" environment, the child more so in the family than the student in the university.

The diffuseness in college is interlarded with equalitarianism since there are few age differences among students. Differences that could be carried into the college setting from the outside such as class, ethnic, and religious differences have, in recent times, been mitigated on the college campus. This diffuseness and equalitarianism foster affectivity among students. In part, this affectivity is a carry-over from adolescence and in part it results from student solidarity. This solidarity is heightened by sharing a similar developmental point in the life course and a common position with respect to environing collectivities: faculty, graduate students and teaching assistants, administration, family. These conditions, plus selection for admission, coalesce to produce a feeling of sharp boundary between student membership and nonmembership, for example, the young in contrast with the old, students in contrast with faculty and administration.

The termination of the oedipal phase means the repression of childhood eroticism centered in the parent-child relationship in order to facilitate the development of autonomy and achievement within the context of formal education.[34] And although there are vicissitudes and contradictions in the development of the young from early grade school to college entrance, the trend of growth is toward increasing differentiation, achievement, and autonomy of the personality. The relative isolation of students and the existence of student solidarity favor repression of certain personality components developed during these earlier phases of socialization. At this stage *diffuse affective loyalties* constitute a strain because

34. Dreeben, *On What Is Learned in School.*

they repress earlier differentiation and interfere with pressures for continued growth. Another strain is equalitarianism which represses past successes, resists efforts for differential achievement and evaluation, and denigrates extant competence differences between students and faculty.

These repressions at the college stage coincide with the repression of constraints and a stress upon available opportunities for freedom in the university.[35] Going to college involves increased freedom in terms of separation from family and community ties and in terms of increased autonomy for courses of action as to the selection of curricula and intellectual interests and in conducting one's own personal and social life. Such increased freedom seems incompatible not only with inequalities of authority in the institution but also with a constraining morality institutionalized in the evaluative and prescriptive powers of the faculty and in their socialization function. Yet these freedoms are a necessary feature for the development of student autonomy and self-regulation. It is where the freedoms are assumed to be limitless (by students or faculty) and not guided by academic values and standards that socialization functions are undermined.

Therapy, socialization, and social and cultural change share a common feature: In the early stages, under strain, there are processes of dedifferentiation, namely, suppression of previous established differentiations in favor of simpler and older patterns. This is a typical regression before further development is achieved. In analyzing the socialization and the therapeutic processes, four features are analogous. Two of these features, *permissiveness* and *support* in therapy, find their analogues in student socialization in *freedom-equality* and *diffuseness of peer-solidarity*. In therapy and student socialization, permissiveness and freedom-equality act as contexts within which previously unexpressed feelings and behaviors can come to the fore and be experimented with. Support occurs in therapy in terms of positive transference between patient and the therapist and willingness on the part of the therapist to accept a wide range of thoughts, fantasies, and, on occasion, acting-out behavior without negative sanction. Although some diffuseness between teacher and student constitutes a parallel condition of transference necessary for student socialization to be accomplished, this relationship is not comparable in intensity to the diffuse support offered by the students for each other. This mutual

35. Dreeben, *On What Is Learned in School.*

support of students must be substantially modified in order to effect socialization in university settings. As in the therapeutic situation, permissiveness and support must not totally dominate the relationship if personality reorganization and growth is to be achieved. Two other features are analogous. In the therapy situation, these features are *denial of reciprocity* and *manipulation of rewards* on the part of the therapist. In the student socialization situation, the analogous features are various activities upon the part of faculty in relation to students directed toward the development of personality *differentiation* and toward expression of legitimate *differential achievement*. Both are channeled through cognitive learning.

Thus, conditions for early or later socialization demand particular structural arrangements. These are conditions which foster emotional and behavioral experimentation associated with growth while at the same time providing mechanisms for fostering and directing that growth within wide ranges of variation.

All members of the academic system live in an environment protected by virtue of its differentiation from other sectors of the society. This environment appears permissive and supportive relative to environments outside academic boundaries. Permissiveness is institutionalized in freedom of choice within the university environment. One aspect of this freedom of choice is academic freedom, meaning that both students and faculty can pursue their desired intellectual courses. Within this context of freedom, support is offered to students by their peer community but also from other parts of the academic community. Faculty must play an important role if transference is to be established between students and the older generation and if the students are to internalize the values of the academic community. Such protected environments encourage dedifferentiation, which makes it more difficult to maintain already internalized repressions. In therapy, transference is a form of dedifferentiation since it tends to move the therapeutic relationship from one of professional practitioner and client to one of parent and child. Since pregenital erotic components were involved in the latter type of relationship, it becomes difficult in therapy to keep such feelings repressed.

The person in therapy or being socialized is placed in a conflict because the permissive-supportive situation is inherently gratifying, but *at the same time* the weakening of the repressions is threatening. Such conflicts have both creative and destructive potentials. Failure to resolve them leads in the therapeutic case to deepening psychopathology, in that of socialization to psychological infantilism. If, however, they can be adequately resolved, new levels of integrated differentiatedness are achieved. In the therapeutic case, the lifting of the repressions of preoedipal eroticism can help to improve the establishment of adult genital eroticism where that has been impaired by neurotic inhibitions. Without the gratifications favored by the permissive-support system, access to the motivational factors which enter into a creative synthesis would not have been possible.

In both psychotherapy and socialization, a balance must be struck between expressing regressive elements of the personality verbally and in fantasy and acting out these fantasies. In both psychotherapy and socialization some degree of control is essential even for creative experimentation. Guidance in therapy and socialization can be achieved only when denial of reciprocity and manipulation of situationally appropriate rewards are utilized. For example, a patient's anger at his therapist in general should *not* be reciprocated with equivalent anger toward him. This would define the relationship as one of *common* participation in the patient's dedifferentiated world of expectations. Denial of reciprocity, if exercised alone, would have the effect simply of frustrating the wishes which permissiveness and support encourage. The therapist must make it seem worthwhile for the patient to consider constructive *alternatives* to the regressive wishes he feels and expresses. The patient must feel that successful adoption of such alternatives will be rewarded, and this implicit promise must in fact be honored if at all possible.

The analogy between this description of psychotherapy and socialization in the academic world is strong. The student is encouraged to experiment within the freedom of the academic environment; the elective system is expressive of this freedom of choice, which encourages the differentiation of their personalities within the pluralistic academic community. In the long run, however, socializing agents cannot permit unlimited diffuse involvement either in the student peer group or in the broadly differentiated university culture. The faculty, while encouraging experience with the multiple alternatives available (a kind of "acting out" in terms of alternatives and differentiations) and encouraging respect for these experiences, denies the legitimacy of continuous engagement with peers and of immersion in the total intellectual spectrum. Manipulation of reward, appropriately situated, then consistently, coincides with this process; that is, reward for achievement within a particular differentiated node supports students and indicates which of the areas of the differentiated environment are most desirable to pursue. The manipulation of rewards suggests to the student the areas in which he is competent intellectually, and in which he finds most personal satisfaction. Through the faculty's manipulation of rewards related to achievement, students gain a sense of success and self-esteem that makes their socialization in the higher educational system possible.

Within this theoretical framework, two clarifications are necessary. We distinguish between levels of affective exchange in the family (or therapy) from affective exchange in university socialization. But the teacher-student relation is not a commerical or political relation. The teacher-student relationship resembles interaction in the family more than relations in the marketplace.[36] Furthermore, socialization may take place in very different contexts from the ones we have described, for example, under conditions of extreme coercion.[37] However, under coercive conditions the effects of the socialization are unstable and produce compliance only as long as coercion is used for reinforcement. In any case, socialization that is primarily the product of coercive force could never produce the autonomous educated citizenry whose personality structure we have described.[38]

Thus family and college socialization emphasize expressive and affective bases of learning to produce the type of personality articulated with a complex differentiated society. However, these bases of action add another dimension of precariousness. Contexts where expressive and affective components are particularly important offer various seductive possibilities. The therapeutic situation gives rise to the problem of countertransference; familial socializa-

36. Talcott Parsons, "Some Theoretical Considerations Bearing on the Field of Medical Sociology," in Talcott Parsons, *Social Structure and Personality* (New York, The Free Press, 1964), pp. 325–358.

37. Bruno Bettelheim and Morris Janowitz, *Social Change and Prejudice* (New York, The Free Press, 1964) ; Stanley M. Elkins, *Slavery: A Problem in American Institutional and Intellectual Life* (Chicago, Ill., University of Chicago Press, 1962) ; Robert J. Lifton, *Thought Reform and the Psychology of Fatalism: A Study of Brainwashing in China* (New York, Norton, 1961).

38. T. W. Adorno, Else Frankel-Brunswik, Daniel J. Levinson, and R. Nevitt Sanford, *The Authoritarian Personality* (New York, Harper and Bros., 1950).

tion gives rise to erotic fantasies on the part of parents as well as children.[39] Again in the therapeutic situation, rigid adherence to conventional morality often occurs as a reaction formation against affectivity.

Some of these reactions occur in the college-student socialization phase with another cycle of repression and development. During this cycle, levels of differential achievement and authority internalized in preadolescence are weakened in favor of peer-solidarity, equality, and demands for freedom from evaluation. Permissiveness of the college environment encourages dedifferentiation. Yet, as it is with the continuity of preoedipal eroticism and its reemergence and reorganization in adolescence and then in genital eroticism, so too it is with cognitive culture learned in the family and during primary and secondary education. Cognitive culture will again emerge, transformed and reorganized at a higher level of expression at the close of the college phase.

The continuity can be viewed in terms both of the changes in student social system participation and of changes in their personalities. True, the regressive isolation of students interposes barriers between students and faculty which can cumulatively escalate antagonisms. If, however, the regression is partial and student behavior is not exclusively motivated by pleasure, there will also appear overtures on the part of students for participation in the intellectual enterprise. This will be expressed by seeking interaction with the faculty and in seeking greater responsibility in community affairs where the value-pattern of cognitive rationality has salience. If these overtures are reciprocated with appropriate rewards from the faculty (both support and recognition of valued contributions), the trend toward such participation will be strengthened.

The capacity of faculty to influence students in this direction depends on the moral authority of the academic community. In the socialization of students, unlike that in the family, the moral authority of the faculty is resisted by student peer-solidarity, a collective obstacle to faculty expectations.[40] Presently this resistance is expressed in derogating cognitive standards by asserting

39. Theodore Lidz, Stephen Fleck, and Alice R. Cornelison, *Schizophrenia and the Family* (New York, International University Press, 1965).

40. Robert C. Wilson and Jerry G. Gaff, "Student Voice—Faculty Response," in *The State of the University: Authority and Change*, ed. Carlos E. Kruytbosch and Sheldon L. Messinger (Beverly Hills, Calif., Sage Publications, 1970), pp. 181–188.

the irrelevance of cognitive learning and in derogating moral authority by charging the university with abdication of responsibility and with immoral complicity in activities extraneous to direct academic concerns.

This difficulty has been exacerbated by an increasing emphasis on research and its associated technologies which has fostered the growth of large administrative organizations. Especially in public institutions, they organize students' lives, which gives rise to the charge of "bureaucratization" of the academic world. In certain respects bureaucratization does characterize the student's environment. However, this term has been used to describe *the totality of academia*. Student resentment is directed against those who have power and authority: presidents and boards of trustees. Although there are legitimate sources of discontent with the distribution of power within the university, a portion of the hostility toward those in authority and living conditions is probably displaced from tensions engendered by the socialization process.

The faculty has been protected from direct hostility by student ambivalence toward them. Part of the ambivalence is a product of the positive as well as the negative transference built up between teachers and students in the learning situation. Such ambivalence is absent from the relation of students to the administration. But students also perceive "countertransference" on the part of faculty, as when campuses politicize and when faculty intercede upon behalf of their students. Further, when faculties' political views are revealed, they are closer to those of their students than to the general population outside of the academic world.[41]

Growth in personal, social, and cultural terms *cannot* occur without some of the manifestations we have described. Oedipal fantasies, rigid adherence to morality in the face of anxieties, and guilts generated by these and many other types of distortions are normal states of emotional turmoil for creative artists, political essayists, scientists, children, parents, students, and teachers during conditions of socialization and change. When socialization is taking place *within a changing* social and cultural order, these reactions will be all the more intense. In the end, such conditions produce ideological counterparts to individual fantasies (wishes, fears, anxieties, and so forth), which infuse into social movements.[42]

41. Everett C. Ladd, "American University Teachers and Opposition to the Vietnam War," *Minerva*, 8 (1970), 542–556.
42. Weinstein and Platt, *The Wish to Be Free*.

*The Academic System under Change: Real and Potential.* The system of higher education has been undergoing changes related to more general changes in society which have affected the socialization of students. We will focus upon societal changes relevant to undergraduate education.

Since World War II, cultural developments and social structural demands have produced extensive growth of research complexes and graduate training within the university. One result has been the differentiation of the academic role so that now faculty are obliged to participate in graduate training and research as well as undergraduate teaching, especially in the better private and public institutions. The consequences of such an arrangement for undergraduates are that they must share faculty interests and emotional investment in them with interests stemming from involvement in laboratories, research projects, and graduate students. Undergraduate student hostility toward research can, in some part, be a type of rivalry for faculties' attention in contrast to competing interests. The growing involvement of faculty in graduate training and research is analogous to that of the differentiation of the father's role in the family and as job holder outside the family as this developed at the outset of the industrial revolution.

At the outset of this type of differentiation, previously with the father's relation to children and presently in terms of the faculties' relation to students, separation arouses anxiety; it is seen as desertion or neglect. These feelings can never be entirely overcome, but they can dissipate as socialization is consolidated. In the family at the turn of the century, the unremitting hostility toward the father's absence from the family filled the novels of Kafka, Lawrence, and Proust and the psychoanalytic writings of Freud. Now that the father's occupational role external to the family has been stabilized (along with moral authority in the family linked with the occupational role) the expression of anger toward fathers has declined. In the mid-twentieth century less tension is recorded between the father and children; but as child socialization shifted further into the hands of the mother, the mother has come in for increased attention in the psychoanalytic literature; the expression of hostility toward the mother has also increased in literary works.[43]

43. This reached its height with the Jewish-mother literature in Philip Roth's *Portnoy's Complaint* (New York, Random House, 1969).

As a result of the structural differentiation of the role of socializing agent, the degree of closeness between father and children or between teacher and students has decreased. As if to compensate for this loss, there is more emphasis on upgraded capacities of the socializing agent and the transmission of these to the individuals being socialized. Thus, in the industrial revolution the father participated in an economic order more complex than the organization of the family firm or family farm.[44] He directed his own economic existence, entered and competed on the labor market, organized a life of self-discipline and control articulated to the factory system, and rationally allocated money for his and his family's wants. Such participation in an industrial order necessitated higher levels of cognitive capacities (rationality) and emotional controls. Even unskilled factory workers developed upgraded skills, intelligence, and personal abilities in order to participate in the economy. The father, as a role-model for his children, passed on to them these enhanced abilities. And these conditions developed, increasingly with subsequent generations, the personality capacities for participation in the industrial system with increasing ease and with decreasing tensions.

In academia a cultural upgrading in knowledge and competence in the intellectual disciplines is reflected in a high degree of specialization in knowledge in the universities and colleges since the end of the nineteenth century. The professionalization of research is a function of that upgrading. Levels of generalization of knowledge have also increased, accompanied by changes in the levels of competence necessary for dealing with those bodies of knowledge. As a result, the role of intelligence as a generalized medium in regulating cognitive matters has become more salient.

During the industrial revolution feelings were expressed that industrial work was incompatible with raising families and might evolve into separate functions; the "desertion" of the father allegedly made fatherhood in the family meaningless. Similarly, some contemporary critics of the academic system feel that the functions of research and undergraduate teaching are incompatible and should be separated. One suggested development is that research institutes be established separate from teaching institutions or that graduate and research universities be established separate from undergraduate schools. Within another context, it is sug-

---

44. Neil J. Smelser, *Social Change in the Industrial Revolution* (Chicago, Ill., University of Chicago Press, 1959).

gested that two different Ph.D.'s be offered: one a teaching Ph.D. and another a research Ph.D. These suggestions arrive by different routes at the same endpoint: the development of separated bodies of personnel involved in teaching and research and physically separated from one another.

Our view, on the contrary, is that these functions can and should continue to be performed by the same groups of people, even in the most prestigious universities. We base this view on the assumption that the undergraduate student should be exposed to academics who are involved in the higher reaches of the cognitive world and who act as role-models and socializing agents for these young people. As with the father in the industrial complex, the young become exposed to and committed to varying degrees of cognitive rationality. This value-pattern is later implemented in societal contexts more complex than previously experienced. Cognitive rationality plays a special role in the ability to deal with modern social systems.

Not all undergraduates so exposed will become academics. Many will move into other contexts and careers. Much undergraduate cognitive learning will be further developed and infused with other values and patterns of behavior. However, the value of cognitive rationality should be internalized at intense and general enough levels so that action will be guided by it; such action is applicable to a variety of contexts. The internalization of cognitive rationality upgrades cognitive potentialities from the capacity to deal with detailed knowledge to the capacity to deal with more generalized knowledge, from knowledge in particular to the competence to gain further knowledge when that becomes relevant. The cognitive rationality value facilitates the use of knowledge gained for further learning in formal educational arrangements and the use of intelligence for general applicability within the societal community. In all these ways, cognitive rationality makes for an educated citizenry, a population whose behavior is importantly guided by this value-pattern.

Exposure to intense levels of the cognitive rationality value-pattern, the general developmental trend within the university, enhances the natural strain in the relationship between teacher and student. However, the benefits tend to compensate for the increased strain, just as benefits in performance-capacity previously compensated for the increased strain of family socialization under conditions of fathers working outside of the home. Within the academic system, higher levels of cognitive learning have been accompanied by the imposition of increased fiduciary responsibility on students. Not surprisingly, students have occasionally rejected this increased burden. But this is only one reaction and we will explore others.

Other changes articulate with the permissive and supportive components of the system. Again not surprisingly, higher levels of demand put upon students give rise to *demands* for increased student autonomy and to the *granting* of greater autonomy commensurate with the increased levels of responsibility and intellectual upgrading. Consider four areas of academic life in which student autonomy has increased and the degree to which this has been accomplished without endangering the academic system. (Of course, a balance must be struck between inclusion and autonomy: such a balance must not undermine the socialization of students or the distribution of fiduciary responsibilities.)

One area of academic life in which student autonomy has increased is the extracurricular aspect of students' lives. With the emphasis on in-college residence (in contrast to the continental European traditions), the academic institution must take responsibility for providing residential space, dining facilities, and so on. The amount and kind of control accompanying these responsibilities have varied: one pattern has been to include some faculty members in the residential community itself, as in the Yale colleges, Harvard houses, and the residential colleges at Santa Cruz. But there has been student pressure against these traditions, especially of parietal rules. What is now called "coresidence" has been gaining ground. The residential life of American students has thus come to be largely autonomous, in contrast both to older traditions and to those still in operation in residential secondary schools, though changes have been taking place in secondary schools also. Autonomy has been growing also in many fields of extracurricular activity, such as art, drama, music, student newspapers and magazines, and to some extent in athletics. This increasing autonomy has given rise to anxiety in the older age groups, both inside and outside the academic community, especially concerning sexual relationships and drug use.

A second area of academic life in which student autonomy has increased is that of curriculum: organization and control of courses of study. The older requirements and grading systems have been substantially modified in recent years. In addition to wide choices among courses and programs, credit for flexible tutorial work, "independent study," "pass-fail" grading, and the like have increased the range of student autonomy, even at undergraduate levels. These changes, like those in extracurricular areas, do not satisfy all student demands, but that there have been major changes is beyond doubt and there will probably be more.

Within the curriculum area, there have been requests for reduction of grading and occasionally demands for the abolition of all evaluation. Although there has been considerable change, there is little possibility that all evaluation can be eliminated from the academic system. As long as academia constitutes a socializing environment, evaluation will always be a necessary component of faculty manipulation of symbolic rewards, necessary for developing in students capacities and desires for differential achievement.

A third area of academic life in which student autonomy has increased is student participation in the corporate decision-making process. There has been a proliferation of student-faculty committees, often into areas where students were virtually unknown before. The division of power and responsibility remains fluid, ranging from advisory participation to equal-voting power in all decisions; indeed some students advocate "full democracy," meaning one participant, one vote. In such an arrangement, students would vastly outnumber faculty. Difficult though it is to work out equitable formulas for student participation in academic decision-making, a shift to greater student participation is occurring.

A fourth area of academic life in which student autonomy has increased is probably the most sensitive: the governance of the university, for example, the rules concerning rights and responsibilities of the different segments of the university community, procedural rules for decision-making, and the distributions of power and authority. Student participation in university governance is now taken for granted, though students have not been included in all aspects of governance of the university nor have they been given a controlling voice in those aspects in which they participate.

Except for the last area, increased student autonomy has reinforced the permissive and supportive aspects of the socialization environment and has accentuated the dedifferentiations and resistances to socialization. There are also positive consequences of the increased permissiveness and support, given the intensity of socialization and degree of personality transformation attempted in college; the general formula is that the more intense the regression, the greater potential for significant personality restructuring (provided that total breakdown is avoided).[45] However, in these early stages of restructuring there has been a tendency to interpret increased autonomy as complete equality between students and faculty and thus for the students to minimize the stratification of the academic community. Effective socialization as well as effective cognitive learning is dependent upon the maintenance of a pattern of stratification between those performing socialization functions and those being socialized.[46] This is also necessary in the university environment so that the faculty can, under appropriate circumstances, deny reciprocity and control rewards and thereby socialize students to develop the differentiated personalities and pluralized involvements required by complex cultures and societies.

*Student Socialization and Modern Society.* At this point we must ask what aspects of the personalities of college students are socialized and for what purposes? How is socialization accomplished within university or college contexts and how does this socialization relate to the structure of the modern societal community?

The rapid increase in the number of the young going on to college in recent years clearly is no accident, yet the explanation of the rising rate of college attendance is variously interpreted. For example, we hear that the prestige of a college education is so great it is sucking into college young people who previously would not have participated and even drawing into college those who would rather not attend ("the compulsory university"). It has also been suggested that higher salaries for the college-educated and demands for technical skills in industrial occupations are forcing more youth to go to college and that this demand by industry has been the impetus for state and private funds to be diverted for such activities.

These explanations are not wholly convincing. Prestige of higher education does not emanate out of nowhere; something must lie behind its rising prestige in order to entice larger numbers of persons to perceive a college education in this way.[47] Conversely,

45. McHugh, "Social Disintegration."

46. Thomas J. Cottle, "Parent and Child—the Hazards of Equality," *Saturday Review*, February 1, 1969, pp. 16ff.

47. The Carnegie Commission on Higher Education reports that a survey indicates that 97 percent of all parents interviewed wanted their children to go to college. See *Quality and Equality: New Levels of Federal Responsibility for Higher Education*, Carnegie Commission on Higher Education (New York, McGraw-Hill, 1969).

why has there been a decline in the attractiveness of the conception of the self-made man? If the need for increased technical capacities were the major force behind growing enrollments, why has the largest growth in undergraduate education occurred in the relatively impractical liberal arts and sciences? A recent *New York Times* article decried the overemphasis on abstract courses and advocated more stress on the vocational in college; the article applauded a shift among some of the young toward the practical. Finally, one might ask, higher salaries for what? The English major with a bachelor's degree has no industrial skills, and even a physics graduate is not competent to make scientific contributions. Thus, the explanation of the rise in undergraduate college enrollments remains to be given unless the undergraduate environment is conceived in relation to the changing society and to the ways in which the undergraduate educational experience links with that environment. The undergraduate environment is not a microcosm of the society, but there must be links between the university and society, just as there are links between the family and society.

The explanation at a general level lies in the role of citizenship in the societal community of the type of society which has been developing in the modern world. The older ascriptive bases of society are becoming attenuated; the particularistic solidarities of religion, ethnicity, localism, and class have been eroding as bases of status and even of relationship. The spread of higher education has contributed to this erosion. Thus, modern society has become increasingly pluralistic on various bases of functional differentiation. In a Durkheimian sense, increasing differentiation can be integrated only through organic solidarity rather than in terms of ascriptive or traditional bases of integration.[48]

Pluralism has been accompanied by an increase of freedom in many respects, such as greater freedom of access to ideas and greater freedom in behavioral spheres (the possibility for participation in wide ranges of activities and groups from leisure to cultural, religious, political, and occupational groups). An upgrading of levels of freedom, however, places an increasing burden of choice on those who must conduct their activities within this less ascriptive framework. There is also the responsibility to make choices in ways that can be integrated into the individual's own

48. Emile Durkheim, *The Division of Labor in Society*, trans. George Simpson (New York, The Free Press, 1969). Originally, in English, New York, The Macmillian Co., 1933.

interests and into a range of social concerns from the narrower ones of family to those of the society, culture, and humanity. Common values are necessary to integrate these choices among the many different persons and the activities of the numerous groups in society.

A general formula for integrating choices through adherence to a common value within the societal community is that of *institutionalized individualism*.[49] The institutionalized-individualism formula must not permit either the individual or the institutional components to take priority if the framework of freedom is to operate within the societal community. Specific freedoms must be grounded in values, which means being embodied in societal normative systems, notably in law, and internalized in personalities. However, institutionalized individualism must be committed to at high levels of generality so that many types of action, persons, and collectivities can be evaluated in terms of it. The value-commitment cannot be so precisely defined that it signals only narrow courses of action if there is to be freedom in the sense of pluralistic involvement.[50]

One reason for a high level of value-generality is the linkage of the academic system to an extensively differentiated society and its subsystems. Value-generality permits transference of orientations from action acquired in the academic subsystem to other systems and subsystems. In contrast, specificity of value-orientations would hinder action in a wide range of collectivities (in pluralistic involvements). We are assuming that the individualism of modern society results from the differentiation of the primary subsystems of action, that is, the differentiation of the cultural from the social system and both of these from the personality system. These systems are articulated with one another through generalized value which must be specified in action under particular circumstances.

This formulation suggests why we have stressed the cognitive as well as the affective components of student socialization. Within the conceptual framework we have been developing, the affective

49. Talcott Parsons, "Durkheim's Contribution to the Theory of Integration of Social Systems," in *Emile Durkheim, 1858–1917: A Collection of Essays, with Translations and a Bibliography*, ed. Kurt H. Wolff (Columbus, Ohio State University Press, 1960), pp. 118–153; also see Talcott Parsons and Winston White, "The Link between Character and Society," in *Culture and Social Structure*, ed. S. M. Lipset and L. Lowenthal (New York, The Free Press, 1961), pp. 89–135. Also see Chapter 1 of this book.
50. Talcott Parsons, "Youth in the Context of American Society," *Daedalus* (Winter, 1962), pp. 97–123.

complex links the individual's personality to multiple *solidary identifications*, while the cognitive complex integrates the personalities of individuals at three different levels. (It integrates multiple social-system involvements; it mediates between cultural and personality systems; and it integrates the individual's affective involvements in a plurality of collective systems.) Most discussions of socialization do not emphasize the cognitive component,[51] but it has been through the differentiation of the cognitive aspect from the rest of culture that the cognitive complex, consisting of knowledge, rationality, competence, and intelligence, has become a generalized resource for the personalities of individuals in modern society. Given the orientations to action guided by institutionalized individualism, citizens are capable of making more intelligent choices; without high levels of knowledge, intelligence, and competence, unconfused by other cultural and motivational components, this would be impeded. But the other side of the coin is that a developed cognitive complex that is uncontrolled by value-commitments, affective solidarities, and so forth, can be disruptive to the solidarity of the societal community.

Weber and Freud understood this problem from different points of view. In the late writings of Freud and in the post-Freudian literature, greater theoretical stress has been placed on ego-control as directives to social action in contrast to unconscious motivations (libido theory). However, neither Freud nor his followers envisioned bringing all action under total intellectual control. Weber understood this too, and he discussed it in his conception of rationalization. Rationalization of action, about which he was so concerned, could never be complete. Weber implied this in his distinction between *Wertrationalität* and *Zweckrationalität*, which do not have equal theoretical status. Wertrationalität can be institutionalized, resulting in progressive rationalization *within a given valued end state*. Although such orientations have brought under rational, conscious control larger segments of everyday actions, it is questionable whether this condition could prevail for every segment of life. The value-pattern depicted by *Zweckrationalität* would achieve this ideal, but Weber questioned whether this could be institutionalized for every aspect of social action without deleterious consequences for individuals' personalities (for example, a sense of anomie) and for social organization.

51. See, however, Kohlberg, "Stage and Sequence."

In spite of the necessary balance between cognitive and affective components, socialization in higher education has taken the rationalization process very far. The institutional arrangements of higher education (in which socialization is now taking place) are directed toward the rationalization of personality, placing stress upon the cognitive aspects of personality and emphasizing rational action guided by knowledge, intelligence, and competence. This rationalization process is not new, but there have been two significant changes: (1) the intensity of education, that is, the depth of penetration of the personality by the upgraded knowledge system within the university and (2) mass participation in the college system. These two conditions suggest that the character of action and its evaluation within the societal community is changing. Such changes are part of what may be implied in the phrase "post-industrial society."

One side of the coin is the increasing freedom of action through upgraded cognitive capacity. The other side is relating this capacity to societal involvements, solidarities, and responsibilities. Institutionalized and internalized values constitute an essential stabilizing base for any social system. For socialization in the college environment, a central problem is value differentiation and internalization at sufficiently general levels to accomplish both commitment and freedom.

A goal of general education is preparation for citizenship in a pluralized, institutionally individualized societal community. Differentiated values constitute a basis for the normative order of such a community, but members are not automatically attached to these values. Through the motivation to emotional attachment to membership roles in the plural collectivities involved in the structure of the societal community, such commitment is achieved. Differentiated values are also involved in personal goal-orientation and its relation to collective interests, especially solidarity. The individual's relation to the collectivity is referred to as "identification" in the sense that, when he is thinking about the collectivity, he will use the pronoun "we."

By means of application and admission, the student begins his identification with a particular academic community—he is, as part of his "identity," a Harvard or a Berkeley student. This identification in a special collectivity, differentiated from college students of the same age-grade in other schools and from those of the same age-grade who have not gone to college, is also a subidentification with a larger collective organization. For example, a Harvard freshman is not only a member of the freshman class but also a member of Harvard University and the "Harvard community." Harvard University is itself a collective system which includes other individuals of many different statuses and roles and many different subunits such as departments, institutes, centers, and so on. The issue becomes: How does the freshman relate these memberships to his membership in the university and how does university membership relate to his eventual status as an educated citizen within the societal community?

On the social-affective side the path of socialization implies that the student utilizes his initial tendency for peer-solidarity and identification but gradually enters into a more ramified system of identifications that culturally are on higher levels than he has previously experienced. Thus the young student is normally involved in collective arrangements where he is exposed to higher standards of cognitive culture than he was in high school. Identification with academic disciplines in lecture classes, seminars, and tutorials (exemplified in the phrase, "I'm taking sociology . . . *with* Professor . . .") exemplifies such exposure, but so does participation in extracurricular activities such as the debating teams and the college newspaper where high cognitive standards usually prevail. In short, the faculty holds higher-level cultural standards than the students and it is their function to expose students to these standards when students register for their classes. Few students will attain the level of cognitive involvement of their teachers, but development to this level is not the purpose of undergraduate higher education. The faculty's aim is to have students internalize a growing level of cognitive rationality for implementation in college and postcollege life.

The university not only provides higher levels of cultural exposure in comparison with the high school experience but also wider ranges of freedom in a more differentiated environment. The college student may pursue a variety of interests, most of these cultural but some not so involved with cultural life. The range of freedom within the academic sphere is exemplified in the selection of areas of concentration and in the selection of courses but also in extracurricular activities, choice of roommates and friends, and romantic relationships. For the noncollege population of the same age-grade, the immediate environment is comparatively less supportive and protective and does not offer such a wide range of choices.

At the same time the academic system is stratified. Higher status groups are selected for their predominantly cognitive achievements. At every level of institutional prestige, the faculty have, *on the average*, greater identification with cognitive concerns and collectivities and have achieved more intense involvements with cultural activities relative to their students. On the whole, faculty are more "cosmopolitan" than their students. They are participants in a ramified cultural world beyond the local institution. The professionalization of the academic role has accentuated this cosmopolitanism, and in leading universities faculty members are prominent contributors to knowledge as well as involved in various professional and public activities. In a national sample of academic men, we found little difference in the degree of cosmopolitan attitudinal identification of faculty at the varying prestige-level institutions; faculty members at all levels generally emphasized their disciplines as a source of identification. In contrast, actual publication record and professional reputation vary with institutional prestige. Significantly, however, faculty at the lesser prestige institutions who are *not publishing* and who *do not have* national reputations still identify with their disciplines. This identification has some effect on their own orientations in teaching and interacting with their students.[52]

The trend in recent societal development has been for the salience of cultural contributions to increase and thus to enhance the status of academic faculty. A special societal status has been given to a few academics who have made spectacular contributions to knowledge. Such academic culture heros are socially assessed in accordance with their professional attainments and not with their class origins. Many come from middle and lower socioeconomic classes. Further, even though academic culture heros are few, they are more numerous and influential than ever before in history.[53]

Some resistance to socialization, from the hardly noticeable to the explosive, is endemic to the process. But presently, because of mass education, stronger peer-solidarities, and more emphasis upon increased cognitive capacities, student antagonism to socialization

52. Gerald Platt, Talcott Parsons, and Sally Nash, "Dimensions of Identification and Loyalty among Academic Men," in Platt and Parsons, *American Academic System.*
53. Don K. Price, *The Scientific Estate* (Cambridge, Mass., The Belknap Press of the Harvard University Press, 1965).

has increased. If antagonisms to the agents of college socialization can be attentuated through cathexis of tutors, teaching assistants, or junior or senior faculty, that is, of those with socializing responsibilities for students, then previously acquired cognitive orientations can be rekindled. The main mechanisms for abating hostility are cathexis and transference but they are reinforced by curiosity, exposure to knowledge, and the *prestige* of opportunities for academic participation. Concerning the prestige of academic participation, the hostility expressed in anti-intellectualism and in the "compulsory college attendance syndrome" of those attending the university under self-defined duress may reflect ambivalence rather than pure antipathy. Thus students also express the positive affective pole of their ambivalence toward participation in the prestige activities of college.

The ability of the faculty to generate affective attachment of the type just noted depends upon their coordination of two sets of factors. First, they must offer students opportunities in the college environment which the larger community defines as valuable: activities having moral authority within the larger community as, for example, acquiring knowledge. Thus, opportunities mean here commonplace activities that students engage in in university settings, for example, taking a course with a particular instructor, choosing a field of concentration and playing in the orchestra. This first set of factors should be conceived of within a pluralistic context. To be sure, the participating student forecloses opportunities by making choices; by making selections in a given semester he or she sacrifices the opportunity to take other courses that might have been participated in. Yet the average student can still take a considerable number of courses during his stay on campus. Of course, there is also a sense in which the faculty, through offering courses in his specialty to students, is carrying out one aspect of the denial of reciprocity. He is symbolically saying, "I have knowledge which you can participate in if you wish to do so, knowledge worthy of learning," and is implicitly denying intellectual equality between him and his students in the realm of this knowledge. His denial of reciprocity should not be based upon mere assertion of legal-bureaucratic authority, which will invariably fail, but on the demonstration of knowledge, intellectual expertise, and cognitive competence.

The second set of factors involves the individual's personal achievement within the opportunity manifold. However unsatisfactory present grading systems may be, some form of differential evaluation of individual performance is an essential aspect of socialization within higher education. In the future such evaluation may take different forms, perhaps as simply differential access to desirable opportunities, but evaluation will continue. *Of course, evaluation in terms of manipulation of rewards which are not of value to the recipient will not socialize.*

The individual's choices within a pluralistic environment must be circumscribed to form a satisfactory pattern of commitment. Since each participation has an affective component, it is impossible for all involvements to have identical intensity of affect. Thus, without a degree of rationality, that is, of intelligent action, no coherent pattern affectively satisfying to the individual and to systems of his participation can be achieved. This, then, is a *direct* link between *cognitive* and *affective components* of the personality systems, although there are other indirect links. *Rational integration of the allocation of affective significance among participations is the most salient means whereby higher levels of socialization are accomplished*—although it is also a focus of resistance. Resistance often takes dedifferentiated forms: minimizing pluralistic involvement and elevating one involvement ("total commitment") to the exclusion of others. The link between the cognitive and affective components of the personality system may be viewed from another angle: the rational integration and pluralization of affect constitutes a form of affective economy in relation to the cognitive complex. This is a parallel to "intelligence banking" which will be discussed in Chapter 7. This parallelism should be anticipated because both intelligence and affect are generalized media.[54]

Affective banking lies in the interchange between social and cultural systems. Affect as a medium circulates among personalities and social and cultural systems. Any of these as holders of affect can function like monetary *depositors* in a bank. They have entrusted some of their affective interests to such an entity, on the average maintaining a positive balance rather than demanding in any given time period the return of the total affective deposit to which they are formally entitled. The analogue to the *borrower* from a bank occurs when a social system gives supportive affect to a member beyond that which he has earned, but, as with a bank, on some kind of credit terms. Students are in this position. Admis-

54. Talcott Parsons, "Some Problems of General Theory in Sociology," in *Theoretical Sociology*.

sion to membership in the college or university is equivalent to a bank loan. Undergraduate students' tenure in the college is essentially a guarantee of affective support for the expected period of time of their education.

The support component of the relationship between faculty and students and between institution and students must be unequal. Students often assess this differential negatively as domination. It is not necessarily domination but may instead be a necessary feature of socialization. Further, the affective support among student peers is not as often negatively evaluated because the levels of mutual support are approximately equal. However, because of this parity, there is little affective upgrading that can accrue from such peer interaction.

The lending function of the college is thus primarily a culturally fiduciary one. The institutionalization of the fiduciary responsibility for cultural standards, centering in the faculty, enables institutions of higher education to function as affective banks and to give students greater emotional support than would be available to them in other contexts—for example, if they had not gone on to college but had gone directly into the labor market. Repayment of such affect loans consists eventually in increased capacity of the student cohort to contribute to the values extant in this kind of collectivity, that is, to participate in collectivities where values of cognitive rationality have some priority. We are not suggesting mere improved ability to perform in labor terms but rather improved performance within a pluralized societal community where action is structured in institutionalized individualistic terms. This creation of new affective resources is essential for all socializing agencies whatever the level of development and for all agencies of social and cultural change.

Pluralization and upgrading of affect through cognitive functions is thus an outcome of successful student socialization. Interdependent with affective development is the pluralization and generalization of *value-commitments* so that moral legitimation of activities need not be confined to specific roles. Greater generality of values is frequently an outcome of student socialization, but it is not automatically internalized by students. Its development in the individual student depends on his feeling of the justice of differentiation among his plural participations, that is, on his feeling that each collective participation within the total system of participation is given fair consideration, although not necessarily equal consideration.

Generalization and pluralization present comparable problems in the cognitive field. Cognitive rationality has primacy in the academic system and underlies the professionalization of faculty roles. Cognitive rationality also constitutes an axis of differentiation of the academic system from institutional sectors of the society in which other value patterns take priority. How does this primacy of cognitive rationality in the academic core relate to the socialization of undergraduates? The answer involves the generalization and pluralization of the cognitive complex. Once membership as student is accepted and socialization pressures take hold, the student makes some room for cognitive concerns among his personal goals. Student achievement measured by competence in cognitive matters, that is, by learning, is rewarded by the faculty. These rewards reinforce initial identification with the higher-level academic strata and, as a result, the student will value cognitive achievement not only during his student days but, if socialization is effective, in his postgraduate life will continue to value it and to derive self-esteem from performance in accordance with cognitive standards.

This process is reinforced by faculty commitment to the integrity of cognitive standards of validity and significance. The mechanism utilized to enforce these standards is again denial of reciprocity to student overtures incompatible with such standards and subsequently selective rewarding. Noncognitive concerns are relevant to the teaching situation, but such concerns are less salient within the total system than the cognitive experiences and needs of the students. One goal in socializing students is to enable them to distinguish evaluation of social action on everyday grounds from evaluation of cultural output on exclusively cognitive standards. In some areas purely cognitive and everyday standards shade into each other as, for example, in expressive assessments of the elegance of science or mathematics. Yet these are separate domains of action and evaluation, and even overlapping areas can be understood by undergraduates.[55]

The internalization of cognitive standards is psychologically difficult. It demands a personal discipline to prevent extraneous factors such as motivations, desires, and ideological commitments

---

55. Harold Garfinkel, "The Rational Properties of Scientific and Common Sense Activities," *Studies in Ethnomethodology,* pp. 262–283.

from excluding or distorting these standards. A mediating mechanism in this process is that of relevance. The faculty can offer examples of cognitive problems and prospective solutions to students in a graded series from the completely "relevant" to pure cognitive concerns.

Relevance to practical, political, and ideological student interests must come to terms with the faculty's commitment to cognitive standards. This commitment provides a link between affective concerns and cognitive meanings. Teachers assist students with their noncognitive involvements while helping them to develop cognitively valid interpretations and alternative solutions to the various problems they, their society, and their culture face. In such a learning situation the issues studied may be relevant to the students and the solutions may help them resolve certain tensions and give them a basis for rational action, but from a socialization point of view the educational experience demonstrates to the undergraduate the value of cognitive standards in achieving solutions.

Such learning can follow a graded series from elementary to more advanced levels of cognitive sophistication. This series involves not only the command of empirical information but also theoretical generalization and generality of relevance of problems and solutions. Solutions to basic human problems cannot be exclusively oriented to those presently faced by students but must transcend, at least in their general formulations, the limits of a specific time and situation.

Cognitive capacities help in assessing probable consequences of alternative courses of action and in understanding antecedents of a current situation. Yet some segments of the undergraduate population crave impulsive action without contemplation of the effects of such action on other aspects of the society. This is a kind of parochialism related to the desire for temporal "nowness": It suggests action in accordance with "my or our beliefs" without concern for future developments. Cognitively rational components have been neglected or submerged by other components to action.[56]

The direction of cognitive development is now clear. Higher levels of generality and cognitive capacities link to controls in the allocative ordering of pluralized affective commitments. But the pluralization of participants has another implication; the division

56. There is much ambivalence among students on this point. Dissidents accuse their elders of acting irresponsibly, which can mean not having taken adequate account of the consequences of their actions, but they also insist on the legitimacy of themselves acting impulsively (spontaneously).

of labor integrated through organic solidarity must produce a plurality of types of subcollectivities, roles, and personalities. The freedom for individuals to seek autonomously what is most meaningful to them has its counterpart in the wide diversity of packages of participation. Enhanced freedom poses problems of integration, because of the probability of mutual interferences in individuals pursuing their respective choices. Such interference has frustrating consequences to individuals and disorganizing possibilities for the society. Some ordering becomes essential. Complementarity of function constitutes maximum integration. The patterning of rules permitting wide variations produces minimal integration.

For a modern society there is no possibility of uniformity in roles, personalities, and styles of life; tolerance of diversity must exist in a pluralized environment. The maintenance of such diversity is dependent upon the institutionalization of procedural rules. The academic world is one of several areas in modern society where procedural rules have been institutionalized and in which one is offered conditions for learning them. Procedural rules take many forms, but a common one is embodied in the principle of academic freedom. This principle offers special protection for expressing opinions, and this protection is universalized for all participants. At the same time it is necessary to observe cognitive standards. The right to criticize claims to cognitive validity of a point of view is balanced by an obligation to cite evidence to substantiate the challenge. Such procedural rules sustain the differentiation of the system while acting to integrate it also. For undergraduates these rules safeguard them against dogma, propaganda, and sectarianism and permit them to develop voluntarily their packages of differentiated commitments and participations. Finally, such rules assist in exposing the student to the cognitive process and to problems of validity as they operate within the academic system; disregard of the procedural rules would be tantamount to suppression of cognitive processes at their highest levels of expression.

Several reports have been disseminated by commissions and committees studying higher education. The reports have been critical of traditional academic education; yet there has been little theoretical integration of their many suggestions for change. We cannot end this section without commenting on suggested changes which have implications for the cognitive and affective socialization of the young.

One suggestion is that higher education should be as universally available as possible. That is, there should be higher education at low cost (federally and state financed) for very large sectors of the relevant age-grade. Behind this suggestion is the explicit desire to draw into higher education many lower-class and minority young. It is hoped that such a policy would reduce the opportunity gap between the middle and lower classes attending college and would ameliorate the accumulative disadvantage of poverty and cultural deprivation. Another suggestion is that college attendance be made available not so exclusively to the 17–21 age-grade and that interested older individuals be permitted to return to the university, perhaps after their children are grown, for continuing their education. This could serve several different purposes, including giving older persons the opportunity to change careers or simply to invest themselves in a more intellectual life.

These changes would affect the composition of the student body and would therefore have implications for student socialization. The inclusion of the poor and blacks in large numbers will change the average backgrounds of students, the nature of their cultural and intellectual experiences, and their degrees of preparation for college. The inclusion of greater numbers of older people into the student body may also bear on levels of preparation, but this is less important than the effect of widening the age structure of the average student body.

There has also been a suggestion summarized in the phrase "more options and less time" for undergraduate education. One form of this is to make structural changes in undergraduate education so that it would include ever more fields of learning, some academic, some more practical or "relevant." There has also been talk of including practical experience with academic experience: various forms of "on the job training" simultaneously or serially with academic training. Finally the suggestion has been made that all of this could be accomplished in less time than the present college career takes. This shortening of time would entail either more intensive work in a shorter period or a net reduction of education while keeping the pace about the same as at present.

It is impossible to predict the extent to which these changes will be implemented. But if these changes were instituted in the academic system, they would affect the socialization process—although the precise impact is a matter of conjecture. The inclusion of disadvantaged minorities will change the character of the student audience. Although faculty are sometimes accused of being oblivious to their students, this has hardly been the case; even within the lecture context, students and faculty are interacting, and faculty respond to student needs.[57] The poor and the blacks have already changed the content of undergraduate education: witness growing programs and departments in Afro-American studies, Third World studies, courses and programs on women, and so on. Such populations will continue to place pressure on faculties to shift the content of courses. Insofar as this is accomplished, the materials taught and learned will have new kinds of meaning for the lives of their students. Thus, broadened population inclusion is a subtle form of influence toward the teaching of relevant, applied, practical, ideological, and politically salient topics.

It is questionable as to how far such changes will go before faculty reactions set in; in academia now, faculty are reasserting their values and interests. But even if a faculty reaction were to go far and a compromise[58] were achieved between faculty and student desires, such a compromise need not basically change the balance between everyday and purely cognitive concerns. That is, teaching will continue to range from the applied to the pure, from the specific to the general, in terms of cognitve content. There is nothing inherent in studies of poverty, the ghetto, ecology, or the environment which prevents the socialization of students to the value of cognitive rationality. There is little chance that the inclusion of practical or specialized problems in college will constitute the exclusive form of learning for the young; alongside such studies will still exist general education. And even these studies will serve as a node for exposure to cognitive problems so that ultimately the learning is generalizable from one problem to many other problems. Nothing in the inclusion of applied programs and departments suggests that socialization in college as we have described it will be substantially altered by these changes.

The "less-time-more-options" restructuring also would not appreciably affect student socialization. Those students who advocate this structural reform seem to desire to achieve the freedom of postcollege adulthood sooner.[59] This might necessitate an intensifi-

57. George Wald, "A Generation in Search of a Future," a speech given at Massachusetts Institute of Technology on March 4, 1969, reprinted in *The University Crisis Reader*, ed. Immanuel Wallerstein and Paul Starr (New York, Random House and Vintage Books, 1971), I, 4–12.

58. Wilson and Gaff, "Student Voice," in *State of the University*.

59. Neil Smelser, personal communication.

cation of student socialization but not a basic change. The "more-options" side of the slogan reveals a continuity with trends of university and societal development. Even if more options imply something other than traditional academic subjects, these new possibilities represent development toward increasing differentiation of the environment. A more differentiated academic environment may increase strain on students in dealing with greater freedoms, but this structural invocation will not appreciably affect the nature of student socialization.

Alteration of student socialization might more likely stem from the influx of older individuals into college. Student peer group solidarity would be weakened. Changed age composition might also reduce the authority of faculty because of the lowered age differential between the average faculty member and student. However, there would still remain a differential in expertise between faculty and their older students which would sustain the authority structure. Further, even the older student, once he returned to the college context, would undergo regressions similar to his younger colleagues. Giving up structural supports such as the occupational role or raising children would facilitate this type of regression although it may not be as severe as that for the young student. Therefore, even for the older college student, socialization would be similar to that of the younger college student.

The effect of older college students on the socialization process depends upon the conditions under which they are introduced to the campus. For example, would they be diluted among the young or would they constitute a critical mass, a special audience similar to that of the poor and minorities? Would they interact with the younger students or would they form a separate entity? If the older student interacts with the younger, participating in activities normally associated with youthful college students, then peer-solidarity would be attenuated. But such participation for the older student hardly seems likely. Thus for the bulk of the students and for the academic structures, the inclusion of older students will not have a dramatic impact.

To reassert what we have already said, college socialization is directed toward the development of larger segments of the society for more effective participation in a particular type of changing societal community; thus, although socialization may change slightly by exposing broader sectors of the society to college, these changes will not have massive effects without massive social regression of the societal community. Since so much of this analysis hinges on the articulation of the academic system to the societal community, we turn to a discussion of this articulation.

*The Societal Community and the Academic System.* Although socialization in higher educational institutions helps prepare for citizenship roles in a societal community which emphasizes institutionalized individualism, the academic community is *not* a microcosm of the society but a differentiated part of the society. This differentiation concerns the obligation to implement the value of cognitive rationality. The implementation of this value-pattern distinguishes the social organization of the academic system and its institutions from three other types of social arrangements: the economic market,[60] administrative bureaucracy, and democratic political organization.

With regard to political democracy, one feature of modern societies is the extent to which government has been differentiated from the societal community. Governmental systems function as collective decision-making bodies as well as agencies to implement decisions in order to achieve collective goals. The societal community, in contrast to the political system, is the relational matrix of solidarity in society; this relational matrix is differentiated into many subsolidarities.[61]

The governmental system and the societal community interpenetrate; they are also interdependent. One mode of articulation is through the institutionalization of political democracy, including equality of citizen status and the delegation of decision-making power and its implementation to elective office. The equality principle is institutionalized in the formula, "one citizen, one vote." And elective officials are periodically held accountable to electorates. A second interface between government and societal community lies in the legal system. The legal system has political aspects beyond the legal foundation of policy decisions and administrative tasks that relate to legislative functions. One political aspect concerns the backing of legal processes by governmental power, another the manning of the legal system, for example, the appointment of judges. The nomination of candidates for elective office and the confirmation of nominations by legislative bodies

---

60. Theodore Caplow and Reece J. McGee, *The Academic Marketplace* (New York, Basic Books, 1959; Garden City, N.Y., Anchor Books, 1965).
61. Talcott Parsons, *The System of Modern Societies* (Englewood Cliffs, N.J., Prentice-Hall, Inc., 1971), chap. vi.

also involve legal considerations. Normatively the legal system is nonpolitical; this independence is reflected in the insulation of the judiciary and the system of courts from everyday political affairs.[62]

These two interfaces are regulated by constitutional provisions, which are protected against the pressures of ordinary politics. At this level the basic pattern of equality, "basic rights," has been institutionalized in such documents as the Bill of Rights. Basic rights are not primarily political but belong to the fiduciary system.[63] There is a zone of interpenetration between the societal community and the fiduciary system that is not political but central to socialization in higher education in preparation for participation as educated citizenry. In this socialization context the legal content of citizenship is of greater importance than is the political. With respect to the patterns of equality, the academic system institutionalizes a synthesis between two references of equality: those of basic rights in the fiduciary system and those of membership status in the societal community.[64] It is this version of equality to which students are socialized and which they are expected to internalize.

The cognitive stress of student socialization is thus formally congruent with the patterning of basic rights. Cognitive validity is intrinsically independent of relational systems at the social level, as basic rights are independent of cultural commitments at the moral-evaluative level. In contrast to this, the patterning of the affective significance of participation is important in membership status. But this means plural memberships, and the specific meaning of political equality is applicable to some, but not all, of these memberships. The internalization of such discriminations is a feature of the academic process. Its accomplishment helps resist tendencies to illegitimate politization of collective relationships in the academic and societal communities; both are contexts in which political bases of equality and participation are inappropriate.

With respect to inequalities in the academic community, the emphasis is upon intellectual achievement evaluated on universalistic grounds. Emphasis upon these bases of evaluation de-empha-

62. The independence of the legal system in the United States has recently been recognized by European writers although it is denigrated by American radicals. In this connection, see Jean-François Revel, *Without Marx or Jesus: The New American Revolution Has Begun* (New York, Doubleday and Co., 1971).

63. Robert Bellah, "Civil Religion in America," *Daedalus* (Winter 1967), pp. 1–21.

64. Talcott Parsons, "Equality and Inequality in Modern Society; or, Social Stratification Revisited," *Sociological Inquiry*, 40 (Spring 1970), 13–72, especially the technical note on pp. 56–69.

sizes differential authority and power, although not denying them a place within the academic system.[65] It is worth noting in passing that the academic and legal systems are closely related through their common commitment to universalistic standards.

Another axis of the societal community concerns the balance between freedom and constraint. In the academic system, the institution of academic freedom (subscribed to by students as well as faculty) stresses freedom but not freedom to pursue any interest, as, for example, hedonistic interests, but rather interests that fulfill the shared fiduciary responsibility of those in the academic community. These interests are defined by the value of cognitive rationality, which is capable of generalization to other value-patterns involved in citizenship and plural solidary membership in the societal community. With this stress on freedom, the balance of constraint shifts in the direction of moral authority (in Durkheim's sense) ; less emphasis is put upon hierarchical or coercive authority and sanctions.

Therefore, the academic system can present to students a model of the institutional patterning of a modern societal community, although that model is incomplete. It is a model which emphasizes the legitimacy of pluralistic differentiation and the development of diversity through the exploration of freedom and equality of opportunity. This exploration is grounded in the institutionalization of fiduciary responsibility, not of the pure cognitively rational variety characteristic of graduate education, but a pattern in which the cognitive values constitute part of a larger complex. Successful socialization to this pattern should yield the beginnings of attainment of a level of value-generalization where cognitive components can be integrated in the same system with others.

After the undergraduate phase, those who have passed through it will manifest varying patterns of behavior and participation and should therefore constitute a differentiated group in society. Christopher Jencks and David Riesman have grasped an implication of this development when they suggest that the company of college-educated men and women are becoming a new upper-middle class in American society: a class based on style of life, patterns of behavior and culture rather than wealth and power.[66]

If the academic system is to continue to transmit its traditional

65. Gerald M. Platt and Talcott Parsons, "Decision-Making in the Academic System: Influence and Power Exchange," in State of the University, pp. 133–180.

66. Jencks and Riesman, "Social Stratification and Mass Higher Education," Academic Revolution, pp. 61–154.

values, to socialize students to these values while at the same time adjusting to the changing conditions and demands of society, it must preserve its cognitive core in general educational programs while permitting wide latitudes of variation within that framework. We can suggest some structures which permit such continuity and change in academia. First, there should be a *combination* of high-level cognitive opportunities and social pressure to take advantage of them within a solidary community, preferably residential, in which students can invest a considerable proportion of their affective interests. The primary trustees of the cognitive interests should be the faculties, but responsibilities should be differentiated and overlap within the stratification system of the academic community. A comparison with families is relevant. Parents and children live together and share differential responsibilities for collective welfare, but each subgroup has its own sphere of activity exclusive from the others. The family and higher education are environments protected by differentiation from outside institutions, but for students and children this means especially permissive and supportive environments. However, such permissiveness and support cannot devolve into a country-club environment, a hippie community, or an asylum for emotional and political problems, although all of these activities should and do exist on campus. Alongside with these and having priority among them, the college must stress intellectual concerns which are seriously pursued by all categories of membership in that community. With respect to what kind of intellectual concerns, we would suggest that for general education the "core body of knowledge" no longer holds. After adequate opportunities to learn and just rewards for achievement are provided, entry into higher levels of cognitive culture depends on a combination of two circumstances. The two circumstances are cognitive standards of validity and problem statements (and conditions of their solution) which can resonate in a progressive series as relevant to students. These cognitive standards can be formulated in abstract terms, but for socialization they must be continuously implemented in varying interaction settings between teachers and students. However, on the faculties' part there must be a special firmness of commitment to these standards and therefore a refusal to reciprocate deviations from them. This is essential for the students' development of competence and of intelligence, not for development of knowledge *per se*.

Cognitive standards need to be related to, not replaced by, interest in problems and solutions. Relevance in this sense can act as a vehicle for cathexis and positive valuation of cognitive standards. By dealing with the noncognitive significance of certain problems, an instructor can reinforce the contribution of cognitive solutions even to areas of noncognitive involvement and concern. He can impress upon the student that concern is not enough for the solution of problems, but that cognitive control of the formulation of the problem, as well as evidence regarding its causes, are necessary for effective remedial policies.

Partly under student pressure, there has been a tendency to widen opportunities for relevant studies. There also probably will be increasing student participation in outside activities, as for example tutoring and teaching children in poor white and black ghettoes. Some of this activity will be during the students' extra-curricular time but some will be for academic credit in connection with courses. This is analogous to clinical aspects of professional training.

In *quantitative* terms, it is difficult to spell out the relationship between cognitive and noncognitive involvements. However, three desiderata can, in broad terms, guide policy for relevant study opportunities. The first of these is the maintenance of a balance between cognitive and noncognitive interests in relevant activities. The university is especially concerned with cognitive matters and should not lend its sponsorship to interests on the part of members of its community where noncognitive aspects overwhelm cognitive aspects. The relation between curricular concerns and matters out-side of the curriculum such as on-campus extracurricular activities and the private lives of students is of course a problem. Keeping cognitive components in balance is most important within the curriculum. In addition to whatever concern for usefulness or other noncognitive interest the student has, if the student is not inter-ested in learning from an activity in a cognitive sense, the activity does not belong in the college curriculum. This criterion presumes that student demands for relevance must fall short of total aliena-tion from cognitive values of the academic institution and its faculty.

The second desideratum has implications for the pluralism of the academic community. This pluralism derives from differentiated-ness of cognitive culture itself, by disciplines and across discipli-nary fields. Pluralism ramifies into ideological areas, such as religious and political involvements, because it is an aspect of the *differentiatedness* of the academic community within the society. This differentiatedness has emerged in part through dissociation of the academic institution from commitment to any *one* noncognitive orientation. In earlier years, insistent pressure came from religion, but today there is as much if not more pressure from political sources. However, the university cannot afford to be officially committed to any one noncognitive orientation; it cannot be an official organ of any religious doctrine, political party, or movement. Hence, its noncognitive interests in relevant matters must be limited by keeping open opportunities for other groups of students whose conceptions of what is relevant differ from those of more presently popular or insistent groups.

The third desideratum concerns the suggestion previously made about a graded series relating the cognitive and noncognitive components in learning. The college student is exposed to more generalized cognitive problems than those which formed the staple of his intellectual diet in secondary school. The culture shock of this exposure is a factor in his tendency to emphasize the noncognitive aspects of relevance. In addition to direct exposure in curricular involvements, there is, especially at the more elite institutions, an intellectual atmosphere, directly represented by distinguished academic contributors to cognitive enterprises.

In this setting, the undergraduate student needs ample opportunity to participate in a graded series from more immediate and personal concerns to those of greater cognitive emphasis. Such opportunities should include attraction to cognitive standards for use in solving personal, political, and social problems, for serious participation as a citizen in the society, and for taking advantage of the opportunities to enhance intellectual abilities in all these respects. There should also be some concern with opportunities for developing cognitive standards for occupational roles and for developing professional and intellectual commitments which can be expressed in going on to graduate work in various disciplines and professions.

As for the role of specialization in general education, we believe that common levels of cognitive capacity (intelligence) and competence in cognitive problem-solving are more important than the content of knowledge of the "common core of knowledge" which was so prominent in discussions of undergraduate education in the forties.[67] Intelligence must be linked to some substance, but the emphasis should be on what one can do with knowledge, on intelligence in handling cognitive problems rather than on what one knows. This is the trend in higher education; it is promoted (fortunately) by the proliferation of knowledge in all fields which no undergraduate could be expected to bring under total control. Does this imply an end to specialization? Definitely not. Opportunity for cognitively as well as noncognitively relevant specializations of interest should be provided in the academic community at the undergraduate level. The attainment of a relatively high level of cognitive capacity and competence for the college-educated implies a respect for knowledge and for cognitive capacities but also the acquisition of actual competence. Therefore some level of concentration in an area is necessary. Undergraduate specialization teaches students how to grapple with intellectual problems while simultaneously instructing them about the difficulties of achieving a cogent intellectual solution, let alone practical results. We are not suggesting a particular field of knowledge but rather some depth involvement in any field which can give the student the cognitive experience we have described.

*The Noncollege Population.* Only a few studies compare matched populations of college and noncollege young. In these studies only a small number of personality dimensions are examined. These are: authoritarianism-dogmatism, religious beliefs, and intellectual values. The changes noted for the college sample in comparison with the noncollege population are increased intellectual interests, decreased religious values, and decreased authoritarianism.[68]

There are interesting details that can be elaborated, such as the finding that for both college and noncollege populations during the four-year period of college there was a decrease in authoritarianism.[69] College students however far exceeded noncollege young in their decreased authoritarianism over the four years. This finding contrasts with the generally positive relationship between

67. Daniel Bell, *The Reforming of General Education: The Columbia College Experience in Its National Setting* (New York, Columbia University Press, 1966).

68. The data relevant to college and noncollege population are excellently summarized in Feldman and Newcomb, *The Impact of College*, pp. 64–68.

69. W. T. Plant, "Longitudinal Changes in Intolerance and Authoritarianism for Subjects Differing in Amount of College Education over Four Years," *Genetic Psychology Monographs*, 72 (1965), 247–287.

age and authoritarianism.[70] The college experience reduces authoritarianism to a much greater extent than does maturing while not attending college.

Using less directly relevant empirical materials but working within a theoretical framework consonant with our conception of the socializing effects of college, we came to conclusions similar to the studies reported above. We suggested that the college population, in contrast to the noncollege population, tended to be less responsive to hierarchical authority, more autonomous, and more committed to a highly differentiated action environment. The noncollege population had greater respect for authority, was less able to challenge it, and was grounded in a smaller range of ascriptive solidarities such as religion, kinship, and ethnicity than was the college population. It is our assumption that the end product of the socialization in the college better equips the individual for participation in the developing societal community of modern America. In this chapter we have elaborated the character of the socialization of the college population and have articulated the relationship between the university and its socialization effects with the societal community. In our earlier formulation we focused on autonomy and pluralistic involvement for the college educated. Now we suggest that the college environment inculcates new values and intensifies previously held values along the following lines : commitment to basic rights of pluralistic membership on universalistic standards; commitment to action based on intelligence (rationality) ; commitment to rationally oriented achievement universalistically assessed; and commitment to moral authority with the capacity based on cognitive capacities to challenge authority.

All of these commitments and capacities are present in the noncollege population; on the average, however, they are exhibited to a greater degree among the college-educated. There is no discontinuity between the college and noncollege populations in terms of values, intelligence, capacities, or biological and sociological maturation. Continuities along all of these dimensions must exist in order to integrate the two communities. Also, if such continuities did not exist, it would be impossible for high school student graduates to continue their education in colleges. We are discussing scale difference, but these differences are large enough so that we may refer to them as categorical differences.

70. Adorno, et al., *Authoritarian Personality*, pp. 140–141.

Why should these features of personality be categorically related to membership in the college and noncollege populations? First, because the noncollege population terminates formal education and therefore intensive socialization earlier than the college population. In American society this limits the noncollege population in terms of financial and occupational opportunities; the college-educated on the average get more prestigeful jobs and over the course of their lives have larger incomes than the noncollege population. But beyond this, termination of education affects the noncollege population in terms of technical capacities as well as its life-style; it undergoes more limited transformation of values and levels of commitment. The noncollege population remains in a less differentiated value matrix and more readily committed to values grounded at the social system level while the college-educated are more culturally oriented and more liberated from societal values.

Since the high school experience is not discontinuous with the college experience, the values institutionalized in each system are congruent. Cognitive rationality permeates both systems, but in the high school system it is not given the priority that it is in the universities and colleges. The intensity of expression of cognitive rationality is only one difference between the college and high school. Another one is the relative immersion of students in the two systems. In high school, the student remains physically connected and financially and emotionally dependent upon his community and family. In college, the student attenuates ties with community and the family. As a result of this difference, there is a greater degree of dependence upon and affective ties with the college community. As with the therapy situation, the student "falls in love" (and "in hate") with college. Some of this dependency ("transference") is manifested in postgraduate hangers-on around the college campuses: a conspicuous phenomenon in places like Berkeley, Madison, Cambridge, and Amherst. But the college experience is truly completed (like the psychoanalytic experience) when the individual can internalize the values of those with whom he has identified and can direct his life according to these standards without continued dependence.

The college environment tends to be a "total" one and therefore one in which students are socialized at more intense levels of their personalities than in high school. Both environments affect the personalities of their students, but with two differences. The first is the degree of intensity of affects, which we have already remarked upon; the second is the variation in the content of affects to which we are about to address ourselves. Although there is a membership component in high school attendance, it does not mean basic rights of pluralistic membership as does attendance at college. High school is compulsory and rarely selective. By contrast, admission into membership at a particular college is from the viewpoint of students a voluntary association. From the college viewpoint it constitutes selection of membership by application of specific and universal criteria. The entering freshman is presumed equal, within latitudes, to other students past and present; indeed he is an alumni member of that institution for life (even if he does not remain the full four years). Further, acceptance of admission obligates the student to share in the rights and responsibilities of college membership including sustaining, changing, and financially supporting the institution. Finally, college institutionalizes relative freedom in such areas as choice of courses, intellectual pursuits, majoring, and extracurricular activity.

Attendance in high school tends to be compulsory. Conversely, high schools ordinarily accept all of the potential students within their jurisdiction, which makes for a wide range of talent among students. Performance and attendance in high school is sustained until graduation or until the student is of age legally to "drop out." On the other hand, the commitment to pluralistic basic rights of membership in the college environment is based on selectivity and voluntary association—a different principle of membership from that in the high school community. The college environment more closely approximates the societal community in this respect. Equally important, in the college environment individuals can more readily develop the commitment to perform in terms of self-guided action within the context of normative freedoms and constraints.

The college environment is more differentiated than the high school environment and the course of permissible action is greater in college. As a result, the average high school student does not develop the same spectrum of toleration of differentiation and pluralization which grows out of the college experience. This difference is not attributable only to the larger number of areas of study available in college but also to the different way in which the two systems are embedded in the values of the larger society. The high school is less free from social values of the society and, although social values are to a degree present in the college environment, the college is more independent of religious, political, economic, and familial concerns. In the high school, teaching is not only oriented to the cognitive culture but it also serves the purpose of giving the student an identity with his nation and past (note how blacks decry the absence of their history from high school courses) and it sanctifies religious, political, and familial values.

A popular suspicion is that the college experience results in an irreverent graduate. The contrary argument is tenable: The college student learns to locate a multiplicity of collective affiliations within a differentiated network, giving relevance to each affiliation and attributing to none an absolute commitment (although some hierarchy should exist among them). The transformation that occurs in the college phase of socialization is acceptance of complexes of solidarities for oneself and acceptance of the legitimacy of still other complexes beyond one's own interests. By contrast, the high school student is more committed to a circumscribed environment grounded in the values of the larger society. He is more affectively bound to a limited number of ascriptive solidarities, such as his family and his religious organizations. His standards of evaluation and potential courses of legitimate action are also circumscribed by these affiliations.[71]

A phenomenon related to the latter situation concerns the transformation of high school and college peer-solidarities. When the college population completes its education, continued dependency upon solidarities formed in college is not typical. The dissipation of college friendships is partly a consequence of geographic dispersion. Equally important as dispersion is college socialization, which pluralizes participation; pluralized participation means fitting in college colleagues and friendships in an extended associational matrix.[72] For the young who have gone only to high school, there is less geographic dispersion. High school graduates remain closer to each other; they more frequently choose post-school friendships from previous neighborhood associates and classmates.[73] Finally, level of education has become the most

71. Eli Chinoy, *Automobile Workers and the American Dream* (Garden City, N.Y., Doubleday and Co., 1955); Morris Rosenberg, *Occupations and Values* (Glencoe, Ill., The Free Press, 1957); William Foote Whyte, *Street Corner Society*, 2nd ed. (Chicago, Ill., University of Chicago Press, 1955).
72. Wright and Hyman, "Voluntary Association Membership."
73. Whyte, *Street Corner Society*.

important factor in mate selection; even more so than the socioeconomic origins of the families of bride and groom.[74]

In college, the highest rewards go to students and faculty whose works are the most creative, cogent, scholarly, and expressive, especially when aesthetic and scholarly achievements coincide, as in mathematical elegance. These standards of evaluation are consonant with the value of cognitive rationality in contrast to the high school experience where creativity is not given the priority it is in higher education.[75] In high school, priority is given to comprehension and the mere possession of knowledge.

A college professor usually knows more than his students. But it is not without precedent that an undergraudate may publish a novel or develop a formula which far exceeds the talents of many professors of the faculty. Such talents are recognized and rewarded in the college environment without regard to age. Faculty are committed to contribution within the framework of cognitive rationality and also to universalistic standards of contribution. That is why "anyone" can make an important contribution to knowledge. By committing themselves to these standards, faculty socialize their students to universalistic standards. Although most students are not able to exhibit extraordinary contributions, college faculty (in contrast to high school faculty) give rewards for such talent. High school faculty, being more instrumentally oriented, make sure that all of their students know their work so that the students can complete high school with a good record and go on to college or have enough ability to get a good job.

The high school authority structure is more *hierarchical* than the college organization. Authority stems more from position (office) than from expertise. Compatible with this greater role for bureaucratic authority, rote learning of facts persists in the high school to a greater extent than at college despite the pragmatic influence of John Dewey. Nevertheless, there is variation among high schools, depending on the quality of the particular high school, the community in which it is situated, the orientation of the school (for instance, vocational or college-preparatory), the educational experience of the staff, and the degree to which the

74. Bruce L. Warren, "A Multiple Variable Approach to the Assortative Mating Phenomenon," *Eugenics Quarterly*, 13 (1966), 285–290.

75. Dreeben, *On What Is Learned in School*; Edgar Z. Friedenberg, *The Vanishing Adolescent* (Boston, Mass., Beacon Press, 1959) ; Robert Rosenthal and Lenore Jacobson, *Pygmalion in the Classroom: Teacher Expectation and Pupils' Intellectual Development* (New York, Holt, Rinehart, and Winston, Inc., 1968).

school organization has changed as a result of the infusion of college value-orientations. Yet, with all these sources of variation and despite complaints of some college students that the university is too "authoritarian," the high school is a more bureaucratic learning environment than the college.

Tension exists between hierarchical authority and the value-pattern of cognitive rationality.[76] Cognitive rationality fosters evaluation on universalistic grounds, that is, an evaluation of contribution without regard to the source of authority. Cognitive rationality also fosters institutionalized conditions for autonomous behavior. Students who do not go beyond high school are *more* likely than the college-educated to be more responsive to hierarchical authority and readier to base evaluations on ascribed positions. They are *less* likely to have developed the tools of rational criticism with which to direct their own lives. Respect for authority and the capacity to challenge it is class related.[77] The issue hinges on whether compliance with authority is based upon universalistic standards of evaluation or upon standards tied to hierarchy. Apart from the differences in the organizational settings of the college and the noncollege populations, the college population tends toward the former set of standards, the noncollege population toward the latter.

The higher educational system, with its emphasis on cognitive rationality as a value-pattern, has institutionalized those orientations of action described by Weber in his analysis of Western history. The college experience extends the socialization process, developing the individual so that his personality can articulate with a differentiating, rationalizing, and changing society. Intelligence, universalistic standards of evaluation, autonomy, flexibility, and rationally oriented legitimate achievement are features of this extended socialization.

*Reactions to Socialization and Contemporary Student Activism.* There is need to comment on the definition of goal-priorities and values, especially value-generalization, before closing this chapter. Levels of differentiation differ between the academic world and other elements of a pluralistic society. However, the rapid growth

76. Erich Fromm, "Origins of Neurosis," *American Sociological Review*, 9 (1944), 380–384.

77. Adorno, et al., *Authoritarian Personality;* Richard Christie and Marie Johada, eds., *Studies in the Scope and Method of "The Authoritarian Personality"* (Glencoe, Ill., The Free Press, 1954) ; Milton Rokeach, *The Open and Closed Mind* (New York, Basic Books, 1960).

of the academic system has resulted in excessive differentiation, which must be counterbalanced through the integration of cognitive interests with other activities. The stress on relevance tends to redress this balance. A balance must be struck among types of goals which have cognitive primacy and those which do not. A balance must also be struck *within* each type of goal-orientation between cognitive and noncognitive components. Development in this direction occurs during the college socialization when evenhanded faculty attitudes demonstrate respect for the different types of orientations. Undergraduate students regardless of the purpose of their college careers (pure, applied, or academic) should feel that their interests are worthwhile, that there are no second-class citizens within the academic community.

There should be other academic contexts within which students oriented to practical values can participate and from which they can develop cognitive values and personal identities. Thus, faculties should not only show respect for traditionally nonacademic activities to a greater degree than they have in the past; it will be necessary to institute colleges, departments, and programs oriented to a balanced mix of cognitive and practical concerns. Such units will lend legitimacy for participation in activities which previously did not exist in academia. Moreover, just as interdisciplinary work among scholarly disciplines closed cultural gaps, these units will bridge the gaps that have been developing between elements of the cultural and social system value-orientations.

Similar considerations apply to the internalization of values. The issue is not one of inadequate internalization of values but rather of attaining high enough levels of value-generalization to permit recognition of the legitimacy of a wide range of specific values.[78] To accomplish this the faculty must be cosmopolitan in the sense of orientation to a scholarly world as well as appreciative of other forms of scholarship and of professional and practical involvements. Taking this stance, they can reinforce high levels of pluralization and of generality in their students. At the institutional level, we have suggested some relevant changes. Another change might be an increased integration of professional with arts

78. This view seems consistent with Erikson's distinction between "moral" and "ethical" levels in personality development, with "ideological experimentation" coming in between. Erikson also speaks of both "premoral" and "amoral" components of child development which come to be expressed in student dissent. See Erik Erikson, "Reflections on the Dissent of Contemporary Youth," *Daedalus* (Winter 1970), pp. 154–176.

and sciences schools in order to provide opportunities for integrating cognitive and practical values and organizing affective interests.

During the recent growth of academia, not enough consideration has been given to some of these problems of integration at both the value and structural levels. One result has been increased difficulties in the socialization of the college young. By pointing to some strains that have been expressed in student discontent we can better understand the changes the academic system has been undergoing, how these relate to changes in the wider society, and how student socialization can be located within the life cycle.

Previously we identified four themes of student discontent. Each theme has a negative and positive component; that is, it points to an objectionable academic trait and a desirable change (both allegedly). The first theme is complicity in societal involvements judged immoral: the Viet Nam war, the military-industrial complex, the disregard of the rights of disadvantaged groups in the immediate neighborhood of the university, the neglect of minority-groups' needs such as access to higher education, and discrimination against women. The suggested change is that academia should revert to its basic values, should circumscribe its involvement in these immoral activities, or get involved in moral ones. The second theme concerns the competitive character of academia regarding both student and faculty success and perquisites. The suggested change is that academia should become a true community, in one version a community of scholars and students with little individual interest separate from that of the community. The third theme is that of student powerlessness; students are unable to control the decisions which affect their lives in the impersonal and bureaucratic milieu of large academic communities. The suggested change is participatory democracy with special emphasis on student power, the limits of which are not defined. This theme is associated with the desire for autonomy in relation to the frustrations accruing from their dependency status. The fourth theme charges the academic system with repressiveness: with preventing needed self-expression and self-fulfillment. Various groups want to be liberated to "do their own thing." The focus of this complaint has been the *in loco parentis* role of college authorities concerning students' private lives, but it also ramifies into curriculum. The suggested change is to lift all restrictions in private and curriculum matters.

These four themes critical of the college community are over-determined from three sources: from real tensions in the wider society, from displaced personal problems, and from the affective frustration resulting from college socialization. The confluence of such sources, normal as they are in such changing situations, complicates the analysis. A link between feelings of grievance inside and outside the academic community is what Erikson has referred to as the "revolt against dependency."[79] Without denying the legitimacy of protests against injustice, we note that student dissenters seem unaware of two facts that mitigate the impact of injustices on students. First, college students tend to come from the most advantaged segments of the population (and to return to them) and they do not suffer economically or socially in a comparable way to the disadvantaged groups with which they identify:[80] blacks, poor, the third-world peoples, women, for whom they speak and who constitute their symbolic allies in "liberation" movements. Second, faculty and administration, in contrast to other professionals and the general population of the society, hold attitudes close to student opinions on political issues.[81] Thus, neither clear status deprivation nor confronting an oppressive establishment lies at the heart of student complaints. These diffuse feelings of exploitation, inferiority, and dependency may better be interpreted as forms of relative deprivation and psychological displacement.

Understanding the dynamics of student dissent requires the analyst to combine social-structure variables with personality-level factors. The links between them are the strains which students have experienced in the course of socialization and the resulting moral orientations, actions, and critical interventions, which they feel to be legitimate in coping with these needs. Naturally such a formulation does not explain away the merits of student discontent nor should it minimize the social problems of the day and the role students have played in bringing these to public attention. It can be said, however, that students in their tension-laden socialization

---

79. Erik Erikson's article, "Reflections on Youth," offers an insightful analysis of these issues. We shall in our discussion rely upon Erikson's exposition. Since there has been no consultation with Erikson and since his position was taken independently of our own, the convergence between the two works bolsters our cofidence, to a certain degree, in the validity of both positions.

80. Jerry Farber, *The Student as Nigger* (New York, Pocket Books, 1970).

81. S. M. Lipset and Everett C. Ladd, Jr., "The Divided Professoriate," *Change*, 3 (May-June 1971), 54–60; S. M. Lipset and Everett C. Ladd, Jr., ". . . and What Professors Think," *Psychology Today*, 4, no. 6 (November 1970), 49–51, 106.

situations are more sensitive to injustices in the society than those in more secure social positions. Only the moral absolutism, the nowness, and the totalistic logic of the young distinguish them from their teachers and many of their elders. The involvement of the young in the Civil Rights movement, in various forms of dissent concerning civil liberties, ecology, population problems, and urban decay has contributed to the solution of serious problems. However, until very recently, their impulsive and sometimes violent actions have also contributed to the polarizing of campus and society.

From the point of view of the sociological analyst, the needs of students, which are reflected in the themes of their criticisms, arise from an interplay between affect and value-commitments. For young students, tension is created by juxtaposition of the value of cognitive rationality, with its emphasis on pluralization, with their diffuse, affective loyalties; loyalty values stress an undifferentiated egalitarian peer-group organization. One way to reduce this strain is to assert an undifferentiated value-orientation linking value-commitments to affective components at an equivalent level of differentiatedness and to further connect these to an ideological cause, such as justice or self-liberation. Linking value-commitments to affective components implies a *dedifferentiation* of cognitive, affective, and moral orientations as well as the social and cultural systems involved. The manifestations of dedifferentiation are moral absolutism and diffuse solidarity which excludes all others from belonging to the significant "we"—thus negating pluralism—and cognitively fosters what Erikson calls "totalistic logic."[82] One manifestation of moral absolutism is to pose polar alternatives where right and wrong, cognitive validity and error, and affective belonging and alienation are fused in a single orientation. Since such an orientation conflicts with social and cultural realities, what is fervently wanted is either projected into a lost past, a prominent feature of *Gemeinschaft* romanticism, or into an unrealized future, commitment to which Erikson calls a "Utopian conviction."[83]

The tensions arising from college socialization underlie the dedifferentiation syndrome although the situations and groups cathected have some realistic basis for identification. The real and

82. Erikson, "Reflections on Youth," p. 164.
83. See Chapter 6 of this book for a discussion of the structure of ideological 'myths."

imagined similarity among these groups and situations provide students with intellectual ammunition with which to attack the university and especially its procedural rules. Obviously procedural rules are vital to maintaining university pluralistic differentiation. It is therefore understandable why procedural rules have become the center of the controversy between the radicals and the establishment. One conflict arises from the establishment view that procedural rules should be observed and, if violated, that appropriate sanctions should be imposed. This view conflicts with the radical belief that amnesty is an absolute right no matter what procedural infractions have been perpetrated. Some "law and order" advocates within as well as outside the academic community need to "act out" a compulsive attachment to such rules, whereas a student minority (equally compulsively) needs to act out its repudiation of rules in general. The orientation to rules is a classic focus in problems of revolution.

Erikson's analysis of youth is compatible with our analysis of the sources of student alienation. Among the four stages of moral education which precede "ethical consolidation," Erikson points to "moralistic antiauthoritarianism" as "condemning the adult world with righteous fervor." Within the academic world, students are prone to condemn value-neutrality especially as institutionalized in the standards of cognitive validity. Students often want to politicize the academic community and thereby collapse the social and cultural components of the system in favor of political orientations. Such efforts are in conflict with the pluralistic character of the academy but also with its political pluralism since such students tend not to be tolerant of political diversity. A counterpoint to this moralistic-political stance is one in which affective concerns predominate. The affective theme stresses "liberation" from establishment repression rather than punishing the establishment for its moral offenses. Erikson suggests that the latter behavior is connected with residua concerning "oral trust" and is manifest among hippie-counterculture type groups; our analysis refers to themes of community, spontaneity, and self-fulfillment.

Erikson discusses two stages genetically prior to that of moralistic antiauthoritarianism. One, the premoral phase, concerns assertive activism and centers in the development of anal-urethral interests and muscular competence during the second and third year of life coincident with demands for autonomy. Erikson related residua from this stage at later ages with violence and obscenity as, for example, in the case of motorcycle gangs. The other early stage concerns the impact of the internalization of the superego during the oedipal period; it occurs about the fourth and fifth years of life and involves "the claim to the right to wield *initiative* of imagination and action . . . without the oppressive sense of guilt which at one time deepened the propensity for repression."[84] When not fully integrated into a coherent moral-ideological pattern, these components account for radical features of dissent: tendencies to react defiantly to imposition of discipline, to derogate the legitimacy of the moral prohibitions, and to be assertively intrusive into domains of parental privilege.

The affective-solidary side has models intermediate between oral trust and the adolescent peer-solidarity underlying the moralistic antiauthoritarian stance. Between the amoral and the oedipal phases, there develops in favorable circumstances an affectively oriented solidarity in the family, where the child has acquired a more autononous membership status than previously. This affective solidarity also underlies the concern for achievement, transferred to the school and flowering in latency. Psychoanalytic theory has stressed the repression of infantile sexuality, but has not given equal prominence to inclusion based on *affective* solidarity that is nonerotic, but involves solidarity on a new basis of cathexis. Certainly much of this syndrome survives into the adolescent peer culture.[85]

One reason why affective solidarity is important lies in the contrast between the strongly egalitarian stress of the adolescent peer-group and the generational stratification of the nuclear family. Such a collectivity, if it is affectively integrated, must develop affective attachment *across* generations as well as within either the parental or the sibling group. The adolescent peer-culture tends to *repress* these cross-generational solidarities in a way parallel to the repression of differentiation of levels of cognitive achievements in the academic system.

If the permissive-supportive aspect of college socialization facilitates the lifting of repressions and if the other components of the socialization system operate successfully, overtures toward affective solidarities across the lines of stratification within the academic community will get encouragement. A dialectic of overture and hesitancy on both sides of the stratification lines is observable.

84. Erikson, "Reflections on Youth."
85. Keniston, "Youth: A 'New' Stage of Life."

The next stratified layer of personality development on the affective side involves the family and, on the moral side, superego internalization of societal norms represented in the family. But student militant antiauthoritarians rebel against familial stratification and differential achievement in favor of age peer-solidarity and total equality. This syndrome is at once moralistic, solidaristic, and ideological, but it also has a creative side. It can mobilize resources for the next step in personality growth. The problem is not only how to increase the levels of cognitive competence and intelligence but how to develop the necessary psychological resources for effective participation in a differentiated world, a world more complex than anything the young individual has experienced before.

On the side of affective solidarity, effective socialization attenuates the rigidities of peer communalism by allowing solidarity across the stratification lines to develop and through teaching that solidarity, especially in qualitatively differentiated groups, does not necessarily mean betrayal of loyalties to those not included in them. Both should be combined with an overall loyalty to the specific academic community. The structural logic is essentially the same as in the case of value-generalization where commitment to the general pattern is firm, but room for differentiated specifications is made.

Parallel developments should be expected on the moral-evaluative side. Erikson speaks of a pattern called "post-moral, pre-ethical pragmatism."[86] This characterizes the majority who have not become mobilized in any of the other earlier patterns, notably that of moralistic antiauthoritarianism, but who also have not yet attained the level of "ethical consolidation." The first two patterns exist concurrently; and under certain kinds of strain the postmoral pragmatists may be mobilized into the pattern of moralistic antiauthoritarianism, as happened in the wake of mass arrests by police at Columbia, Wisconsin, and Harvard. Erikson, however, regards this pragmatism as an intermediate stage, thus linking it with vulnerability to dedifferentiation under stress.

The pattern Erikson calls "ethical consolidation" is therefore the value-pattern appropriate to successful socialization relative to participation in the pluralistic, institutionally individualized, societal community. This participation needs to be congruent with

86. Erikson, "Reflections on Youth," p. 171.

affective loyalty, to a differentiated and stratified solidary community, which practices *a far reaching toleration of difference* but also recognizes functionally necessary status distinctions of achievement and authority as well as similarly necessary constraints on freedom or expressiveness where collective interests are involved.

What is the place of the cognitive component in all this? Erikson refers to "ideological experimentation" in youthful dissent as having its origins in the period between oedipal moralism and ethical consolidation.[87] Cognitive learning can provide leverage for reducing rigidities in the type of personality organization we have been discussing; it can have this effect on ideological commitments as well as on other and more general inflexibilities. The psychotherapeutic situation is analogous; verbalization with cognitive interpretation of affective-moral sentiments affects their impact on the personality and changes their meaning. Thus, although this is not the only reason, it is one reason why later stages of socialization have become associated with high levels of cognitive learning.

This chapter has emphasized student socialization in relation to the recent development of mass higher education, which involves the evolution of a new type of societal community characterized by pluralistic differentiatedness and institutionalized individualism. Evolution implies adaptive but not necessarily moral superiority. Our analysis does not glorify this type of societal community, especially if its merits are interpreted as apologies for the territorial national state. We are not putting forward a rationale for chauvinism.

There is, fortunately, a groping toward affective community beyond national limitations.[88] Indeed, one feature of the American societal community has been its capacity to integrate by inclusion diverse ethnic and religious groups which, in their European locations of origin, had been more often antagonistic, as, for example, groups of English Protestant and Irish Catholic origin. Transitional feelings of solidarity, though with many setbacks, have been gaining ground. The ecumenical movement in the religious field, first within Judeo-Christianity, but increasingly beyond it, is a manifestation of that trend.

87. "Reflections on Youth," p. 161.
88. Robert Bellah, *Beyond Belief: Essays on Religion in a Post-Traditional World* (New York, Harper and Row, 1970).

Moreover, a trend toward greater ethical universalism is discernible; this is one connotation of Erikson's concept of ethical consolidation. There is a connection between this trend and the cognitive emphasis of the educational revolution. Compared to previous stages in the development of Western society, the educational revolution upgrades cultural interests relative to economic and political interests, and in general cultural foci of organization are more cosmopolitan than are social systems or personality foci. Moreover, in the cultural system the cognitive complex is the most unequivocally *universalistic*. This universalism is a basis for the utilization of the system of higher education as a socializing agency as well as an instrumentality for the development of technical knowledge and its competently expert use. The two functions necessarily go together.

# 5

## THE UNIVERSITY AND
## THE APPLIED PROFESSIONS:
## THE PROFESSIONAL SCHOOLS

The second main context to which the university's knowledge and competence functions in the wider society are relevant is that of practical goals, which are promoted through the services of the principal professions. In a historical sense, training for professional service was the matrix within which the modern university took shape. The four standard faculties of the older European university, namely Theology, Philosophy, Law, and Medicine, were all in the first instance professional faculties, that of Philosophy being primarily a training school for teachers, especially at higher levels of secondary education, namely, the *Gymnasium* and the *Lycée*.[1]

As Ben-David has shown, the current American conception of a Faculty of Arts and Sciences constituted a structural innovation, the result of which was the differentiation of the core functions of the university, namely, of graduate training of prospective academic professionals and of research, from training for the applied professions. Thus a student of the European university system, as of the middle third of the nineteenth century, would not have made the distinction between the material of Chapter 3 and that of the present chapter. He might, however, have distinguished English higher education on the Oxford-Cambridge model as concerned with the education rather than the training of undergraduates from the Continental universities which were concerned with training for the professions.

Given that this process of differentiation has occurred in the American system, the problem arises of why there has not

1. Joseph Ben-David, *American Higher Education: Directions Old and New* (New York, McGraw-Hill, 1972).

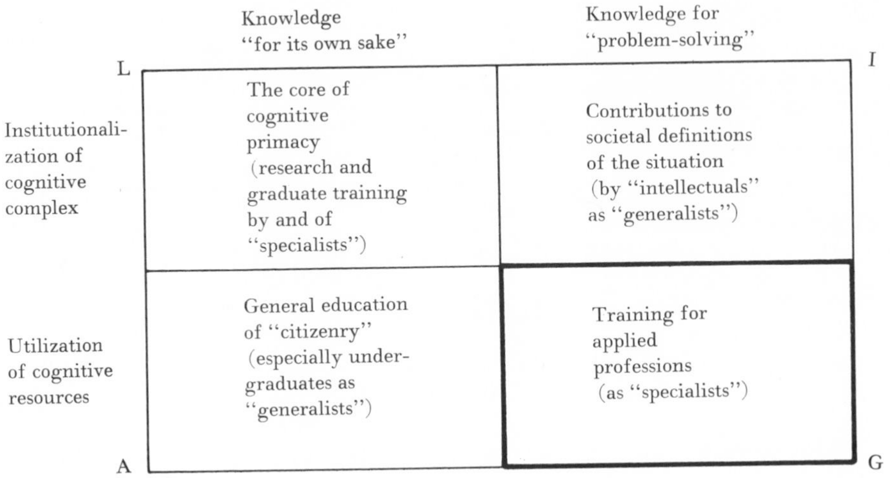

|  | Knowledge "for its own sake" | Knowledge for "problem-solving" |
|---|---|---|
| Institutionalization of cognitive complex | The core of cognitive primacy (research and graduate training by and of "specialists") | Contributions to societal definitions of the situation (by "intellectuals" as "generalists") |
| Utilization of cognitive resources | General education of "citizenry" (especially under-graduates as "generalists") | Training for applied professions (as "specialists") |

L ... I
A ... G

Figure 5.1. Institutionalization of Cognitive Rationality in the Structure of the University

*Note:* The heavily outlined subsystem is the substantive focus of this chapter. For a more formal analysis of this figure and its relation to other subsystems, see the appendix to Chapter 2.

emerged a process of organizational separation between the core sector of the university and the professional schools. This is a problem in some respects parallel to that of why the core functions of graduate training and research have not become organizationally separated from that of general education in the undergraduate college. A distinguished school of professional training with no university connections scarcely exists in the United States. The trend has been to hold that good professional training is to be found only in *university* professional schools, where the faculty of the professional school in question is treated as part of a general university faculty.[2]

The integration of professional training in the university is thus an empirical feature of the American system of higher education. Why it has worked out this way, instead of the development of a plurality of independent training schools, profession by profes-

2. The case of medical training is instructive. Rightly or wrongly the pendulum swung drastically from a quantitative center of gravity of medical education in proprietary medical schools without any university affiliations to the point where now only graduates of university—"Class A"—medical schools are eligible to take the "Board" examinations for a license to practice. This policy, interestingly, was put through by the American Medical Association, that symbol of arch-conservatism, spurred by the Flexner Report.

sion, is a background question that will underlie the whole discussion of the present chapter. That the American solution to this problem is not the only possible one is attested by the existence in the Soviet Union of professional schools, both in medicine and in law, wholly dissociated from the universities.

Thus there is an apparent paradox, namely, as the cognitive complex and its institutionalization in the university have become more highly differentiated *from* other institutional complexes, the university system has tended to draw into itself institutional complexes which earlier had been more loosely connected with it, such as professional training. Part of the explanation of the apparent paradox lies in the process of general upgrading of the cognitive complex itself. Medicine is a dramatic illustration. As late as most of the nineteenth century, the competence of the physician was based on clinical experience, not in the modern sense on applied science. A similar situation existed for engineering, where only elementary science was needed; nothing existed like the contemporary involvement of pure science in fields of practical technology.

Once it was recognized that universities were coming to be the main locus of the institutionalization of the sciences, the upgrading of professional practice demanded closer relations of the applied or clinical side to basic intellectual disciplines than had prevailed before. This also was a time when the contributions of the learned professions were beginning to permeate the life of the society as a whole to a greater degree than before.

The process of cognitive upgrading entailed not only a quantitative increase in available knowledge but also internal structural changes in knowledge.[3] As Daniel Bell has put it, the postindustrial society has become, as never before, dependent on *theoretical* knowledge, and the university has been the locus of its development.[4] The previous chapter stressed the importance for general education of the cultivation of intelligence and the use of intelligence in dealing with complex human relationships at affective levels. The center of gravity will probably move farther from command of specific bodies of knowledge, even of core significance, toward the development of capacity to use cognitive resources effectively in coping with an indefinite range of life problems; this

3. Talcott Parsons, "Professions," in *International Encyclopedia of the Social Sciences*, ed. David L. Sills (New York, The Macmillan Co., and The Free Press, 1968), XII, 536–547.

4. Daniel Bell, "The Post-Industrial Society: The Evolution of an Idea," *Survey*, 72, no. 2 (Spring 1971), 102–168.

means integrating the cognitive components with those focusing on other categories of interest.

In a sense, among the aspects of the cognitive complex, competence has a special significance for the applied professions. They are focused on the effective achievements of concrete practical goals where serious interests of their clients are often at stake. Professional competence in this sense is central to the clinical performance of the professional function. Increasingly, such competence has to be grounded in bodies of theoretical knowledge, just as the basic sciences underlie the practice of medicine. This circumstance complicates the structure of the professional world. Hence though more focally concerned with competence than other participants in the cognitive complex, the applied professional must articulate this both with theoretical knowledge and with the kind of higher-order competence that enables him to mobilize cognitive resources for the purposes at hand. It is not so much what you know initially but how competent you are in coming to know what you need to know and in going about informing yourself.

This change has been accompanied by a parallel process of upgrading of the intellectual levels required by the applied professions as illustrated by the emphasis on basic sciences in medical training and similar developments in other professional fields. This has been an uneven development, but it is part of the process of bringing the professional schools into closer relations to the universities, indeed into a kind of symbiosis. However, one of the reasons for their continuing differentiatedness, both from faculties of arts and sciences and from each other, is the fact that the axes of organization of knowledge in the intellectual disciplines do not correspond with the organization of competence in relation to practical goals—recall that the so-called science of medicine is not a discipline, but a mobilization of relevant knowledge from a number of disciplines. This differentiatedness between the intellectual-discipline level and an applied concern has been accentuated recently by both cultural and social changes.

This set of cross-relations contributes to instability in the definition of the fields of specialization in applied professional fields. The cultural developments to which we have referred tend to broaden the conception of relevance of cognitive fields. Thus in the earlier phases of its scientific development, medicine was thought of as the specific application of *biological* science to the exclusion of the *psychological* and *social* disciplines and to be subdivided by organ systems. More recently, psychological medicine has acquired professional respectability, and a sociologically oriented component is gaining ground. This sociological emphasis is not limited to the narrowly practical problems of the delivery of health care or to those of the supply of health-care personnel.[5]

This tendency for the conception of relevance to broaden is reinforced by the tendency for academic specialists and applied professionals to share the cognitive orientations of the educated citizenry and of intellectuals, both of which have a predilection to be generalists. As such, they are continually raising questions of whether the applied professionals define their roles and responsibilities too narrowly and, obversely, whether academic specialists define theirs too abstractly and hence irrelevantly. The interplay of these reference points throws light on the position of the cognitive complex in modern society.

We will proceed on the assumption that the specialized competence of the applied professional is oriented primarily to practical goals which are initially noncultural but are in general social, although there are both personal and organic references involved as well. We emphasize the social because of our special concern for the framework of social organization within which these functions are performed and which bears on the problem of rationality.

The effectiveness of professional performance is dependent on two sets of factors: (1) the availability and proper combination of the factors of effective goal-attainment, translated from the general action level to that of the society, and (2) the demand aspect —the suitability and acceptability of the output for the needs of the beneficiaries and clients and, on the other hand, the reciprocal outputs (including allocative priorities) which they can make available to the practitioner system.

Our concern is not with the whole of this complicated nexus, but with the genesis of *one* factor in professional effectiveness, namely, competence, seen in relation to other aspects of the larger nexus.

One contrast to be drawn among highly educated groups for modern society is on the axis of specialization vis-à-vis concern with generality. The academic and the applied professionals are by this criterion both specialists but on a different basis. For the academic, the basis lies in the structure of knowledge, which is

5. Cf. David Hamburg, ed., *Psychiatry as a Behavioral Science*, Behavioral and Social Sciences Survey Series (Englewood Cliffs, N.J., Prentice-Hall, Inc., 1970).

essentially a *cultural* focus. For the applied professional, it lies in the practical goal-structure which is in the first instance *social*, but also *personal*. This difference makes for different patterns of *cognitive significance*—as distinguished from validity—in the two cases. In short, the stress on generality characterizes the orientation both of the educated citizen and of the intellectual, in senses which will be discussed later in this chapter.

As we stressed in Chapter 3, for the academic the cognitive stress is on learning with cognitive primacy, even where the learning is not his own but that of students and others, such as lay audiences or readerships. His fiduciary responsibility is to the cognitive enterprise. For the applied professional, the fiduciary responsibility is to the utilization of cognitive resources for practical goals. Hence it focuses on the *contribution* of competence and intellectual integrity and on integrity in his trusteeship of the welfare of clients dependent on his services. A case in point is the traditional concern with the welfare of the patient as the paramount obligation of the physician. The responsibility for the utilization of knowledge thus implies, on the cognitive side, that *selection* within the available corpus of knowledge by criteria of *relevance* for the interests of clients must play a major part. The physician-in-training is not a general biological scientist, no matter how much biological science he must learn, nor is the law student a general student of society. This is not to say that interpenetration in cognitive content does not exist. Indeed the general process of the advancement of knowledge has probably increased the overlap rather than diminishing it—because of the element of generalization built into the structure of knowledge itself.

This in turn is related to the increasing stress on relatively generalized competence and the use of intelligence. Less and less are students in professional schools required to memorize vast bodies of information. They are increasingly oriented to the more general nature of the problems and of the cognitive resources available to deal with them.

Here a phenomenon emerges which has its counterpart in the academic sector but not so conspicuously. This is the seeking of help in dealing with a case from a specialist with a kind of competence which the referring practitioner does not adequately command. This phenomenon calls attention to a distinction between two levels of competence, namely, the operative competence needed to perform the practical task—for instance, a surgeon called in by an internist—and, second, the competence to judge the necessity for specialist help and the kind of help needed and to evaluate the quality of performance. This division of labor should not be identified with that operating within the system of cognitive disciplines. Its rationale still focuses primarily on the practical goals of the professional function—this is its basis of relevance.

Similar considerations apply in the field of research. The essential difference, however, in ideal type lies in the primacy of cognitive values in the research case and hence in the secondary role of the practical goals of the applied professions and of their corresponding fiduciary responsibilities.

The considerations just reviewed make clear that the cognitive structures of knowledge and of competence relevant to the applied professions, though articulating with the primary intellectual disciplines, are also different. The modes of social organization of the applied professions are also increasingly different from that of the core academic profession itself.

Another trend of professional education in the United States, in contrast to some other countries, has been bringing professional schools more closely within the structure of the university and, in a good many cases, establishing new professional schools within it. Further discussion of this trend can best be undertaken after a review of the structure of the professional world. There are typical differences between the applied professions and the academic, although the applied professions cover a range of variation among themselves. There has been little attempt to analyze this range of variation systematically.

The applied professions are simultaneously rooted in the structure of the culture and in the practical needs of the society and its members. There is not a direct match between them; the cultural organization of the intellectual disciplines is different from the cognitive bases of professional competence because the concrete needs served by the latter require mobilization of knowledge from a number of sources, as in the case of medicine. Another direction of mobilization of cognitve resources, that toward theology, philosophy, and ideology, should be distinguished from that for practical goals and will be discussed in Chapter 6.

It is essential to build this difference into our scheme for analyzing the institutionalized application of knowledge from intellectual disciplines to practical concerns; the applied professions reorganized knowledge in terms of relevance to the practical goals and interests which the profession serves. At this point knowledge, competence, and service meet in a clinical focus. On the knowledge side, such expressions as the "science of engineering," the "science of medicine," and perhaps the "discipline" of law are appropriate. None of these are intellectual disciplines in the sense in which physics, biology, psychology, or economics are. However, they are nonetheless rather highly rationalized and systematized. Still, there remains the problem of articulation with bodies of knowledge organized on another basis.[6]

### The Structure of the System of Applied Professions[7]

Two antecedents of the modern professions need to be distinguished from each other. One antecedent is the older, more traditional professions falling in the cluster of engineering, medicine, and law. These concern the more general levels of human practical interest and have been established for decades and perhaps centuries. The second antecedent is more recent and consists of social foci: administration, both public and private, welfare, social work, and education, especially at levels below higher education. In some respects, banking and accountancy are on the borderline of the professional complex.

The three types of applied professions in the primary cluster concern the practical management of man's relation to the physical environment, to himself as organic and psychological individual, and to the society in which he lives. In all three cases, the cognitive base of the relevant technologies has remained predominantly empirical. In the case of engineering, this interfered with the establishment of close connections with natural science in the universities. Thus when engineering schools developed in Germany (*Technische Hochschulen*) they were for a long time denied the privilege of granting doctoral degrees parallel to those of the universities in law and medicine. In the United States as well

6. This situation gives rise to two-way pressures. Thus in the social science area, political science has wavered between self-definition as a predominantly analytical science of political factors and as the "science of government" which would make it the cognitive underpinning of the profession of public administration, in turn raising questions about the relevance of economics, sociology, and psychology to public administration. Conversely, the concern with clinical problems of government can provide a stimulus to raising problems of interdisciplinary relations. The maintenance of balance between these two foci of attention is a problem facing the whole modern world of knowledge.

7. For a formal paradigm of the detailed structure of the applied professions, see Figure 2.10 of the appendix to Chapter 2 of this book.

as in Great Britain a number of separate technical schools were established. However, the more elite of them, such as M.I.T. and Cal. Tech., have tended to develop, first to high-level schools of natural science as well as engineering and then in the direction of more general universities, especially by expansion into the areas of the humanities and of social science.

*Engineering and Architecture.* In terms of the paradigm just set forth, engineering appears to be a simple case, but this may be questioned. Empirical technology grounded in the knowledge acquired by practical men has for long been intertwined with explicitly science-based technology, the more scientific component of which has resulted more from pure research than from urgent technological problem-solving, from inventions as distinguished from discoveries.

The clinical focus of engineering should be the solution of practical "how to" problems presented by clients, such as how to build a building with certain functional specifications, how to build a bridge, how to manufacture a given product efficiently, or how to land a man on the moon. These shade off into scientific problems. At the highest levels of new technological development, substantial numbers of scientists as distinguished, by professional identification, from engineers, have come to be involved in practical work. This does not, however, invalidate the basic distinction between the roles of scientist and engineer.[8]

By contrast with medicine and partly with law, the clients of engineering practice have been collectivities rather than individuals. Most engineering enterprises are relatively costly and involve interests wider than those of the particular individual, for example, a municipal government, a manufacturing enterprise, or, in some cases, such as military technology, national government. Nevertheless, orientation to the practical task, defined largely by the needs of the client, seems to be central to the functions of engineering in relation to the cognitive system, as in the case of the other applied professions. This is its clinical focus. It is one part of the demand for professional services.

On the practice side, the training process and the competence resulting from it must integrate relevant cognitive components with the social and psychological bases of the practical interests

8. Joseph Ben-David, *Fundamental Research and the Universities: Some Comments on International Differences* (Paris, Organization for Economic Cooperation and Development, 1968).

involved. For engineering, these center on the needs of human organisms in their relations to the physical environment, in the case of medicine on the psychosocial needs of the individual in relation to the integrity of the organism, and in the case of law on the needs of the social system—often as they impinge on individuals—with special reference to its normative order and the latter's cultural base.

The cognitive side needs to be articulated in the developing corpus of the intellectual disciplines, partly through the institutionalization of the cognitive resource base of the profession in basic sciences. Under the modern conditions that emerged within the present century, this is the basis for integrating training for the applied professions and research into problems bearing on them in the university system.

Genuine science-based technology is surprisingly recent, having developed on a large scale only in the present century. This has led to considerable numbers of scientists, not only engineers, playing technological roles in such fields as the uses of nuclear energy and in electronic communication. Indeed, a kind of marriage between these two social groups has been developing with respect to the new phase of the technological revolution; this marriage has become a storm center in the relations between the academic system and the rest of society. In spite of the intimacy of the connection, a structural differentiation has emerged between academic "pure" science and its engineering applications, between "development" as distinguished from the routine management of technological installations, even of the most sophisticated types, and "research" in the sense of developing the underlying knowledge of scientific principle which will be applied through technological processes.

Another profession, architecture, has historically been associated with engineering and may be included in the same complex with it. However, it shades over into the fine arts and certain aspects of the cultural realm other than the cognitive. It also has social connections, ranging from the design of monumental government buildings or churches to domestic architecture much of which comes close to the family consumption level. Architecture in recent times has also been associated with another profession, city planning, which relates to engineering somewhat as public health does to medicine. Again, city planning has verged into the social sciences just as architecture has verged into the fine arts, but it has also emphasized its relation to engineering and hence to the physical environmental base. Both of these cases underline the complexity of the larger world of the applied professions.

*Medicine.* For historical reasons, medical education was more closely involved with the universities than was engineering, especially in Continental Europe. This probably had to do with the humanistic concerns of the universities and with the fact that medicine dealt with the human individual and not with impersonal physical "nature." Indeed, medicine was historically a principal matrix of concern with the individual, first with his biological ills, but ramifying in various directions.

For decades the overwhelming focus was on clinical experience and, so far as knowledge was involved, with what could be gained from direct contact with and observation of sick people and the various vicissitudes through which they went. This began to change only with major developments in the biological sciences toward the end of the last century, such as those which had practical pay-off in ways of controlling infectious disease, as, say, in bacteriology.

Once this combination was established, a set of basic sciences came to prominence in the faculties of medical schools; their status competed with that of the clinical branches. Out of this has grown a complex of science laboratories, teaching facilities, and teaching hospitals. The latter also are permeated with research activities in widely varying relationship to the actual training of physicians. Thus, animal laboratories on the roofs of hospitals have become common. The relationship between animal laboratories and human medical care has proliferated in the field of the clinically scientific aspects of medicine. For example, with respect to the testing of new drugs and studying the rejection phenomena of transplanted organs, there has been continual intellectual traffic between animal study and experimentation on human patients. The former can tell much about most of these problems without endangering human lives, but the conditions are never exactly the same in human contexts, so that in the transfer from animal to human subjects there is always an element of uncertainty. At the same time, it has become standard doctrine that it is unprofessional to carry out new procedures without exploration of the problems at the animal level.

Medical science started with an overwhelming concentration at organic levels, but has gradually spread into psychological areas, building on older clinical traditions of psychiatry. Psychoanalysis, and other developments in the field of psychiatry and brain research, have introduced some basic science into this aspect of medicine, including some social as well as psychological considerations.[9]

American scientific medicine invested in expensive personnel, laboratory, and clinical facilities. This investment, plus the emphasis on science, partly accounts for the identification of medical education and research with the universities. This identification has had something to do with the hiatus between academic medicine and the rest of the profession, which contributed to the political vicissitudes of organized medicine.

More than engineering even, medicine has been the model of the science-based applied profession, partly because good health is a widely shared object of positive valuation in modern society. There is also positive valuation of engineering in terms of the desirability of control of the physical environment. For a variety of reasons, however, the previous good reputation of technology has become somewhat tarnished, not only because of the issue of pollution but also because technology is said to have created such dangers as those of nuclear warfare and, more generally, a prison for human life instead of its liberation from environmental constraints.

Perhaps similar doubts will develop in the case of medicine. Meanwhile both engineering and medicine—and related professions such as public health—have institutionalized a massive involvement of science with the practical concerns of the everyday world and have thereby forged a relationship of interdependence between the academic system and other parts of society. Some of the phenomena involved in this interdependence contribute to the current strain in the relations of academia to the rest of society; we will take this up in discussing the ideological problems of the academic system.

*Law.* The third major professional complex, law, has special functional importance for modern society and for the place of the academic system within it. The tradition of university faculties of law in Europe, having been established at nearly the same time as medicine, was transplanted into the American academic system. The expectation developed that quality legal education should be conducted in *university* law schools which were integrated into the university as a whole.

9. Hamburg, *Psychiatry as a Behavorial Science.*

Whereas engineering deals with the physical environment and medicine with the individual, law deals with the normative order of societies and thus focuses on social systems. Part of the legal system is concerned with rules that are declared to be binding through the coercive sanctions of government, but this is not the whole of it, either in the sense of normative rules or of social organization. The law of the state merges into customary law[10] and moral obligations.

Enforcement is primarily a political rather than a legal function; police forces and prisons apply the consequences of legal decisions—often imperfectly, but their main personnel are not lawyers. Thus with respect both to normative content and to social organization, the legal system is relatively autonomous vis-à-vis the government.

At the level of social organization two different components of the legal system overlap. The first is the courts, which in certain respects are governmental institutions; but the independent judiciary, the participation of the lay public through the jury system, and the much more extensive professional involvement of the legal profession prevent courts from being a mere branch of government. That judges are appointed or elected through governmental processes and that the decisions of courts are enforced by governmental agencies is balanced by these other factors, for instance, that judges are required to be professional lawyers de facto if not always constitutionally. At the same time lawyers have a governmental status through their membership in the bar; they are "officers of the court" to the bar of which they have been admitted.

This official status does not prevent the legal profession from being a private profession in the sense in which those of engineering and medicine are. The lawyer deals privately with private clients, though he may also accept employment in a governmental agency or in a private organization. This differentiation of the legal system from government has gone substantially farther in the Anglo-American world with its Common Law tradition than in Continental Europe, where most members of the higher civil service have been, by the definitions of their jobs, professional lawyers. Except for specialized legal officers in governmental agencies,

10. Lon L. Fuller, "Human Interaction and the Law," *The American Journal of Jurisprudence*, 1 (1969), 1–36.

there is no presumptive expectation in Great Britain or in the United States that civil servants will be legally trained.

One of the criteria in terms of which law is a profession is its intellectual content. There are not only laws but something which can be called "the law" in which a good lawyer must achieve a modicum of cognitive mastery. As cognitive content, "the law" with its related methods of analysis may be compared to the "science of medicine." Although not an intellectual discipline in the sense of the basic sciences or the specific humanities, but rather an eclectic mobilization of knowledge relative to legal processes and thus predominantly empirical, the law is not without structured conceptualization on highly general levels.

Indeed, the role of clinical experience in the definition of the situation for medicine is parallel to that of experience of the judicial process for the law. An even better parallel exists between the role of the hospital in medicine and of the courts in law; each functions as the public sector of the profession. There is also a large, indeed quantitatively predominant, sector of legal practice outside the courts. The role of the lawyer as counsellor to individual or corporate clients is traditionally and in some respects legally protected by privacy. Much of it does not even involve issues which could be litigated and where it does involve such issues they are not usually brought to court, either because lawyers' advice is to the effect that the client "does not have a case" or because they are settled out of court.

The parallel holds up in another respect. With the development of scientific medicine, the hospital, especially the teaching and research hospital, has come to be the frontier of medical knowledge and of the technology of its successful application. Its public character focuses, however, on the knowledge and technology side; it may be thought of as an extension of Merton's conception of the "communality of science."[11] Thus the more scientific that medicine becomes, the greater the pressures toward a form of social organization which facilitates professional-level communication, both of information and of evaluation. For this facilitation to grow, the relevant communications must circulate within a community which comprises scientists, clinical practitioners both inside the hospital setting and outside, and those in course of training to be

---

11. Robert K. Merton, "Science and Democratic Social Structure," in *Social Theory and Social Structure* (Glencoe, Ill., The Free Press, 1957), chap. xvi, pp. 550–561.

practitioners and teachers but also scientists with medical "know-how."

This setting creates a problem involving the position of patients who can no longer be treated only as objects whose return to a satisfactory state of health is the predominant consideration in their relations to physicians. However, if the operation in the system is in any sense clinical, patients are an indispensable component of the social system of medical innovation and education as well as routine practice. These circumstances contribute to the salience recently, especially in connection with medical research, of the theme of the protection of privacy.[12] The patient in this situation is no longer a participant solely by virtue of his own health needs but is under pressure to participate in multiple roles: the traditional role of patient cooperation in facilitating his own recovery and also that of a case to be demonstrated for teaching purposes and of research subject. This differentiation of patient roles should match that of the medical team producing a more complex but more productive system from the point of view of the system's contribution to the health of the larger community, not only of particular patients.[13]

To complete this digression into the medical complex, a special relation exists between the increased complexity of the patient role and the affective aspects of the physician-patient relationship. It is an oversimplification, but not wholly inaccurate, to describe the two components in the traditional, undifferentiated doctor-patient relationship as the patient's affective needs involving his reactions to disability, suffering, anxiety, and their alleviation, matched on the physician's side by compassion, that is, concern, for the welfare of a human being in trouble and needing emotional support. The patient needs competent help which compassion alone cannot provide, for instance, certain acute pains could be diagnosed as indicating an infected appendix in danger of bursting and the only effective remedy lies in competent surgery. The competence of the surgeon obviously cannot be reduced to the level of his compassion for the sufferings of patients without regard to cognitive and technological operative components.

In the simpler tradition of medical practice, the primary institu-

---

12. *Ethical Aspects of Experimentation with Human Subjects, Daedalus* (Spring 1969), including an article by Talcott Parsons, "Research with Human Subjects and the 'Professional Complex,'" pp. 325–360.

13. Renée C. Fox, *Experiment Perilous: Physicians and Patients Facing the Unknown* (Glencoe, Ill., The Free Press, 1959).

tional problem of medicine was to integrate the affective and the cognitive-technological components of the physician-patient relationship as a social system. In the new, more highly differentiated situation just sketched, the greater complexity necessitates greater extensity of the relevance of scientific considerations beyond the health problems of particular patients and higher levels of generality of the principles from which specific therapeutic orientations are derived.

The cognitive-instrumental aspects of these developments seem clear. There has been immense advancement in knowledge of the functioning of the human organism and in the borderline of its relations to the personality of the individual. This in turn has involved advances in many branches of the technology of medical care of which hormone therapy and organ transplants are examples. The question is whether and, if so, how such differentiations on the instrumental side of the therapeutic relationship can be matched by complementary differentiation in the affective sphere.

It is our view that there is such a match. Medical practice is focused on the personality of the individual, and this defines the consumption market for medical services. Capacity to manage health problems, however, requires factor inputs which, on the affective side, are not confined to the concern of the physician for the plight and prospects of his particular patient, but must be generalized to include concern for the welfare of all patients.

The first order of concern is limited by the fact that any given physician can treat only a limited number of patients in a given time period, and he cannot cathect in this individual sense the myriads of sick people who are not *his* patients. However, he can have affective orientations on a general level. The generalization of such orientations will occur laterally to include concern for all sick people and, more broadly, for the disabled, the suffering, and the anxious. But it will also include concern for the continuation of availability of good medical care and for the future of the health-care complex.

The commitments of medical teachers are in considerable measure motivated in this way; their students will carry on the function of caring for a population of unspecified sick persons in the future, much of it after the teacher can no longer practice. Such care may improve, not only through the training of new cohorts of students but through research which will give future physicians tools their predecessors did not have. In short, an affective involvement in the plight of sick people generally is as much a feature of commitment to medical teaching and research as it is to the care of particular individual patients. In the case of research, however, and to a lesser degree in that of teaching, this concern is combined with more purely cognitive interests, so that many medical researchers working on predominantly scientific problems may care about patients only in preconscious or unconscious layers of their personalities; they do not often face the distressing aspects of the plight of the individual.

On the side of patients also there is a parallel process of involvement with more generalized levels of affect than that involved in the plight of a particular patient. Patients do not usually object to being used as cases for teaching purposes, and indeed patients can become intensively involved in wanting to help members of research teams with work which cannot benefit them as individuals.[14] This is a process of affective engagement. The most general statement is that all participants in the health-care complex, in varying ways and degrees according to their roles, participate in both the cognitive-technical and the affective aspects of the functioning of the social systems of health care. In the present century, these systems have come to be further differentiated with respect to the role structure on both sides than was the case with the earlier traditional doctor-patient relationship.

In theoretical terms, the transition from the older doctor-patient relationship to the more recent orientation of the medical complex has been accompanied and in part made possible by a process of generalization of the symbolic medium of affect, in some ways analogous to the process discussed in the last chapter. As involved with the personality of an actor, affect not only motivates cathexis and identification with particular sick people but becomes a medium capable of extending the relevant attitudes to contexts where the mobilization of motivational and cultural (moral) resources and their allocation in contingencies that may arise become possible. To be affectively concerned then is not limited to the relatively particularistic contexts of traditional medical practice.

Let us now return to the legal complex. It is essentially similar to the medical case despite two differences. The first is that affective engagement with the "existential" plight of clients does not have the same order of salience for lawyers as it does for physicians;

14. Fox, *Experiment Perilous*.

concern for clients' relation to the normative order of the society in most cases takes precedence. The second difference is that, with respect to differentiation of the social system of professional service, the legal case has not advanced as far as the medical; legal research and hence the involvement of both professionals and clients in it has not advanced relatively as far.

Just as illness may be conceived as a disturbance in the normal state of health of the individual, the legal problems of clients may be considered to indicate disturbances in the relations of the units involved, which are not only individuals but include collectivities, to that aspect of the normative order defined as "legal," one which is oriented to the public forum of the courts, though only a minority of actual transactions enter that forum. The practice of law, including the process of adjudication itself, has functions analogous to the therapeutic in the medical field, namely, that restoration of integrative balances, of which one aspect is the settlement of disputes—or the working out of a course of action which will minimize the possibility of disputes—but on terms which can be sanctioned as legitimate by the authoritative legal agencies.

Like all therapy-type processes, this is one of the adjustments to an environment the principal features of which are given but which at the same time presents contingencies of unpredictable variation. From the point of view of the units exposed to situations of disturbance, the relevant environment is the social environment (the *milieu social*), as this concept was used by Durkheim, especially in his early work.[15] But as Durkheim came to demonstrate in some of his later writings, a property of this environment is the combination of its normative status—a set of norms or rules empirically given for the guidance of conduct—and the *moral authority* by which such norms are legitimized. Thus the legal system functions not only to settle disputes and to forestall potential disputes but to assert and reinforce the moral authority of the system of norms itself in the requisite situations of detailed relevance. Merely asserting the moral grandeur of the Constitution does not accomplish this; it is necessary to specify what particular constitutional rights mean in concrete action situations and to mobilize realistic support for them.

As Durkheim insisted, the milieu social is the structure of the

15. Emile Durkheim, *The Division of Labor in Society*, trans. George Simpson (New York, The Free Press, 1969). Originally, in English, New York, The Macmillan Co., 1933.

society as seen by its participating member units. This structure is not statically given, though it is given for any particular unit in a particular situation. The givenness is, however, relative, and two modes of departure from it should be distinguished. One consists in fluctuations ubiquitous in all environments in their relations to more stable systems. The other is innovative (or degenerative) change.

Interpretation of the nature of these changes depends, as does the view of the legal focus expressed here, on recognition that the system reference is the general action system, so that the society can be seen to constitute an environment for personalities contained within it. The source of the moral authority of institutionalized order lies in the cultural system, that is, values at the cultural level, which transcends the values of the society. There is always, in advanced systems of law, a trans-social reference to some philosophical or religious basis of the moral authority of law and hence of justice. In the background of modern societies, this has been conspicuous in various conceptions of Natural Law. In the American legal system, it is embodied in the Preamble to the Constitution, in the Bill of Rights, and in the two underlying conceptions of "equal protection of the laws" and "due process of law."[16]

The milieu social consists not only of a normative structure but also of a fluctuating relational system perceived by the participating units. These fluctuations are caused by varying combinations of the determinants of social processes including the physical environment, the biological exigencies of life, and human psychological reactions, but among the most important determinants are economic and political vicissitudes.

From this point of view, the legal system is a mechanism of adjustment which irons out the conflicts and maladjustments resulting from these fluctuations. As such, it employs a generalized code and a set of rules of procedure for its use to help "define the situation" for the actions of the units involved from the double point of view of attempting to integrate the unit interests and those of the collective system in which the law obtains, often at the cost of imposing frustrations and penalties on losers in processes of litigation.

16. An analysis of this aspect of the status of law, which takes this point of view, has been worked out in a seminar paper by James Koch, "The Progress of Law and Legal Education in America," unpub. MS, Harvard University.

In the light of these considerations, the primary function of the legal system is to define the situation, both for units which are actual or potential litigants and for the larger social system. Enforcement of norms and decisions is primarily a political rather than a legal function. The successful definition of the situation, however, requires not only making known what is expected of social units but acceptance by those involved of the justice of the rulings which impinge upon them—a principal aspect of the problem of social integration. The salience of this problem is accentuated for Anglo-American law by the adversary system whereby, when it comes to actual litigation, one party must lose—a consequence parallel to electoral victories in majoritarian political democracy. This problem of acceptance revolves around an affective component, but one which should be treated, unlike the medical case, as secondary to that of defining the situation with moral authority.

Any society, any milieu social, is a system of human action; hence the fluctuations of which we have been speaking are man-made. The same is true of the legal order itself. As man-made, it is subject to change by processes of human action. Focusing at the social system level, we may speak of four processes by which this takes place. Perhaps the most problematical is that of legislation, the others being administrative rulings, judicial decision, and the development of customary law.

In traditional societies, including those in our own background, legislation has been minimal. However, with the changes brought about in the course of the democratic revolution, it became ideologically tempting to treat legislation as the sole legitimate source of legal order. A classic formulation of this was the Austinian formula that "law is the will of the sovereign" on the assumption that the people constitute the sovereign in the sense of Rousseau's General Will.

In an analytical sense, this view politicizes the conception of law, merging it with collectively legitimate policy decisions, a view not identified solely with representative democracy but also central to early Communist theory.[17] Administrative rulings become completely subordinated as mere applications, while judicial decision is eliminated altogether—if it occurs as more than

17. Harold Berman, *Justice in the U.S.S.R.: An Interpretation of Soviet Law*, rev. ed. (Cambridge, Mass., Harvard University Press, 1963).

application, it is a usurpation of legislative authority—and customary law is relegated to its premodern status.

For the American case, a basis exists for asserting a different view in the existence of a written Constitution providing for the separation of powers and a federal structure; these enable the courts to acquire a position essentially independent both of legislatures and of executive branches. When independence was combined with the adoption on a large scale of English Common Law, which functioned through the courts, a legal system was established which, from some points of view, is undemocratic.

The legal processes focusing on the judicial system mediate between the law-making activities of the other two branches of government and the requirements of federalism; this guidance occurs under an intentionally generalized Constitution. As Lon Fuller has recently made clear, however, the grounds of judicial decision also extend to customary levels, not so much set usage in the community as waves of informal sentiment in the community not fully articulated in formal governmental action.[18]

Parallels to the other two applied professional complexes, especially in terms of the bases for their increasingly close affiliation with the universities, can be found in the judicial system; for example, the processes of *generalization* of the definition of the situation for social action parallels the development of the scientific base for engineering and medicine. In these terms, law is not simply the will of the sovereign, whether the sovereign be interpreted as a legislature or an executive (president or Communist party). Neither can the legal system be considered simply an expression of a *Volksgeist* through the channel of customary law. What is *distinctive* about the legal system is its rationalization of the societal normative system through the combined agencies of the judicial process, of the thinking and writing of members of the legal profession independent of the holding of judicial office, and of university-trained professionals in the law schools.

University lawyers often are, like their medical colleagues in the clinical fields, also practitioners. However, by the nature of their university status they are *teachers* of law, and their teaching role implies generalization of the base of cognitive competence and

18. Thus, some of the directions taken by the Warren Court were in advance of formal governmental action and reflected an egalitarian trend of sentiment in such fields as civil rights, the organization of legislative representation, and the rights of defendants in criminal cases. See Fuller, "Human Interaction and the Law" (n. 10 above).

of affective acceptance of law from more immediate interests of particular clients. Although this generalization process is currently less advanced than in the medical case, law professors are increasingly coming to be researchers in the field of law, a process involving a developing liaison with social science disciplines, a parallel to but later in development than that of the reliance of medicine on the basic sciences.

This process of rationalization is presently largely on the equivalent of the clinical level. An impetus to it derives from the tradition of the appellate courts to require opinions as well as decisions from their judges; these opinions not only set forth facts and considerations of law but *justify* the way in which the particular case was decided. In courts with more than one judge, there is the tradition of dissenting opinions if there is a divided court. This clinical literature of judicial opinions is articulated with unofficial discussion within the profession, centering in its academic branch in journals (Law Reviews) published by the university law schools. This cognitively oriented literature is beginning to articulate with relevant parts of the social science disciplines. Thus, the general direction is parallel to that in the other two professional complexes: to underpin the grounds for particular decisions and classes of them with more generalized and systematized bodies of legal principle.

### The Newer Professions:
### One Step Further Removed from the Cognitive Complex

A cluster of new professions has become prominent in the last generation.

*Primary and Secondary Education.* Perhaps primary and secondary education has been a special case that became prematurely professionalized in the early part of the present century. Part of the problems of education as a profession reflects the fact that, unlike the academic profession, primary and secondary education did not concentrate on cognitive content with its special relation to the research function but rather on pedagogy, the processes of transmitting knowledge at elementary levels, accompanied by some concern for aspects of socialization. Socialization, because of the public character of the educational system, tended to be colored by considerations of nationality and patriotism, though the progressive school movement introduced other emphases.

A serious source of difficulty for the older profession of education was the relative weakness of a cognitive base for professional competence in respects other than the rather elementary subject matter taught. This helps explain the slowness of universities in establishing professional faculties of education—Teachers' College at Columbia remained unique for a long time and had difficulties in gaining academic recognition as the equal of other professional faculties. This gap is being closed, facilitated by developments in psychology and the social sciences, but it is a slow process.

*Social Work.* A second cluster of the professions has been called the welfare cluster; among these social work has been the most important occupationally. Even more than teaching, social work has been linked to the "softer" areas of human concern; and, like teaching, it has lacked the cognitive base in physical and biological science which rescued medicine from identification with mere do-goodism. Even more than education, social work has been caught up in complicated areas of controversial public policy and has not benefited from the same order of value-consensus which has underlain medicine and law.

Social work has shared with education the problematic character of its cognitive base. The clinical scope of social work has not been as clearly focused as has the scope of medicine or law. Prevalent conceptions of case work and group work attempt to define such a scope. Social work clients lack a clear conception of the extent to which their problems are their own fault, comparable to the conception of illness as a state the sick person himself cannot control, or to the legal conception of the individual's "responsibility" for his acts and their consequences. On the professional side, social workers are uneasy because of the precariousness of their cognitive basis of competence and because they are uncertain whether applying knowledge and professional competence, along with concern, is the appropriate way of dealing with the problems of people who, at the level of their personal and family lives, have troubles that cannot be diagnosed as either medical or legal.

Another complicating factor, which allies social work with law more than with medicine, is the difficulty of drawing the line between the problems that should be handled at the level of the particular case and those that can more appropriately be handled by collective measures. This circumstance puts social work in politics to a far greater degree than engineering or medicine, as far as the actual operations of the profession are concerned.

These circumstances contribute to social work's difficulties in establishing its status as a profession. Many of these difficulties have little direct connection to the system of higher education, but some do. The American academic system seeks to discover the limits of its capacity to make contributions to the welfare needs of the society, as in other professional areas, not primarily through the university itself taking corporate responsibility for community welfare, but through producing and channeling cognitive resources which can be utilized in professional functioning in this area.

*Administration.* The third professional complex of the second tier is administration, both public and private. Administration brings the analysis of predominantly executive functions, previously relegated largely to entrepreneurial genius, into a more rationalized framework in which formal training in relevant cognitive fields and the mobilization of the resources of such fields can be applied to organizational management. This movement has enjoyed conspicuous success in the field of business administration and moderate success in the public field. The principal difference seems to lie in public administration's greater exposure to the sensitivities and vicissitudes of politics.

There are two other fields of applied knowledge, accounting and banking, which fit into the roster of the professions. Accounting has been formally professionalized but has failed to assume an independent professional focus in the universities. Probably this is because of the narrow specificity of its clinical focus, which does not give much scope for cognitive generalization. Banking, on the other hand, played an important role in the processes of development of the economy, but did not become highly rationalized. The field of banking may be rationalized through the involvement in it of certain classes of economists and systems theorists in ways that shade into the wider field of administration.

The business executive's nonadministrative responsibility is oriented to the efficiency of his firm as measured by financial balances. The public administrator is oriented to the delicate balances between the effectiveness of the organization and the interests of the constituencies to which it is accountable. The former is the least sentimental focus of accountability, except perhaps for cases where survival through political power is at stake. Both kinds of administration are relatively insulated from the social-ethical complications that plague the welfare complex, perhaps because administration as a professional complex overlaps the big-power subsystem of the society in a sense in which the other two professions do only indirectly.

On the cognitive side, administration has the advantage of a well-focused clinical concern, namely, the effectiveness of the organization in which the executive assumes responsibility. In this area considerable codification of relevant knowledge has occurred, especially in accounting, such as elaborate cost-benefit analysis and developments in general science as cybernetics and the theory of games. Back of these resources lie the resources of economics and of some branches of political science, psychology, and sociology.

These three newer professional complexes have in common that they are organized mainly around their clinical task. The field of administration seems the most successful, in part because of the definiteness of this focus, but also because of the availability of more satisfactory techniques of measurement than the others and because it articulates with the big-power structure of the society in relatively uncontroversial ways.

Although a science of administration is more closely approximated than a science of education or a science of social welfare, there has been scientific progress in all three fields. Their articulation with a cluster of basic sciences at the general intellectual discipline level is, however, less advanced than in the fields of engineering or medicine, although not so far behind law. However, development of a clinical-science complex and the beginnings of a basic-science complex in all three fields testify to the mutual advantages to these fields and to the universities of integration into the university system, predominantly in the form of establishing professional faculties within the university. Involvement with the universities can be expected to accelerate the process of rationalization of the cognitive resources available to these professions and to contribute to the attainment of higher levels of cognitive generality (especially through articulation with the relevant basic sciences).

### Clinical Priorities of Applied Professions:
### Some Latent Functions

This general action cluster of the applied professions emphasizes in the *first* instance the clinical focus of their functioning. In the clinical area the *demand* for professional services is most evident.

The demand for trained and competent services is analogous to the demand for knowledge in the academic professional's relation to the market of ideas.

The utilization of knowledge and competence institutionalized in the applied professions could scarcely have developed as it has without utility to clients' interests, thought of in a pragmatic sense. In all three cases, however, at least two layers of contextual elements define latent functions of the professional groups in question. These concern functions in system-references at higher orders than are the manifest functions.

To begin with the case of medicine, the manifest function of medical practice, the treatment of illness, focuses on the individual, both as organism and as personality, whereas the first-order latent function focuses at the social-system level and concerns the conception that the sick role is a social category within which some forms of social deviance find expression and may be partially legitimized. Sickness can secure for the ill individual certain elements of permissiveness and support. These indulgences depend on self-definition as sick and the acceptance of therapeutic help. In these self-definitions are included mechanisms of social control by which the motivations of what has been socially defined as deviant behavior can be undercut, and social control reasserted in recovery from illness. If this is correct, then the functions of medical practice are not confined to helping individual persons who are in distress, but also include services to various social system needs involving the protection of social order through the control of certain kinds of deviance. There is, of course, a fine line between control of deviance and repression of what may be desirable motivations toward social change. Both aspects are empirically important, but it is difficult to draw the lines, and the lines themselves are likely to shift with various changes in circumstance.[19]

The legal profession involves the analogous syndrome. In the first instance, legal practice has been oriented to helping to cope with the legal problems of clients; consequently the attorney has been concerned with protection and furtherance of the client's interests. The structure of the profession and in particular the

19. A telling example of this function concerns the family as a social system. From the point of view of its functioning, the therapy of one of its members—not only psychotherapy but often somatic cases—may help the family to maintain its integrity as a family. John Spiegel, *Transactions: The Interplay between Individual, Family, and Society* (New York, Science House, 1971), pt. 3, pp. 143–312.

lawyer's quasi-official status as an officer of the court, a public institution, mean that the handling of the client's interests must be brought into juxtaposition with conceptions of the public interest.

Physicians and lawyers have in common that they represent particular clients and hence the interests of their clients. But in the medical case the patient, by entrusting his interests to a physician, defines it as belonging in the realm of socially relevant health problems and is hence required to accept the institutionalized procedures for dealing with such problems. Similarly the client of a lawyer, faced with difficulty which involves potential conflict with others, might conceivably fight it out with his adversary. In going to a lawyer, however he implicitly accepts the jurisdiction of law through the courts and if the matter goes to court will allow his interests to be represented by his attorney who is bound not only by fidelity to his client's interests but also by his commitment to the public interest through law. From this point of view, which emphasizes the *duality* of the focus of these two professional groups, the individual patient's or client's interests is transcended by a social interest in the outcome of the professional handling of "cases."

Is there an equivalent of this social responsibility of physicians and lawyers for engineers? The clients of engineering services are concerned with the efficient achievement of specific practical goals. The engineer, however, is a professional whose competence is grounded in applied science. In this context, he has the interests of his clients to consider but also his integrity as a professional practitioner; one aspect of this integrity is the assumption of fiduciary responsibility *not only* for giving his client what he ostensibly wants but also for the possible side effects of the various alternatives. It is difficult to evade the problems of the social consequences of engineering procedures, as is illustrated by the problem of pollution.

Thus, social responsibility is implicit in the clinical role of the engineer because the practical problem with which he is called upon to cope is always part of the larger complex of the utilization of physical science in the interest of human adjustment to and control of the environment. Similar continuities apply to the physician's treatment of particular illnesses shading into considerations of the place of medicine and the health complex in the functional equilibrium of the social system. For the lawyer, the relationship is even more direct because of the explicit duality of his role.

The ramifications of context and latent function extend farther. Though at the first contextual-latent level, the main focus is on social-system function, at the second a spreading out occurs in terms of the respective places of the clinical functions in the general action system. Engineering and law stand at the extremes with medicine in the middle.

Engineering, as it has matured, has become the paramount field of applied science and that part of science most concerned with the *instrumental* significance of knowledge for human interests. The first contextual layer concerns the fact that no one discrete instrumental use of physical science can be isolated from a wider context in terms of societal interest—the case of the social consequences of the harnessing of nuclear energy for weapons is a classical one.

Beyond this, however, is the cosmological significance of physical science. Starting with Galileo's invention of the telescope, the instrumentation of research into the physical universe has been intertwined with engineering contributions; scientists have increasingly come to be among the major clients of the engineering profession. This is conspicuous in the nuclear energy field and spectacularly so in the technology of the exploration of space and in the field of information processing through computers; the two fields overlap substantially.

In such contexts the scientist and the engineer become partners in developing and scientifically verifying new and more sophisticated understandings not only of man's immediate physical environment but of the physical universe in which it is placed. A long road has been traversed from the geocentric views of Ptolemaic astronomy, via Copernicus, Newton, and Einstein to the views of the macrouniverse opened up by developments in radio-astronomy and subatomic physics. These new understandings have implications for the *meaning* of human existence on one small planet. In all of these developments, science and engineering technology act as partners. Despite a current wave of skepticism as to whether trips to the moon are worthwhile compared to other uses of resources, the fascination with what can be found out by space exploration has become so deep-seated that concerns for more immediate social welfare are unlikely to lead to its radical suppression. In an interesting way, the cultural impact of this cosmological concern is likely to prove a long-run reinforcement of the position of the university because its effective pursuit is dependent on competent *scientific* as well as *engineering* performance.[20]

The case of law is at the other end of this spectrum. The retardation in the development of its articulation with the intellectual disciplines (compared with the articulation of medicine with *its* basic sciences) has been due to a kind of cross-pressure; this interest has been crowded out between the clinical functions of law and its second-order latent function.

Not only is the profession of law responsive to the public interest, it is concerned also with the legitimacy of normative order in society. Legitimacy in this sense can never be fully grounded at societal levels alone. It must reach into cultural levels, in the first instance the moral-evaluative complex, but also more generally. Eventually this ramifies to the level of religion, but in modern societies there are delicate issues here because of the separation of church and state.

This latent function of the law in the United States becomes salient when great Constitutional issues are involved, as in the freedoms guaranteed by the first amendment, which require a great deal of interpretation. Such men as Justices Holmes, Brandeis, and Cardozo and Chief Justice Warren are just as integral to the American legal profession as are the stereotypical corporation lawyers, or the legal defenders of the political dissidents of our time. Constitutional law has become the structural focus of the legitimation problem; the formulae through which it is handled shift from what the Constitution authorizes or forbids to what is the morally *good* normative order for a society.

The status of medicine involves problems of social responsibility other than problems of deviance and social control. In some quarters medicine and public health are held responsible for negative natural selection and the population explosion and are condemned in these terms. Another type of responsibility concerns the decisions as to who is to benefit from scarce and expensive resources, such as access to kidney dialysis.

Back of these problems lies a series focusing on problems of meaning in Weber's sense as they concern the fate of the human

20. This upgrading of the immediately pragmatic concerns of the engineering profession, first to the level of concern for new social responsibilities and then to that of participation in cosmological concerns, has facilitated the development of certain engineering schools first to include graduate faculties of science and then, with the inclusion of the social sciences and humanities, into general universities. M.I.T. is the premier American example, but there are several others, such as California Institute of Technology, Carnegie-Mellon, and Case-Western Reserve.

individual. Illness is only one of the ways in which the problems of the meaning of human experience become salient, and the medical profession is not the only profession having to work in situations where this is so, but in modern times its role has become conspicuous.

The use of advanced knowledge and technology to intervene in what otherwise might be the natural course of events has become salient at both ends of the life cycle. Contraception and abortion raise the questions of moral rights to decide whether human lives will or will not come into existence, and the principal implementers of preventive techniques are medical. For a long time, the postponement of death has been a medical obligation, but with recent developments it is becoming more problematical. Intermediate medical functions involve similar problems. Disability and suffering are the most significant foci, variant as are these categories.

In serious cases, the physician is confronted with the problem of coming to terms with the ultimate problems of the human condition. Indeed his perspective is especially poignant because he often deals with the deleterious impact on individuals of irrational forces for which neither he nor the victim could reasonably be held responsible. On one level his function is to contribute to making the chances of the individual life more reasonable than they would otherwise be.

All three of these applied professions have a common pattern of dual relation to the cognitive complex in general and the academic profession in particular. In their clinical capacities, they are users of cognitive outputs, a function which necessitates substantial reorganization both of knowledge and of competence in order to fit the needs of their clients. At the same time, they bring to focus, from their respective angles, salient problems of the *meaning* of knowledge and competence for the human condition. This occurs first at the level of the relation of client interests to those of the wider society, but it extends to the level of consideration of the place of their clinical functions (and of the knowledge and competence their effective performance requires) for trends of development of the human condition generally.

In this latter respect, the applied professions are sources of pressure to broaden specialized cognitive interests in the direction of integrating such cognitive concerns into the more general scheme of human orientation. An ivory-tower organization of the intellectual disciplines would be more insulated from such pressures. This path of transition is from the articulation of the cognitive complex with the applied professions to that with the role of the intellectuals.

The structure for the three clusters of applied professions applies in principle to the second tier, to education, welfare, and administration, as these are embedded in the structure of society and responsible for functions on its behalf. However, they are less immediately concerned with extrasocietal problems, that is, with the physical environment via the organism, with the individual personality, and, in the case of law, with the normative order of the whole society. Hence they probably are more involved in the dialectical relation between client-interest and the public interest, although in all three cases they also address more general-order concerns.

Both public and private administration impinge on the legitimacy of the goals of their client organizations as well as of the methods chosen to pursue them. Thus many of the problems of bureaucracy versus community participation are being fought out at levels which transcend that of efficient administration. The welfare field is particularly sensitive to charges of bureaucratic insensitivity, especially in our egalitarian climate of opinion. The issue of justice for the poor thus merges with the issue central to law, the legitimacy of the normative order. The case of education is interesting; the line between higher education and primary and secondary education results from the special involvement of higher education with the cognitive complex and particularly the intellectual disciplines. Though in certain respects intrinsically continuous, there has developed an especially clear line—some would say an arbitrary one.[21] All three of these professional

21. Many different ramifications of these problems could be explored. Our conception of the primacy of the three applied professions implies that they enjoy a higher level of prestige than those in the second tier. In the second tier, the cases of administration should be distinguished from welfare and education. Administration concerns an instrumental role relative to clients, although these clients may have high centrality (in Shils's sense) in the social structure. See Edward A. Shils, "Centre and Periphery," in *The Logic of Personal Knowledge: Essays Presented to Michael Polanyi* (London, Routledge and Kegan Paul, 1961), pp. 117–131. Contrast administrative clients with welfare clients who by definition have low centrality. Professional intervention on their behalf has stigmatized them as dependents. On quite a different level, the earlier phases of education involve not people directly implementing the main societal goals and values but those in a state of preparation, which also connotes dependency. In the light of the current rallying of movements for change about groups symbolically defined as disadvantaged and dependent, it may be significant that the professions concerned with the poor, the young and their teachers, and women tend to be in this

groups are necessarily involved in the kinds of strains in society and reactions to them that raise questions transcending that of how well they are contributing to the welfare of their particular clients, defined in terms of the clients' demands. In the case of administration as a profession this leads into the controversies over the "establishment" and the legitimacy of its position, in the case of education into a mixture of considerations, and in the case of welfare into tensions over social justice.

A source of difficulty in previous attempts to cope with the problem of the coherent classification of the professions was a failure to realize that the two main groups of professions reviewed here lay on different levels of function for human action. The first group, the academic profession itself and the cluster of engineering, medicine, and law, are anchored at the *general* level of action; they are custodians of the society's central cognitive resources, their utilization in relation to the physical environment, the needs of the individual, and the normative order of society.

The second group, consisting of education, social welfare, administration, and (on the periphery) accounting-banking, concern functions *within* the social system. This distinction implies that the first group of professions have more to do with the role of cognitive resources in determining the preconditions and setting of life in the society, the latter more with operative problems *within* that setting. Their scope of reference is more limited, as are their points of leverage for change.

### Applied Professional Patterns of Organization and Articulation with the Cognitive Complex

There is, however, a basic pattern of organization common to all the applied professions. Their paramount feature is the orientation of each to a clinical focus. The level of rationalization of the knowledge and competence which can be applied in each field is a matter of the development of bodies of knowledge comparable to the science of medicine. There are points beyond which increasing the level of this rationalization, through bringing more advanced knowledge to bear, involves articulation with the basic-science

second tier. Is the disproportionate involvement of women in the professions of social work and primary and secondary education related to the difficulty of these professions in achieving prestige-equality with the primary tier of professions? A combination of factors appears to define both the clients and the practitioners of these professional groups as relatively deprived.

disciplines that root organizationally in faculties of arts and sciences and in the intellectual disciplines which have their home there. The clinical focus of the pure academics in arts and sciences lies in the main recipients of their services: graduate and liberal arts students and the consumers of research outputs.

This pressure toward utilization of more advanced knowledge and competence makes for the involvement of the applied professions with the university. This is a two-level articulation. The cognitively lower level is the clinical science. The development of a clinical orientation among teachers of future professional practitioners is facilitated by the fact that they teach in university professional schools and are thereby stimulated to live up to university standards of cognitive rationality. The second level of articulation involves a cross-cutting set of ties with the basic disciplines so that, through interpenetration, the professional faculty becomes an extension of their relevance beyond the ivory tower of the purely academic faculty. Development of this second level is uneven, but with the definition of practical needs in the various fields and of relevant cognitive resources, development of this level will spread in the coming period so that not only law but education, social welfare, and administration will become more similar to engineering and medicine. This will be the cement which binds the practicing professions to the academic system.

Within this structural setting, the university system functions as a source of outputs to the applied professions and through them to the society as a whole. It is necessary to further analyze these outputs at two levels. The first is that of the general system of action at which the primary function of academia is cognitive and the categories of output are knowledge and competence. They become important insofar as the respective professional complexes begin to transcend the empirical levels where clinical experience alone can be the source of professionally relevant knowledge and competence. The academic contribution occurs mainly through training relatively independently of clinical experience, though integrated with it, and through the results of research. The resources thereby acquired by the applied professions are then utilized in the interests of clients through the work of trained practitioners who have acquired the requisite knowledge and competence.

This output of resources can become greater than before at the higher levels of differentiation and structural elaboration of the systems we have outlined, where on both professional and client sides there is no longer a simple service relation. Furthermore, at this more differentiated level, the attempt should not be for the direct transmission of knowledge and of the competence characteristic of the pure academic role for practical professional use; instead, this transmission should be mediated by a process of adjustment to the needs of practice, essentially through the clinical focus appropriate to the profession. The clinical science must be articulated with the appropriate basic sciences, and the former must be embodied in the necessary clinical competence of skills essential to the good practitioner.

The articulation with the university of schools of professional training depends on the importance to the profession of the cognitive base of the requisite practical knowledge and competence. At the same time, the faculty of the university professional school must pay adequate attention to its clinical branches and bring about some kind of a synthesis between the roles of its basic scientists and its clinicians both on a cognitive level and on one which involves ingredients of successful performance of professional functions, that is to say, the promotion of noncognitive goals by rational means.

Certain aspects of this synthesis were illustrated by the place of affective concern for patients in the case of medicine and the place of sensitivity to the problem of the moral status of the normative order of society in the case of law. Insofar as professional education becomes an integral part of the academic system, its units must be capable of adequate output of these essential noncognitive components of orientation as well as of the central cognitive components.

The primary focus of the applied professions is on the performance of important noncognitive functions for societies. Thus, engineering is concerned with socially useful adaptation to the physical environment, medicine with the social concern for the health of individuals, and law with the integrity and adaptability of the society's normative order. If this emphasis is correct, the balances and the integration between intelligence, as the generalized medium primarily concerned with the cognitive system, and affect as the medium concerned with the solidarity of the social system are especially important. This theme was prominent in our discussion (in the previous chapter) of the socialization function in relation to undergraduate education. It seems appropriate to the social responsibility of the cognitive complex as well as to its commitment to cognitive rationality as a value. As in the medical case, the concept of social responsibility can integrate the interests of the individual personality and of the cultural system in defining the social situation as moral order. On this basis, medicine and law are the focal applied professions, flanking a central social concern on both sides. If that is the case, the affective focus of socialization for citizenship in a system of institutionalized individualism becomes purely social in emphasis.[22]

With respect to all of the applied professions but particularly medicine and law, there seems to be a recent shift of orientation on the part of students in professional schools. Whether this shift can be interpreted as jeopardizing the integrity of the cognitive foundations of professional competence is questionable, but it suggests an enhanced concern for the moral and affective aspects of the professional role as one of service as distinguished from the pursuit of self-interest. Connected with this is an increased concern for existential problems, such as those deriving from the fact that medical practice has a close relation to death and the process of dying.[23]

An increasing number of students going into the applied professions are verbalizing this conception and are requesting greater opportunities for this type of service. This trend seems to be a compromise of the conflict between proponents of the pure pattern of cognitive rationality and those of "total relevance," the dedication of the university to particular political causes.

22. The synthesis of intelligence and affect (central to the present analysis) was formulated some years ago by Renée Fox and Miriam Massey Johnson (originally in a seminar paper) in the concept of *detached concern* with reference to the medical case. Dr. Fox used the concept in her study *Experiment Perilous*. The component of detachment designates the necessity, for those committed to values of cognitive rationality, to use knowledge and competence with maximum effectiveness. The component of concern states the imperative of doing this in a framework of affective solidarity, in this case with the patient, so as not to dehumanize the relationship. This argument can readily be extended to the legal case where the affective component would not be identification in a personality-focused sense, with feelings of justice. Dr. Fox has recently suggested that in addition to competence and detached concern, there should be a component of "informed concern" in the orientation of the physician. This would derive from the mobilization of knowledge, not so much in its instrumental significance for diagnosis or therapy as in its existential meanings with respect to patients' situations and their human significance.

23. See Talcott Parsons, Renée C. Fox, and Victor M. Lidz, "The 'Gift of Life' and Its Reciprocation," *Social Research*, 39 (Autumn 1972), 367–415.

## Applied Interchanges at the Social System Level

These considerations also indicate the transition between the status of the cognitive system at the level of the general action system and the academic system at the societal level. At the societal level the academic system is a set of social organizations, pluralistically differentiated but interpenetrating. In spite of hierarchical components, in the bureaucratic aspect of university administration, in the teacher-student relationship, and in the senior-junior faculty relationship, the main structural type is associational rather than bureaucratic, but because of its fiduciary and collegial characteristics it is not a pure democratic association.

Since academia is anchored in the fiduciary subsystem of the society, its outputs to the other sectors of the society should be special cases of those involved in the interchanges of the societal system. In the paradigm of double interchanges generalized from economic theory, in each case one of the two pairs constitutes an interchange of product outputs, while the other constitutes an interchange of factors, for example, factors of production in the economic case or factors of effectiveness in a political sense (A–G). At the level of the general system of action, emphasis should be placed on the *products* of the academic system: knowledge, competence, and the intelligent organization of affective interests. At the level of the social system, emphasis should be shifted to the *factor* outputs. The justification is that the significance of academic output at the social-system level does not lie in functions analogous to those of consumers' goods as an output of the economy, but rather as providing resources which, when combined with others, facilitate the relevant societal functions.

The relevant case is the output of labor capacity as governed by value-commitments. Among the subsectors of the fiduciary system, that of kinship is obviously involved in the output of labor in the original economic sense. However, the academic system is the source of special categories of educated and trained manpower beyond what is ordinarily meant by labor-capacity. In these terms the output of trained labor-capacity should be interpreted as a contribution of the academic system to the provision of professional service in the society. The output from the academic core must be mediated through the social structure of professional training before it can become optimally effective. Indeed our analysis implies that the socialization function of general education needs to be *combined* with that of professional training in the cognitive and affective operation of the professional schools to produce optimum labor-capacity for performing applied professional function.

In the interchange between the fiduciary system and the societal community, the factor output from the fiduciary system is commitment to valued association. The associational aspect of the academic community is important for its own functional significance as well as for a symbolic prototype of good solidarity. This significance, prominent at the level of general education, is propagated from the academic system into its more immediate environments. For the applied professions, this implies an effect, both on the associational character of professional groups themselves and at the next remove between practitioners of the professions and their clients. In this context, the concept "association" is quite different from that of bureaucratic hierarchy.

Through this channel, the academic system has a pervasive, though unobtrusive, influence on the structure of the society in which high-level academic functions are institutionalized. This should not be interpreted to mean that the university is a microcosm of the society. Rather, in a succession from aspects of the Christian church, the religious orders within it, and even aristocracies, academic pressure tends to favor the combination of universalistic norms with the egalitarian component of the collectivity defined as a company of equals.

The third category of fiduciary output is legitimation of authority. Although legitimation of authority was formulated with Max Weber's political usage in mind, it is also relevant to the present context. Since the academic system is committed to the value of cognitive rationality, one component of professional fiduciary responsibility is defined by this component, whereas the other component is commitment to the values underlying the functional goals which the profession serves. For medicine it is concern for patients within the field of health, for law concern for the integrity of the societal order and the welfare of clients. The authority thereby legitimized is that entailed in taking responsibility to implement these *combined* value-commitments within the limits of professional role-opportunities.

Just as the academic system's fiduciary commitments at the value level are anchored in generalized value-patterns institutionalized in it, albeit differentiated into cognitive and other functional categories, so at the level of the general action system the cognitive component is anchored in the cultural status of knowledge as a cultural product and in the organic facilities for the implementation of these commitments. The applied professional sector of the academic system must synthesize these anchorages with the values and cultural commitments involved in the applied functions of the respective professions.

This outline of output categories from the academic system to the applied professional complex shows what the academic system contributes beyond the direct satisfaction of its own interests. However, since this contribution occurs in the context of an interchange system, the contributing should be linked to processes of receiving.

If we continue to emphasize the primacy of *factor* exchanges at the societal level and *product* exchanges at the general action level, the processes of receiving at the societal level should be thought of as acquiring the factors necessary for implementation of the fiduciary commitments of the academic system. The three primary factors, other than the fiduciary commitment itself, are wage income (A–L), justification of the allocation of loyalties (I–L), and assumption of operative responsibility (G–L).

Wage income means money inputs to the academic system. Farther out, at the boundary between practitioner and client, there has been a tradition that, except for the indigent, clients should pay the full cost of the services rendered to them, though modified by the sliding scale. In some cases, such as law, this has been extended to the principle of having students pay nearly the full cost of legal education, though this seems to be changing. Medicine has a different tradition. The concept of wage income should be extended from wages for services rendered to claims on the part of the academic system to adequate financial support for the fulfillment of its commitments. Such claims need not come only from the recipients of specific services. Where there is no direct correspondence, the motivation to financial support must be traced to sources other than the supporters' direct benefits from the academic function. One such motivation is expectation of future societal benefit, if sufficient investment is made under the right conditions. This would seem to underlie the massive government investment in medical education and research in the last generation. Here, the particular recipients of the eventual benefits are not expected to pay the costs.

This interpretation seems compatible with an emphasis on the fiduciary character of the academic system. It is also compatible with the fiduciary aspect of kinship; taking responsibility for children and their socialization is a fiduciary obligation in the sense that parents do not directly benefit from their investment in the oncoming generation. Professional education and research are on the borderline of producing pay-offs but are still predominantly on the fiduciary side of the line.

The second category of societal input parallels the commitment to valued association and is an input of influence within a framework of prestige. This input helps in the integration of the academic system in the society or, conversely, promotes its malintegration. Commitment to valued association must be thought of in the context of pluralism and of loyalty to collectivities. Commitments to association in the interest of implementation of values is a way in which the academic system can ensure adequate loyalty on the part of the various categories of participants.

The inclusion of professional education and the attendant research in the academic system has, under optimal conditions, the virtue of linking cognitive rationality with certain service functions in the interest of the implementation of other societal values. The failure of these two value-components to be adequately integrated can accentuate academic vulnerability to what (in Chapter 7) we will treat as deflationary pressures.[24]

Part of the strength of the academic system lies in the plurality of the noncognitive value components of the professional complex. Thus, on the whole the contemporary medical and legal complexes have not been as vulnerable to loss of confidence as the complexes of physical science and engineering. Further problems arise concerning the second tier of professional groups which are probably more vulnerable than the first. We will discuss these problems briefly in the next chapter. For now, we wish to be clear about the nature of the input-output relations of the academic system, both directly on the level of cognitive rationality and indirectly through the applied professions, for which cognitive rationality

24. Engineering seems to be the victim of one such pressure, namely, that coming from the ideological left concerning the status of the "military-industrial complex." Here an integrate of academic science, professional engineering, business enterprise, and some aspects of government is charged with having abandoned the service of beneficent control of the physical environment—and avoidance of its pollution—in favor of serving the interests of imperialism, exploitation, and oppression. Without the university connection with engineering and science-based technology in industry, this ideological complex could not be very significant to the academic world.

has become an indispensable source of knowledge and competence.

One further input to the fiduciary system at the societal level requires comment. This input, the assumption of operative responsibility, is exchanged for the legitimation of authority. The assumption of operative responsibility means that individuals and subcollectivities involved in the academic system, although given authority to implement the academic and the combined academic-professional values through the use of power within certain limits, are expected to assume responsibility for their part of the process. This has implications for the various components of the academic system. On the positive side, it points to a relative eagerness to assume responsibility but also to the dangers of going too far— especially because the academic system must be regarded as a differentiated subsystem of society that cannot assume too general responsibilities.[25] On the negative side, there are vulnerabilities connected with certain kinds of academic passivity, such as expecting to be supported without reference to the contributions which have become so appreciated.

The inputs to the academic system at the general action level have a special bearing on its integration with the complex of the applied professions. With respect to the return for the output of knowledge, there must be a balance between the cognitive considerations basic to knowledge and the noncognitive ones necessary for justifying and legitimizing its uses. Knowledge at the general action level parallels goods at the societal level. The return to the producers of knowledge is therefore analogous to consumers' spending and has to do with questions like the balance between utility and taste in the field of consumption and beyond taste, with the commitment of resources to noneconomic functions. Thus, the professions must consume knowledge in some appropriate balance with the noncognitive goals and interests of their professional functions. The demand for knowledge in the professional context should be expected to reflect such integrative needs.

Another context of input involves the return for outputs of competence. This concerns the problem of the development of effectiveness for attainment of goals at the personality level, in psychoanalytic terms on the level of ego-function. Education in general involves investment for future effectiveness, but education has a special meaning in the professional context because of special

25. McGeorge Bundy, "Were Those the Days?" *Daedalus* (Summer 1970), pp. 531–567, discusses the Harvard University tendency to "run the country."

kinds of competence which cannot be instantly acquired. Simple manifestations of the actor's benevolent sentiments will thus not cure a sick person. On the professional level the *technical* level of the functionally important competence is noteworthy. The costs of its acquisition must be motivated by a sufficiently strong demand for the parallel of capital in the economic case, which in some sense implies delayed gratification. Put banally, no matter how deep the surgeon's compassion for the sufferings of persons with operable conditions of cancer, he cannot help such people much (except as a priest-counselor) without acquiring sufficient competence in the relevant branches of surgery. This takes personal investment *and time.* If being an effective helper in such situations of distress constitutes gratification, and it is difficult to argue that it does not, such gratifications are necessarily delayed.

*Applied Professions: Historical Perspective.* At a more general level, both the previous chapter and the present one have considered the subtle interplay between intelligence, as a regulator of knowledge and competence and their uses, and affect as a regulator both of the recognition of achievement and of the social definitions of situations. In some ways this interplay is the major regulator of balances in the professional field, except for cultural definitions of the situations themselves. We shall attempt to analyze these interchanges more fully in the next chapter. The present chapter is intended to establish the thesis that professional education and its closely associated research activities have become integral parts of the American academic system. This is not attributable to a historically fortuitous combination of circumstances alone, but is rooted in the nature of the academic system as part of modern society.

The more general processes of differentiation, inclusion, adaptive upgrading, and value-generalization make this integration an essential development. With the development of the cognitive complex itself, a differentiation along the broad lines of pure and applied relevance of cognitive considerations has had to take place. This process of differentiation posed the dilemma of exclusion of the applied professions from the academic system—in line with the ivory-tower conception—or its compatible inclusion. A necessary condition for inclusion is the protection of the integrity of the cognitive enterprise which is in turn a basis for its serving as an effective resource-base for the practical goal-interests about which the applied professions have been organized.

The institutional opting in favor of the inclusion of the complex of professional education within the academic system, although interpenetrating with its nonacademic environment, constitutes a step in the upgrading of the adaptive capacity of the society as a whole. The harnessing of knowledge and competence to practical needs does not necessarily derogate the autonomy of the basis of its significance; it has to be something in its own right before it can claim any usefulness as instrumentality. For this integration to take place, the value-base of the academic system has to be generalized. So far as it is academic, the value-base can remain primarily cognitive, but it must be in terms of a conception of the cognitive that does not exclude the relevance of contributions to the practical goal-attainment interests of the professions. This suggests that the value of cognitive rationality is part of a more general value-system which includes most of the applied complex but is not necessarily restricted to it.

The development of the academic-professional complex has been made possible through increasing interpenetration with other sectors of the society. As in so many other contexts of increased division of labor, this development entails at the same time increased access to opportunity but also increased vulnerability because of the more ramified relational context within which particular events take place, be they corporate decisions, commitments to research projects, faculty appointments, or students' decisions to enroll in particular programs or courses.

The problem of the relation between the core academic complex and the professional complex is a case of the general problem of the relations between functional autonomy of a societal subsystem and interdependence with other subsystems, which includes mutual benefits from the interdependence and mutual costs, interpenetration, and service to other subsystems.

We have followed this line of analysis, starting with the core functions which constitute the basis of a claim to autonomy, through the contribution of a relatively autonomous system to the general education of the new citizen and that of the professional practitioner. We will now examine a more diffuse sector of the cognitively oriented population of modern society, the intellectuals, after which we will attempt to synthesize these various threads of analysis into a coherent dynamic pattern.

# 6

## THE UNIVERSITY AND
## THE "INTELLECTUALS"

We now turn to the last of the three contexts of the relevance of the academic system to societal concerns outside of its own cognitive core. This context brings cognitive resources to bear on problems of the cultural *definition of the situation* for the society and of society's relations to the status and functions of the primary bearers of these processes, groups we loosely call *intellectuals*, which are found both inside and outside the university world. In order to put this discussion into an intelligible setting it will be necessary to explicate somewhat the conception of definition of the situation, and what, at the sociological level, we mean by the intellectuals.

The concept, "definition of the situation," derives from W. I. Thomas.[1] It is the fourth member of the family of generalized symbolic media operating at the level of the general system of action.[2] The other three are intelligence, performance capacity, and affect. We did not discuss it at length in Chapter 2 because we had already imposed a considerable theoretical burden on the reader at that point and it seemed to us more relevant to the subject matter of the present chapter.

We have not tried to remain puristic in use of the term "definition of the situation." The *primary* reference is to its conception as

1. Edmund H. Volkart, ed., *Social Behavior and Personality: Contributions of W. I. Thomas to Theory and Social Research* (New York, Social Science Research Council, 1951), chap. xv, "The Individualization of Behavior," pp. 238–258. See also William I. Thomas, *The Unadjusted Girl* (Boston, Little, Brown and Co., 1931).

2. Talcott Parsons, "Some Problems of General Theory in Sociology," in *Theoretical Sociology, Perspectives and Developments*, ed. John C. McKinney and Edward A. Tiryakian (New York, Appleton-Century-Crofts, Educational Division, Meredith Corp., 1970), pp. 27–68. The formal paradigms dealing with the general system of action have been substantially revised. The revised version is presented in the technical appendix of this book.

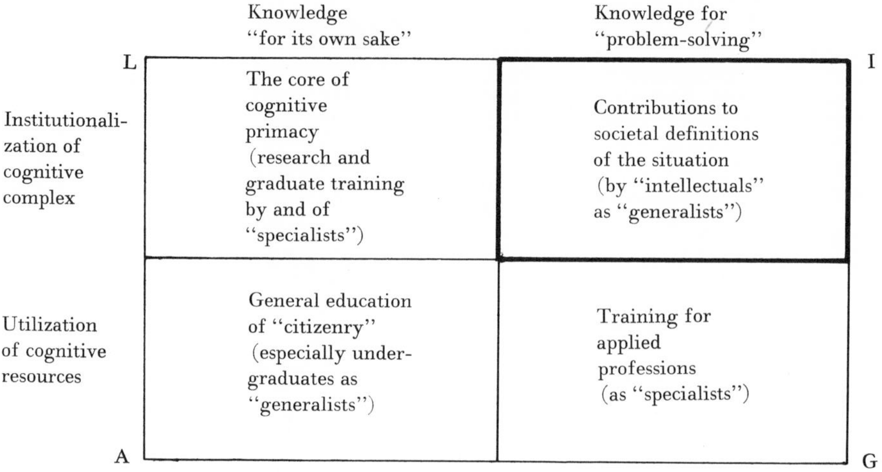

| | Knowledge "for its own sake" | Knowledge for "problem-solving" |
|---|---|---|
| **L** | | **I** |
| Institutionali-zation of cognitive complex | The core of cognitive primacy (research and graduate training by and of "specialists") | Contributions to societal definitions of the situation (by "intellectuals" as "generalists") |
| Utilization of cognitive resources | General education of "citizenry" (especially under-graduates as "generalists") | Training for applied professions (as "specialists") |
| **A** | | **G** |

Figure 6.1. Institutionalization of Cognitive Rationality in the Structure of the University

*Note:* The heavily outlined subsystem is the substantive focus of this chapter. For a more formal analysis of this figure and its relation to other subsystems, see the appendix to Chapter 2.

a generalized symbolic medium. On occasion, however, we shall use it to include the more particularized valuables at the cultural level which can be acquired through its expenditure and the value of which is measured in such terms. These are actual patterns of symbolic organization in constitutive, moral, and expressive contexts, a meaning close to that of Thomas himself. We are following a tradition in the economic field where distinctions are made between money and real goods. Both together constitute wealth. Hence, it seems reasonable to mean by "definition of the situation" the generalized medium, and the real entities, and the sum of them from the point of view of level of meaning, analogous to wealth assessed in monetary terms but including both financial assets and real goods.

Definition of the situation is parallel to *value-commitments* at the social system level,[3] that is, in the same sense as intelligence is a generalized medium parallel to money and affect is parallel to influence. In all these cases, at least one difference between the medium at the social-system level and that at the level of the general system of action is that certain constraints operating at the

3. Talcott Parsons, "On the Concept of Value-Commitments," in *Politics and Social Structure* (New York, The Free Press, 1969), chap. xvi, pp. 439–472. Reprinted from *Sociological Inquiry*, 38 (Spring 1968), 135–160.

social-system level, a subsystem of action, may be conceived to be lifted at the general action level. Thus in Chapter 2 we suggested that "exclusive rights of possession" were central to the property complex at the social-system level and applied to money but that they did not apply to knowledge and the other components of the cognitive complex at the general action level, even though, in the special sense we outlined, intelligence is subject to the general imperative of scarcity.

Definition of the situation shares with value-commitments its place as the medium anchored in the pattern-maintenance subsystem of the larger system of reference. It is thus an embodiment of the primary *code* which regulates the boundary-definition and self-reproduction of the system in question, though the exact sense in which it is dominated by the code as distinguished from other components remains to be clarified. In comparison with genetics, it is probably closer to the level of template or program than of code. This code-template affects the concrete action system through two channels. The first is through specification, the second through incorporation in a generalized medium of interchange, namely, the definition of the situation.

Specification is analogous to the spelling out of the genetic code in particular genes or gene-clusters. In action terms we mean, within a series of levels of pattern-maintenance systems, a structuring which maintains constancy of *pattern*, from higher to lower levels of generality, but introduces new and more concrete contexts of relevance for its implementation, both at less general levels and in more specialized contexts.

Specification from the most general code level should follow the outlines of an inverted tree. The first branching concerns the focus of functional differentiation of the cultural system itself. We have designated that as the differentiation into patterns of constitutive, moral-evaluative, expressive, and cognitive symbolization. We have already dealt (Chapter 2) at some length with the relation of this paradigm to cognitive symbolization, especially through the role of cognitive standards of validity and significance as well as through the output of knowledge. As can be inferred from Durkheim's final position, the focus of the specification of the code to the moral-evaluative level concerns the integration of action systems and leads to the relation between the cultural and the social systems with respect to the institutionalization of values.

More problematical is the relation of expressive symbolization at the cultural level to the personality of the individual as subsystem of action. Our suggestion is that the primary mode of specification of normative-symbolic culture to the *personality* system is expressive, meaning that the core of personal identity is organized about a normative conception or pattern of personal style.

These three contexts of the specification of the constitutive *cultural pattern* of the action system provide a base for its institutionalization and internalization in the noncultural subsystems of action. Since cultural patterning is *always* normative from the perspective of action, all three constitute matrices of meaning within which normative structures in each of these functional contexts can be defined. These definitions are not simply or predominantly cognitive. The same problem arises here as with Kluckhohn's use of the term "conception" in his definition of values,[4] which we altered to "pattern of orientation." There are constitutive definitions as patterned sets of symbolic meanings and also moral, expressive and cognitive definitions.[5]

The definition of the situation conceived as a medium of interchange thus must be more general in reference than its social-system counterpart, value-commitments. Its functional significance is not confined to levels of *institutionalization*, which concerns the relation between moral standards and values at the societal level. But besides the all-action concerns of the constitutive complex itself, the more general action-level medium must include relevance to *both* expressive and cognitive standards, their relations to each other and to the moral and the constitutive standards.

As a generalized symbolic medium, definition of the situation must be conceived as contentless in a sense parallel to intelligence and affect as we have discussed them. To be valuable, it must be used in transactions of interchange, both to acquire control of other valuables and to serve as a measure of their value. These other

4. Clyde Kluckhohn, "Values and Value-Orientations in the Theory of Action: An Exploration in Definition and Classification," in *Toward a General Theory of Action*, ed. Talcott Parsons and Edward A. Shils (Cambridge, Mass., Harvard University Press, 1951), p. 395.

5. The paradigm being outlined here is congruent with that outlined by Durkheim in the conclusion of *The Elementary Forms of the Religious Life*, trans. Joseph Ward Swain (Glencoe, Ill., The Free Press, 1954). He there spoke of the three contexts of organization of action systems: the cognitive, conceptualized in Kantian terms, the moral, which had been a preoccupation of his earlier career, and the religious. See Talcott Parsons, "Durkheim on Religion Revisited: Another Look at *The Elementary Forms of the Religious Life*," in *The Scientific Study of Religion: Beyond the Classics*, ed. Charles Y. Glock and Phillip E. Hammond (New York, Harper and Row, 1973).

valuables, however, are the particulars which are important relative to the generality of the definitions of the situation.

The standards of meaning for this particularization are the three just outlined, namely, the moral, the expressive, and the cognitive. Of the three, the reader of this book is most familiar with the cognitive. Cognitive standards link the organic cognitive potential of the individual (through the brain but grounded in his genetic constitution) with the cultural standards of what constitutes valid and significant knowledge. In this interchange context the medium which matches and integrates with definition of the situation is intelligence. If action is to be intelligent it must so far as possible conform to the standards of cognitive validity and significance.

The second context is the moral. Within the pattern-framework of the constitutive definition of social systems, a cultural provision of moral standards (the moral community in Durkheim's sense) is relevant. Insofar as these moral standards are institutionalized, they constitute the basis for a going system which, from the point of view of its individual members, defines their social environment. This dual nature of the social system anchors affect as a general action medium. In the relevant interchange, the definition of the situation is particularized by integration with affect as the basis of identifications with the institutional order and also with respect to the sense of justice of its participating members.

The third context of interchange concerns the interchange of culture and personality systems; it comes to focus in the *cultural* patterning of modes of personal identity or style. Here the definition of the situation is particularized by stress on expressive standards and integrated with the performance-capacity of individuals; definition of the situation also has an expressive emphasis in that it integrates situational exigencies, cultural standards, and the motivational interests of individuals.

The moral reference is irrelevant here. As Durkheim believed, the focus of the moral component lies in the institutionalization of values in the social system by virtue of which the latter becomes a moral community. This social system becomes the environment in which the individual person acts and is the internal environment of the general action system. As such, it has dual meaning for the individual actor: as a factual state of affairs and also as a normative order. In both respects, but especially in the latter, the social environment becomes internalized as part of the individual personality, the moral component forming the focus of his conscience, which is close to what Freud meant by superego, and the cognitive-factual part close to what Freud meant by the ego. By virtue of internalization as conscience the normative aspect of the social system acquires, in Durkheim's term, *moral authority* and has a determining role in his action. This is a special case of interpenetration.

In a sense parallel to that in which Chapter 2 discussed pure affect integrating two or more persons without involvement of institutionalized solidarity, we may now speak of pure definition of the situation guiding orientation without particularization to cognitive, expressive, or moral standards and their respective modes of full structuring, especially by institutionalization and internalization. Moral standards internalized in the personality constitute one aspect of the particularization of the individual's identity or style, namely, that which articulates with his role-integration in the pluralistic social system, including grounding of his personal moral critique of that system. On this basis *recognition* as a sanction (in Thomas's sense)[6] becomes meaningful. There are parallel senses in which the individual personality is constituted by the relevant *expressive* patterns that have become part of his identity and is also constrained (in Durkheim's sense) through internalization both of cognitive and of moral standards. This was the focus of our analysis of student socialization in Chapter 4.

As a generalized symbolic medium, definition of the situation is both contentless and scarce. We have just tried to explain what being contentless means; definition of the situation should *not* be interpreted as an outline of the structure of the cultural system. Definition of the situation is scarce in the sense that its use to make meaningful culturally symbolic patterns precludes by their very selection action-commitment to alternative patterns. Units of an action system which have cultural primacy thus have limited resources at this level and are also bound by conditions analogous to the imperative of solvency for a firm. Capacity to define the situation, if it circulates, can only be maintained if expenditures are balanced by income. Thus, playing fast and loose with cognitive standards may result in deficits in the income of knowledge; defective definition of moral standards may result in shaky institutionalization of the social milieu; and the failure to fit expressive standards with personal needs may result in a lowering of senses of

6. Volkart, *Social Behavior*, and Thomas, *Unadjusted Girl*.

personal obligation, in cultural as well as in societal contexts, that is, in "alienation."

*Intellectuals and Their Concerns.*[7] We wish to examine in this chapter the possible impact of the university's activities and outputs on the cultural world other than the impact of purely cognitive activity. This rounds out consideration of the impact of the university, since its contributions to the applied professions and their functions are primarily social, and its contributions to socialization through general education consist primarily of outputs to the personalities of individuals.

Our concern then is not only with definition of the situation as a medium of interchange but with the structures and processes by which the different cultural subsystems are interrelated and influenced by cognitive considerations. Religion is a constitutive base of cultural systems. The relevant symbolic frameworks, for example, in the form of "myths of concern,"[8] permeate the entire action system, including subtle relations to the cognitive complex. The intellectual disciplines most directly involved in this connection are philosophy and the equivalent of the clinical discipline of an applied profession, theology and some of its neighbors.

The *moral* complex is associated in particular with the social order. The cultural grounding of moral sentiments and attitudes must articulate with the social science disciplines, but involves levels other than those of strict social science. One aspect of this cultural grounding is social criticism, especially if social criticism is construed to include critical analysis of the moral grounding of social institutions and political policies rather than only their negative evaluation. It seems legitimate to refer to this context as that of *ideology*. What is distinctive about ideology as distinguished from theology is its concern with the existing or potential society which is inherently part of this world, but, though it must be concerned with knowledge in the full sense and with cognitive standards, it must also be concerned with specific evaluative judgments. Secondly, ideology goes beyond value-relevance in Weber's sense to the frank advocacy of specific evaluations, both positive and negative. We can thus regard ideology as another clinical discipline.

In cultural terms, the third complex of relevance is that of the

7. For a formal paradigm of the more detailed components of the concerns of intellectuals, see Figure 2.11 in the appendix to Chapter 2 of this book.

8. Northrop Frye, "The Critical Path: An Essay on the Social Context of Literary Criticism," *Daedalus* (Spring 1970), pp. 268–342.

arts with their special relevance to expressive symbolization. Here the humanities constitute the primary discipline focus in the organization of the university. The point at which humanistic scholarship meets problems of artistic creativeness and function may, following Frye, be called *criticism*,[9] which again is analogous to a clinical discipline.

Of these three foci, we shall be concerned here mainly with the ideological, but, in view of the many complex interrelations, it is unwise not to take account of the other two. In all three contexts, our problem concerns the ways in which the cognitive complex can be integrated with these other bases of cultural concern and also of conflict arising between cognitive and noncognitive interests. This latter problem area is particularly important today because of the extensive revolt against rationalization which, in all three of these borderline fields, seems for the extremists to imply repudiation of everything having to do with the cognitve complex.[10]

Who then are the intellectual mediators between the university as the institutional core of the cognitive complex and those especially concerned with the noncognitive aspects of culture? Unlike teachers of undergraduate students, of future professional practitioners, or indeed of core academics, they do not constitute a corporate body. The theological faculties of universities can scarcely be said to be the equivalents of the "Doctors of the Sorbonne" of Rabelais' day, or of the theological faculties in the early Protestant German universities, which were the "keepers of the Prince's Conscience." Even within the university, the intellectual concern with religion has been diffused from theological faculties to include philosophers, historians and sociologists of religion, and members of general "Departments of Religion" within faculties of Arts and Sciences. In the ideological field, a large part of the function is performed in departments of philosophy and in the social sciences.

Some criteria concern the level at which such people try to communicate and the type of audience they are concerned to

9. Frye, "The Critical Path."

10. With special reference to the functions of criticism, Frye (ibid.) speaks of the university as the base of this function: "The university is the source of free authority in society, not as an institution, but as the place where the appeal to reason, experiment, evidence and imagination is constantly going on. It is not and can never be a *concerned* [italics ours] organization like a church or a political party" (p. 335). And on the following page, "In its relation to literature the university is primarily a place of criticism. The university is a first-rate place for studying literature, but at best a second-rate place for producing it" (p. 336).

reach. *Qua* core academic, a professor is primarily interested in communicating to his disciplinary colleagues and to graduate students. *Qua* undergraduate teacher, he is concerned to reach an institutionally defined "public" of students with whom he is systematically placed in contact. Finally, for a teacher in a professional school, his public is the actual or potential practitioner. For the intellectual in our sense, it is a diffuser public, both inside and outside the university, but *always* with a segment outside. Furthermore, the intellectuals who are members of the university, mainly at faculty levels, are matched by those who do the same thing, but from locations outside the university. They are a very diverse group; some are writers, some journalists, some politicians, some are attached to religious organizations, some are creative artists.

The common core is concern—in a sense close to but not identical with Frye's—with the patterning of cultural symbol systems, not as a pure object of cognitive study, but as a component in more broadly *meaningful* orientation and with the involvement of these meanings in various aspects of life, especially for the social world. The basis of the concern, and hence the nature of the meanings, cannot be purely cognitive but must *also* be constitutive (religious), moral, expressive, or some combination of these categories.[11]

With respect to level of communication, one criterion fits the conception of a parallel to the clinical focus. This conception is that, in contrast to the conception of cognitive specialization, for instance, in the intellectual disciplines and their subdivisions, the intellectual is an intellectual *generalist*. This almost goes without saying since he wants to tap concerns *not* congruent with cognitively specialized interests. The question then arises of how cognitive standards can or cannot be integrated with these noncognitive concerns or how far the cognitive standards must be altered by their association with the others. An earlier era saw "warfare between science and religion"; today something approaching warfare exists between the cognitive complex and a good deal of ideology as well as between the cognitive and the expressive complex.

With respect to social organization, illuminating evidence comes from a study by Charles Kadushin, Julie Hover, and their associ-

---

11. Robert N. Bellah, "Religion and Social Science," in *The Culture of Unbelief*, ed. R. Caporale and A. Grumelli (Berkeley, Calif., University of California Press, 1971), chap. xiv.

ates.[12] Their preliminary findings suggest that the organizational focus in the United States is to be found in authorship in a small number of periodical publications which are neither strictly academic, like disciplinary journals, nor popular. They found the *New York Review of Books* to be the leading channel, with the *New York Times Book Review* a rather distant second. To be a frequent author in one of these and a few other publications is to be an "intellectual."[13]

*Intellectuals, the University, and Secularization.* Providing background for the current role of intellectuals is the differentiation between religion and secular culture which has taken place over some centuries; an outcome of this differentiation has been the predominantly secular character of modern universities. On the cultural level, the Reformation by the seventeenth century had resulted in the rise of the new philosophy in the work of Descartes, Leibnitz, Spinoza, Hobbes, and Locke and of natural science with such figures as Galileo, Newton, and Harvey. A line of differentiation emerged between religion as the focus of denominational commitments and loyalties and secular cognitive culture. The Renaissance had already emancipated the arts to a considerable degree.

This did not mean that religion was eliminated from intellectual purview but rather that religion as cognitive object became pluralized and generalized. One outcome of the process of differentiation was a continuing decline in legitimacy of the claim of particular religious positions to monopolize legitimate intellectual points of

---

12. Julie Hover and Charles Kadushin, "The Influential Intellectual Journals: A Very Private Club," *Change Magazine*, 4, no. 2 (March 1972), 38–47. See also, Charles Kadushin, "Who Are the Elite Intellectuals?" *The Public Interest*, no. 29 (Fall 1972), 109–125.

13. An antecedent of the term, "intellectuals," was the concept of Karl Mannheim, the *freischwebende Intelligenz*—the unattached intelligensia. By calling them unattached, he wished to emphasize that this group did not fit any of the conventional categories of class affiliation, especially in a Marxian sense. See Mannheim's *Ideology and Utopia*, trans. by Louis Wirth and Edward Shils (New York, Harcourt, Brace and World, 1936). Perhaps the most influential recent formulation of what the intellectuals are is that by Edward Shils, "The Intellectuals and the Powers: Some Perspectives for Comparative Analysis," *Comparative Studies in Society and Culture*, 1 (October 1958), 5–23; also, Edward Shils, "Intellectuals, Tradition, and the Traditions of Intellectuals: Some Preliminary Considerations," *Daedalus* (Spring 1972), pp. 21–34. See also Edward Shils, "From Periphery to Centre: The Changing Role of Intellectuals in American Society," in *Stability and Social Change*, ed. by Bernard Barber and Alex Inkeles (Boston, Little, Brown and Co., 1971). The first-mentioned essay by Shils provides the title for a recent collection of his essays. See Edward Shils, *"The Intellectuals and the Powers" and Other Essays* (Chicago, Ill., University of Chicago Press, 1972).

view.[14] The general pattern of cross-cutting emerged between basic intellectual orientations and the cognitive grounding of particular bodies of religious doctrine. From this point of view, philosophy has formed an interface between the cognitive aspect of religion and the structure of secular cognitive culture. This implies a sense in which religion, relative to what continued to be general in the cognitive tradition, came to be particularized and privatized, though continuing in the background.

Even theology began to transcend its particular denominational anchorage; it became reasonable to speak of problems at least of *Christian* theology shared by Catholic and Protestant branches. But the intellectual lead was taken by philosophy which increasingly discussed religion without specific denominational references. The range of concerns then broadened to include Judaism on a basis of presumptive legitimacy other than its antecedent relation to Christianity alone and later a new awareness of religions outside the Judeo-Christian tradition as something other than "heathen." Religions became objects of study from other than a philosophical point of view, notably through the development of history, anthropology, and sociology in the nineteenth and twentieth centuries.

Institutionally, then, the academic system has in a variety of ways come to be secularized. Two patterns may be distinguished. In the Continental European tradition, universities were treated as an organizational and financial responsibility of the state. Hence, with the general process of secularization of the state, it was regarded as illegitimate to impose any denominational religious pattern on state universities. (As religious pluralization developed, separation of church and state meant that religious institutions came to be private.) However, theological faculties were sometimes allowed to retain their denominational affiliations while the other faculties were secularized. In the United States, it was clear almost from the beginning that public institutions of higher education had to be secular.

The other pattern has been the voluntary secularization of the private sector of the academic system. Most American institutions which antedate the Civil War were established with denomina-

14. Thus a history of political thought in the 16th century by John William Allen, with *one* exception, organized the material around the "points of view" of specific religious groups. The exception was Machiavelli. See Allen, *A History of Political Thought in the Sixteenth Century* (London, Methuen, 1951).

tional affiliation or sponsorship—a pattern followed later by the Catholic institutions. The impact of religiously neutral secular learning helps to account for the fact that the new university system which emerged after the Civil War, in the development of which the private institutions took the lead, was mainly secular.

These circumstances, both in the development of the general culture and in the academic system, mean that recently the cultural interaction between the academic system and the rest of the society has been predominantly secular. In paradigmatic terms, the noncognitive cultural complexes with which the cognitive primacy of the academic system comes to be juxtaposed are moral-ethical and expressive-aesthetic complexes. Religion does not disappear, but remains in a somewhat neutralized status in the background. Contrary to much contemporary opinion, this neutralization of religion need not mean a decline of religious commitment but rather the attainment of a level of generalization of that commitment which makes the old religious quarrels less meaningful than they were before.

Relative to the other two cultural components, American intellectuals have shown a tendency to vacillate between giving moral and giving expressive considerations precedence. Giving moral considerations precedence seems to have predominated in our intellectual history, but it can be argued (as Daniel Bell does)[15] that there has recently been an increase in expressive concerns, though this change may not be a long-run trend but only a cyclical swing. In any case, the relative neutralization of religion implies that the *cognitive* problems involved in defining these two areas of basic orientation and the balances among and between them will remain central.

Indeed, the rise of the university complex to its position of prominence and the participation in it of intellectuals seem to throw doubt on Bell's thesis of the developing radical hiatus between American "social structure" and "culture," as he calls them. As Bell himself recognizes, the hiatus between instrumental and expressive concerns goes back at least to the Romantic movement and has been prominent in France for several generations.[16] To

15. Daniel Bell, "The Cultural Contradictions of Capitalism," *The Public Interest*, no. 21 (Fall 1970), 16–43.

16. See Priscilla and Terry N. Clark on the division between the Cartesian spirit which animated the Durkheim circle and the culture of spontaneity which animated the Left Bank literary and artistic world. Priscilla P. Clark and Terry N. Clark, "Writers, Literature, and Student Movements in France," *Sociology of Education*, 42, no. 4 (Fall 1969), 293–314.

some extent, Bell's position continues views advanced in *The Lonely Crowd* by David Riesman[17] and also by Clyde Kluckhohn in his paper on the changes in American values.[18] Our view is that these changes are not as far-reaching as has been alleged. In the next chapter we shall present some evidence that the inflation-deflation type of fluctuation probably accounts for a substantial part of the observed phenomena. If this view is correct, the observed phenomena do not necessarily constitute a turning point.

The emergence of the academic system as differentiated both from societal and from noncognitive cultural concerns with emphasis placed on its cognitive functions means that integration of the cognitive components with the moral and the expressive must involve nonacademic participation. With respect to their role in this process of integration, intellectuals are persons concerned with the general definition of the situation, for the human condition as a whole but especially for the meaning and status of social systems.

Institutionally the importance of intellectuals has increased with the development of broadcasting, namely, the dissemination of symbolically significant messages to publics the membership of which is not specifiable in advance. The first great step in this direction was the invention of printing so that books, pamphlets, and eventually newspapers could reach wider readership than was possible with hand-copied manuscripts. Printed materials were published in the sense that authors and publishers could not control in detail the access of readers to them; they were in the public domain. The penny press was a further development—a by-product of the industrial revolution in England. The present century has witnessed an enormous expansion of informational technology, probably the most important technological complex of our time. Radio and television as mass media are now familiar, however incompletely understood their impact is. These, however, are only the visible parts of a broader complex which includes methods of data or information gathering, storage, retrieval, and processing. These have the effect of multiplying the qualitatively new properties of written as distinguished from spoken language, which has had the potentiality not only of extension of access to recipients of

17. *The Lonely Crowd: A Study of the Changing American Character* (New Haven, Conn., Yale University Press, 1950).

18. Clyde Kluckhohn, "Have There Been Discernible Shifts in American Values during the Past Generation?" in *The American Style*, ed. Elting Morison (New York, Harper and Bros., 1958).

communication horizontally but of extension *in time*.[19] Both the academic profession and the outside intellectuals rely on the technology of externalized culture, starting with the printed page.

Despite indistinct boundaries, this world of institutionalized culture is socially organized in professions and quasi professions, some of which interpenetrate with the academic system. Thus, conservatories of music are usually outside the universities, as are schools for dramatic arts or dance, but university departments of music, fine arts, and literature often contribute to the training of artists. Furthermore, such recent tendencies as the resident poet or writer bring the arts more closely into the university orbit.

The worlds of newspaper and book publishing and radio and television broadcasting have a more cognitive-informational emphasis. The editorial function in publishing houses is close to the academic, and, although private publishers are numerous, there are university presses, often with faculty participation in editorial functions. For journalism, including electronic broadcasting, some training takes place within the university in schools of journalism. Harvard, though without such a school, has the Nieman Fellowship program. Indeed, journalistic circles convey the feeling that journalism is not a business but carries fiduciary responsibilities, including commitment to the value of cognitive rationality.[20]

It would be a mistake to attribute the proliferation of these predominantly nonacademic cultural complexes in modern society entirely to technology, although technology has been prominent. More correctly, this proliferation is part of the same general movement in both the cultural and societal systems of which the expansion of the academic system itself is also an outcome. Indeed,

19. The senior author has noted: "As I write this, I have been listening to a record of a Beethoven piano sonata played by Artur Schnabel. Not only has Beethoven been dead for nearly 150 years—hence his music has survived only because it was written—but the performing artist, Schnabel, died a number of years ago. The recording, played with modern equipment, is not quite the same as hearing Beethoven play his own sonata in person, nor hearing Schnabel, on the actual concert stage, play Beethoven. Nevertheless, musically it is very good, hardly an example of the corruption of real values by technology. In principle, the case is parallel to that of the contention that readers of Plato's *Republic* cannot possibly understand his philosophy, since they did not personally participate in the dialogues in the Academy at Athens in Plato's time. Both Plato and Beethoven have *survived* as cultural figures." On the general issue, see Robert K. Merton, "Insiders and Outsiders," *American Journal of Sociology*, 78, no. 1 (July 1972), 9–47.

20. Thus in the 1970 election campaign Vice-President Agnew stirred up resentment among journalists with an accusation of deliberate destructive criticism of Administration policies and actions. The reaction had the ring of genuine moral indignation.

since technology is dependent on the development of science, the technological factor is as much a product of academic developments as are these other phenomena products of technology. The academic and the nonacademic parts of that sector of the society with cultural primacy share common developmental origins and are interdependent with each other.

This information-dispensing complex of institutional arrangements and the settings in which they operate (the press, newspaper, magazine and book publishing, radio and television, the nonverbal arts) are functional equivalents of the clinical focus of the applied professions. This sector of the society constitutes an interface between the academic system and the nonacademic recipients of the relevant categories of its outputs. As clients (readers, listeners, viewers), they relate to the practitioners on various sorts of terms, some paid, some gratis, some with collectivity membership, some without.[21]

However, the same *order* of interpenetration exists in this sector of nonacademic consumers of academic output as in the applied professions, though it is not so intimate. The same order of differentiation in the role structure as in the applied professions closest to the academic system has taken place. Thus, the influence of those oriented to the publics in which intellectuals participate and sometimes aspire to lead does not depend only on being in practice and prepared to serve the interests of clients. Influence depends often, especially for leading members of the field, on the teaching function, sometimes in academic settings, sometimes not. For example, Walter Lippmann, over his long career, has done more than supply the readers of his column with informative comments on public affairs; he has served as a model for political journalists, and his books belong in the main literature of political science. Other examples are Raymond Aron in France, who has in fact been a university professor, and perhaps James Reston, who has not.

Not surprisingly, there is a problem of the academic respectability of views expressed by high-level journalists and T.V. commentators. A major faction among intellectuals of these types is antagonistic to the academic establishment and shades into the world of the dropouts. A minority of academics participate actively in the discussions of nonacademic intellectuals—a promi-

21. Hover and Kadushin, "The Influential Intellectual Journals." Their findings support this view.

nent example is John Kenneth Galbraith. In short, the pro- and anti-academic orientations among intellectuals articulate with internal tensions and conflicts within the academic system itself.[22]

Although it is justifiable to treat the interface between the academic system and intellectuals as distinct from that between the practitioners of applied professions, there is also structural continuity between these interfaces; empirically the boundaries are fluid even though an analytical distinction may be valid. The analogy to the *client* population of the applied professions lies in the intellectually interested public, the members of which constitute the readership and viewership of the statements of such people. Where this public is academic, their interest is only partly with the cognitive concerns in material they pay attention to.

The university makes a major contribution to this complex, both by contributing substantive ideas and by holding up cognitive standards. Although some academic intellectuals with a following in the general public are looked at askance by colleagues who restrict their audiences to academic circles, nevertheless both academic and nonacademic intellectuals are sensitive to considerations of cognitive rationality in a sense in which most politicians, for example, are not. The output of the universities to this sector of the society is indispensable to the functioning of the intellectual milieu, which is in turn necessary for a modern society.[23] These references to the structural and interchange settings provide background for a discussion of problems of the intellectual content of ideological activity.

### Ideological Developments and the University

Our interest is thus with the interrelations of the academic system and those parts of the nonacademic system involved in cognitive concerns at high levels of generality and should follow two main directions of noncognitive cultural concern, namely, the moral-evaluative and the expressive-aesthetic. Furthermore, a par-

22. There have been a number of other American academic men besides Galbraith who can qualify as prominent intellectuals. Examples from the social science area are Milton Friedman, David Riesman, Erik Erikson, Norman O. Brown, and Hans Morgenthau, and from other areas Noam Chomsky, I. I. Rabi, Edward Teller, and the late Robert Oppenheimer. Such figures are matched from the nonacademic side by Lewis Mumford, Norman Mailer, William J. Buckley, and others. There are also persons in the worlds of theater, music, films, and arts who could be included in such a list.

23. Clifford Geertz, "After the Revolution: The Fate of Nationalism in the New States," in *Stability and Social Change*, ed. Bernard Barber and Alex Inkeles (Boston, Mass., Little, Brown and Co., 1971), pp. 357–376.

tially secularized religious concern plays into both, perhaps especially the expressive-aesthetic.

The process of secularization, as it impinged on the academic system, has had its counterpart in the world of intellectuals as an enhanced concern with problems of meaning rather than with empirical explanation alone.

In terms of Western intellectual history, the evolution of the main themes of the secular intellectuals' concerns can be traced in orderly sequence involving differentiation and the other processes of the development of action systems.[24] A few highlights of this developmental history will be touched upon here. Probably the first developmental process was oriented about the status of science vis-à-vis religion. This theme was central to the new philosophy launched by Descartes. Soon, however, under the twin conceptions of a divinely ordained order and of the order of nature, a concern emerged for defining the situation for social man. Social and political conceptions tended to merge in the line running from Hobbes through Locke to Rousseau with a dialectical tension between the individualistic emphases of English utilitarianism and the collectivism of Rousseau. (Rousseau was followed not only by the French but by the Continental tradition more generally.) In its societal references, this definition of the situation did much to set the cultural tone for the two processes of societal transformation subsequent to the establishment of the first phase of modern societies, in England, Holland, and France in the seventeenth century, namely, the industrial and the democratic revolutions.[25]

The two main conceptions were that of society as a contractual network of relations among discrete and independent individuals, each acting in terms of his natural rights and self-interest and that of a solidary secular collectivity, where the concept of people as a political entity fused the analytically distinct categories of polity and societal community. Set against this political concept of a society was the English one which emerged in the classical economists' conception of a market system embodying an indefinite plurality of contractual arrangements. The Rousseauistic conception underlay the democratic revolution by legitimizing the *inclusion* of the whole citizen body in the societal collectivity, thus destroying the legitimacy of a society in which privileged

24. Talcott Parsons, "The Sociology of Knowledge and the History of Ideas," unpub. MS, Harvard University.

25. Talcott Parsons, *The System of Modern Societies* (Englewood Cliffs, N.J., Prentice-Hall, Inc., 1971).

classes (including the Church as a privileged collectivity) held the ascendancy. The utilitarian conception which emphasized freedom of individuals to engage in enterprise in their own interests with the probability that the net outcome of such endeavors would be beneficial to society as a whole was the ideological foundation of the industrial revolution, especially in the English-speaking world. These lines of ideological difference persisted between France and England into the eighteenth century, were reflected in social structure, and set the stage for the nineteenth-century polarization between the idealized conceptions of capitalism and socialism as the basic alternatives open to secularized Western society and later to the world as a whole.[26]

Leaning on the background of secular philosophy and of the developing sciences, interpretation of what was happening in Western societies was intertwined with early phases of the development of the social science disciplines. In a rough sense, the differentiation of focus we have outlined was that between an older conception of political science, somewhat in the tradition of Aristotle, and the emergence of economics as a technical discipline. Politics continued to incorporate the older conservative traditions, and economics was susceptible of a conservative interpretation because of its relation to the vested interests of the rising bourgeois classes. At any rate, the association of the secularizing movement with processes of societal differentiation and thus with social change was symbolized by the fact that the industrial and political transformative processes were labelled revolutions. This association has left an imprint on the

26. In Chapter 3 we treated the focal type of social organization of faculties, the collegial association, which is prominent in the fiduciary sector of the society, as one of four possible types, the other three being the economic market, the democratic association, and administrative bureaucracy. In the capitalism-socialism polarization, the market was the type used to characterize capitalism, though Marx synthesized this with a formula for the structure of the capitalistic firm as a two-level power structure consisting of owners and workers. In short, the socialist movement tended to borrow from Rousseau in emphasizing the unitary societal collectivity; the public interest was contrasted with the self-interest of capitalists. Among the two political types of structure, however, its tendency was to emphasize the democratic side and leave the role of bureaucracy in actual organizations, especially those of economic production, little discussed. Weber more than any other author called attention to bureaucracy as an organizational type, and he did so particularly with reference to economic production. Bureaucracy has become the bête noire in the ideology of the recent left as the market was for the socialists. The collegial-associational type, which is not confined to universities but permeates the world of the professions, has scarcely surfaced in ideological discussions yet. Negative characterizations of the professions, although not absent, tend either to treat them as bureaucracies or as monopolies, the latter being a version of the market model. Perhaps the feeling remains that as estates, collegial associations are medieval and have no place in the modern world.

status of the social sciences in relation to the more diffuse role of modern intellectuals. Although most of the main themes were already familiar by the mid-nineteenth century, Karl Marx succeeded best in synthesizing the economic and political themes of the two revolutions taken together and the radical theme of the conflict between the exploited and alienated elements and the ruling classes.[27] Implicit in the Marxian view was a romantic bias (derived from Rousseau) in favor of the elimination of classes and exploitation by the absorption of all classes into an undivided societal community with a unitary general will.

The materialistic conception of history legitimizes the view that in the last analysis what counts in human affairs is the economic interests of the population and their power relations as delineated in the Marxian scheme. This intellectual situation set the stage for the ideological controversies of the later nineteenth and the earlier twentieth centuries, where the main issue was capitalism versus socialism. The socialist and labor movements in Europe formed a realistic reference point, culminating in the Russian Revolution. The clarity of the dichotomy was, however, blurred by such factors as the fascist movements (alleged by the left-socialists to be capitalist), the sharing by democratic socialism of commitment to political democracy with certain capitalist elements, the fact that many liberal capitalists considered socialism and fascism to be brothers under the skin, and the continued existence of preliberal and preindustrial conservatism.

Although the secular interpretation of the social world constituted a major preoccupation of intellectuals in this period and although the processes of development in the social sciences, notably economics and political science, were one point of articulation with the academic world, there were also stirrings in other cultural areas. The processes of industrialization were understood to involve developments of science and technology rather than only economic and power interests and class conflict. The turn of the century also saw new developments in the aesthetic-humanistic sphere, such as those of painting in France, but ramifying into the humanities in the academic world. In the background, in spite of its integration with Marxian socialism, the version of secular humanism which tended to be expressed as scientific materialism

27. Karl Marx and Frederick Engels, *The Communist Manifesto*, trans. Samuel Moore (Chicago, Ill., Henry Regnery Co., 1954).

began to falter in its nineteenth century aura of apodictic certainty—for example, that the claims of religion had been refuted and hence that rational men were necessarily atheists.

Nearest to the ideological core, however, was a weakening of the rigidity of the socialism-capitalism dichotomy. This in turn was related to a diminution in the dominance of economics and political science over the other social sciences in the universities.

A combination of two aspects of this shift is of special interest to us. Historically, the intellectual creators of the capitalism-socialism ideologies were, even on the conservative side, socially located outside the university setting despite exceptions like Adam Smith. This was true of Edmund Burke, Bentham, Ricardo, John Stuart Mill, St. Simon, Marx, Engels, and Lenin. Since the turn of the present century, however, the intellectual resources for ideological structuring have been provided by the universities with the development of academic economics, political science, philosophy, history, sociology, psychology, anthropology, and certain of the humanistic disciplines. Now even the nonacademic intellectuals are usually university trained.

This circumstance gives the universities a different order of importance in shaping the process of ideological definition of the situation than was the case in the nineteenth century. It also increases the universities' vulnerability from both the ideological right and the left. Lipset's studies[28] show that academic people are, in their political opinions, typically on the left of the American population. Nevertheless, academics find it necessary to defend themselves from pressures and sometimes realistic attacks not only from the political right, but, more recently, they have undergone the disconcerting experience of being under pressure and attack from the political and cultural left, charged with being guilty of complicity with the exploitative, repressive, and imperialistic establishment.[29]

28. Seymour M. Lipset, "Youth and Politics," in *Contemporary Social Problems,* 3rd. ed., ed. Robert K. Merton and Robert Nisbet (New York, Harcourt, Brace, Jovanovich, Inc., 1971), pp. 743–791. See also Seymour M. Lipset, "The Politics of Academia," in *Perspectives on Campus Tensions: Papers Prepared for the Special Committee on Campus Tensions* (Washington, D.C., The American Council on Education, 1970).

29. This dual vulnerability is related to a third institution of academic organization (in addition to academic tenure and academic freedom), the institution of *corporate* political neutrality. We have not undertaken to discuss this institution at length in the present book, but an autonomous university system in a pluralistic society clearly cannot as a corporate entity be identified with any partisan position. What the New Left radicals offer as an alternative to "complicity" is not autonomy but instrumental dependence on *their* political movement. See the Carnegie Foundation for the Advance-

This institutional change has been related to one of substantive cognitive content, namely, the shaking of the near monopoly of prestige in the social science disciplines formerly held by economics and political science through the rise to prominence of sociology, psychology, and anthropology and to shifts of emphasis within the discipline of history. Sociology, psychology, and anthropology only began to be institutionalized in university faculties in the late nineteenth century.[30]

From the longer-run point of view, the spearhead of the change may prove to have been the rise of sociology. Both psychology and anthropology were regarded for a long time as ideologically innocuous because of their relation to biological science, which was linked with ideological conservatism. Indeed, it was not until the spread of psychoanalytic thinking that an ideologically different tendency appeared. Anthropology had the potentially disturbing connection with the concept of culture. Sociology, though it often was indistinguishable from psychology and anthropology, did not have such firm roots in either biological or cultural traditions. It was therefore under cognitive pressure to assert its independence from these two sister disciplines as well as from economics and political science in spite of historical relations to them.[31]

With respect to the cognitive analysis of social systems, this academic shift constituted a new order of concern with the fiduciary system and the societal community as distinguished from concern with the polity and the economy. It reflected the differentiation between the conceptions of the polity as collective goal-oriented subsystem and the societal community, a differentiation which could not take place on the basis of Rousseau's postulates or on those of Marx. Concern with the sociological problems of the

---

ment of Teaching, Bulletin #34, 1971, for an informed discussion of this problem. See also Alexander M. Bickel, "Political Involvement—Notes," prepared for a conference of the American Academy of Arts and Sciences, November 13–14, 1970, unpub. MS, Boston, Mass.

30. As late as the 1930's there was no independent Harvard Department of Psychology, but one of Philosophy and Psychology, and no official recognition of Sociology until 1931, long after the University of Chicago, Columbia, and several other American universities. Anthropology was nearly contemporaneous with psychology in its institutionalization. On the institutionalization of sociology, see Edward Shils, "Tradition, Ecology, and Institution in the History of Sociology," *Daedalus* (Fall 1970), pp. 760–825. On the institutionalization of psychology, see Joseph Ben-David and R. Collins, "Social Factors in the Origins of a New Science: The Case of Psychology," *American Sociological Review*, 31, no. 4 (1966), 451–466.

31. The meeting at which the founding of the American Sociological Association took place was actually a meeting of the American Economic Association, to which all the American sociological "founding fathers" belonged.

professions, as distinguished from the traditional treatment of the market system, constitutes a less salient parallel. Interest in the sociology of religion and of kinship fit in the same intellectual context. Many of the more general problems of this intellectual shift come to a head in concern for education, particularly higher education.[32]

Anthropology and psychology, though overlapping and inter-penetrating with sociology, have been primarily concerned not with social systems but with cultural and psychological (personality) systems. From the point of view of the roster of the intellectual disciplines, this development has rounded out the Comte-Spencer classification of the sciences. It links the social sciences with the humanities, notably history, philosophy, and the critical analysis of cultural products in literature and the arts.[33] It also links them, through psychology and through aspects of anthropology,[34] with the natural sciences by way of biology.

The consequence in the intellectual sphere has been to focus attention on a ramified set of problems concerning the human condition, the scope of which is parallel to that of the religious controversies of the Reformation period but which, in cognitive terms, enjoys the enhanced sophistication of three centuries of intellectual development. The original secularization of social thought associated with the Enlightenment made a convincing case that the real social forces were economic and political when they were not biological. The process of differentiation in modern societies and its relations to culture and personality have made this case less plausible at the societal level as well as at the interpenetrating ones, especially of culture. This change of emphasis has been associated with the emergence of the behavioral sciences other than economics and politics.

Not many years ago, there was much talk about the "end of ideology."[35] Although disputed, it seems justified to contend that the classic ideological division between capitalism and socialism has been receding from salience. The symbolic polarization between

32. This line of theoretical development helps to explain why *sociologists* are writing the present book.

33. Frye, "The Critical Path."

34. Talcott Parsons, "Clyde Kluckhohn and the Integration of Social Science," in *Culture and Life: Essays in Memory of Clyde Kluckhohn*, ed. Walter W. Taylor, John L. Fischer, and Evon Z. Vogt (Carbondale, Ill., Southern Illinois University Press, 1973), pp. 30–57.

35. Daniel Bell, *The End of Ideology: On the Exhaustion of Political Ideas in the Fifties* (Glencoe, Ill., The Free Press, 1960).

"left" and "right" continues, however. Moreover the New Left uses Marxist rhetoric, including categorizing what it calls the right as "capitalist." Nothing as clear-cut as the older socialist ideology in either its Communist or Democratic Socialist versions has yet emerged despite significant, though subtle, shifts. One hears about alienation and about class conflict, but little about the economic aspects of Marxian theory; indeed, one sometimes gets the impression that the author of *Das Kapital* is considered to have been past his intellectual prime and writing about trivialities; it was the young Marx who was "authentic." Alienation is no longer focused on labor but rather on the relation between persons and social roles in any institutionalized situation, and the economic meaning of exploitation has shifted to an allegation of diffuse repressiveness into which psychoanalytic ideas have entered as well as economic and political.[36]

On the conservative side, it is no longer easy to identify those who are not left-radicals with a strictly capitalistic ideology. The key concept here is "liberalism." Ever since the capitalism-socialism dichotomy took shape, those on the left have tried to identify liberalism with capitalism as well as with the remnants of preindustrial conservatism and, more recently, with newer versions of the radical right, notably fascism and its subsequent relatives, such as McCarthyism in the United States in the 1950's. This identification has been prominent among Communist intellectuals, who have tried to argue that there are two and only two possibilities. On the right, certain factions have tried to argue the converse position: that anything except orthodox laissez-faire attitudes constituted creeping socialism and would end up as Communist-type dictatorship.[37]

36. In Chapter 2 we called attention to the affinity in cognitive structure between (a) the economic system and its theory at the social-system level and (b) the cognitive system at the cultural level. Since left-radical ideologists, like any intellectuals, try to articulate their views in as cognitively rational terms as they can, perhaps they are generalizing from their felt opposition to the academic establishment as institutionalized in the universities to the older traditions of the evils of capitalism. Hence they find the suggestion congenial that the evil part of the modern university derives in essence from its capitalistic associations.

37. The more extreme wing of the Old Left has been the Communist movement. In spite of a common ideological excoriation of capitalism, there has been on the whole little mutual sympathy between this wing and the New Left. Partisans of the New Left are unsympathetic to the Soviet Union and the socialist societies, with the partial and somewhat ambivalent exceptions of Mao's China and Castro's Cuba. Orthodox Communist ideologists for their part are also not impressed with the New Left. The antagonism came to a head in France in 1968 when overtures from the student radicals to the Communist party and trade unions were rebuffed.

The rigidity of this dichotomy has been broken by the existence and growing importance of a center which could not reasonably be driven into either of the polarized positions. On the left, a role has been played by democratic socialism, which shared the main patterns of political democracy with nonsocialist democratic movements but refused to let itself be identified with the dictatorial elements of Communism. Only this has made it possible for much of the Western European intellectual world to maintain an identification with American democracy. In the political arena, the problem came to a head in relation to the fascist movement, notably German Nazism which the democratic socialist groups refused to identify with capitalistic democracy such as the New Deal movement in the United States or the state of British society when the Labor Party was out of office.

On the right, there has been a dissociation between the liberal, shading into a conservative, position and those of the variegated groups classified as the radical right. Only this center, differentiated from both the radical left and the radical right, has made workable what the Western world understands as political democracy. Although not devoid of internal conflicts, these can usually be sufficiently modulated so that loyal opposition is possible, including the acceptance, without resort to violence, of political defeat on particular occasions. Thus, political democracy is bound up with structural pluralism in the society. This in turn implies that both plural economic interests and interests grounded in other bases, locality, religion, ethnicity, and indeed social class itself, can be integrated into a system of order not inherently repressive or exploitative. This integration is dependent on a high degree of differentiation between the polity and the societal community, differentiation the legitimacy of which the romantic tradition of Rousseau has denied.[38] The logical extreme of Rousseau's point of view is that *all* relations of solidarity between individuals and societal collectivities must be totally integrated in a unitary community of interest and service.[39] The pluralistic point of view, on the other hand, is that formal collective decision-making should not comprise all fields of every interest but should become a differentiated function, limited in its performance to contexts where there is,

38. Jean-Jacques Rousseau, *The Social Contract and Discourses* (New York, E. P. Dutton and Co., 1923).
39. In this respect, Rousseau was the spiritual father of Lenin.

in extensity of function and in time, a specific urgency of collective action.

The liberal ideological position asserts the legitimacy and functional significance for a modern society of this sphere of pluralized political interests and commitments and its relation to a structurally pluralistic societal community. These radicalisms of both right and left function to dedifferentiate this pluralistic differentiatedness by asserting that legitimacy is confined to commitment to a *single* position, which unites goal-attainment orientations (the political component) with legitimation by undifferentiated value-commitments.

Although we have treated the academic system as specifically differentiated from the economic, political, and religious contexts and from the local community, and so on, it must articulate with all of them. For the reasons already discussed, especially in Chapters 2 and 3, the autonomy of the academic system is vital to the effective performance of its differentiated functions. One way of coping with this problem is to assert the right of academic control over these other differentiated sectors. This has been expressed in the ancient fantasy of philosopher kings, but in spite of tendencies in this direction from time to time[40] it has not been the major trend in any but the more primitive Communist societies. Since intellectual man rests his case on persuasion, he is not well suited to be the primary wielder of political power.

Another extreme solution is expressed in the German term, *Gleichschaltung*, a major slogan of the Nazis. *Gleichschaltung*, the sacrifice of autonomy by giving primacy to participation in a movement in which the academic role is defined as instrumental, has been the trend in the definition of the academic function in all totalitarian systems, both Communist and fascist. This type of solution harks back to the status of religion before the processes of differentiation, both cultural and social, took place.

*Structural Issues Defining the Situation.* The present analysis concentrates on a process of interchange between the academic system and the predominantly nonacademic intellectual community concerned with contributions to a general definition of the situation rather than with specific practical services. Since academic secularization, the focus of this interchange has been on the meanings of the state of contemporary society and its changes.

40. McGeorge Bundy, "Were Those the Days?" *Daedalus* (Summer 1970), pp. 531–567.

Cognitive grounds of intellectuals' general orientation to the social situation are needed, but as with the applied professions this cognitive interest must be synthesized with an interest in a morally, politically, and affectively satisfying solution of problems of orientation. This latter need articulates with the structural divisions within the social system and, underlying these divisions, those of different classes of personalities and different modes of involvement with cultural concerns. Ideological structures are the *result* of the interaction of cognitive and other orientational needs. There are ramified complexities, for example, whether a more political-science or more sociological perspective enters into an ideological formulation or whether the intellectuals in question feel closer kinship with aesthetic or political-activist elements in the society.

As in the case of the applied professions, the articulation between the cognitive resources of the university and the felt needs of its intellectual clientele must occur through a rearrangement and different selection of cognitive content analogous to that occurring through the clinical focus of the applied professions. Certain of the academic disciplines play the role of basic sciences for ideological utilization.

This role implies pressures impinging on the disciplines most closely involved and helps to explain Lipset's findings that politization has gone farther in such disciplines as sociology, philosophy, political science, and, to a lesser degree in economics, than in the natural sciences.

Before secularization of universities occurred, theological faculties performed an equivalent of these ideological functions internal to the university (or college); furthermore, they were linked to an external intellectual leadership group, the Protestant clergy. Professors in divinity schools and some at the college level were in effect clinical professors in the ideological field.

There does not now exist any specific organizational framework within the university structure for meeting this ideological need, and so far there has not been a strong demand for it. This structural vacuum may have been a factor in the vulnerability of the universities in situations of pressure to which they have recently been subjected.

The foregoing considerations suggest, if not a plan for such organization, at least principles by which this ideological function could be carried out relatively smoothly. The modern university has an affinity with liberal democracy with its pluralization of legitimate political affiliations. This pluralization underlies the principle of corporate political neutrality as distinguished from the granting of rights for individual political opinion and participation.

These rights, essentially rights of the citizen in liberal democratic societies, are closely connected with academic freedom, which is the right to conduct cognitive exploration and communication with minimal preimposed constraints. It includes the right to express and advocate extreme views. However, academic freedom demands, if it is to be generalized in a community, *procedural* regulation in the interest of civility and intellectual integrity. Civility and intellectual integrity impose constraints on freedom of *political* action within the academic community—and indeed of some kinds of expressive action. Such constraints have to do with preservation of the freedoms of all groups in the community from being suppressed by particular militant groups and with preservation from exposure to offensive actions. Some consideration must also be given to the protection of the institution's position in the larger community. Specific lines are notoriously difficult to draw, but the principles just stated seem reasonable.

There is an illuminating analogy in psychoanalytic procedure. The analysand is given an unusual freedom for verbal self-expression; he is encouraged to say anything which occurs to him in the course of treatment. A line, however, is drawn between use of this verbal liberty and what psychoanalysts call "acting out," namely, converting fantasies into overt action, between expressing hostile feelings toward the therapist in the analytic situation and of physically attacking him. The analogy goes a step farther in that the analyst's interpretations are meant to provide emotionally significant cognitive clarification of the analysand's motives, situation, and problems.[41]

The academic clarification of the society's ideological problems, this time in a public forum, is analogous to the analyst's interpretations. They must be intellectually respectable; the cognitive component must not be simply subordinated to other interests. The standard academic organization of knowledge and competence, however, must also be adapted, by selection and reorganization in

41. Marshall Edelson, "Toward a Study of Interpretation in Psychoanalysis: An Essay in Symbolic Process in Psychoanalysis and the Theory of Action," in *Exploration in General Theory in Social Science*, ed. Johannes J. Loubser, *et al.* (New York, The Free Press, 1973).

terms of relevance, to concerns which include noncognitive components.

Thus continuity exists among all three of the contexts of relevance of cognitive concerns outside the realm of clear primacy of cognitive values. All three functions can be fruitfully furthered through the institutionalization of a clinical focus or its equivalent. Within this pattern, a process of synthesis between cognitive and noncognitive components can take place. In each case this involves a protected environment where the harsher pressures of the world of everyday responsibility can be relaxed. The institution of academic freedom, as well as tenure and corporate neutrality, provide this protected environment[42] and belongs in the same broad class with the institution of privileged communication in the applied professions. More generally, it is a case of the institutionalization of *privacy*.

If anything, the desirable direction of change is not to weakening the hard-won boundaries of the academic system in favor of its assimilation to other parts of the surrounding society, but rather to make them clearer and stronger than before, though by no means impermeable. This need for clearer institutionalization seems to us to be particularly most urgent in the field of the present discussion, namely the relation of the university world to the needs of intellectuals and their client publics.

## The Ideological Outlook

*Cultural and Social Levels.* In developing hypotheses about dynamic processes and trends of change in Chapter 7, we will attempt to take into account the balance of input-output relations on which ideological outcomes depend. For the present, it seems sufficient to establish a pattern of articulation concerning general sociopolitical ideological movements. This can be construed as the legitimate successor of the division of Western society and culture in earlier centuries into dialectically interacting religious groups,

---

42. The reader will recognize that in Chapter 4 we treated this protected environment as important for the student socialization function in the undergraduate college. We adopted the terms "permissiveness" and "support" from the paradigm used to analyze psychotherapy to characterize features of that protected environment. The present discussion is meant to generalize this conception of a protected environment to the other two concepts of university function without full cognitive primacy. Academic freedom and tenure are part of the same family of institutional patternings. See Alan Heimert, *Discussion Memorandum on Academic Tenure at Harvard University*, The University Committee on Governance, Harvard University, November 1971.

on the surface furiously combatting each other, but with underlying cultural consensus.

A parallel may be drawn between the polarization of Western Christendom, divided into Catholicism and Protestantism, in the Reformation and post-Reformation periods and that of capitalism and socialism in the period of the culmination of the democratic and industrial revolutions. In both cases, the sharp dichotomy did not turn out to be stable nor to lead to the definitive victory of one or the other position. Current Western society is at the same time an ecumenical and a secularized civilization.

The society currently in process of formation will be neither capitalist nor socialist in the older senses. There has been a decline of ideology parallel to the process of secularization at religious levels. The cognitive role parallel to that of philosophy in the seventeenth century and in the Enlightenment is in our time being played by the social-behavioral sciences in combination with philosophy. As in the capitalism-socialism polarization, the Western intellectual world is again moving toward a secular-ecumenical phase, in which economics and politics are no longer sacred interpreters of the societal aspect of the human condition.

These considerations as well as actual trends of social change help to explain the New Left's structural location and orientation. Consider the tenacity with which Marxist rhetoric is affirmed. Marx was concerned with using the analysis of the classical economics, whereas the New Left is not interested in Marx's economic theory and even less in post-Marxian economics. Instead there is a pervasive fear that the new social science—and even psychoanalysis—is too firmly bound up with the establishment. What is the cognitive foundation for these attitudes? Although Marxism is authentically revolutionary and espouses the causes of the currently underprivileged on many fronts, its position in the socialist establishment, notably the Soviet Union, is embarrassing. Nevertheless, the leftist intellectual can emphasize the political context as an instrumentality of change in the directions he advocates and to be "with it" in terms of sensitivity and participation in the newer noninstitutional and indeed noneconomic and nonpolitical movements that are often summed up as "the counterculture." The balance between the political and the counterculture emphases is probably precarious, but they are held together, in part at least, by their relation to the common enemy, the establishment and "squareness." The fact that Marxian sociology and philosophy have *not* stood at the center of the stage of academic development is an ideological point in its favor for the left.[43]

Consider also that although the academic community is politically left of center in general, the highest concentration of left radicalism, among faculty and among students, is found in sociology and philosophy. This is not a chance occurrence, but it indicates that these disciplines are storm centers of the social and ideological tensions impinging on the academic system. That this should be the fate of sociology is perhaps clarified by the foregoing discussion. Sociology is concerned with the characteristics of the differentiating societal community and many of its subsectors and not primarily with economic and political problems.

The concentration of left radicalism in philosophy has a related significance, which leads to the last main consideration of the present chapter: a broadening of the focus of the ideological problem from its social system core on the capitalism-socialism issue. Psychology on the personality side and anthropology on the cultural side have played an important role with respect to academic disciplines. Anthropology has also been a vehicle of broadening the range of comparative references within which modern contemporary society can be understood.

There has been a current of revolt against the alleged parochialism or culture-boundness of earlier generations of social scientists. In American anthropology, emphasis has been on the study of values,[44] which feeds into the trend toward emphasizing moral problems. Given sufficient bias against the status quo, it is easy to cite almost any difference of value-pattern from the established

43. One social-psychological source of the tension between the academic social sciences and the ideologists, especially ideologists of the left, lies in the fact that a major aspect of the ethos of science—i.e., all the intellectual disciplines—is organized skepticism. See Robert K. Merton, "Science and Democratic Social Structure," in *Social Theory and Social Structure*, rev. ed. (Glencoe, Ill., The Free Press, 1957), chap. xvi, pp. 550–561. The *duty* of a scientist—a *Wissenschaftler* in Weber's sense—is to *question* the cognitive validity and/or significance of propositions which are current and and relevant to his interests and to seek evidence to confirm or disconfirm whatever doubts he may have. The ideologist, on the other hand, always questions the level of his *commitment* to the ideology, including the cognitive belief component of it. Ideologies constitute forms of rhetoric which seek to mobilize *faith*. Repeated conflicts occur over this issue at both religious and ideological levels. Currently, antagonism on the part of New Left ideologists to establishment social science may be as much based on objections to this pattern of organized skepticism as it is on objections to substantive generalizations current in these fields. The tension is compounded by the claim by dissidents to the same freedoms to express their views as the establishment academics have. They cannot, however, reciprocate by granting the legitimacy of the skepticism which underlies the latters' tolerance.

44. Ruth Benedict, *Patterns of Culture* (Boston and New York, Houghton Mifflin Co., 1934). Kluckhohn, "Values and Value-Orientations."

ones as evidence of how narrow the latter are. This relates to a process of value-generalization occurring in the general society and culture, but is not only reflected but in part guided by the academic version of the relevant intellectual developments. In a phase of turbulence, values radically different from the institutionalized ones are avidly grasped at as allegedly the truly authentic ones. Thus, the Judeo-Christian tradition is often declared to be bankrupt, not only because of anticlerical secularism but in the broader perspective of religio-cultural development, and oriental religions are extolled. The Judeo-Christian tradition, like the bourgeoisie, will be superseded by the genuine values of the cultural proletariat : Buddhists, Hindus, and perhaps Muslims.

There is a link between attraction to Marxism and attraction to the oriental religions, allegedly victimized by the prejudiced and culture-bound West, and to the attraction of Marxism in non-Western societies, notably China. The link is that Marxism is a secularized version of the main pattern of Christian theology; its secular status neutralizes many of the rationalistic and political objections to the historic Christian transcendentalism and other-worldliness.[45]

The analogue of the Judeo-Christian tradition includes a definition of the world as essentially evil, for original Marxism the world of capitalism, for the current New Left, the Establishment. To lead the faithful out of their involvements in this evil world, there has appeared a savior, who is reviled and persecuted because his true nature is not appreciated, indeed cannot be by those not possessed of the Spirit. This time, however, the Savior is not an individual but a collectivity, originally the proletariat, specifically defined as of the humblest origin and having had to suffer humiliation and persecution. The Spirit seems to be class consciousness. This, as Erikson has noted for the New Left youth,[46] is a bridge to the conception of the revolt of the dependent who are youth, the poor, the racial minorities, peoples oppressed by colonialism, and (with some ambiguities) women.

In the New Left version, the figure of the proletariat becomes indistinct since neither its self-appointed vanguard, the Communist parties, nor the allegedly co-opted trade unions and labor move-

45. Talcott Parsons, "Belief, Unbelief, and Disbelief," in *The Culture of Unbelief*, ed. R. Caprole and A. Grumelli (Berkeley, Calif., The University of California Press, 1971), chap. xii.
46. Erik H. Erikson, "Reflections on the Dissent of Contemporary Youth," *Daedalus* (Winter 1970), pp. 154–176.

ments, are acceptable. Hence, the tendency is for radical young people to appoint themselves to the role of savior. Another feature common to radical ideologies and the Judeo-Christian tradition lies in their eschatological view. In secular versions, the Second Coming has been replaced by the Revolution, after which all the evils of the world will allegedly disappear, for the older Marxism in the state of Communism, for the newer movements in a vaguely defined state of universal brotherhood and love.[47]

This similarity of patterning between the Christian myth and ideologies of the Old and the New Left helps to clarify the differences between the cognitive structure of the academic intellectual disciplines and of ideologies. Because of the historic and current interpenetration between religion and ideology and between the academic world and religion, these different cognitive structures pose problems. One attempt to build a cultural bridge has been the *liberal* myth, which in turn relates to the stake of the academic system in the pluralistic structure of modern societies.[48]

Clearly the conflict between the ethos of organized skepticism of science and the call to faith of "myths of concern" or ideologies is, as noted above, a major source of tension and hence a barrier to full integration. In addition to this, however, there are fundamental differences of symbolic structure. To adopt Frye's term, myths of concern, which seems to cover all three of the primarily noncognitive types, perhaps the most striking difference is that primarily cognitive symbolism minimizes both teleological and genetic orientation; it is primarily concerned with knowing in a sense in the here and now. This is not to say that it is not interested in predictions and possibilities of the future nor in the history of current states of affairs, but it is not, *qua knowledge*, constitutively, morally, or expressively engaged in the *non*cognitive meanings of the future or the past. This of course is an ideal type.

Certainly for the Western world, the Christian and the Marxian myths have, grounding as they do at constitutive levels, been the most influential. Whether and how either or both can be integrated with the cognitive complex at levels which are compatible with the modern university system and the possibilities of its further development remains an open question.

47. Frank E. Manuel and Fritzie P. Manuel, "Sketch for a Natural History of Paradise," *Daedalus* (Winter 1972), pp. 83–128; Judith N. Sklar, "Subversive Genealogies," *Daedalus* (Winter 1972), pp. 129–154.
48. Frye, "The Critical Path." See also Kenneth Burke, *The Rhetoric of Religion* (Boston, Mass., Beacon Press, 1961).

*Personality and Organism Levels.* The second extension of the problem beyond the societal focus is in some ways more difficult to analyze cogently. Really far-reaching processes of differentiation and its concomitants in systems of action involve not only the social and cultural systems but that of personality and indeed the behavioral organism itself. In some respects this process of reorientation of definitions of the situation is as important as that within the societal system itself.

On the side of the empirical development of systems of action, we agree with Robert Bellah[49] that the process of development of social systems as part of action involves not only the differentiation of the social system itself but the differentiation of both cultural and personality systems *from* the social system and of each category of system internally within itself. The development of the intellectual disciplines and the process of secularization are processes of the differentiation of the cultural system from the social and concomitantly of differentiation internal to the cultural system itself.

Similarly, there has been in the modern period a process of differentiation of the personality system from the social system and from the cultural system. This has been manifested in a variety of facets of individualism and related modes of institutionalization of individual freedom and autonomy, as in the complex of rights discussed in T. H. Marshall's analysis of the development of citizenship in Great Britain.[50] Among the intellectual disciplines, individualistic concepts have seeped into psychology and certain parts of philosophy, but also into the other social-behavioral disciplines, and indeed into law and medicine. There has been much analysis of various aspects of the autonomy of the individual and of various contexts of the character of the personality and of the organism.

Eighteenth- and nineteenth-century economic analysis converged with the social advocacy of economic individualism in an early version of the modern phase of this trend. Among the many currents, two nearly contemporary ones, psychoanalysis and existentialism, are self-defined as in conflict with economic individualism but are in our opinion closely related both to each other and with it.

49. Robert N. Bellah, "Religious Evolution," in *Beyond Belief: Essays on Religion in a Post-Traditional World* (New York, Harper and Row, 1970), pp. 20–50.
50. T. H. Marshall, *Class, Citizenship, and Social Development* (Garden City, N.Y., Doubleday and Co., 1964; Anchor Books, 1965).

From the point of view of a sociologist, psychoanalysis, existentialism, and economic individualism have all been deficient in their appreciation of the significance of social systems as a component of the human condition, positive as well as negative. In their more extreme moods, some of their proponents have talked as though the great imperative is the total emancipation of all human persons from all social control as inherently repressive[51] or inherently incompatible with the dignity of total human responsibility.[52] The utopian situation expected after the eschatological boundary has been crossed is always excepted, but the new society will have practically nothing in common with *any* previous society. Conversely, radicals often accuse psychoanalysts of being concerned only with reconciling their patients to conformity with the establishment. Thus, Freud is given little credit for his stance with respect to traditional religion,[53] to say nothing of his contribution to the loosening of hang-ups with respect to sex, though it must be conceded he was not an unrestricted libertarian in sexual matters.

Freud's work is almost prototypically significant for our present discussion because he stood in the academic tradition of the use of cognitively rational methods.[54] But the *objects* of his concern were not, as for the physical scientist, nonacting entities nor, as for the economist human action, assumed to be rational until proved to be otherwise, but the nonrational aspects of human action shading off into the specifically irrational. In the analytical terms we have been using, Freud was concerned with two components of action which were minimized in the utilitarian and Marxist traditions, namely the affective-expressive and the moral. In Freud's work, the affective-expressive component of action emerged in concepts like libido, cathexis and in the rooting of their motivation in what, often ambiguously, has been called "instinct." The moral aspect entered psychoanalytic theory through the concept of the super-ego, though it has more pervasive ramifications.

So far as the personality as object of study is concerned, the effect of psychoanalysis was to relativize the rational aspects of

51. Herbert Marcuse, *One Dimensional Man: Studies in the Ideology of Advanced Industrial Society* (Boston, Mass., Beacon Press, 1964).

52. Jean-Paul Sartre, *The Age of Reason*, trans. Eric Sutton (London, Hamish Hamilton, 1957).

53. Sigmund Freud, *The Future of an Illusion*, trans. W. D. Robson-Scott (London, Hogarth Press, 1949); also, Sigmund Freud, *Totem and Taboo*, trans. A. A. Brill (New York, Mossat, Yard and Co., 1918), and Sigmund Freud, *Moses and Monotheism*, trans. Katharine Jones (New York, A. A. Knopf, 1939).

54. Sklar, "Subversive Genealogies."

motivation, although the analyst of personality may himself be committed to rational procedures and standards. These two non-rational foci, the affective and the moral, being in a sense justified by psychoanalytic thinking, have been taken as guides to action on the part not only of scientific students of action but of individual actors and movements.

The emergence of psychoanalysis was connected with trends of development of modern, Western society and culture. The themes which have dominated the intellectual movement Freud founded have resonated in the society beyond psychoanalysis. From our analysis in Chapter 4 of the undergraduate student situation, this resonance seems particularly strong in the student community with its sensitivity to . problems of authority, of expressive-autonomy, and of moral legitimacy.

At the philosophical level rather than the level of behavioral science, existentialism's thematic structure is similar to that of psychoanalysis. One strand is the relativizing of the conceptions of rationality, especially as represented in the tradition stemming from Descartes, a relativizing process to which Kant made an early contribution. A second is a stress on the individual as contrasted with institutionalized religion in the theology of Kierkegaard[55] and against *any* societal establishment (in the writings of Sartre).[56] A third strand is the dual emphasis on the moral and the affective-expressive. In Sartre's case, the moral component becomes the heroic moralism of the principled atheist renouncing all hope of rewards in heaven, and the affective-expressive component takes the form of the liberation of human spontaneity and affect from the constraints not only of traditional institutionalized religion but also of any established societal structure.

There is in both movements a duality of contrasts and conflicts which may have coincided recently but need not always do so. One is the theme of the necessity of enhanced individual autonomy seen relative to the constraints, real or alleged, of a society defined even in its institutionalization of tolerance as inherently repressive.[57] This is a new version, new in its included range of

---

55. Sören Kierkegaard, *Either/Or: A Fragment of Life,* trans. David F. Swenson and Lilian M. Swenson (Princeton, N.J., Princeton University Press, 1946) .

56. Sartre, *The Age of Reason.*

57. The popularity of Marcuse arises from his combination of a radical, antisocietal, and eschatological interpretation of the psychoanalytic tradition with a Hegelian-Marxian orientation that preserves the continuity of the tradition of conflict and revolt but loosens orthodox Marxian commitments to the primacy of economic and political de-

relevant considerations, of the old dilemma of the individual *versus* society, a dilemma which modern sociology regards with some skepticism.

The other conflict lies deeper : at the level of the general system of action. This is the poignant conflict between the process of rationalization and those human concerns that conflict with the claims, seen as constraints, of rational behavior or rational social organization. However unstable and temporary it may turn out to be, the *coincidence* of these two thematic conflicts in the current situation constitutes the core of the current ideological controversies and explains why the academic system has become a storm center of such controversy.

By the usual standards of the balance of freedom and constraint, the university is one of the more tolerant sectors of any known society. But the Marcusian stance alleges that, by this very fact, it is an agent of repression. That two-edged sword, the intellect, liberates from previous conformities but *of necessity* imposes new conformities for all those who would follow the rule of reason. Marcuse seems to protest against *any* standard of conformity; when this protest is applied to reason itself, it becomes the advocacy of irrationalism. This existential dilemma, translated to the level of social organization, produces tension between the institutionalized academic system and the radical intellectuals of the New Left, many of whom claim the designation of intellectual but at the same time deny the legitimacy of things intellectual, that is, cognitive.

This seems to be an essentially new phase of the capitalist-socialist ideological discussion. In accord with the double structure of the dilemma, it has constituted a double upgrading of the location of the tensions. With respect to the society, the upward displacement has been from the level of economic and political interests to the level of the societal community, conceived both as *differentiated* from the polity and as related to the institutionalized values in the fiduciary system.

This upward displacement has been a necessary condition of

---

terminants. Marcusians, however, lean more to the affective counterculture than they do to militantly activistic political revolutionism.

Professor Smelser (personal communication) suggests that one basis of the vogue of Marcuse's doctrine of the repressiveness of tolerance may lie in the increased societal dependence on self-restraint and self-discipline cultivated in the independence training of the present youth generation. The dictates of a more fully internalized conscience may be felt to be even more painfully restrictive than the disapproval or punishment of others. If correct, this is an application of the principle of relative deprivation.

raising the question of the status of the individual (both in the psychological references of personality theory and in the cultural references having to do with moral responsibility) as well as the question of accepting guilt oneself or attributing all guilt to the establishment. This means a new statement of the problem of individuality from what, after secularization, was treated as almost wholly intrasocietal to a more inclusive frame of reference which is societal, cultural, organic, and psychological all at once.

This frame of reference is not a simple epiphenomenal product of nonrational developments in the structure of the human condition but is one aspect of the intellectual development of the cognitive sector of the Western cultural tradition. This intellectual culture is institutionalized primarily in the university system. It is an indispensable ingredient of the total mix, but has contributed to the emergence of forces with which it cannot easily come to terms. The ideal of the liberation of the id could not have gained currency in its modern form without Freud's *intellectual* work, guided by the values of cognitive rationality. This may serve as a parable of the debt owed by the anti-intellectuals to the achievements of the intellect. On the other side, the stabilization of orderly opportunities for the continuing expression of the newer nonrational concerns is dependent on a society and personality structure with a major component of competence and cognitive rationality.

# 7

## DYNAMIC PROCESS IN THE UNIVERSITY
## SYSTEM: THE NATURE OF THE CRISIS

In this chapter, selective dynamic processes will be analyzed in two contexts central to the academic system; however, this coverage leaves a wide range of dynamic processes only alluded to or untouched.

Although our interest in higher education preceded the recent crisis, the impact of that crisis has influenced our thinking.[1] How can the nature of the crisis be understood in theoretical terms? We will start by focusing on two generalized media of interchange and their relation to recent tensions in the higher educational system.

*The "Banking" of Intelligence and Influence.* Monetary inflation and deflation in the economy serve as models of similar processes in academia; our focus, however, will be on the inflation and deflation of intelligence and influence rather than of money. The recent academic crisis is in some respects analogous to a deflationary economic crisis. This academic deflation follows an inflationary period. These phenomena are our concerns as well as whether the conditions of recovery are currently being met.

Conditions of recovery and long-range structural changes in the university will be considered in the final chapter of the book where we will give attention to continuities and discontinuities in change and, without quantification, point out some of the possible limits of change.

The analysis of inflation and deflation of media, other than that of money, is preliminary. A systematic analysis would entail a discussion of all eight media, but such an analysis would be

1. Talcott Parsons, "Higher Education as a Theoretical Focus," in *Institutions and Social Exchange: The Sociologies of Talcott Parsons and George C. Homans,* ed. Herman Turk and Richard Simpson (Indianapolis, Bobbs-Merrill, 1971), pp. 233–252.

beyond the scope of this volume.[2] And yet we cannot confine the analysis to one medium. We will therefore deal primarily with intelligence and influence and secondarily with affect and value-commitments.

Intelligence is the medium focal to the cognitive complex at the general action level, whereas the influence medium is focused in integrative functions at the social-system level; both are important to the university system. Since the university system is a point of interpenetration of the cultural and social levels, both these media must be examined in relation to each other. Further, it would be a distortion to conceive of the academic system only in terms of the cultural or the social level; higher education must be understood in terms of both cultural and social processes and groundings.[3]

A feature of media not appreciated by common sense is that the amount of the medium in circulation may increase by processes analogous to the increase of money by credit creation through banking operations. Although our terminology smacks of the economy, we are referring to the creation of *any* medium in circulation.

For the medium of intelligence, two points must be clarified. First, we are not dealing with intelligence as a trait of the personality. Treating intelligence as a personality trait would not provide insight into the instabilities which the process of intelligence creation introduces into action systems. In our conception, the total amount of intelligence circulating in an action system can be increased, but increasing the flow of intelligence in circulation will have consequences for the social stability of the system.

Second, it is necessary to describe *how* intelligence is increased in an action system in a manner analogous to that of the increase of money through credit creation. Our position is that the university, as a general action-level unit, functions as an intelligence bank and as a social system unit as an influence bank. The first step in creation of intelligence is achieved through deposits of intel-

---

2. The eight media are: intelligence, performance-capacity, affect, and definition of the situation at the general action level; and money, power, influence, and value-commitments at the social-system level.

3. Although in some circles academic organization is viewed as just another type of social structure giving little significance to its cultural groundings, the *fiduciary* aspects of academia, namely, its collegial association, academic freedom, and tenure, are not intelligible without reference to its cultural interpenetrations. Treating the academic system as predominantly a power-system must bypass an understanding of these features of higher education.

ligence—rather than through improving the genetic constitution of individuals. In this sense, the upgrading of intelligence in society is in the first instance the result of social processes, although the organism will necessarily be involved at some point.

Individuals and some collective members such as student classes, faculties, and departments deposit intelligence by entrusting some of their cognitive interests to the institution. Selective admission of students and faculty (through appointment) helps to ensure that members of the academic community have a good deal of intelligence available for deposit.

Intelligence depositors, like bank depositors, retain the right of withdrawal and make actual withdrawals from time to time for their own uses. Leaving an institution is equivalent to closing out a bank account.

But what can institutions of higher education do besides perform a custodial function with the intelligence deposits they receive? As Chapter 2 suggested, through an input of performance-capacity, a part of the intelligence can be invested in the production of higher levels of knowledge, competence, and potential for rationality than would otherwise be possible if the individual or collectivity did not become part of the university community. The academic community is an environment organized to develop intelligence in its own right, but also by directing part of it into new channels the university enhances the position of the cognitive complex as a whole within the society. Without membership in such a community and without the entrusting of intelligence to such an organized environment, it would be more difficult to upgrade the amount of intelligence in circulation in society.

We are not referring to individual cases. We refer to a capitalization of intelligence in societal action, a capitalization to which a society is committed and to which the commitment is institutionalized in an organized environment directed toward such capitalization. By contrast to capitalization of intelligence, there are many self-educated individuals in society, but no modern society could be totally dependent upon self-education in order to achieve substantial cognitive upgrading. The university system makes this societal-process level better organized and more efficient. Similarly, a department within a university can, by virtue of its subcollectivity status, accomplish more within the realm of cognitive endeavors than if it were a collectivity organizationally separated from all other departments outside of its own subject matter.

The addition to the amount of intelligence in circulation consists of the fact that units in the system can act more intelligently than they otherwise could; that is, they have readier access to relevant knowledge, better opportunity to build up competence, and greater capacity for rationality than they would have had they been dependent upon their own resources alone.

Moreover, pooling resources of intelligence not only gives participants access to each others' intelligence but implies accepting role obligations involved in cognitive activities within the university; this condition also contrasts with the self-taught individual. Thus, students assume binding obligations to fulfill requirements, to be engaged in some form of pursuit of specialized knowledge, and to use the university environment to enhance personally directed intellectual interests (an analogy to faculty's research). Faculty assumes obligations to teach, to keep abreast of developments in their fields, and to do research. These commitments to perform, officially sanctioned by the institution, impose constraints on the investment of intelligence so that some (but not all) activities can be legitimately engaged in. By cultural and institutional standards intelligence is constrained to be invested in particular kinds of activities the end product of which is an increase in the amount of circulating intelligence.

The institution can justify lending its sanction to commitments to perform because it is the organized focus of *fiduciary* responsibility for the implementation of cognitive standards. Thus, the university can assume corporate responsibility for judgments as to what *kinds* of performance of cognitive significance should be encouraged. The *combination* of access to the pooled intelligence and the sanctioning of performance underlies the university's special intelligence-creating capacity.

As in the case of loans by a bank for productive purposes, how the extra intelligence is used is generally left to the loan recipient; academic freedom operates to ensure such freedom of use. Thus, the faculty's right to pursue research interests of their own choice and the students' right to direct a portion of their education themselves and in both cases to have available and use the pooled resources of the university environment illustrates the free use of intelligence loans. Of course the university has institutional responsibility for the choice of those to whom such loans should be made. This is principally controlled through admission and appointment. Finally, such intelligence loans involve enforcing standards of pay-off, analogous to schedules of amortization and interest rates in the case of monetary loans.

The status asymmetry in the academic community affects the operation of intelligence banking. Those in higher tenure positions, like officers of a bank, have responsibility for decisions about what kinds of performance and by whom shall be made conditions of loans. Some risky loans are made; dubious cognitive endeavors are underwritten by the university. Thus 'the university may invest in adventurous and inventive programs not directly involved with accepted cognitive priorities or unproven as to their cognitive contributions. But, as with a bank, the university must remain cognitively solvent; an application of cognitive rationality is one part of its fiduciary responsibility. Cognitive solvency is relevant not only to evaluation of the performances of borrowers but to collective depositors. The intelligence entrusted to the university by students and faculty cannot be squandered on intellectual misadventures that leave the institution bankrupt with respect to its previous relative intellectual position in the total academic system.

The intelligence value of performances made on the basis of the loans must be measured by standards of cognitive validity and significance of the outputs achieved in terms of knowledge, competence, and rationality. By these standards some loans will fail, but on balance there must be more successes than failures. Successful outcomes create intelligence not only for the unit but for the system in a sense parallel to that in which successful use of investment funds *makes* money both for the borrower and for the system.

For the university as a social community, the relevant medium is influence as distinguished from power, money, and value-commitments.[4] Influence is a medium of persuasion but not through giving intrinsic valuables, as, for example, factual information; influence is contentless in the same sense as the other generalized media. Influence is persuasion from a position of relative and relevant prestige, which justifies the use of influence in terms of contributions to the welfare and solidarity of the community. In the university, which is a pluralistically organic soli-

4. Talcott Parsons and Gerald M. Platt, "The American Academic Profession: A Pilot Study," unpub. MS, Cambridge, Mass., 1968. Also, Talcott Parsons and Gerald M. Platt, "Considerations on the American Academic System," *Minerva*, 6, no. 4 (Summer 1968), 497–523.

dary community, the institutions of tenure and academic freedom provide the principal framework within which influence operates.

The university can be an influence bank just as it is an intelligence bank. Participants in the community deposit influence, entrusting loyalty and solidarity to the university and to its subunits. As a fiduciary system, the university holds these influence deposits in trust and (as with intelligence) invests them.

As with intelligence, the depositor of influence may withdraw his deposits. Further, within the university as part of a pluralistic society, all of one's loyalty cannot and should not be invested in the university; furthermore, shifts in loyalties are also to be expected. But, as in the case of monetary banks, there ought to be a sufficient balance of deposits of influence so that lending operations are reasonably safe.

The university as an intelligence bank is linked to the cognitive complex through the interpenetration of the cultural system with the fiduciary system. The university as an influence bank is linked by interchanges of the fiduciary system with the societal community and in particular through value-commitments to the fiduciary system. Through the interchanges of value-commitments for influence, the university can act as an influence-creating bank.

The university solidary community is defined by the values institutionalized in it; among these cognitive rationality takes precedence. Those who have entrusted their deposits of influence to the university share commitment to these values. These mutual value-commitments define both the right of the institution to lend influence and the obligations undertaken by the recipients of such loans. They should be made and used in the interest of legitimate undertakings, that is, with cognitive standards either primary or standing in appropriate combinations with other values.

Over the long run, credit-creating institutions must be solvent; however, at any particular point in time, as a lending institution the university will be "insolvent." This means that an institution has invested more influence than it has unrestricted rights to control. Thus, should there be a demand for full repayment by all depositors at the same time, no lending institution can successfully comply with such demands. Under normal circumstances, such a run on the bank is not encountered because the lending institutions have balances on hand to fulfill normally expected demands for repayment. A balance of deposits in excess of the proportion which has been properly invested is an essential condition of generating more of the media, but in the nature of the case is not sufficient to protect the institution against all risks.

Thus, if a university plays a banking role with regard to influence and intelligence, it is vulnerable to runs on its influence and intelligence balances on hand. The equivalent of an intelligence run would be for enough participants in the university to start thinking, saying, or acting as though the *intelligent* thing to do is to cease participation in these cognitive enterprises, for example, by dropping out or by involvement in predominantly noncognitive activity. The equivalent of an influence run would be to withdraw trust and loyalty from a particular institution and to transfer them to "worthier" or "more relevant" contexts. Withdrawals can, of course, be accompanied by attempts not just to break contact with the institution but to transform it into something other than an intelligence or influence bank. Since intelligence is cognitive in focus, a common shift is to try to use the influence or prestige of the institution for functions in the larger society other than those falling under the values of cognitive rationality, for example, making it predominantly an instrument of radical political action.

The affect medium, which connects the individual with various groups, may be affected by disturbances in the intelligence and influence media, that is by such runs on the bank as we have been discussing. This is a topic to which we will return shortly.

## Inflation and Deflation of Intelligence and Influence

Media operate in interchange. In this process there are ratios between the values of the medium and of what it can obtain; this is the amount of the medium exchanged for the valued object: an analogue of price. Moreover, insofar as a medium functions in a system of interdependent exchanges there must be price *levels*, not only particular prices.

The absence of inflation or deflation is constancy of the value (amount) of the medium exchanged for valuables (acquired objects) as measured over a period of time. Thus, constancy of media other than money can be referred to as the "constancy of interchange value" over time. An inflationary trend is a process by which the medium loses value relative to the valuable objects for which it is exchanged. A process is inflationary only when the loss of value is generalized, that is, when the loss of value occurs with respect to most objects and not simply one or two objects.

At the general action level, inflationary trends mean in our paradigm the loss of value of two media especially. In the recent past the rising inputs (costs) of intelligence into the educational system and the rising affective investments in the cognitive complex mean inflation for each investor at the expense of investment in other general-action-level functions such as expressive and moral symbolizations. At the social-system level, inflation means a rising cost of entrusting loyalties and value-commitments to the academic system. These costs have been at the expense of investment in other activities and solidarities for students and faculty.

A deflationary trend, a process where the value of the medium undergoes a rise in value relative to valuables it can purchase, constitutes a rise in the interchange value of the medium. The deflationary trend in academia has been in the direction of redressing the rising costs of intelligence, affect, influence, and value-commitment of participation in the cognitive complex and, more specifically, of participation in higher education. Inflationary-deflationary trends tend to spiral; there is sometimes overcompensation in the deflationary direction following an inflationary period.

In order to measure rise or loss of value of media (intelligence, affect, influence, value-commitments) it is necessary to devise indices similar to those economists have developed for money. However, these media are probably not measurable by cardinal scales and therefore may not be amenable to quantification in a fashion similar to money. In spite of this obstacle, a crude account of the inflationary and deflationary trends of these media in relation to the recent crisis in academia is possible.

We suggest an adaptation of the economist's proposition that the stability of price level (interchange value) is related to stability of the economy; this is what Schumpeter called the circular flow. Such a stability may or may not be desirable. Many economists believe that a mild inflationary trend is favorable to economic growth. Similarly a mild inflationary trend in terms of the four media we have been discussing may be favorable to the growth of higher education in society.

A feature of inflationary and deflationary trends is their cumulative tendency arising from social interaction. All human action involves uncertainty compounded by mutual expectations: the double contingency of interaction.[5] As ego and alter interact, each makes his next move contingent on what the other has done. But in looking ahead, each will plan on the basis of what he thinks the other will *probably* do, without waiting, before making commitments, for the actual event. Such a system of mutually oriented expectations can readily, as a function of a set of interlocking expectations, get out of touch with the realistic probabilities of development of the interaction system.

A generalized medium is a structured expectation as well as a symbolic mode of communication to others and to the actor himself. Hence the value of a medium tending cumulatively to decline or rise relative to what can be done with it is an instance of the structuring of expectations. The more developed the media of interchange, the greater are the structured degrees of freedom open to actors. These degrees of freedom create uncertainty beyond the inherent uncertainties of action (as for example in relation to the physical environment). Within this field of uncertainty inflation and deflation occur. Unrealistic expectations are not the sole factors leading to inflation and deflation, but expectations *are* central to them.

In modern societies where banking of media exists there is increased vulnerability to inflationary and deflationary pressures. Most readers, aware of the monetary stringencies to which universities are currently being subjected, will find it natural to analyze the sources of stringency in terms of inflationary and deflationary monetary trends. Readers will be less familiar with inflationary and deflationary trends in other media. With respect to both intelligence and influence and, in part, affect in relation to intelligence and value-commitments in relation to influence, the recent growth and upgrading of the system of higher education has been inflationary. This has resulted in instability and vulnerability of the academic system. A deflationary spiral began in the early 1960's and developed in the later 1960's into a crisis analogous to a financial panic, putting severe strain on some of the more over-invested academic banks. This helps explain certain elements of the recent academic crisis which remain perplexing to most observers: the suddenness with which a critical situation developed at Berke-

5. Talcott Parsons and Edward A. Shils, eds., *Toward a General Theory of Action* (Cambridge, Mass., Harvard University Press, 1951), chap. i, pp. 3–29. Talcott Parsons, "Interaction: Social Interaction," in *International Encyclopedia of the Social Sciences*, ed. David L. Sills, (New York, The Macmillan Co. and The Free Press, 1968), VII, 429–441.

ley in 1964 and then spread to other institutions; the paradoxical mixture of reasonableness and unreasonableness of the demands of student groups which tended to polarize observers into sympathizers and opponents of the demonstrating students; and the sudden decline of acute forms of the deflationary trend followed by a continued depression, the acute phase of which may erupt again dependent upon whether specific conditions of recovery are met or not.

*The Context and Background of Inflation and Deflation.* Academia is part of the social system; it is the adaptive subsystem of the fiduciary complex of society and is allied with other fiduciary subsystems including kinship, national citizenship, and civil religion. The academic system is also linked to the cultural cognitive complex, to the behavioral organism at the general action level, and to the societal community in the social system.

In illustrating recent inflationary and deflationary trends in higher education, we will make only passing reference to higher education's relation to kinship, national citizenship, and religion. Our focus will be on the relations at three levels: the cultural, the general action, and the societal. Later in this chapter we will return to this same topic in a more systematic fashion, employing the cybernetic hierarchy-of-control model as the framework for analyzing inflationary and deflationary processes.

## Inflation-Deflation at the Cultural Level

At the cultural level four types of symbolic systems orient intended action. In cybernetic terms the cultural system is grounded in *constitutive symbolism* which centers in that part of *religious symbolism oriented* to problems of ultimate concern;[6] this is the pattern-maintenance subsystem of culture. *Moral-evaluative symbols* play an integrative role; at the cultural level, moral-evaluative symbols are the focus of societal values including cognitive rationality. *Expressive symbolization* is oriented toward goal-attainment at the cultural level with special links to the personalities of individuals. Finally, *cognitive symbolization* (knowledge) is oriented to adaptive cultural functions.

In the academic system the cognitive complex has a certain autonomy especially as institutionalized in graduate education and research. This autonomy has been dependent upon a delicate

6. Paul Tillich, *The Courage to Be* (New Haven, Conn., Yale University Press, 1952).

balance of cultural symbol systems. But a delicately balanced system is open to encroachments of the subsystems upon each other. Although we have not specified the media of exchange internal to the cultural level, encroachment of one subsystem upon the other can be viewed metaphorically as a kind of expectational inflationary and/or deflationary process. Since our focus is on cognitive culture, we will refer to its encroachment on the other cultural subsystems as expectationally inflationary and their inroads on cognitive symbolization as expectationally deflationary.

Thus, the rationalism and scientism which have grown in the West since the seventeenth century are suggestive of inflated cognitive orientations to action. For example, that Marx's later writings attempted to ground socialism in scientific materialism is an indication of the rising need in the mid-nineteenth century to legitimate the socialist movement in scientific terms. Similarly in the twentieth century, have not such works as those of Bertrand Russell, P. W. Bridgman, George Lundberg, and of the psychological behaviorists[7] indicated an inflation of cognitive culture in the physical and social fields? Parallel examples exist for the humanities during this same period.

However inflated the expectations for cognitive culture since the seventeenth century, a strong belief in cognitive rationality was necessary for establishing the autonomy of the knowledge complex. Thus, secularization, in and outside of academia, was needed to protect cognitive culture from transgressions from other symbol systems. Significantly, conflict between science and religion has passed from the scene. Indeed, men of the cloth now have in their pastoral counselling become in part psychiatric social workers; in another direction the major Catholic universities have sought to have their curricula defined as secular.

At the cultural level contemporary conflicts are in terms of cognitive encroachments on expressive and moral-evaluative symbolization. Inflated expectations for cognitive culture have been expressed in various forms, such as the position that a moral-ethical code can be built on scientific grounds alone, a position recently developed in the works of B. F. Skinner.[8] On the expressive side we

7. Bertrand Russell, *Human Knowledge, Its Scope and Limits* (New York, Simon and Schuster, 1955); P. W. Bridgman, *The Logic of Modern Physics* (New York, The Macmillan Co., 1927); George A. Lundberg, *Foundations of Sociology* (New York, David McKay Co., 1964).

8. B. F. Skinner, *Behavior of Organisms: An Experimental Analysis* (New York, Appleton-Century-Crofts, Inc., 1938); B. F. Skinner, *Walden Two* (New York, Mac-

have witnessed in the recent past a disdain for the arts and in the academic realm something approaching second-class citizenship for the humanities.

Deflationary currents have been the recent anti-intellectualism among students and more generally the attack against "materialism." Among the student left there has been a tendency to eschew the more scientific writings of Marx and to emphasize his humanistic papers and his concept of alienation. These positions in the expressive direction articulate with political criticism, especially among students, but not all deflationary movements in the expressive direction can be attributed to the young—although our concern with higher education gives them particular significance for us. Student culture blends into other expressive positions such as the "do your own thing" ideology, the drug culture, and other activities giving priority to expressive symbolization. Not all of these expressive forms are on the boundary of legitimacy, so that in some respectable academic circles there have been calls for the priority of the experiential over the cognitive.[9]

On the moral-evaluative side, the cultural legitimacy of autonomous intellectual interests has been challenged in the name of a preference for the immediate implementation of moral commitments. The form this has taken is the moral injunction to get involved without much specification as to what one should get involved with. The assertion here seems to be that involvement with cognitive culture is amoral and is tantamount to no involvement (apathy).

Another form of moral symbolization has been the rising concern with the moral implications of cognitive culture. This concern has focused on issues such as the moral consequences of scientific technology and the moral-political implications of scientific frameworks. There is felt a need to examine these frameworks and to make implicit commitments explicit. In the case where scientific frameworks are found morally wanting, there is presumably an obligation to abandon such positions.

These have been partly accurate criticisms of the limitations of

millan Company, 1960); B. F. Skinner, *Beyond Freedom and Dignity* (New York, Alfred A. Knopf, Inc., 1971); Clark L. Hull, *Principles of Behavior* (New York, Appleton-Century-Crofts, Inc., 1943).

9. Norman O. Brown, *Love's Body* (Westminster, Md., Random House, 1966); P. E. Slater, *Microcosm: Structural, Psychological, and Religious Evolution in Groups* (New York, John Wiley and Sons, 1966); Charles A. Reich, *The Greening of America: The Coming of a New Consciousness and the Rebirth of a Future* (Westminster, Md., Random House, 1970).

cognitive culture. But during its period of growth and its auton-omous establishment, these issues were not as salient as they have now become and therefore were not predominant. The deflation-ary movements of moral-evaluative and expressive symbolism are directed toward redressing expectations held about rationalism and science. However, as noted earlier, these symbol systems are related to each other in a delicate balance; none of the factions demanding redress have been aware of the need for balance nor have they offered stable solutions.

## Inflation-Deflation at the General Action Level

Inflationary and deflationary processes at the general action level take place primarily between culture and the behavioral organism and secondarily between personality and the behavioral organism. The principal medium of exchange for the behavioral organism is intelligence. Since it regulates the exchange with both the personality and the cultural systems it will be the medium upon which we will focus our analysis of inflationary and defla-tionary processes at the general action level. Our concern is with loss and rise in value of intelligence in its exchanges with other subsystems.

In general action terms, the behavioral organism has adaptive primacy. It provides generalized resources for action; notable among these resources is cognitive capacity (as distinguished from knowledge content at the cultural level).[10] Intelligence is *not* a trait of the personality but a circulating medium in action. Thus, the capacity for intelligent action requires not only tapping re-sources at the organic level but combining cognitive capacity with motivational resources at the personality level, integrative re-sources in the societal community and cognitive standards and content of knowledge at the cultural-symbolic level. The intelli-gence organism interpenetrates as well as interchanges with other subsystems of action. In these interchanges inflation and deflation with respect to intelligence occur.

The primary substantive outputs of culture to the behavioral organism are knowledge and cognitive standards of validity and significance. Desired items of knowledge are varied and must be acquired from many sources and, like the consuming household's

10. Gordon Pask, "The Meaning of Cybernetics in the Behavioral Sciences," in *Progress of Cybernetics*, ed. J. Rose (New York, Gordon and Breach Science Pub-lishers, 1970), I, 15–44.

standard of living, must be put together in a coherent pattern by the consumer. Utilization of cognitive standards must be mobile: transferable from one problem area to another. There can be no one-to-one correspondence between items of desired knowledge and the standards of their use, as compared with the standards involved in their production.

In the market of knowledge, the buyer and seller-producer exchange is regulated by the exchange of intelligence. The cultural system as the consuming unit allocates incomes of intelligence from behavioral organisms to many problem areas of knowledge production and, conversely, the behavioral organism expends intelligence to acquire the use of such knowledge and of the cognitive standards of their evaluation and use. Such knowledge and standards are part of the cultural heritage and not part of the organism and therefore are acquired by the expenditure of intelligence.

For the consuming cultural unit, two problems are analogous to household consumption: (1) the allocation of intelligence for what cultural products (the problem of the use of limited resources) and (2) the evaluation of the worth of the product consumed. Solutions to these problems make possible the rational distribution of the uses of intelligence.

On the production side, there are also choices to be made. The first of these is the use of intelligence for long-term capitalization of knowledge in contrast to its use for the satisfaction of the immediate needs of consumer wants. The second choice for the cultural system is that of the use of intelligence for cognitive and noncognitive purposes.

Finally, on the consumer side there tends to be pressure for the expenditure of intelligence for knowledge which satisfies immediate wants. Special conditions have to develop for the consumer to make investment in the long-term capitalization of intelligence.

These are the problems for intelligence inflation and deflation: (1) the state of the demand for knowledge and the pressure for short- or long-term investment of intelligence; (2) the balance of cultural uses of intelligence for cognitive and noncognitive purposes; and (3) the condition and volume of the employment of cognitive standards of culture in knowledge production. An inflationary period is characterized by strong demands for cognitive knowledge. Intelligent investment is in long-range knowledge production, including both the advancement of knowledge and the dissemination of prior knowledge of a cognitive character. Cognitive standards of validity and significance are employed for evaluating knowledge production. In a deflationary phase, the demand for knowledge slackens, especially as touching its longer-run significance. This is associated with oversaving of intelligence and/or with its investment in noncognitive cultural and social activities. Cognitive standards as resources for evaluation are not fully employed. Under these conditions knowledge production of both types falls off.

Institutions of higher education and research are in one sense knowledge "factories" that advance and disseminate knowledge. In the phase of rapid expansion of higher education, intelligence inflation was created. The resources necessary for the increase in the volume of knowledge and in its diversification were not, and probably could not be, increased rapidly enough to meet the demand; the effect was an upward price spiral for knowledge, that is, an increasing amount of intelligence was required for advancing and disseminating the same output of knowledge. The consequence was a depreciation of the unit of value of intelligence—one effect of which was the relative improvement in the unit value of other general action level media. In particular, the value of affect has risen and the demand for definitions of the situation from intellectuals and also from academics has grown. In short, the inflationary process of the recent past proceeded along the following lines: Holders of unspent intelligence in society, notably young potential students, were willing to deposit their intelligence into the care of academic institutions as fiduciary trustees of cognitive interests. On this basis, the universities made commitments of the generalized intellectual resources entrusted to them by student and faculty participants. These intellectual loan recipients are the four tenure classes of membership.[11] The phenomena of expansion are sufficient to account for an inflationary state having developed at this sensitive point.

It is sensitive partly because expansion has been investment in the *increase* of intelligence and knowledge over their previous relative positions in the action system. At a time when the cognitive system is under pressure, this investment means the sacrifice of many other potential pay-offs which would have been available had the sector of the system where relatively pure cognitive rationality prevails not been increased so rapidly. The rapidity of

11. Both students and faculty can function in the capacity both of intelligence depositors and of intelligence borrowers.

development of the cognitive system exceeded the growth in the other three sectors where greater stress on noncognitive concerns is concentrated. The result has been the expansion of the core sector at the expense, first, of the socialization of undergraduate students and, second, of the effective contribution of academic disciplines to cognitively sound ideological definitions of the situation through the discussions of intellectuals. Perhaps there has also been an overintellectualization of some of the applied professional sectors at the expense of social responsibility in primarily noncognitive fiduciary respects.

We need not dwell on the deflationary process here: the withdrawal of trust and the unwillingness to make new intelligence deposits, diverting them either into saving or into spending in noncognitive areas. Such action has not been equal for all four types of tenure members nor for all types of academic institutions; thus the deflationary panic has been somewhat uneven across the academic system. However, it has been serious enough in some inflated but central "knowledge factories" to threaten the stability of the entire system. The reasons for withdrawal of confidence and the unwillingness to make intelligence deposits, particularly on the part of students, lie in the concentration of resources in the expansion of pure cognitive culture at the sacrifice of the other sectors. The result of the deflationary trend has been to raise the unit worth of intelligence in exchange for cultural knowledge and standards. The extent of the deflation is difficult to assess, although it is probably not as great as some critics of academia implicitly contend.

A similar inflationary-deflationary analysis could be essayed in the exchange between the behavioral organism and the personality. In this exchange lies the core of intelligence banking. The problem here is the old one of the balance between short-run consumption in contrast to long-term investment of intelligence. Unlike the hoarding form of saving, the presumption is that delayed gratification combined with attempts to increase the level of intelligence can be expected to pay off in the future in increased performance-capacity, regardless of what goals are adopted. The role of personality in the intelligence-banking operation is to make commitments to a considerable flow of investments, not only to use available resources intelligently by *current* standards. This is the meaning of the differentiation of an academic system from the ordinary world of social life; it is a "capital-goods industry" for the production of knowledge and intelligence, "financed" by the commitments of personalities to devote greater proportions of their resources to *learning* than would otherwise occur.

Like all banking systems involving generalized media, this one is vulnerable to runs and more generally to deflationary pressures owing to the asymmetry between obligations to depositors and borrowers. Loss of confidence in the system will be manifested in ideologies that downgrade the importance of intelligence, knowledge, and rationality in favor of expressiveness, morality, and immediate goals. The problem of defining proper balances among such concerns is a legitimate and important one.

Thus, the essential deflationary theme is impatience with the delays and other sacrifices involved in investment in cognitive learning processes. In extreme instances, it takes the form of a demand that these be jettisoned in favor of noncognitive solutions and other pay-offs *now*. Clearly, tensions come to focus about the status of the cognitive system. In historical-evolutionary perspective, this focus is closely related to the problem of the status of the process of rationalization upon which Max Weber laid such stress, especially in his later work.[12] The present controversies resemble the controversies over the status of the economy in the postindustrial revolution period when modern society became polarized over coping with the increase of productive capacity which the industrial revolution had brought about. (A formal explanation of the preceding analysis will be found in the technical appendix.)

## Inflation-Deflation at the Social-System Level

The focus of inflation and deflation at the social-system level is in the influence and value-commitment exchanges between the fiduciary subsystem and the societal community. This process is initiated by deposits of influence and value-commitments into the academic system through membership by means of admission and appointment. Such deposits imply interests and commitments to learning (in both senses) and to the acceptance as valid of the relevant cognitive values. These grounds of association contribute to the solidarity of the institution.

As a fiduciary system, higher education provides a protected environment for exploration and learning. Academic freedom and tenure provide the structural conditions for protected freedoms. In

12. Max Weber, *General Economic History*, trans. Frank H. Knight (New York, The Macmillan Co., 1961).

such a system the primary mechanisms of integration cannot be those on the side of power and the use of force but rather those on the side of trust and the use of persuasion. Thus, in this context influence plays a major role in relations between students and faculty, faculty and faculty, administration and faculty, and so on.

The role of trust and persuasion can be illustrated in the student-faculty relationship. Obviously, cognitive information cannot be the sole binding force between faculty and students. Indeed a built-in tension exists in the form of the information and competence gap between faculty and students; in competence and information the faculty are of necessity superior to their students. Despite the frustrations of the learning process, that tension can be breached by the influence medium: by the capacity to persuade on the basis of solidarity and shared value-commitments. With this capacity as the basis of integration, students can be motivated to accept the frustrations of learning and the notion that learning in itself is a good thing without immediate knowledge or control of the concrete pay-offs for such effort. The same model holds for other collective relationships within higher education. Thus, a faculty member will not make a commitment to endure the long hours of research solely on the basis of economic pay-off; he has to believe that this type of effort, even if it fails to produce anything tangibly worthwhile, is a good thing.

In a different domain, influence works in another way. Faculty members from different disciplines cannot precisely assess the validity and significance of knowledge in another field. On the basis of influence one faculty member takes the word of another concerning the value of the contributions of a particular man in a different field.

Deposits of influence are made by all tenure-level members into a particular academic community. The cumulative effect of such deposits comes to be the creation of more influence than any single depositor has and in the end more influence than the sum of the deposits. The cumulative effect is to create influence banks. Academic institutions are influence banks (as well as intelligence banks) where members are both depositors and borrowers and where members may thus receive "interest" on their influence investments.

For example, there is influence interest from his institutional affiliation accruing to a particular faculty member in attempting to get a research grant or to have a paper published.[13] In both instances these efforts are assessed on universalistic grounds but also in part assessed on grounds of the institution from which the grant application or paper came.

The faculty members and students repay such loans of influence when they contribute more to the institution than it contributes to them. Thus, students earn the resources to repay influence loans when they have combined cultural, social, psychological, and organism factors in actions focused on cognitive components of culture and become referred to as educated men and women. Given their level of initial influence investment, they have, by increasing their influence on society, repaid their influence loan from the academic institution.

Naturally there are, as with banks, larger and smaller depositors and borrowers of influence. Full-tenure members of an academic community are larger and more secure depositors of influence and commitments; they offer the institution an influence security-base. Their influence interests may be narrower than those of junior faculty or students but their permanent appointments give them special borrowing privileges and perhaps "influence stock" in the academic influence bank. The full faculty members are usually most concerned with the academic institution, its development, its curriculum, who is admitted, and who is appointed and on what criteria; they make sure that the institution does not squander its influence and that a certain level of influence, even an increasing influence ratio, is achieved. In spite of this special position of the faculty, a higher educational institution needs depositors and borrowers at all levels. An institution's prestige is built upon diversification and not solely on its senior faculty. The level

13. The well-known paper of Robert Merton, "The Matthew Effect in Science," seems to us to constitute an excellent empirical demonstration of the phenomenon of "credit-creation" in a primarily cognitive field which is clearly not monetary. In this paper Merton analyses the "reputations" of Nobel Prize winners as evidenced by references to their work in the scientific literature. His finding is that these reputations have been on the average substantially enhanced following the receipt of the award. Clearly this cannot be accounted for by actual improvement in the quality of their scientific contributions—Merton carefully considers this possibility—but must derive from their membership in the very select company of Nobel laureats. We interpret this finding to mean that the Nobel awards serve to create influence which is placed in the hands of the actual scientists, and through them enhances the prestige of the type of scientific contributions which their work exemplifies. This should then be a net addition to the volume of influence circulating in the scientific world. Merton selects his title from the well-known passage in the Gospel according to St. Matthew, "To him who hath shall be given and from him who hath not shall be taken away, even that which he hath." See Robert K. Merton, "The Matthew Effect in Science," *Science*, 159, no. 3810 (January 1968), 56–63.

of influence of an institution is dependent upon the quality of research and teaching, its junior and senior faculty, and the quality of the graduate and undergraduate students it produces.

Within this context the problems of inflation and deflation of influence and of value-commitments can be considered. The rapid expansion of higher education over recent decades produced a rising cost in unit influence input and in value-commitment to the cognitive rationality necessary for participation in higher education and especially for participation in the more prestigious institutions. The key to this inflationary process has been the enhanced prestige of the academic system in society and within that system the enhanced position of the elite institutions. Part of this enhancement has been solidly based in the increase of cognitive outputs and their increased importance in the society. Unfortunately the increase has also tended to outrun the supplies of relevant factors. The scarcity led to overpricing; overpricing operated both on the fiduciary aspect of the academic system and on the community aspect, with consequences for cognitive commitments and for the influence of academic roles and institutions.

This situation has affected societal value-systems concerned with commitment to cognitive rationality. The problem is the *proportion* of the value-commitment devoted to cognitive functions. The academic system gives salience to cognitive values and, in so far as societal value-commitments constitute a fluid medium, there is a problem of deciding the share of value-commitments invested in cognitive functions in contrast to those invested in short-run noncognitive pay-offs.

In an inflationary state the value-commitments actually made in the cognitive field have been overextended; they are excessive as compared to alternative commitments and realistic possibilities of implementation. Such a state is precarious because doubts about the legitimacy of *such heavy* commitments in this direction may react on the influence system by stimulating influence depositors to withdraw their deposits on bases other than current needs. Both with respect to influence and to commitments to the values of cognitive rationality, a source of the inflationary process has been the mutual reinforcement of the expansionist tendencies of both institutional and individual participants in the more elite sectors of the academic system.

This expansion has built on genuine growth and with it has come not only quantitative increase but also qualitative upgrading.

Furthermore, it has been stimulated by massive inputs from outside the system, notably the immense demand for higher education among potential students, the great increase in the levels of financial support for research, and the pressure to recruit candidates for professional training.

Our analysis is consistent with the fact that a major manifestation of a state of crisis has been found among undergraduate students in such elite institutions as Berkeley, Wisconsin, Columbia, Michigan, Oberlin, Harvard, Chicago, and so forth. A relevant consideration is that, as part of the general growth and expansion of the system, the elite sector had gained not only in absolute but in relative prestige. A telling index lies in the increased selectivity of these institutions at the level of admissions.[14]

The deflationary disturbances have been greatest among undergraduate students for two main reasons. In the recent past, admissions to elite universities and colleges have been at the cost of large deposits of influence and large commitments to the values of cognitive rationality, levels of investment which almost preclude investment in all other statuses save that of student. Second, the potentiality for pay-offs for such large investment, while potentially greater than that for many other tenure levels, was not immediately visible. Such conditions created panic possibilities.

The same influence and commitment pressures developed for graduate students and faculty, but these segments of the higher educational system have not as readily been swept up into the deflationary panic, perhaps because these tenure levels were seemingly less cut off from potential investment repayments; and for senior faculty, such repayment was close to being guaranteed. Indeed a linear relation seems to hold between involvements in the influence and value-commitment deflationary movements in academic tenure levels and perceived potential return on influence and commitment investments.

The deflation of influence and value-commitments on the part of undergraduates has been vividly manifest: (1) in the realm of value-commitments by an increasing interest in "relevant" studies and lowering commitment to the more cognitive fields and (2) in the realm of influence in the decline of authority of faculty to implement policy and in diminished student regard for academic

14. John McBrearty, Gerald M. Platt, and Talcott Parsons, "Demographic Characteristics of Academic Faculties," in "The American Academic System: A National Survey of Faculty," Gerald M. Platt and Talcott Parsons (forthcoming).

decision-making organs. Such influence processes are analytically distinguishable from hierarchical power, but another symptom of influence deflation has been for students to treat these relations with faculty *as if they were power relations* in which political power was the sole basis of social control.

### The Inflationary Process: A Cybernetic Point of View

Up to this point we have treated the inflationary-deflationary process only in intrasystem terms. Such a framework has simplified a process which is actually more complex. Obviously, in an inflationary-deflationary spiral there will be effects across system boundaries producing resonating consequences at higher and lower levels of society. We did not take up the problems across boundaries in the previous section because we wished first to illustrate the feasibility of an inflationary and deflationary analysis with media other than money. Holding the level constant made possible a simpler illustration of this.

We now take up this same problem with *intra* and *inter*system effects of inflation and deflation. Simultaneously we will employ the cybernetic hierarchy of control as the framework within which to place the *inter*system effects; moving from the cultural to the personality and the organism levels and then within the social system from the fiduciary and solidary to that of the political and economic systems.

Because we are coming at the same problems from a different perspective there will be some reiteration of materials previously discussed. The repetition may help in illuminating a complex problem.

We will comment on six areas in which inflation and deflation have taken place. These are generally ordered from higher to lower cybernetic levels. One major advantage of ordering these areas is that it will give us the opportunity to pinpoint the level of society in which the eye of the inflationary-deflationary storm was located.

1. Cultural level—the inflationary-deflationary process exclusively internal to the cultural system. Since this has already been discussed in the previous section it will only be briefly remarked upon.
2. General action level—the connection among culture, personality, and behavioral organism. The focus here will be

on the balance of the intelligence medium, knowledge, and cognitive standards with those of personal competence and noncognitive interests; particular attention will be given to intelligence credit and its potentials for inflation.

3. General action level—the social system in relation to personality and the behavioral organism. The main issues here will be the relation of intelligence to affect but also to performance-capacity. In substantive terms this level is relevant to the research and graduate functions and socialization discussed in Chapters 3 and 4 respectively.

4. Social-system level—the fiduciary-societal community interchanges. This area concerns the problem of rationality of action in the allocation of loyalties, and in interchange between value-commitments and influence, and the problem of influence credit-creation.

5. Social-system level—the societal community subsystem of higher education. Here again the problem is that of rationality but concerning commitments to social structures and moral authority of the academic community as a normative order. In this context we are concerned with the allocation and exchange of the affective medium in relation to participation in the university.

6. Social-system level—the political and economic dimensions. In this section we will focus on power and money as media and their theoretical place in the university and their relations to influence and value-commitments.

*Culture.* Exclusive to this level is the emphasis on the *rationalization* of cultural symbolism. This has been at the expense of other cultural components including religious, moral-evaluative, and expressive symbolism. Historically, this conflict evolved in terms such as "science versus religion" in the seventeenth and eighteenth centuries, "science versus moral authority" in the nineteenth and twentieth centuries, and recently "science versus expressive-aesthetic culture."[15]

The rapid growth of higher education has exacerbated *intra*cultural tensions in these areas. The enhanced prestige of science in the last generation and the achievements of the physical and

15. Robert N. Bellah, *Beyond Belief: Essays on Religion in a Post-Traditional World* (New York, Harper and Row, 1970). Daniel Bell, "The Cultural Contradictions of Capitalism," *The Public Interest*, 21 (Fall 1970), 16–43.

biological sciences, followed by attempts to extend their methods and points of view to the behavioral and social fields, are forms of cultural inflation of the cognitive component at the cost of encroaching upon the other cultural components.

We have already dealt with this topic in the previous section. Here we wish only to underline that the expectational inflation of the capacity of cognitive culture to solve contemporary man's problems began to come under suspicion and then attack as it continued its inflationary growth. Thus, the inhuman consequences of the atomic bombs and nuclear weapons, the Nazi concentration camps, and, more recently, scientific and technological encroachments on human and natural environments have brought into prominence other cultural concerns. Given the position of the university with regard to cognitive culture this inflation has made the higher educational system vulnerable to deflationary pressures along these lines.

*General Action—Culture, Personality, Behavioral Organism.* Much has been made of the growth of higher education in reactions to the Soviet Union's launching of Sputnik. The trends of growth since the turn of the century show a direction of growth which belies the exclusiveness of such an explanation. However, it is correct that since World War II[16] special emphasis has been placed on cognitive orientations in our society. Perhaps this is best signified by the high level of prestige that universities, professors, and college graduates have enjoyed until a certain reaction set in. This interesting sociological phenomenon cannot be explained solely in terms of practical pay-offs, although these too are involved. Most faculty are not men of affairs, nor do they possess high practical know-how. Similarly most college-educated young people are not vocationally trained[17] but in spite of this they have been sought after by both industry and government.

Given favorable postwar social circumstances, rational cultural and historical trends were able to penetrate deeply into the social orders of our society and became highly evaluated. This condition generated growth most manifestly reflected in numbers of the

16. A. Hunter Dupree, "The Great Instauration of 1940: The Organization of Scientific Research for War," in *The Twentieth-Century Sciences,* ed. Gerald Holton (New York, W. W. Norton and Co., 1972), pp. 443–467.

17. Clark Kerr, *The Uses of the University* (Cambridge, Mass., Harvard University Press, 1963). David B. Palley, "The Aims of American Colleges and Universities," unpub. honors thesis, Harvard University, 1968. Jeanne S. Binstock, "Design from Disunity: The Task and Methods of American Colleges," unpub. diss., Brandeis University, 1970.

young attending college and in activities which increasingly approximated pure cultural standards, namely, research and graduate training which in the 1950's and 60's became the sine qua non of university output and evaluation. These activities were judged in terms of cultural standards of cognitive validity and significance; watering of the cognitive stock was not tolerated.

Such growth and such *emphasis* on the cognitive complex encroached on what from a longer-run point of view are legitimate personality, social system, and behavioral-organism interests. The problem became that of the cost of knowledge in terms of intelligence inputs and of noncognitive personality interests. In Keynesian terms the production of knowledge could not keep up with the demand in the form of the willingness to expend intelligence for knowledge. The intelligence price of knowledge was driven up, especially as compared to possible uses of intelligence in alternative action processes.

One possible side effect of this inflation could have been a tendency to dilute the rigor of the strictest application of cognitive standards to knowledge production.[18] For whatever reasons both the principal producers and purchasers of knowledge, between World War II and the mid-1960's, were unwilling to do so. It was conditions such as these which caused the productive limitations and the scarcity of knowledge—relative to demand, of course.

Cognitive standards of validity and significance were the factors of evaluation of production of knowledge and competence. The conditions of production could be changed only if, in the interchange between definition of the situation and noncognitive value-commitments, there would be a relative reduction of the commitment to cognitive values. This would change the balance of exchange of intelligence for cognitive standards as given in the definition of the situation. The events of the mid-1960's unstabilized this exchange and thus put pressure on higher education to diversify its categories of knowledge output. In our formal terms this exchange was focused between culture and the behavioral organism.[19]

18. This would be parallel to economic producers attempting to hold manufacturing costs constant in the face of rising costs of factors by lowering the quality of products and thus maintaining price levels.

19. A case can be made for the view that the pattern set for medical education in the United States by the Flexner Report of 1910 and the policy adopted by the Johns Hopkins Medical School in the early part of the century and widely emulated was a prototype of inflation and had repercussions beyond the field of medical education. The slogan was "scientific medicine"; the attempt was to mobilize the entire body of scientific knowledge bearing on health questions and to insist that a maximum proportion of this be mastered by all those to be qualified for the practice of medicine. This

In exchange with personality, intelligence was not as important to cognitive output as the development of competences, that is, capacity of personalities to use inputs of intelligence and other media for effective and meaningful performance. Meaningful performance involves other dimensions; intelligence is only one component of action. Thus, meaningful performance involves affective interchanges. The personality identifies with collective associations and solidarities which underlie the individual's desires for meaningful association and sanctions of group belongingness.[20] Affective inputs to collective association must be balanced in terms of expressive needs and of opportunities for personality development. Inflation in this dimension gives undue weight to competence and the conditions of access to it over other personality interests. The result has been the rising cost of competence as compared with other personality developments and interests.

The university was drawn into this inflationary spiral because of its place in developing both specific and generalized competences. Specific competence in the university is especially prominent in its contribution to the applied professions. The university also contributes more generalized competences, especially those at the undergraduate level, such as the development of an educated citizenry. It also develops scholarly competences necessary for advanced and professional training and even vocational competences, although until recently these have not had explicit prominence.[21]

---

policy within the medical field underlay the high standards of excellence attained by the best American physicians. At the same time, it created a gap between this top level and those falling short of these scientific standards. Our impression is that quite adequate medical care could be provided by professional groups whose training was on a somewhat lower level than the Johns Hopkins standard in most cases other than those of special complexity.

This development in medical education, extending as it did to research, had something to do with the widespread pressure in the arts and sciences area to give priority to the graduate school-oriented standards of the more elite institutions. We have commented at various points on the effects of this idea in raising the professional standards of the academic world. At the same time a case can be made for the view that somewhat more modest aspirations on the part of a sector of the academic world could have produced a better-rounded system with greater educational potential. It may turn out that change will occur in the gap between scientifically oriented professionals and the marginally qualified. See Smelser's California system study for the impact of the "Berkeley model" on the academic system as a whole. Neil J. Smelser, ed., *Public Higher Education in California: Growth, Structural Change, and Conflict* (Berkeley, Calif., University of California Press, 1973).

20. In the terms of W. I. Thomas this is "response." See William I. Thomas, *The Unadjusted Girl* (Boston, Mass., Little, Brown and Co., 1931).

21. Palley, "Aims of American Colleges and Universities"; Binstock, "Design from Disunity"; also, Parsons and Platt, "Considerations on the American Academic System."

The balances between cognitive and noncognitive values and motives help to define societally meaningful goals. Specifically, the balance involved here is competence as performance-capacity with cognitive priority and other performance capacities where noncognitive interests are found in combination with the cognitive. The problem of balance exists in the core academic disciplines and in the professions. One example in the area of medical research, which borders on the pure and applied disciplines, lies in the balance between the human rights of subjects in contrast to research goals. There has been a general tendency toward inflationary commitments to cognitive concerns in the service of advancing medical knowledge over the personal rights of subjects (who frequently are also patients).[22] An analogous illustration could easily be offered for undergraduates in their education, particularly at elite institutions.

*General Action—Social System, Personality, Behavioral Organism.* A transition from the general action level to that of society becomes necessary because our focus shifts to affect, the medium anchored in the social system. Our previous discourse on the socialization of educated citizenry defines this problem in a Durkheimian sense in which the university can legitimately be considered a moral community where this socialization takes place. In this context cognitive inflation occurs as a consequence of the diminution of the capacity of intelligence as a medium to command (through exchange) involvement in the academic community. Specifically it means loss in the unit value of intelligence in comparison with affective commitment.

Cognitive inflation created vulnerability to withdrawal of affective involvement in the university community. Intelligence banking is vulnerable because it cannot perform its own functions and simultaneously satisfy all presumptively legitimate claims on it. Such vulnerability, inherent in all banking operations, is accentuated during inflation. The cognitive inflation in some of the elite colleges and universities made the balance between intelligence and affect difficult to maintain. Not surprisingly, these schools became most vulnerable to demands for full and immediate repayments of their intelligence inputs. When payment was not forthcoming, these institutions became centers of disturbance.

22. Talcott Parsons, "Research with Human Subjects and the 'Professional Complex'," *Daedalus* (Spring 1969), pp. 325–360.

It seems to us legitimate to call these disturbances symptoms of alienation.[23] Alienation is a disposition to be distrustful of the commitment of affect to any context of social organization or cognitive enterprise, to downplay the meaningfulness of the cognitive complex and the functions associated with it. This trend bifurcates either downplaying cognition in terms of absolutistic attempts to implement moral values or dropping out, that is, withdrawing, not only from the cognitive complex but from society generally and into expressive patterns of interests.

A medium anchored in a system but involved in mediating inputs and outputs from other systems to the system of reference in terms of the internal relations of the system also functions as a medium of *cost* control. Thus in a modern economy money not only mediates the sale of goods and services *to* and the acquisition of factors of production *from* systems outside the economy but also is the measure of value in terms of which the economic legitimacy of the incurring of cost is assessed. Affect performs this function in relation to the internal processes of the social system. The functional equivalent of the solvency of a firm in the economy is the affective adequacy of the operations of units of the system. Alienation is the danger signal that this evaluative criterion is not being adequately met. Hence widespread alienation is evidence of inflation in the affective context.

Affective imbalance in exchange from the point of view of the university to the student investor is analogous to imbalance in the circulation of money from firms to households and from households back to firms. It suggests that universities and colleges have not been putting back into circulation amounts of affect equal to or larger than those which have been invested in them. Thus, affect has been committed excessively to the development of purely cognitive interests. The result is a shortage of affect in circulation between participants and the academic community. The example given earlier in this chapter illustrated the high costs to students of affective investment or collective involvement. The present one illustrates the same point from the point of view of the producing organization. The affective circular flow was imbalanced, causing inflation; the value of intelligence as a medium had been lowered

23. Gerald M. Platt and Fred Weinstein, "Alienation and the Problem of Social Action," in *The Phenomenon of Sociology*, ed. Edward A. Tiryakian (New York, Appleton-Century-Crofts, Inc., 1971), pp. 284–310. Peter L. Berger, *The Sacred Canopy* (Garden City, N.Y., Doubleday and Co., 1967), chap. iv.

so that it could not command the same level of inputs of affect as it could before inflation had set in.[24]

*Social System—Fiduciary Subsystem and Societal Community.* In the last section we discussed the transition from the general action level to the societal level. In this section we discuss inflation-ary-deflationary processes within society and especially within the fiduciary subsystem. More than any of the other societal subsystems, the fiduciary is concerned with the implementation of value-commitments.

Education is part of the rationality subsystem of the fiduciary complex. Education involves implementing the values of cognitive rationality but also combining this value-pattern with those of socializing the young (see Chapter 4), with the application of professional knowledge (see Chapter 5), and with intellectual activities (see Chapter 6). Cognitive rationality, the principal value-commitment upon which the university accepts the moral obligation of lending influence, is the basis upon which influence banking operates. Hence the main concern at this level and the focus of inflation will be the influence medium.

The recipient of influence loans assumes obligations and respon-sibility for the disposal of other people's influence deposited in the university. This is analogous to the obligations and responsibility assumed by monetary bankers in lending other people's money deposited in their banks. In the university, the more fiduciarily

---

24. This *dual* function of affect as a medium is relevant to the anchorage of affect in the *social* system. Participating individuals, as personalities, have incomes of affect linked to their social participations and also spend their holdings of affect, the latter in the form of identification in collectivities. There is a parallel here with the Keynes-ian paradigm. Just as consumers-workers can diminish their participation in the economy through oversaving of money or through the withholding of commitments to supply labor as a factor of production, so personalities in their relations to significant collectivities (such as the academic) can diminish their participation either by slowing their spending of affect or by withdrawing from significant participation in the form of withholding cathexes. In both cases affect may be transferred to other contexts of identification, although the case of expressive-aesthetic withdrawal suggests the min-imization of societal involvements, equivalent to a kind of voluntary unemployment. (See General Action Interchange paradigm—G-I set—technical appendix, Figure 7.) The interchange just referred to is the focus of the affective attachment of in-dividuals to any sector of the societal community, in this case, of the academic com-munity. Intelligence as a medium is not directly involved in it; the most relevant involvement of intelligence is in the A-I interchange (Figure 7, technical appendix); the balances in the A-I interchange are important to the socialization function, as that was analyzed in Chapter 4. The "Keynesian" balances of affect, however, underpin the integration of affect with intelligence so that serious disturbance of the personality-social-system balance should be expected to have repercussions in the affect-intelligence area, which is manifested as the activation of resistance to socializing forces by with-drawal of identification in the academic community.

responsible persons are charged with investing and lending other people's influence deposits. These responsible persons tend to be faculty members and administration personnel.

Influence comes to the university from many sources. A portion of influence deposits come from student influence investment but deposits are also granted to the university from other participating members, such as the faculty and graduate students, from alumni, other funding sources, and from the general public. All tenure levels in higher education are both depositors and borrowers of influence.

Fiduciary responsibility is the basis of the internal stratification of institutions of higher education. Levels of competence combined with levels of commitment to cognitive rationality undergird the stratification system; the faculty in general stands higher on both of these than students, in part because of the length of time in which they have been involved with academic careers and in part because these are institutionalized aspects of their occupation and life-style. This higher level of commitment and involvement legitimates the faculties' responsibility with regard to influence investment and loans. Further, if the system is functioning adequately, these higher levels of competence and commitment give the faculty appropriate resources with which to implement fiduciary responsibilities. General and differential access to resources is correlated with the prestige of the faculty, the department, and the institution—and their reputations for distinctive academic achievement.

An inflationary trend is a situation where the unit value of the influence medium depreciates in its capacity to command value-commitment to cognitive rationality and to command relevant, more concrete resources for academic purposes. Even in the best colleges and universities the average entering students do not have the capacity in the form of personal competence to contribute much to implementation of the values of cognitive rationality, certainly not on a level equal to those of the faculty, nor have they yet developed the performance capacity to contribute significantly to cognitive outputs. One function of influence loans to students is to assist in developing these value-commitments and personal capacities so that the gap between faculty and students is narrowed and eventually closed.

Students in elite colleges have become an increasingly privileged group because they are the winners in an intense competition for admission to a limited number of places. As a quid pro quo, they are expected to assume higher obligations for performance during the period of their stay on campus and also subsequent to their college careers. Thus, a special strain exists between such students and their faculty which can produce a reaction in the form of students relaxing either commitments or efforts to implement them. At this level the focus of inflationary tension lies in the decreasing value of influence as a means to acquire academic commitment; the influence loans of the college have a diminished capacity to convince the student to develop higher-level commitments and higher-level cognitive capacities. The disposition to expend effort to close the gap between faculty and students is impaired.

This is further compounded by a typical form of influence inflation in any socialization context: the decreasing value of abiding by the rules set by those most responsible for the socialization process. The presumption tends to be that socializers have set unfair expectations on individuals being socialized who therefore can repudiate the legitimacy of such expectations, which are caricatured as unfair burdens. In the influence for value-commitment exchange, this is parallel to relaxation of cognitive standards of evaluation at the general action level and in the economic realm the lowering of product quality in order to maintain price.

*Social System—Societal Community Subsystem of Higher Education.* The university constitutes a unit of the societal community. Citizens at the university's value center are its faculty whose value-commitments and competences are acquired over an occupational career supportive of their values. Other members of the university community are more explicitly under value and social structural cross-pressures: future educated citizenry, professional practitioners, and intellectuals.

On the larger and more elite campuses classes of persons exist who are not part of the core faculty but are committed to the values of cognitive rationality and whose performances are vital to the functioning of the university. Smelser has referred to these classes as new estates: such people as research faculty, research associates, faculty with joint appointments in the arts and sciences and professional schools, part-time and visiting faculty, teaching and research assistants, and so on.[25] Naturally some of these

25. Neil J. Smelser, "Growth and Conflict in California Higher Education: 1950–1970," *Bulletin of the American Academy of Arts and Sciences*, 25, no. 8 (May 1972), and personal communication. See also the epilogue to this book.

classes overlap with others previously noted and are not totally independent (or entirely new) university statuses.

For all of these classes, there is also national and local citizenship, national and local academic and disciplinary ties, and personal and familial lives. In these contexts faculty members and other persons pursue their private concerns and priorities. This complex set of associations within the university is an extensively variegated environment of commitments and obligations for all those community members involved in it. In spite of this, the faculty remains at the value center, acting as models of academic values and drawing other classes toward their commitments even as they themselves are drawn outward.

The prototype of this process exists in student socialization. Parallel to the sense in which intelligence as a medium has tended to decline in value in student socialization, there has been a decline of the value of influence as medium in the faculty's exchange with students. Influence within the societal community operates as a mode of persuasion for students to enter into one of the paths of cognitive development demanding higher levels of involvement in cognitive endeavors. Influence is a reward at the disposal of the socializing agents. Until recently, the faculty could command a considerable student commitment to shared academic values. From the faculty's point of view this was a deflated state similar to the sense in which groups with fixed salaries, like faculty members at secure universities in the 1930's, benefited from the price deflation of the economy. Recently the reverse has been the case. The ability of the faculty influence to command student commitment has declined. Thus in this dimension an inflationary trend has reduced the value of influence in exchange for student loyalties. If higher education is an influence-creating bank, the investment value of commitments came to be inflated for certain classes, such as students, while the faculty could command such investment at relatively little influence cost. This trend was reversed in the mid-1960's.

A similar condition held for the new academic statuses. These estates in the university community experienced increasing relative deprivation. For example, teaching assistants and research personnel made large commitments to cognitive rationality but received little reward in terms of acceptance in the solidary community for such investments. Teaching assistants, although not treated as faculty members in terms of privileges (inclusion), have performed a large share of faculty functions including on occasion teaching their own classes. And research personnel often were denied privileges such as access to the faculty club or independently soliciting research grants. In solidary terms persons in these statuses became vulnerable to alienation and thus to withdrawing their value-commitments and affective investments, which in many instances they did.

Thus, from the point of view of the faculty and such new categories of personnel, the value of the two academically central generalized media, intelligence and influence, has been depreciating. The impact of this depreciation has been unequal among the various classes of members within the academic institutions. The impact has presumably been least for senior faculty but increasingly greater on lower status levels, being most intense for certain undergraduates. This deflation is related to the real and potential rewards, including influence and its accretion. For most academic classes, save that of the senior faculty, rewards have in recent times become increasingly precarious.

*Social System—Political and Economic Dimensions.* The political and economic aspects of the university are not at the core of the phenomena we have been discussing but are conditional to it.[26]

The current stress on the power aspects of the academic system is less an accurate description of the forces at work than a symptomatic symbolization of tensions and ideologies which reduce all conflict to that of political struggles. True, in crisis situations concern with power rises rapidly, but with subsiding of the tensions this concern can decline equally rapidly. That the academic system is not primarily one of power relationships is suggested by our survey of academic men; we found that faculty members were not power hungry; quite the contrary. Most faculty members wished to reduce their administrative involvement, and most would rather be influential than powerful in their departments, universities, and colleges.[27] There is little indication that faculty members attempt to protect their power positions by keeping outsiders at bay.

26. Clifford Geertz makes the same point with respect to Balinese cockfighting and betting. The heart of the fight is in the expressive symbolism of the status competition and not in the betting, but a "deep" fight would not have importance without the betting. Just as betting is conditional to cockfighting, so money is conditional to the operations of higher education. See Clifford Geertz, "Deep Play: Notes on the Balinese Cockfight," *Daedalus* (Winter 1972), pp. 1–38.

27. Parsons and Platt, "The American Academic Profession"; Platt and Parsons, *The American Academic System.*

A second political problem concerns the position of the academic system in the larger community. The status of the system of higher education has been greatly enhanced as many different indices show. As part of this process of status enhancement, it is probable that there has been a power inflation of considerable magnitude, both internally and externally. Internally there has been the increasing power of administration vis-à-vis all the other components of the university rather than of faculties only. However, in the context of the Durkheimian notion that organic solidarity and the political organization of the state must grow concomitantly[28] and not in any zero-sum relation with respect to each other, such power inflation as there has been on the part of administration will ultimately be redressed by a catching up by the nonpower elements in the system. The system is still in flux, but there are signs that in the recent struggles both the faculty and students have gained an improved position with regard to the administration.[29] The realities of this situation are as yet not fully clarified.

In societal terms the inflationary trend in the relation of the academic to the political system has mainly involved decisions about the financial status of universities. State legislators and the national Congress have begun to worry of late about the magnitude of commitment that has been made to the universities and have been concerned about justifying continuing the growth rates of the recent past.

This is a point at which the university is particularly vulnerable to backlash from the political right involving a variety of factors. The more flamboyant features of student life-styles and political activism have played their part. When the latter led to acute disturbances which have involved confrontations, questions of public order have been raised. Back of this are also the traditional components of tension between the liberal university and more conservative general society. Thus, recent research has documented that university faculties, in political attitudes, stand well to the left of other professionals and the general public.[30] Thus,

28. Emile Durkheim, *The Division of Labor in Society*, trans. George Simpson (New York, The Free Press, 1969).

29. Talcott Parsons and Gerald M. Platt, "Decision-Making in the Academic System: Influence and Power Exchange," in *The State of the University: Authority and Change*, ed. Carlos E. Kruytbosch and Sheldon Messinger (Beverly Hills, Calif., Sage Publications, 1970).

30. Seymour M. Lipset, "Academia and Politics in America," in *Imagination and Precision in the Social Sciences*, ed. T. J. Nossiter (London, Faber, 1972), pp. 211–289; see particularly Table 1, p. 225.

they are often the recipients of right-wing backlash as a form of deflationary influence.[31]

Vulnerability of the university is in part a result of the fact that it is not self-sufficient with respect to political power but has to be subsidized from the outside. Such immunities as tax exemptions have constituted a major subsidy to private institutions; financial support by state and federal governments constitute another form of political-economic subsidy. To a considerable extent political and economic subsidies have been bound together in a single package in that financial subsidies have been made by governmental agencies.

The massive growth of higher education since World War II occasioned large increases of budgets. This meant a shift in the composition of the financial support, with an increasing fraction coming from federal, state, and local governmental sources. This pouring in of funds, including the rapidly increasing Federal support of research and graduate training, has had an inflationary effect at the economic level in the sense that the margins of a variety of types of academic output have been lowered: (1) with respect to student elements; (2) with respect to training qualifications of teachers; and (3) with respect to research. The dollar spent on academic affairs therefore, has not bought as much as it did before—even apart from general inflation.

Another inflationary factor has been that, in the strictly economic sense, the productivity of labor in the academic enterprise has not been rising substantially, because it is overwhelmingly a "service industry." Money costs, however, have been rising because academic incomes must remain competitive with other occupations, including the standards of living of subsidized students, as, for example, graduate students.[32] It should not be inferred from this lagging economic productivity relative to the rest of the economy that the academic enterprise is "unproductive" in other than economic senses. What it means is that as an economic investment it has been becoming relatively more expensive. This element of financial strain probably increases vulnerability because it is so difficult for subsidizing decision-makers, such as legislators,

31. Talcott Parsons, *Structure and Process in Modern Societies* (Glencoe, Ill., The Free Press, 1960), chap. vii, "Social Strains in America," pp. 226–247.

32. Howard R. Bowen, *Efficiency in Liberal Education: Study of Comparative and Structural Costs for Different Ways of Organizing Teaching-Learning in a Liberal Arts College* (New York, McGraw-Hill, 1971).

to understand why it is so difficult for colleges and universities to check the rate of rise in their financial costs.

In addition to these two factors, the difficulties of the academic world have coincided with an inflationary phase in the development of the national economy. The monetary inflation increases the money costs of operating universities, whereas the combination of this with recession puts pressure on funding agencies to slow the rate of growth in financial support, if not to cut it absolutely.

In discussing these six levels we have touched upon all of the main points of tension and inflation that we envision within the academic system and in relation to its environments. Nevertheless, we have not been entirely systematic in our analysis. To do so would have necessitated the development of a paradigm of media at the cultural level and a discussion of all media and of exchanges among them where sociologically (not logically) these occur. The magnitude of such an analysis exceeds the purposes of this chapter, of this volume, and indeed our capacities. But we have accomplished an *inter*system analysis of inflation within the cybernetic framework in some detail. In the last section of this chapter, we turn to a discussion of the deflationary panic of the 1960's and an attempt to pinpoint the levels of deflation and the mode of involvement of the media.

## The Deflationary Panic

The cognitive-influence panic in higher education of the mid-1960's was analogous to financial panics in the economy, for example, that of 1929. The eye of the panic was at level 4 in the exchanges between the fiduciary and societal community systems. Secondarily, it was severe on the borders of level 4; at level 5, within the societal community of higher education; and at level 3, in the relationship among the social system, personality, and organism. This means that there were deflationary trends in influence in relation to value-commitments, in intelligence and intelligence banking, and in intelligence in relation to affect.

Such assertions demand empirical verification of an extensive nature which we cannot undertake. However, we can suggest that, though there has developed some distrust of cognitive culture, this has not gone too far (level 1). True, on the other end of the spectrum (level 6), there have been severe financial stringencies. State and federal legislatures as well as alumni have been less free with their funding and more concerned with return on investment, but even this has not gone too far. Such distrust as has developed has been uneven from state to state; but at both the federal and state levels there has been continuing political support for the belief that a college-educated population is desirable. Furthermore, in spite of the ambivalences on the part of parents and students that became manifest, there is still a widespread desire to go on to college and a willingness to pay for it.

In short, the most intense expressions of the panic have *not* focused at levels 1 or 6. We can then note at other levels what form the panic did take. One symptom is the widespread resistance of college students to commit themselves to traditional cognitive learning and the decline of the capacity of faculty and institutions to persuade them to do so (level 4). Secondarily, students went through a phase of intense distrust of much of academic authority and of the value of a large part of academic organization and rules of conduct, although recently this problem has been somewhat alleviated (level 5).[33] The process of long-range investment in intelligence and development in the purely cognitive fields has been under attack in favor of immediate and noncognitive competences and relevance (levels 3 and 2) despite the undiminished numbers of students who want to go on to graduate work (although at this level too there has been pressure for relevance

33. During our final revision of this chapter (early May 1972) student disturbances have revived, although it seems unlikely that they will be either as intense or as widespread as the last major episode in the spring of 1970 when the expedition into Cambodia coincided with the killing of students at Kent and Jackson State Universities. The renewal of disturbances seems to be a direct result of the renewal of intensive bombing of North Viet Nam (starting in April 1972). The war is probably the most sensitive issue on a continuing basis, both because of the general moral status of war itself and because symbolically war is highly disruptive of the lives of young people.

The war issue, however, has converged with certain others. Thus at Harvard, not unlike many other institutions, financial stringency has occasioned financial cutbacks in the support of graduate student teaching fellows. These measures were reacted to by the organization of a teaching-fellow/graduate student union and the calling of a strike, which was absorbed into the antiwar strike, but both subsided soon. In addition, the sensitivities of the black students have been involved in charges of university racism, manifested in attacks on the views of one member of its faculty and connected with the theme of imperialism by the university's ownership of stock in the Gulf Oil Company, which operates in Portuguese South Africa. See the *Harvard University Gazette* during the first half of 1972.

These events show that there is still sensitivity to panic reactions in the deflationary direction, but short of something like major re-escalation of the Viet Nam war, we doubt that another massive mobilization of student negativism is likely soon. Significantly, there is this time a greater effort to discriminate the University as target from the Federal Government (*Harvard Crimson*, April 28, 1972). Even the mining of Haiphong Harbor did not provoke as massive a student reaction as might have been expected and certainly as would have occurred in 1969 or 1970.

and noncognitive interests). It is difficult to say what subsection of the undergraduate population wishes to go on to graduate work and in what sense there is continuity with undergraduate populations prior to the panic. In any case, the deflationary trends at levels 3 and 2 are much more salient among undergraduates than among graduate students.

While such illustrative discourse hardly constitutes verification of our theoretical position, it does indicate the potential value of such a framework for investigating these problems. It organizes some previously disparate data and events, as, for example, why certain issues have had staying power among students while others have drifted in and out among student discontents, why certain issues have been able to mobilize large numbers of students while others have mobilized only the most radical activists. Naturally, the answer to these and other related issues revolves about the degree to which issues were related to the center of the panic.

But our assertion of its centrality need not mean that the main *precipitating* events of the cognitive-influence panic were located at level 4. More of these events seem to have been initiated at level 5, in various ways criticizing the university's conduct and organization regarding students, teaching, research, the local community, and the society. In Berkeley, for example, the initial complaints of 1964 concerned the regulation of student rights to use university premises and facilities for political purposes. At Columbia in 1968, the problems of the uses of the proposed new gymnasium, the degree to which the gym was to be used by the local community, and suspicions regarding the research of the Institute for Defense Analysis were the central issues. And at Harvard in 1969 the status of ROTC as a symbol of the United States' involvement in the Viet Nam war along with Harvard's encroachment on the local community, the so-called Harvardization of Cambridge, were the symbolic occasions for student activism. Other issues involved in precipitating student demonstrations were recruiters on campus from dubiously moral industries (for instance, Dow Chemical) and from the military; the university's treatment of the poor and the blacks in the local community; the university's treatment of workers and minorities already in their employ; and the ratio of minorities among students, faculty, and staff.

From these precipitating foci, disturbances spread rapidly to other areas of conflict. In most cases this took the form of conflict with those in authority concerning student control over their lives (especially regarding the morality of their private dormitory lives) and concerning student involvement with campus decision-making including the allocation of university resources, the types of research conducted on campus, the curriculum, and the hiring policy of the university. These issues more directly relevant to their status as students broadened the basis of participation in the various strikes.

A typical radical-student technique during the period of ferment was to take over a building, an action which violated established rules about the sanctity of working premises for administrators, staff, or faculty. Student lack of organization and cohesion was repaired by the often overreactive police actions administratively ordered against the student demonstrators in the building. In spite of the clear illegality of the occupation, resort to police intervention was perceived as unfair and unjust even among students opposing the radical dissenters as, for example, among the athletes at Columbia University who initially taunted the demonstrators and then went over to the activists' side following the "bust."

The bust, in which students were often injured, was seen as repressive action on the part of the administration; perceptions of an inhumane administration drew wider and wider proportions of the students into the demonstrations. At Harvard and at Berkeley it did not help that the administration reneged on promises of negotiations with students.[34] The use of authority perceived as arbitrary intensified the sense of peer-solidarity which exists among students even under normal circumstances (see Chapter 4 on this point). In a kind of oedipal drama, the conflict polarized along generational lines and in terms of authority and power. Especially salient symbolic slogans became "student power" and "never trust anyone over thirty," which became tantamount to the students not trusting the faculty.[35]

The vulnerability of the university can be understood in terms

34. Gerald M. Platt, "Harvard Student Dissent and Higher Educational Reform," unpub. MS, Amherst, Mass., 1971; also see several relevant excerpts in *The University Crisis Reader*, ed. Immanuel Wallerstein and Paul Starr (New York, Random House and Vintage Books, 1971), I and II.

35. Interestingly enough, many student activists—undergraduates in elite colleges who are the children of educated, liberal, and successful parents (see Lipset)—have already, as citizens in terms of class status, been the *full* equals of *both* their parents and their teachers. In terms of the principle of relative deprivation, their inferiority in generational status with its concomitant lack of competence and experience may seem all the more galling. See S. M. Lipset, *Rebellion in the University* (Boston, Mass., Little, Brown and Co., 1971).

of the position of influence and value-commitments as integrative mechanisms within the university and of the university as an influence bank. In a sense, the university has no way to deal with force, coercion, or violence.[36] An educational institution operates primarily on the basis of the willingness (that is, commitment) of the participants to act according to accepted rules of conduct. Disrupting a lecture is a simple matter; all that is needed is a handful of individuals willing to out-shout the lecturer.

Similarly, the student tactic of nonnegotiable demands to be implemented immediately cannot be dealt with by the university because the university has no way to compel negotiation or arbitration. Within the list of demands there have been reasonable proposals for university reform within the purview of university control. Often, however, the list extends well beyond the potential control of the university or, if within the university boundaries, some of the demands on the list take time and major resources to implement. Others have been in radical conflict with the value-commitments of the university. Nonnegotiable and immediately-to-be-implemented demands are analogous to a monetary run on a bank; they are requests for total payment of all obligations immediately. As an influence bank, with multiple investors, investments, and obligations, the university cannot satisfy all student demands short of bankruptcy.[37]

The major effect of these runs on university influence-banks was deflationary; the withdrawal of confidence in the institution created a tendency to sharpen the natural rift in the solidary

36. A university can call in the police or the militia when under siege, but in a very real sense it is an institution more vulnerable to force than most others. No university or college can perform its learning or teaching functions when besieged; note, e.g., the capacity of the Japanese students to shut down the University of Tokyo for a full year.

37. Another feature of the panic syndrome was the demand on the part of the student activists for total amnesty, i.e., no punishments of any kind for action which they knew to be not only contrary to the normative order of the academic community but also, as in the case of seizure of buildings and destruction of property, to be illegal. This has been a demand which has been difficult, if not impossible, for university administrations and faculties to comply with. It would be tantamount to surrender of the legitimacy of the university position.

For student groups, total amnesty has at least three tempting meanings. First, if they could bring themselves to believe that they had a *right* to amnesty, this could reinforce their claim to a position of moral superiority to their opponents in the confrontation. Second, the demand for amnesty exploits their position of dependency in the protected environment to which we referred in Chapter 4 by saying, "you, who are so benevolent, surely would not do anything to injure your 'children' even when they 'act up'." Third, it reinforces their solidarity as a peer-group. This last motif has underlain the reluctance of students to play any part in disciplinary procedures even though they clamored for greater rights of participation in other contexts.

relationship between students and faculty, deflating the faculty's capacity to influence students. The faculty influence-deflation was partly caused by the expenditures of influence during these trying periods in efforts to achieve accord with the students and to maintain order rather than, for example, spending it on the socialization of students. However, the deflationary consequences were more permanent than this.

What these disturbances did was involve the university in social and political issues which put deflationary pressure on the core functions of the university. When this pressure grew severe enough, it was propagated to higher cybernetic levels. Initially, influence functioned at levels 5 and 4 and then up the cybernetic hierarchy to levels 3 and 2, which then began to generate deflationary effects on intelligence banking.[38]

The propagation upward to the intelligence-banking level was manifest in the anti-intellectual component of the movement. We have sufficiently dwelt on the two foci of that trend. One of them has been the concept of relevance in its New Left sense rather than in the more specifically social science sense in which we have generally used the term. Its focus has been on social change brought about by militant political action and has challenged the legitimacy of the value neutrality of the academic community. The second focus has been the expressive-aesthetic axis and has been manifested in the weakening of cognitive interests in favor of liberated self-realization of various sorts.

Finally, there have been vulnerabilities at the level of the general cultural situation in the university and its concerns. The status of the cognitive component of culture generally has been controversial for many centuries and still is and will continue to be controversial. The manifestation of tensions at this level includes such phenomena as the treatment of a figure such as Freud as an apostle of the nonrational, thereby ignoring his contribution to the extension of rational observation and analysis into the new psychological areas of the unconscious.

38. This argument is in accord with Smelser's analysis in his *Theory of Collective Behavior* (New York, The Free Press, 1963). We take this opportunity to set forth our opinion that Lipset in *Passion and Politics* (with Gerald M. Schaflander, Boston, Mass., Little, Brown and Co., 1971, chap. ii) is not quite correct in his hypothesis that the political ideology of students, especially in relation to the Viet Nam war, was the main source of the student disturbances since 1964 (see pp. 43–44). This factor may have been decisive in the selection of *which* students were to be the primary activists in the disturbances, but in explaining the disturbances themselves the features of the university system reviewed in this chapter have in our opinion been the basic factor.

There has been a disposition to regard Western culture as biased in favor of cognitive interests and to maintain that people who are up-to-date will be critical of tendencies to put strong emphasis on cognitive interests. We regard these attitudes as symptomatic of general tension and as leading to deflationary reductions in the amount of intelligence in circulation. Such inflationary-deflationary swings, however, although they can proceed cumulatively for a considerable time, also tend to reactivate forces which may, given time and other conditions, restore a balance which need not be exactly the same as that of the status quo ante but which are incompatible with permanent institutionalization of the extreme positions prominent in the acute phase of disturbance.

# 8

## CONTINUITY AND CHANGE:
## SOME PROBABLE TRENDS

What changes in higher education are probable? The circumstances that now confront higher education and society suggest that *some* changes are in the offing, and an analysis may indicate which are most likely. But we embark upon this analysis also because it is the logical outgrowth of the discussion of inflationary and deflationary trends in Chapter 7; in this chapter we take up the long-term consequences of these processes as well as of the underlying history of growth.

We are not the first to attempt to predict changes in higher education. However, our analysis will be built upon a theoretical framework rather than on hope for this or that change or fear of it, although hopes and fears will not be entirely eliminated from our analysis. Consequently, our analysis is more likely to be valid; we will accept as axiomatic that any change which occurs will incorporate large portions of the system as it has already developed; and our previous analysis will give us a handle on what portions of the system are more likely to be incorporated into changed forms.

We are justified empirically in assuming that the new forms will incorporate parts of the old. Even the most radical historical changes, such as the French Revolution, brought with them into the new regime major portions of the old culture and social structure although there was an intense effort to expunge all of the past.[1] Even Marx believed that a new system would be a combination of the old and the new.

1. Fred Weinstein and Gerald M. Platt, *The Wish to Be Free: Society, Psyche, and Value Change* (Berkeley and Los Angeles, Calif., University of California Press, 1969), chaps. ii–iv.

## A Synoptic Criticism: The Structural
## "Bundle" in Higher Education

A contemporary issue regarding higher education in society is that of its raison d'être (its definition of the situation as discussed in Chapter 6). Meaning, purpose, consequences, and functions are at the center of the controversies regarding higher education. Intellectuals, students, and politicians, pulling in several different directions, have contributed to this controversy in their efforts to define a new situation for higher education. Every suggested change in mission has implied also important social structural consequences. Although some of this discussion was touched upon from the point of view of the students (in Chapter 4), we will summarize these suggestions for change because they constitute an excellent background for our own views.

One of these critiques centers around the value of cognitive rationality and its institutionalization in higher education. The issues are too numerous to review in their entirety; they range from the desire to eliminate cognitive rationality to the desire for its intensification to the point where it is the sole basis for action in higher education undiluted by other cultural or social orientations. In between these polar suggestions are structural arrangements which would modify the cognitive orientation such as extruding the research function and graduate schools from higher education or, alternatively, differentiating these activities from the undergraduate teaching function and developing separate research and graduate centers.[2] Also in connection with cognitive rationality we hear criticisms (and defenses) concerning irrelevance and value freedom in higher education and research. Further, references to this value-pattern accompany attacks upon science-based technology and its alleged consequences for dehumanization and for pollution and desecration of the environment. These arguments are made by extension of the involvements of science rather than directly against scientific activity, although the latter has also been heard.

A second critique concerns the academic community itself. The focus is upon such features as its stratificaton, authority structure, and bases of evaluation. These are attacked from both sides; by those who would eliminate all forms of hierarchy as, for example,

2. Neil J. Smelser, ed., *Public Higher Education in California: Growth, Structural Change, and Conflict* (Berkeley, Calif., University of California Press, 1973).

by the elimination of tenure levels and of all forms of evaluation and also by those who claim that the university system has gone too far in this direction already and that college environments are now too permissive. We hear complaints about grading (again from both sides), competition, meritocracy, and about the rights and responsibilities of faculty and students.

A third critique centers on the question of the aims of education, especially undergraduate education. Does it serve to produce cogs for industrial wheels and brain-washed middle-class consumers? Does it provide training and thus advantage for an already established elite in society? Or should it offer advantages mainly to those previously excluded, for instance, to blacks and the poor? Or again, should it be an environment of personal exploration in which affective and expressive values are given free expression, an environment where the young can discover their own values and identities and where they can come to feel and experience rather than to know and reason? There are innumerable points of view on these issues, including those who would suggest combinations of all these purposes. Our answer to these questions and issues is given in some measure in Chapter 4. Here we will explore the limits of change in this dimension in light of the purposes of higher education in teaching the young.

The final critique concerns the practical involvements of the university. These issues span the gamut from undergraduate and graduate education to preprofessional and professional training, from research for applied ends to any research funded by external agencies. For example, undergraduate education is accused of being entirely vocational training or not sufficiently enough vocationally oriented.[3] Questions such as "What are nursing and agricultural departments doing on a liberal arts campus?" are asked and then as if the first question had not been asked, the other side of the coin appears: "Why don't we have a 'Man and His Environment' Center or Program at the university?" Similar criticisms are made of graduate education; it is too professional or not professional enough. Psychology, sociology, and anthropology Ph.D.'s are accused of knowing only their fields and not having enough practical knowledge to apply to such problems as urban decay. And, with regard to professional schools such as medicine and engineering, they are accused of having done more harm than

3. Report of the President's Committee on the Future of the University of Massachusetts, Boston, Mass., December 1971.

good, of not being concerned with relevant problems such as the health care for, and delivery to, the poor and the blacks. In contrast to the advocacy of involvement, there are suggestions that the professional schools should go their own way, should split off from the arts and sciences; it is pointed out that these schools are expensive and practically oriented and that they divert the interests, talents, and finances of the core faculty of the university. Parallel criticisms of research are also made: that it is too practically oriented or too rarified, that research detracts from teaching, and that it is controlled by funding agencies outside the university such as the government or industry or that research vitalizes teaching.

No review of contemporary disputations about higher education can do justice to the variegated and opposing criticisms, the differences in nuance, and the sectarian positions held to with varying fervor. Smelser comes close to offering a summary when he suggests that the university is "functionally overloaded." We agree that what he refers to by this term makes the university vulnerable, but it is also a source of strength. From a structural point of view Smelser refers to the focus of this functional overloading as "the bundle."[4] Throughout this book, we have attempted to describe this "bundle," to explain why it grew this way and how it sustains itself in the manner it does.

This bundle of related structures will be the starting point from which we discuss the criticisms already noted and from which we will talk about potential changes in the system. The bundle is part of our theoretical model and a major aspect of the structure which will have to be taken into account when change is considered. Some of the structure will be carried forward in changes of higher education. What parts are more vital than others is what we wish to analyze. Thus it is advantageous to recapitulate the nature of this bundle and why it has developed in this way, the advantages of such an organization, and the limitations on its change.

## The Development of the Bundle in Higher Education

Historically and comparatively, the structure of the modern American university is unique. It is a functionally differentiated system, but despite this differentiation the various subsections have

4. Neil J. Smelser, "Growth and Conflict in California Higher Education: 1950–1970," *Bulletin of the American Academy of Arts and Sciences*, 25, no. 8 (May 1972); see also the epilogue of this book.

held together in a kind of bundle. This packaging is a curious sociological phenomenon. On the one hand there has been increasing specialization in areas of knowledge (the disciplines) ; on the other hand there has been resistance to the development of specialized schools and research centers separated from each other and from the university. Given the Western tradition for organizational rationalization, this packaging is something of a paradox, which requires explanation.

Let us begin with a description of the bundle. In the full university, private or public, there is a combination of functions performed by a number of faculties in corporate association with each other and forming a single institution. Many of these functions are performed by a single faculty, such as the arts and sciences faculty that teaches both undergraduate and graduate students. Although on occasion there is talk of making graduate centers, as, for example, Berkeley and UCLA, into centers which serve *only* graduate students and making the other campuses of the University of California undergraduate teaching environments, this has never occurred. Coming at the same "double function" from the opposite pole, we note that where institutions such as the Johns Hopkins and Clark University began as graduate schools, they soon evolved, for one reason or another, to incorporate undergraduate instruction by the same faculty. And institutions such as Columbia University, in which a sharp distinction once existed between the college and the university (graduate) faculty, such a demarkation became more vague with the passage of time. Furthermore, among the core arts and science faculty the obligation developed of doing both teaching and research rather than one or the other exclusively. These combined functions are a source of much strain; we will return shortly to this topic from a theoretical as well as empirical point of view.

Another aspect of the bundle, this time at the institutional level, is the simultaneous existence of an arts and science faculty integrated with a plurality of professional schools. In Chapter 5 we have discussed joint appointments in both these faculties as a node of integration, but we should also note that both the arts and science faculty and the professional faculty tend to remain under a single corporate association; and both faculties are involved with the operation of the total university.[5]

5. Recently at the University of Massachusetts, there was established a Committee on the Future of the University. Although most of the members on the Committee

Another feature of the bundle is the incorporation of the entire spectrum of disciplines in the university, notably in its faculty of arts and sciences, rather than focusing on a small range of disciplines. Some critics have considered this a wasteful use of resources duplicating efforts already found at other institutions and forcing competition among institutions for the best staff for all these disciplines. In spite of this criticism, this across-the-board attitude is found at most American colleges and universities.

The final element of the bundle is homogeneity of values. Although there are some 1200 four-year liberal arts colleges and universities and although these are stratified by quality, size, and prestige,[6] and they are diverse in many other respects, they are oriented by and strive for the same educational and scholarly goals. In this sense, there has been pressure on the less prestigious institutions to upgrade by emulating (in structural terms) the more elite colleges and universities. The consequences of this aspiration for faculties and for institutions have been considerable; at this point, however, the interesting point is that these colleges have not gone their own way, trying to emphasize particular disciplines and special interests. Indeed, where this has occurred, we have witnessed a transformation in the direction of the described bundle insofar as this is possible given the realistic circumstances each institution has faced.

### Development of the American University: Comparative Perspective

The above description constitutes a bare outline which needs to be filled in with some detail of how the American university developed and how it compares with other university systems. The

---

were from walks of life outside the University, three faculty members, one from each of the campuses, were asked to participate on the Committee. The Worcester campus is exclusively a medical school, although plans exist to develop other professional schools and a limited undergraduate college there. A faculty member, a pathologist, from that campus sat on the Committee. The report of the Committee had little to suggest regarding the Worcester campus and concerned itself primarily with undergraduate education. Despite this, all members of the Committee felt it legitimate for the medical doctor to serve, and he was one of the most concerned members regarding the *quality and nature of undergraduate* education on all of the campuses of the University.

6. Allan M. Cartter indicates that there are 2500 institutions of higher education in the United States, but only about half of these are classified as four-year liberal arts colleges and universities. The remainder are two-year colleges or teacher and vocational schools. See Cartter, *An Assessment of Quality in Graduate Education* (Washington, D.C., American Council on Education, 1966).

developmental baseline of the American university was the nine-teenth-century undergraduate college. There were at the turn of the century some 300 such colleges in the United States, most of which were private and religiously controlled. A second source of colleges were those public institutions established by a series of federal land-grant acts beginning in 1862.[7] But these colleges (and the instruction in them) were not comparable with contemporary undergraduate education. The public colleges provided mainly vocational training, while the private institutions offered a classical curriculum of rote education in Greek, Latin, mathematics, morals, and religion.

As these colleges differentiated from their practical and religious bases, graduate schools began to be established in them. The graduate school adapted to the American system was a modified and upgraded version of the one American scholars had experienced while studying in Germany. The graduate schools became intellectually oriented not so much to their institutions as to the national disciplinary associations which were being formed at about the same time.[8] The combination of graduate education and national disciplinary identification focused formal credentials for scholarly work and advanced training in a field in the graduate school; and the Ph.D. degree became nearly the sine qua non for entry into a discipline as a qualified scholar. In the course of this professionalization of the universities and colleges, branches of the teaching profession gave increasing attention to achievement in scholarship and research to the point where these became predominant criteria for appointment and promotion, especially in prestigious institutions.[9] This particular combination in the arts and science field is distinctively American.[10] The philosophical faculty of the nineteenth-century German university was not really a faculty of arts and sciences in the American sense and definitely not a graduate school of arts and sciences. Continental Europe did not have the equivalent of our undergraduate college either.

7. Christopher Jencks and David Riesman, *The Academic Revolution* (Garden City, N.Y., Doubleday and Co., 1968).

8. Bernard Berelson, *Graduate Education in the United States* (New York, McGraw-Hill, 1960).

9. David Riesman, "Educational Reform at Harvard College: Meritocracy and Adversaries" (forthcoming).

10. Joseph Ben-David, *American Higher Education: Directions Old and New* (New York, McGraw-Hill, 1972); and Joseph Ben-David, *The Scientist's Role in Society: A Comparative Study* (Englewood Cliffs, N.J., Prentice-Hall, Inc., 1971).

The development of American graduate schools did not displace the undergraduate colleges in the same institutions. Instead coexistence occurred with overlap in personnel and teaching arrangements. Though these conditions vary from university to university, the majority of the faculty members at most institutions teach undergraduates as well as graduate students. For example, junior faculty members in a department may teach undergraduates primarily but may also teach graduate students in the middle-level courses and sometimes graduate seminars. Senior faculty members may primarily teach graduate students but they also teach middle-level courses, and undergraduates will occasionally participate in graduate seminars.

The German philosophical faculty was largely a professional faculty concerned with the training of teachers for advanced secondary schools, that is, the *Gymnasia*. There was no organized provision for the training of future university professors. To be sure, they usually got their degrees in philosophical faculties if they were to be in the arts and sciences field. But from then on, they functioned mainly as private scholars. Exceptions developed first in the natural sciences in the research institutes, the heads of which were senior professors and where seminars and assistant appointments gave opportunities for advanced training.[11]

Simultaneously with these developments, the classical undergraduate curriculum began to give way to the elective system for undergraduates.[12] This was associated with an establishment of new intellectual disciplines. The continuity with the old curriculum was greatest in what is presently called the humanities. The natural sciences gradually gained a foothold in the curriculum and were then followed by the social sciences. This process has taken a long time to complete itself. Thus, Harvard did not have a department of psychology, independent of philosophy, until the late 1930's and Amherst College only recently established an independent sociology department; Williams College has yet to establish one. In spite of this expansion of the range of disciplines in faculties of arts and sciences, the *same faculty* covers essentially the whole of the range. The tendency has not been for separate faculties of humanities, natural sciences, or of social sciences to

11. Ibid.
12. Jencks and Riesman, *Academic Revolution*. Also see Laurence R. Veysey, *The Emergence of the American University* (Chicago, Ill., University of Chicago Press, 1965), and Abraham Flexner, *Universities: American, English, German* (New York, Oxford University Press, 1930).

spring up. Nor have we anything comparable to the London School of Economics and Political Science, although there is in New York City the New School for Social Research.

There were technical schools centering on engineering. But the tendency for undergraduate engineering schools was not only to upgrade a larger proportion of advanced graduate training and research in natural science but also to become diversified at both undergraduate and graduate levels. For example, M.I.T. is presently hardly an engineering school; in addition to its basic sciences it has one of the most distinguished economics departments in the world; and its strength in the other social sciences and humanities is considerable.

The institutionalization of the research function came later than the development of graduate education and the proliferation of the range of disciplines, but these trends were related to each other. The institutionalization of research transformed the college teacher from an amateur scholar to a professional researcher; from the scholar who pursued research because of private interest to research and scholarship as an obligated component of the faculty role. However, only relatively recently (post-World War II) was research promoted by massive government and private foundation financial support as well as being encouraged by the universities themselves.

There has been no tendency for the teaching and research obligations and functions to splinter off from each other and to separate into research and teaching faculties or groups.[13] Both teaching and research even at the largest and most prestigious institutions are required of almost all faculty members; our national survey of faculty indicates that most faculty at all colleges and universities prefer a combination of the two.[14]

One further aspect of the academic package should be noted. The nineteenth-century development of university level faculties of arts and sciences sometimes included *affiliated* professional schools. Harvard, for example, had both a medical school and a law school. In the subsequent development, however, existing professional schools were brought closer into the university. There are some exceptions; the Berkeley campus of the University of California

13. As in such cases as the Soviet Union where research is centered in the Academy of Sciences, not the universities.
14. Gerald M. Platt and Talcott Parsons, "The Allocation of Role Time among Academics," in "The American Academic System: A National Survey of Faculty" (forthcoming).

does not have a medical school. The main trend, however, is unmistakable. In medicine this has been influenced by the growing importance of what physicians call the "basic sciences"; much interchangeability of personnel and type of training occurs between arts and science departments in chemistry and biology and basic-science departments in the medical schools. This is closely related to the increased role of research in the medical field. Law schools have been slower to develop this kind of pattern, but it is now under way; and very likely there will be something similar in the relation between the academic social sciences and law schools to that prevailing between the medical schools and the basic sciences.

Another American innovation was that of the department instead of the usual European pattern of the individual chair. This has become the organizational subunit of faculties of arts and sciences and, in varying degrees, of professional faculties also. A distinctive feature of the department is that it, like the faculty itself, is a predominantly *collegial* body, of which a number of full professors in the discipline are simultaneously members, but it also includes all four of the "estates" discussed in Chapter 3.[15]

A comparable organizational phenomenon has evolved at the institutional level. The American university has come to be a kind of "federal state" (in German a *Bundesstaat*, not a *Staatenbund*), not a federation of faculties, departments, institutes, and schools but a federal *complex*. Its federal structure is fundamental, but is closely articulated. The units of this federal structure are predominantly *collegial* also and not bureaucratic in social structure. The primary units are faculties and departments, though some other types, such as interdisciplinary committees and centers, have achieved prominence.

These units are internally stratified, for example, by the tenure levels previously noted. But this stratification is not incompatible with a substantial level of solidarity (as noted in Chapters 3 and 4). Furthermore, the stratification hierarchy is cross-cut by strains to equality, for example, by the basic status equality of different departments organized about different intellectual disciplines in the same faculty. Somewhat similarly, there is a basic equality between the faculties of arts and sciences and those of professional schools. To be sure, these equalities are not absolute. In a department with ten full professors, all ten will not be expected to

15. Ben-David, *American Higher Education.*

enjoy the same level of professional distinction or of organizational influence. Similarly, though in one sense all departments are equal, in other senses they are not; every faculty will have distinguished departments and others which are in a shaky position. Furthermore, it would be rare for new professional schools like those of social work or education to have prestige identical to that of schools of medicine or law. These collegial groupings cross-cut and interpenetrate with each other in complex ways; furthermore, they interpenetrate not only within but outside the university, as in the activities of faculty members in disciplinary associations and other bodies which cross-cut the segmentation into particular universities.

A node of integration exists in the fact that the bulk of the arts and science faculties see themselves as oriented by similar missions and values with regard to the education of the young. Although there may be conscious differences between a faculty at a small state college and faculties at Chicago and Wisconsin, the former sees itself as involved in similar educational endeavors. There are myriad structural ways in which this integration is maintained. Meetings of deans and of presidents, AAUP meetings, academic publications, and faculty and student exchanges perpetuate this solidarity. Consequently, with all the apparent strains and difficulties, the national arts and sciences faculties see themselves as constituting a single system and strive to maintain that systematic association. In sum, there are numerous ways in which the higher educational institutions are associated and integrated and not simply on the basis of disciplinary lines.

## The Bases for the Bundle in Higher Educational Organization

Two foci for explaining the development of the bundle, even in the face of strain, are the influence and intelligence media, including their creation and the extent of their exchange. Each of these media is related to different levels of action; influence is involved with the diversity of the full university on the social-system level, and intelligence has implications for the cohesiveness of the plurality of university functions at the nexus between the social and cultural dimensions.

The American system of higher education (referring here to the approximately 1200 liberal arts colleges and universities) is not financially supported or controlled by a central agency such as the Ministry of Education in France or Japan or the Central Committee of the Communist party in the Soviet Union. In the absence of such central endorsement, the rapid and extensive growth of the system has been phenomenal.

This lack of central support is relevant to the cohesion of the multiple functions of the university. In place of a single institution of financial and moral support, the American system of higher education depends upon a plurality of supporters: alumni, students, state, local, and federal governments, philanthropic institutions, and the good will and moral support of large portions of the general population (which is translated into economic and political support and sponsorship). Such a variegated system is dependent upon the capacity of the higher educational system to influence (to convince) the relevant communities that it is worthwhile supporting such an endeavor.[16] Furthermore, the university as a system must remain connected to a plurality of solidarities rather than to a narrow segment in order to maintain support from a pluralized societal community.

With this in mind, recall Adam Smith's dictum that "the division of labor depends on the extent of market."[17] Smith did not refer only to the division of labor as advanced specialization but also to the integrative mechanisms of the market economy and to the fact that an extensive economy has a much higher potential of productivity than one broken into isolated segments. For the higher educational system, the social organization of the market involves not only the economic market, although this is present also, but also at the social-system level the influence market.[18] Not every buyer and seller needs to be in direct personal touch with every other potential buyer and seller in an economic market; similarly not every participant in the same influence market

16. The term "support" means here more than financial support, although financial support is crucial. The term also implies moral support, good will, legal support, and commitment, which can be exchanged for other things such as financial support. Too often the support issue is reduced to one of financial support, as if all other considerations about willingness or not to give money were independent of these other factors and financial support was the fundamental issue. From an analytic point of view, money is a concrete symbol of the other levels of commitment. By suggesting that perhaps the picture needs to be reversed to some degree, we will doubtless be accused of not being realists.

17. Adam Smith, *An Inquiry into the Nature and Causes of the Wealth of Nations* (London, Henry Frowde, 1776).

18. Talcott Parsons, "On the Concept of Influence," *Politics and Social Structure* (New York, The Free Press, 1969), chap. xv, pp. 405–438; reprinted from *Public Opinion Quarterly* (Spring 1963), pp. 37–62.

has to be in personal touch with every other one. What is important is the existence of a ramified *nexus* of optional relationships operative at any one time and of opportunities for shifting relationships. Thus a basis for the advantages of solidarity of the bundle of functions is established by this nexus, which in turn lies in the generalized mutuality of access of its participants to each other, not on an all-or-none basis, but as part of a differentiated nexus of particularized opportunities, decisions, and participations. Cases of isolation within this system occur, but compared with other kinds of social systems the relative fluidity and mutuality of access is greater. For example, an undergraduate student has presumptive rights of access to his peers at the same institution, and he also has the right of access to faculty members without regard to their reputations and to many other facilities on the campus. There are dangers of the attenuation of this kind of access, which to some degree has recently occurred. But as long as the bundle remains together, there continues to exist the presumptive. legitimacy of access.[19]

A similar analysis applies to the relation of the higher educational system to external communities. The multiplicity of functions means a differentiated influence market for all potentially interested parties drawing from a broad spectrum of intellectual and practical interests at varying levels of sophistication and at all levels of society.[20] Such a situation offers a broad market of access to those who desire to be more formally involved with the academic system. At another level, higher education is legitimately seen as a relatively open system with regard to general exchanges with communities. Thus, there is the presumption, for both private

19. With regard to this point, the senior author notes, "When many years ago I undertook a field study of certain aspects of medical practice, I was warned by some advisers within the medical profession itself that I would have severe difficulties of access to medical people. It was said to be a closed fraternity, the members of which were very jealous of their prerogatives. I was not personally well known at the time, but I think that the main key to such success as I achieved lay in the fact that I was able to use the name of Harvard University in approaching the medical personnel of the Harvard medical school and teaching hospitals. Once contact with such a network is established, it is possible to go beyond it to other contexts, which I did—in the Boston area, to the Tufts and Boston University medical groups. Not every young sociologist in an arts and science department wants to approach clinical professors, talk with them, and accompany them on rounds. But had I been a total outsider, unable to use the Harvard symbol, I am sure my task would have been more difficult."

20. This condition is relevant to the demand for access and thus to the availability of higher education to those previously excluded: the poor, blacks, Spanish-speaking people, etc.

and public institutions, that they are open forums for all interested parties insofar as no sectarian advantage is offered to any. This makes the university an open forum for ideas (for instance, speakers) but also for practical matters (for instance, recruiters). These forms of access facilitate the influence of the system over a broad spectrum of the general population and external solidarities; on the other hand, such openness makes the university vulnerable to criticism from both the left and the right.

At least from one perspective, we have evidence that there is a desire for a continuation of the bundle of functions. From the point of view of a national sample of arts and sciences, vocational, and technical faculty,[21] a preference exists for continued involvement in both teaching and research. Since research and graduate teaching have a certain pre-eminence, faculty at less prestigious institutions expressed a desire to increase their time spent in these functions, but there was only a small preference for a shift in these directions among faculty at the most prestigious schools. Clearly, however, there was no desire for a separation of these functions, and even among the most research-oriented faculty members at the highest prestige colleges and universities, there was an expressed desire to continue to be involved with some teaching. If any functions suffered (in the sense of "desertion"), it was not the primary academic ones but rather that of administration (such activities as committee duty, faculty and departmental office, paper work) where there was an across-the-board desire among all faculty members for a reduction of these involvements in favor of teaching and research.

Faculty members do not constitute the entire population involved in such decisions; therefore their opinions cannot be translated directly into policy. But it is obvious from our data that in spite of the strains, personal conflict, and tensions created by the multiple functions instituted in the faculty role, the common stereotype of the faculty member wanting a split in these in order to escape into research is incorrect. If the total system of institutions is taken into consideration, whatever validity that image might have for a few prominent faculty at the most visible institu-

21. These findings are taken from our national survey of academic men. In the sample, 21 percent of the faculty in liberal arts colleges were in vocational and technical departments such as nursing, business administration, and engineering. See Gerald M. Platt and Talcott Parsons, "The American Academic System: A National Survey of Faculty."

tions, it is inappropriate for the vast majority of faculty in higher education.

Thus we suggest that the bundle is not a result of an antiquated tradition mistakenly carried forward into contemporary academic organization. Nor, given the difficulty it engenders, can it be seen as a simple result of the conservatism of faculties who want to maintain authority and control over a spectrum of organizational domains. It is more properly interpreted to be a combination of activities consonant with the professional identity of the faculty role and beyond that an arrangement interpenetrated with a social structure generating a broad influence market vis-à-vis the general public and many pluralistic interests in society. This generality would be sacrificed if the functions were segregated into a number of isolated submarkets.

One more consideration touches upon the development of the research complex. One of the difficulties in undergraduate teaching as an alternative to research rather than as a balanced component of the same package lies in the contrast, familiar to sociologists, between locals and cosmopolitans.[22] Those faculty who are predominantly undergraduate teachers tend to be on the local side of this typology. When research-oriented faculty members have national or even international reputations in their fields and many contacts outside their institutions, this extends the influence market system across segmentary divisions, making it a national and indeed an international system. Under inflationary pressures, the frantic competition for scarce talent has revealed some undesirable potentialities of such a situation. But this should not obscure the positive side; this extension of the academic system into the interdisciplinary and interinstitutional *nexus* and the maintaining of openness to the wider society creates a single influence market with its many potentials for creativity.

The preceding analysis was exclusively on the social-system level and therefore concerned itself with a ramified influence market with regard to academia's multiple functioning at that level. However, the same considerations should obtain for the intelligence medium and the cognitive complex to which higher education is central.

22. Robert K. Merton, *Social Theory and Social Structure* (Glencoe, Ill., The Free Press, 1949) ; and Alvin W. Gouldner, "Cosmopolitans and Locals: Toward an Analysis of Latent Social Roles," *Administrative Science Quarterly*, 1957. Dec. 1957, March 1958, Vol. 2, pp. 281–306, 444–480.

If we use the logic of the model of economic analysis, an extensive market for intelligence-controlled cognitive activities makes it meaningful for the academic system to develop a wide range of significant outputs, not only within the academic system but in its relations to other sectors of society. We have already stressed four categories of outputs: one central to the academic system itself and three to external functions. The internal output is the advancement of knowledge and the development of competence to perform such functions. The outputs relevant to other sectors are: (1) contributions to the socialization of an educated citizenry where the cognitive and affective components are combined but both are indispensable; (2) services and knowledge to the applied professions; and (3) cognitive contributions to the work of intellectuals and to definitions of the situation.

These latter three are not so predominantly cognitive outputs as the first, but they are obviously valued by society. There is a good deal of societal ambivalence and even hostility about the universities' relationship to these outputs, but there is still on balance a favorable attitude toward the continuing involvement of universities in these outputs. For example, a recent survey reported by the Carnegie Commission indicates that 97 percent of all parents questioned wanted their children to go to college.

In order to achieve the internal and external outputs just mentioned at acceptable levels of quantity and quality, the cognitive system must have access to the relevant resources. These are cultural, social, and personal and are analogous to the factors of production. The "extent of the market" at the cultural level (where intelligence is important) is crucial to the successful functioning of the cognitive system. This is a basis for the institutionalization of the standards of cognitive validity and significance, the primary measure of the value not only of knowledge but of competence and rationality.

The issues here are explicit. The multiple functioning of the higher educational system has its costs—especially nonmonetary —but the separation of these functions into isolated units would have long-range consequences for the contributions of the higher educational system to a society and for the support of the system of higher education itself. Both would be sacrificed through the delimitation of the extensity of influence in the societal and academic communities and of intelligence-controlled contributions to cognitive and noncognitive activities.

*Change and Its Limitations in Relation
to the Main University Pattern*

At the structural level many suggested changes are directed toward the simplification, differentiation, separation, or elimination of various aspects of the university bundle. Such changes would tend to restructure the university itself. Other consequences of such changes were alluded to at the close of the last section: those affecting the "extensity of influence in the societal and academic communities and of intelligence-controlled contributions to cognitive and noncognitive activities."

The controversies outlined at the outset of this chapter involve such issues as the status of the value of cognitive rationality and related standards of cognitive validity and significance and attempts to implement them. There is a range of perspectives all the way from a dogmatic view of the imperative of cognitive purity for the academic system to a view that radically downgrades the status of cognitive interests in favor of expressive interests, especially for undergraduate education.

Another possible change concerns access to higher education generally and to specific types of institutions. Important problems operate on the boundaries of the academic system, especially with reference to the access problems for the disadvantaged in society. A third possible change concerns practical involvements of the academic system in both local and national communities. This includes professional training and the various kinds of consultant services performed by university people. It includes the extent to which the cost of such quasi-academc functions is borne by client groups. This problem merges into the relation of theory and practice, with certain pressures toward politization of the academic system in the interest of particular, morally sanctioned programs of action. Finally, there is the possibility of changing the internal structure of the academic community itself, including the stratification among administrative, faculty, and student components.

Obviously the issue is one of balance between stability and change. The content of the bundle will be the outcome of a process of organic growth and development in both the culture and the social structure of American society. One feature central to this development concerns the differentiation and adaptive upgrading of the cognitive complex, proceeding from aspects of the cultural, social, and personality systems to aspects of the behavioral organism. The structural autonomy of the system of higher education, including its leading universities, is a consequence of this process of institutionalization. The preservation of autonomy is necessary if the society of the future is to continue making available the contributions of the cognitive complex to its many different values and interests. Another feature concerns the institutionalization of modes of articulation of the cognitive complex with the wider culture and society. General education, training professionals for application of cognitive resources, and the cognitive contribution to ideological definitions of the situation constitute the axes of this articulation.

Some of the criticisms of the university system pose challenges to the maintenance of one or both of these features. They deny the relevance of cognitive rationality to social and cultural interests and downgrade the autonomy of fiduciary guardianship of cognitive concerns. Another line of criticism denies the legitimacy of the modes of articulation of the university in society and culture which are not predominantly cognitive. Still another line insists on the purity of the ivory tower and admits the legitimacy only of the pursuit of knowledge for its own sake.

This combination of autonomy and forms of positive societal and cultural articulation is a central issue as the university system develops in the near future. With regard to the components of the bundle, autonomy and the position of leverage necessary to make a positive contribution to both society and culture depends on the maintenance of the integrity of the core of the system. In turn these components are linked to the professionalization of the academic role and its involvement in research and the training of future academic professionals. Moreover, the development of the spectrum of intellectual disciplines represented in faculties of arts and sciences are part of the cosmopolitan national and international status and organization of these fields.[23] Whatever may be the situation for special categories of undergraduate colleges, for universities the maintenance of the organizational prestige of competence in the main intellectual disciplines is essential—as is commitment to the continuing relevance of competence to the system of higher education.

General education involves articulation between aspects of the

23. Merton, *Social Theory and Social Structure*; Gouldner, "Cosmopolitans and Locals."

cognitive complex and the socialization process in postadolescence. This articulation has to do with the nature of the academic community and the combination of cognitive, moral, and affective concerns which it is capable of presenting to the young. A special contribution can be made by an educated citizenry but only if there is a close articulation of the moral and affective components of socialization with the cognitive component. A synthesis of cognitive concerns and standards with these others is the hallmark of that contribution.

With the professions, the synthesis has to be between cognitive factors and practical needs, as analyzed in the discussion of the clinical focus and its functions. In this area professional ethics becomes the counterpart of the commitment to moral values involved in general education.

In relation to intellectuals, still another balance occurs between cognitive and noncognitive components. In this case the cognitive element is primarily critical in Northrop Frye's sense of that term.[24] To use the Marxian phrase, a balance of theory and practice is the imperative. This synthesis has a cognitive component and a commitment to noncognitive values and goals for the society. These should be considered analytically independent of each other. The term "unity," which appears in many discussions, raises the question of whether there are analytically distinguishable components. We feel that these distinctions should be maintained.

Involved with these functional clusters of the academic system, the institutions of the university system should be considered as a social system. One institution is academic freedom, which is a function of the differentiated autonomous status of the academic system. Academic freedom not only provides an environment favorable to intellectual work but also legitimizes the permissive and supportive aspects of the college community related to undergraduate socialization. A second institution is tenure in the broad sense that includes junior faculty, graduate students, and undergraduates as well as senior faculty. Changes away from this pattern in the direction either of market orientation or of a bureaucratic model could be injurious to academic functions. Tenure is related to collegiality, treating those involved at their respective levels as essentially members of a company of equals. Bureau-

24. Northrop Frye, "The Critical Path: An Essay on the Social Context of Literary Criticism," *Daedalus* (Spring 1970), pp. 268–342.

cratic organization is opposed to that of the collegial association.[25] Throughout the book we have attempted to demonstrate the functional value of these status distinctions. The involvement of the cognitive complex in the training in the mastery of intellectual problems of experience, as well as in socialization functions, suggests that some such pattern of stratification is necessary for the perpetuation of the cognitive complex.

Since World War II, structural strains were an inevitable result of developments which the system of higher education underwent. These strains made higher education vulnerable to a variety of attacks and of disturbances. Many of these attacks and disturbances could be interpreted as deflationary processes induced by the inflationary states in which the system had become involved. This aspect of recent events has been largely overlooked by students of higher education. A paniclike deflationary phase followed the inflationary one. The survival of the main sociostructural complex depends on the extent to which deflationary pressures become cumulative so as to induce structural changes. The relevance of the bundle lies in the complex system which the academic has come to be, involving as it does mechanisms of integration. Under deflationary pressures, these integrative bonds tend to rupture, allowing components that have been integrated to develop independently, without reference to each other. Proposals such as the separation of research and teaching and the separation of professional training schools from the core university complex are in this category. If pressed too far, they could reduce the system to a more primitive level of operation, sacrificing the advantages of the division of labor and the extent of the markets mediated by both intelligence and influence.

Short-run advantages could be gained by such measures. The transfer of most university research to specialized institutes or academies, especially if these were generously financed, could lead to an efflorescence of activity in the fields which were thus organized and supported. However, such activity would be at the potential expense of the advantages of the current articulation. Among the potentially negative consequences would be a reduction in the exposure of undergraduates to research activities; an attenuation of the relation of professional training with such activities; the circumscription of the spectrum of endorsed research to

---

25. Richard M. Hall, "Professionalization and Bureaucratization," *American Sociological Review*, 33 (1968), 92–104.

those areas especially focused on the concerns of the institutes or academies; and the cutting off of undergraduates from more diffuse concerns that would indirectly affect the cognitive contributions to the work of intellectuals. Nevertheless such an arrangement could produce increased research productivity in particular areas, possibly reaching an inflationary level. Thus it would be wrong to pose an absolute contrast between deflationary and inflationary possibilities of such structural changes.

Another suggestion concerns the differentiation of the cognitive complex from the expressive and the moral complexes. These proposals are for the diminution of the cognitive emphasis in undergraduate education, instead stressing expressive and affective concerns. This is acceptable if a balance between the cognitive and the other factors permits the continuing centrality of cognitive concerns within the university.

Similar considerations apply to proposals for politization of the university. Recently these have come mainly from the left, which advocates subordinating cognitive interests to the moral imperatives and political action goals of such movements. However, somewhat comparable possibilities exist on the right, which advocates the reduction of the autonomy of the university in favor of its service to religious or right-wing political interests. The common feature of these pressures is reduction of the autonomy of the academic complex in favor of an instrumental role relative to noncognitive concerns or merging it with others from which it has come to be more fully differentiated. It is necessary to distinguish between a balanced articulation of cognitive and noncognitive concerns and the subordination of the cognitive to these noncognitive components.

An upgrading trend has characterized modern society and culture; there have also emerged new areas of freedom and greater inclusion within the sphere of institutional legitimacy of different interests and practices than previously.[26] The autonomy of the cognitive complex itself exemplifies these developments, particularly the struggle for cognitive autonomy in relation to religious authorities. Comparable problems of intellectual freedom relative to political constraints have preoccupied modern intellectuals, especially in relation to fascist-type totalisms and to Communist regimes. The university, though open to various liberal move-

---

26. Talcott Parsons, *The System of Modern Societies* (Englewood Cliffs, N.J., Prentice-Hall, Inc., 1971).

ments as, for example, new styles of life in student living arrangements, must introduce such movements into the academic system without subordinating it to them at the expense of its cognitive functions. Making an undergraduate college into an affective-expressive commune or making it into an instrumentality of radical political movements would be tipping the balance toward subordination of cognitive functions.

These new freedoms are actually dependent on the cognitive complex and its institutionalization. Academic freedom is one of the institutional expressions of differentiated autonomy. Academic freedom includes not only intellectual freedom, so dear to faculty personnel, but also the opportunity to maintain an exploratory environment.

Tenure-collegiality is essential to the fiduciary character of the academic role. Tenure is a symbol of membership in the type of collegial collectivity organized about the implementation of fiduciary responsibilities. Reducing these in favor of either the competitive market model or the bureaucratic model would de-emphasize the fiduciary component, in the latter case in favor of the responsibilities of higher administrative authority, thus making faculty members employees.

This fiduciary theme is relevant to the pattern of stratification of the academic community, which involves legitimating evaluation by faculty of the promise and performance of students. This evaluation has been under attack in the name of egalitarianism. However, the fiduciary responsibilities of the academic profession cannot be discharged if the faculty is not free to evaluate performances. This evaluation need not be a mere continuation of recent practices. Evaluation also occurs among faculty peers as well as by superiors relative to lower-status echelons. Faculty members review each other's publications, teaching, and service on the basis of cognitive standards; they are expected to do the same regarding students' performance.

Thus, the bundle institutionalizes a balance between the autonomy of a differentiated fiduciary system within the culture and society and its articulation with the noncognitive complex. The balance concerns the healthy condition of the various components as units in a system and their subtle modes of interdependence. The balance is maintained through interchanges involving intelligence and influence. The bundle thus is the principal structural outline of the "market" system involving these media.

The bundle is not a rigid structure. Its flexibility and resilience results from the fact that it did not develop as the result of the implementation of a centrally conceived plan but by a diffusely complex evolutionary process. Few particulars can be considered essential, but in the foregoing discussion we have attempted to draw the analytical line between what we think is essential and what is not. The *diversity* of the pressures operating in favor of change seems connected to the flexibility which is a factor in the internal diversification of the system. The lines of probable change compatible with the continuing integrity of the bundle reflect these diversities.

A disproportionate amount of controversy has taken shape over the research-teaching issue, a sensitive topic closely connected to the professionalization of the academic role.[27]

This sensitivity derives mainly from the fact that the research function incorporates cognitive values and standards; the problem of the value-freedom of the intellectual disciplines also comes to a head here. Just as labor became the focus of ideological controversy over the economy in the aftermath of the industrial revolution, so research has become the focus of conflict in the aftermath of the educational revolution. In theoretical terms, the common element in the two cases is the differentiation of a factor in the production of outputs of the functional subsystems in question. In the economy, it is the institutionalization of labor as a mobile factor of production; in the cognitive case, it is the institutionalization of differentiated cognitive standards of validity and of significance as factors in the outputs of the cognitive complex.

Labor is a factor of production, not a category of output. For the economy, the two categories are goods and services, and labor should not be equated with service because of the theoretical distinction between a factor of production and a category of output. In a corresponding sense, the two outputs of cognitive process are knowledge and competence. Cognitive standards should not be equated with knowledge; they constitute a factor essential in the production of knowledge. Neither should capacity to use cognitive standards be equated with competence because competence is an output resulting from the combination of cognitive standards with other factors including cognitive commitments; the combination includes commitments to the values of cognitive rationality, the

27. Joseph Ben-David, *The Scientist's Role.*

use of intelligence in the allocation of aspects of competence, and the affective meanings of the various alternatives.

Cognitive standards in research have become such a focus of controversy because of the differentiation of the relatively pure cognitive complex from certain matrices in which it has been embedded historically, such as undergraduate teaching. After all, it was on the basis of undergraduate colleges that the modern American university evolved. A parallel exists between the notion of alienation experienced as a result of this cognitive specificity and the notion of alienation of labor in Marxian theory.

Marx defined labor both as a factor in production and as a commodity in a labor market like other purchasable commodities. Contemporary writers concerned with alienation tend to stress the Marxist commodity definition rather than a factor-of-production definition. However, commodities tend to be economic outputs, not to be production factors. Sociologically speaking, the institutionalization of labor involved the development of occupational role systems, thus emphasizing labor as a factor of production. In a way similar to those who stress labor as a commodity, many contemporary writers on the academic system have tended to equate cognitive standards with knowledge itself. Actually, knowledge should be treated as an output of the cognitive process and not as a factor.

This strain is accentuated by the upgrading of the corpus of the cognitive complex; the strain tends to focus over *theoretical* knowledge, a point also made by Daniel Bell. In terms of cognitive standards the standards of cognitive significance rather than of validity have been the focus of attack. These standards become salient when an intricate body of cognitive concerns is involved rather than particularized items.[28]

The crisis of the univerity system is related to changes in the American economy, particularly the ending of a long period of increasing economic prosperity and the descent into a recession. This recession has been associated with structural changes in the economy in the direction of decreasing salience of manufacturing and increasing salience of service functions. This shift has put pressure on units of government to finance more activities because the service sectors do not increase in economic productivity at the

---

28. An extension of the above analysis of the "bundle," its significance and modes of working, has been written since the above for the volume edited by Smelser centering on the California system of public higher education. See Smelser, *Public Higher Education in California.*

same rate as the manufacturing sectors. Recession has, of course, accentuated this financial pressure on government.

These developments have had repercussions on the academic system because the system depends on outside agencies for its financial support, including a variety of different governmental agencies. Financial stringency, a deflationary factor in the general context of our analysis, leads to increasing pressure to simplify. Many of the integrative features of the bundle are factors of complexity, which are financially expensive. Therefore financial stringency is a factor of substantial magnitude reinforcing the other tendencies discussed. A further complication lies in the intimate interconnections of financial support with political factors. In particular, the financial burden of the support of higher education on the various levels of government agencies, including research, has tended to activate resistances. Naturally many of the phenomena of change in the academic world have also had backlash repercussions on the political scene.[29]

There has been a tendency in some quarters to think of these financial difficulties as the main problems of the system of higher education.[30] Important as financial factors are, it would be a mistake for people involved in the policy problems of universities to underestimate the nonfinancial considerations that we have been reviewing in the preceding discussion. Correlations exist between economic and political factors and those involved in the intelligence and influence markets. They are, however, correlations and not direct relationships of cause and effect. What happens in the university world is not a *simple* function of the financial resources available to it.

Up to this point, our focus has been on the structural changes and their consequences for the university bundle. We have not said enough about potential consequences of change for the media central to higher education: intelligence and influence. Our concern is with the potential effect of changes in the bundle on the scope and efficacy of these media. We will stress deflationary cconsequences; however, there can be simultaneous inflationary consequences for these media produced by certain types of

29. The California legislature, on Governor Reagan's recommendation, refused any salary raises for two successive years to members of the faculties in the California public system when all other civil servants of the state were receiving cost-of-living raises. This was an expression of gubernatorial and legislative displeasure with the "goings on" in the university.
30. *Boston Globe*, May 28–31, 1972.

changes. The market for intelligence and for influence is an extensive one; therefore simultaneous contradictory trends are possible. On balance, however, especially with regard to scope of influence and intelligence exchange, suggested changes, if pressed too far, would be deflationary.

The key to the analysis is the formula "the extent and the diversity of the market." The general proposition is that the more extended and diverse the market the more potentially extensive the range of intelligence and the influence media exchanges. Most suggestions for change, however, have been in the direction of dedifferentiation of structural units of the bundle and of the bundle's relation to the society. The consequence of these is generally to reduce the extensiveness of the market and therefore to deflate the media.

We will be selective in our review of these issues. Intelligence is at the heart of the cognitive complex. In the cognitive complex it is institutionalized in its most pure form in the research function. Research excellently illustrates the problems involved here because the growing involvement in research has been a major source of strain in higher education.

The pressures for change impinging on the research complex have moved vigorously in two directions and less vigorously in a third, namely, that research be abandoned in favor of expressive and aesthetic concerns. Although this criticism has had some effect upon the university, the literal interpretation of the suggestion has not proceeded far. More significant pressure on the cognitive complex has come in the form of moral criticisms addressed to the type of research that it is engaged in. A second pressure on the cognitive complex has come in the form of advocating the separation of teaching from research. In the former criticism it is alleged that research should be performed in the service of specific moral considerations, considerations specified from partisan points of view. Such an arrangement would undermine the legitimacy of the diversity of scholarly pursuits and debase the grounds for evaluating cognitive contributions. The significance of research outputs in the broad sense of scholarship would be judged on the basis of moral criteria rather than on the basis of cognitive standards. The diversity of the research endeavor would thus be circumscribed, in turn affecting the intelligence-banking function of the university by more narrowly defining the scope of the market for intelligence investments. Intelligence upgrading through involvement in the research complex would be limited to a narrower set of morally sanctionable activities. In the economy this would be analogous to limiting monetary investment to a narrow range of productive endeavors and thus circumscribing the possibility of capital growth to particular industries.[31]

The pressure to split research from teaching and to place each in separate institutions could have similar consequences. Here the deflationary effects on intelligence-banking would be with regard to particular research activities which would not be fostered outside the research institutes. We see again that potential areas of intelligence-banking would be adversely affected while others might flourish.

With regard to the separation of teaching from research, there are other ramifications for the intelligence medium. This type of structural arrangement would lead to the diminution of the number of persons exposed to the highest levels of cognitive activity. What would then be affected is the circulation of that medium at this level of involvement. This condition might well produce a small elite research-oriented group of persons cut off from most others in higher education and to some degree self-perpetuating. Under these circumstances, the broad segment of the population (for example, undergraduates, graduates, and lay audiences including potential intellectuals) presently being upgraded in terms of intelligence could not be systematically and routinely exposed at the levels of present commitment. These are intelligence deflationary conditions because, although there will still exist large intelligence investors in the cognitive complex, the smaller investors such as the developing educated citizenry would be circumscribed as to their potential intelligence growth and expenditure. This condition would in the longer run produce a slowdown in the growth rate of capitalization and circular flow of the intelligence medium in society.

There is in the teaching relationship a circumstance available for intelligence investment on the part of students in the cognitive complex. Intelligence investment on the part of the students can contribute to research activities as long as teaching and research functions are not sharply separated in faculty role obligations. However, a separation of teaching from research would truncate such sources of intelligence input into the cognitive complex. This

31. On both levels this is precisely what the Soviet regime has done.

is one basis for our conception of teaching and research as mutually reinforcing in intelligence capitalization.

Similar deflationary possibilities could affect the influence medium. These too concern the diversity of the structural bundle. Suggestions for change to give priority to service or vocational learning or to a particular political point of view would tend to narrow or suppress the broad spectrum of disciplines incorporated in the university bundle. So too would suggestions to emphasize one area, such as social science, over others have similar consequences, as would separating graduate from undergraduate teaching functions.

The implementation of these suggestions would be inconsistent with the pluralistic intellectual tradition of universities, that is, the tendency for inclusion of increasingly diversified content into the cognitive complex and would impinge upon the structured autonomy of the system. Under these conditions only a narrow set of disciplines would be permissible. Disciplinary circumscription would have deflationary effects on the influence exchange with the widest spectrum of the societal community; the possibility for solidarities between the university and community would become more restricted. A similar deflationary consequence for the influence medium and its efficacy vis-à-vis the societal community would accrue from a split in graduate and undergraduate teaching.[32]

Another suggestion analogous to the previous ones is separation of the professional schools from schools of arts and sciences and, antithetically, involving professional training more deeply in the liberal arts; this latter point harks back to the concern with service and vocational education just discussed.

In the recent past there has been an inflation of cognitive purity in the arts and sciences, and the professional schools have drifted in this direction also. This produced a cognitive inflation. Corrective measures should be formulated cautiously in order to prevent a deflationary spiral in the applied direction. Professional schools have special missions and values which orient them, as do the special missions of the university; neither should be submerged in favor of the other; what is needed is a delicate balance of the two.

Further splits between the schools of arts and sciences and professional schools would have deflationary consequences in terms of

32. Talcott Parsons and Gerald Platt, "Considerations on the American Academic System," *Minerva*, 6 (1968), 497–523. A more detailed analysis of these same issues was made in this article.

influence of the university on wider segments of the society. The applied professions constitute a bridge between the purely cognitive culture of the core of the university and the social concerns of the societal community. To maintain influence exchange between the university and the community, this bridge should be maintained. This analysis is predicated upon a continuation of the pluralistic type of support the higher educational system has experienced over the last hundred years. If higher education should become supported by a central agency such as a ministry of education, as is the case in nations like France, Japan, and the Soviet Union, inflationary and deflationary processes of certain aspects of higher education might result. We do not, however, envision this type of centralization for the higher educational system in the United States in the foreseeable future.

Our discussion here of the conditions faced by the full American university parallels the discussion of the cycle of inflation and deflation made in the last chapter, except for one cautionary point. If deflationary pressures go too far, they would lead to a depression of the state of the university system to a level below the optimum level of its functioning before the crisis, would impede its recovery from such a depressed state, and would block its further development. Though full empirical disentanglement of normal functioning under conditions of inflationary and deflationary pressures is not possible with the analytical tools at our disposal, a worthwhile distinction can be made between (1) an essentially cyclical process of inflation in the state of the principal generalized media, particularly influence and intelligence, and an ensuing deflationary process and (2) the underlying developmental processes of the system which determine its longer-run patterns of continuity and change.

The two are empirically interdependent. To use the economists' language, a depression as distinguished from a deflation may be thought of as a state of subnormal functioning of the system of reference, which may be persistent and indeed may enter into a deflationary spiral. Recovery, defined as resumption of a normal pattern of development, may in the extreme case not occur at all; instead, some continuing disintegration of the system may ensue. Nevertheless, we think we have been able to establish a pattern of normal development of the university system in its internal structure and functioning and in its articulation in the wider society and culture. Although not a rigid pattern of development, it can maintain certain directional characteristics and yet have flexibility in relation to variations of conditions for the system as a whole and various parts of it differentially.

On the background of this pattern the present chapter has been speaking of various pressures for change, originating both internally and externally to the system, as having a "deflationary" effect. Deflationary means essentially that, if such pressures are acted upon to a sufficient extent, they would undermine some set of the conditions under which the university system has been able to function in the past as well as it has; they would thereby contribute to the prolongation of the state of depression or would create new conditions that would counteract the possibilities of developing new levels of growth beyond those of the precrisis period.

By using the analytical device of raising the question of deflationary effect, we intend to stimulate the reader to consider the probable consequences of the proposals under discussion. We have had to take up their implications for defining the situation for various sectors of the university system one at a time, but a survey of their whole range, tested against the developmental model presented in the book as a whole, may give something better than an ad hoc basis for judging actual trends and their probable consequences. Thus, though it is true that there are serious financial deflationary problems confronting higher education today, there are also serious deflationary potentials at other levels of the system. Many of the suggestions for change or reactions to them could as readily undermine the university as its financial difficulties, but some proposals may facilitate its further development.

### Recovery and Change in Higher Education

The previous section illustrated the limitations of change. This is not to suggest that change in higher education is not needed. However, whatever change occurs, the conditions for recovery require that the university system be treated as a fiduciary system and, therefore, it cannot give primacy to interests external to it. Within the fiduciary subsystem of the society, the university system must define values and goals in terms of the primacy of cognitive educational functions. But as long as relatively stable boundaries can be maintained, the recovery of the higher educational system is a potentiality. Should higher education be invaded by economic, political, communal-expressive, or religious orientations to the point where cognitive functions are submerged, its recovery in a recognizable form is uncertain.

One change compatible with recovery will be the inclusion of wider segments of the society, segments previously only partially included or included with lower status: such groups as the poor, minorities, and women. There is pressure on institutions for open-admissions policies; insofar as an open-admissions policy does not undermine the cognitive values and standards of higher education, the system should move in this direction. When financial resources become available, universal higher education may well become the national policy.

The trend to include wider ranges of age grades will be part of this same movement and will have interesting effects. By permitting the young to come and go more freely to campuses, taking periods of time off or attending other institutions here and abroad, and by including more mature persons as students, pressure will be put on curricula and curricular sequences which will in turn be made more flexible to fit the changing character of the student body and student mobility onto and off of campus. Thus, criticism of the rigidity of higher education will in the future be less pertinent.

The inclusion of older persons will also change the age distribution of the student body to the point where there may be considerable overlap with the faculty. Thus it will become more difficult to identify students with the young and faculty with those who are older. Older students will play an integrative role and thus soften the sharpness of the stratification system.

With regard to sex and race, we have previously noted their effect on the differentiation of the curriculum. But there will also be effects stemming from the increasing inclusion of women and minorities on faculties, namely, increased participation of these groups in advanced education and scholarship. The results of such changes in education will ramify through the applied professions and the societal community at large, thus contributing to the upgraded status of women and minorities. Rigid quota systems, however, are not, in our opinion, to be encouraged.

A second change potentially compatible with recovery is change in the stratification system. There are two dimensions here: institutional stratification and the tenure system internal to institutions. Among those institutions that survive as liberal arts colleges and universities (those that do not fail financially or are converted into technical or vocational schools), there may be a general reduction of prestige distinctions. Those lower on the scale may be brought closer in status to the more elite schools. This will be true especially for public institutions underwritten by the states and upgraded as they have been in the past, as, for example, in the California system of public higher education. Drastic outside pressure in this direction, motivated by nonacademic concerns, may be dangerous.[33]

A similar reduction of stratification will occur *within* the university; but these changes are more difficult issues to assess. Institutions will vary. One initial way in which stratification can be reduced without injury to the cognitive complex and to the system of rewards accruing from performance according to these standards is by reducing the number of classes within the faculty. Thus, the distinctions presently extant might be simplified to a two-level system of tenure and nontenure (instead of graduations such as instructor, assistant professor, associate professor, full professor). This has already occurred in a number of institutions, as, for example, at Harvard. A more sensitive question is the place of students, although the change in age distribution among students can soften faculty-student stratification. Another softening factor may be upgraded training of graduate students because of improved undergraduate education. Insofar as graduate students are more readily defined as faculty (for example, as teaching assistants) or as coworkers (for example, as research associates) some degree of increased egalitarian-colleagueship can be anticipated between faculty and graduate students. However, since the tenure system is based on commitment, competence, and performance, complete parity between graduate students and faculty is impossible—as is parity between faculty and undergraduates.

Governance and the tenure stratification system, being distinct issues, are not organized upon the same bases. Governance, the political-power system in the university, is the problem of running the academic institution. Faculty are involved in this process, but in actuality governance is mainly the responsibility of administration. However, when decisions have to be made with implications for the cognitive complex, these are usually turned

33. Robert K. Merton, "The Matthew Effect in Science," *Science*, 159, no. 3810 (January 1968), 56–63.

over to the faculty. Such decisions as appointing faculty members are on the boundary of the governance of institutions and the implementation of the cognitive-rationality value-pattern.[34]

It is possible to list types of activities where students *might* be involved in the governance of higher educational institutions; some have been suggested in Chapter 4. But at this point we wish to address this problem in terms of the relation of governance to that of the fiduciary responsibility of the faculty for the cognitive complex. Instead of listing areas of potential student involvement, let us suggest a general rule to be applied to concrete cases: *In so far as student involvement does not seriously undermine the cognitive-rationality value-pattern, they should be part of the governance of departments and institutions.* In particular cases this might mean either student voting power or advisory roles.

This is not an easy rule to implement. But different institutions face different problems, circumstances, and varying quality of students and faculties. In the light of these varying conditions, no universal set of concrete structural patterns for student involvement in college and university governance can be laid down.

A major change to be expected is a turn toward greater concern with the teaching function, especially at undergraduate levels. This can be expected to involve much experimentation with new methods and a trend toward a less passively receptive student role. This may well include a considerable student role in the evaluation of teaching performance but probably not at the expense of teachers' evaluation of student performance. Formal grading can be considerably modified, but if there is a continuing stress on intellectual achievement, there cannot be radical objection to explicit evaluation, especially the negative criticism of shoddy work and the rewarding of excellence. Thus we regard the recent objection to evaluation as a deflationary phenomenon. Recovery from deflationary crisis should lead to a recession of this wave, though this need not preclude changes in evaluation practices.

Substantial improvements in teaching need not be at the expense of research. We have throughout this book stressed the essential unity of teaching and research.[35] From this point of view graduate teaching, including teaching in professional schools, can pro-

34. In most high-prestige institutions they are in fact shared between faculty and administration, with the former recommending and the latter formally appointing, which means a power of veto over recommendations.

35. This is another case where we do not think they stand in a zero-sum relation to each other.

vide a bridge, as has also happened in many undergraduate honors programs where the student does substantial research work. With some expected exceptions, the best teacher is the creative investigator or scholar whose own interests are genuinely on the frontiers of knowledge and who can give a sense of the significance to mastering the already known as the necessary foundation for being creative. We regard the dilemma of research versus teaching as one of the many false controversies which have so plagued our society, like the one of heredity versus environment.

Beyond these changes, the academic system has been caught up in a process of structural change in society that has contributed considerably to the problems internal to the academic system. A clue to the kinds of structural change to expect lies in the subprocesses of the action system in the evolutionary paradigm.[36] Processes oriented to differentiation and adaptive upgrading are likely to continue, the latter especially being ingrained in the academic system. The subtler problems concern the other evolutionary processes: inclusion and value-generalization.

If the anticipated recovery takes place, the processes of differentiation will continue at both the cultural and the social-system levels. In earlier phases differentiation of the various aspects of the system of intellectual disciplines has occurred; the most recent phase of differentiation has been the emergence of the social science disciplines relative to the humanities on the one hand and the natural sciences on the other. A second process of differentiation has been between the relatively pure intellectual disciplines and the fields of their application through the applied professions, especially the differentiation between the cognitive disciplines and the clinical foci of their application, but also through articulation with socialization and through involvement with the ideologies of the intellectuals.

Clarifications of these earlier patterns of differentiation, however, are not sufficient to meet recent exigencies. The main line of development is likely to be the clear differentiation of the cognitive complex from the other complexes of culture and social structure with which it necessarily articulates. This argument applies especially to the socialization and the ideological components and involves the relation to the expressive and moral complexes.

We have argued that the faculty-student status scale of the four

36. Parsons, *System of Modern Societies*; also, "Comparative Studies in Evolutionary Change," in *Comparative Methods in Sociology*, ed. Ivan Vallier (Berkeley, Calif., University of California Press, 1971).

main grades of tenure is not likely to differentiate further, but neither is it going to be erased. On the other hand, in faculty-student areas dealing with primary academic functions, further differentiation is to be expected. The development of cognitive foci other than the discipline will continue along the formation of operative units based on non- or interdisciplinary interests (various kinds of centers, committees, programs, and so forth). These should operate in the relatively pure fields of intellectual concern such as the complex of biochemistry, biophysics, and microbiology and also in fields of more applied concern, including definitions of the situation in intellectual terms and in those relevant to socialization at the undergraduate level. Such further differentiation should enhance the degrees of freedom open to faculty members and students in defining their own roles; it is viable as long as cognitive commitments are maintained.

The differentiation of administrative organization will also go further, although limits of scale are perhaps being approached, especially for operative units occupying the same campus; the situation may be different for larger state or municipal systems. The technological complexity of many functions will increase, producing growth in the bureaucratic component of academic organization concomitant with the growth of the collegial component.

Defining the respective boundaries of the bureaucratic and collegial components will necessarily remain complex. A recent development preceding the crisis has been the transfer to administrative organs of many functions previously performed by faculty members in order to relieve them of burdens which they found difficult to bear because of the growing demands on their energies and time. The process has been analogous to the provision of secretarial services and teaching and research assistance. Under the pressure of crisis, however, faculties have tended to take back some of these functions.[37] Administrations in these respects, like faculties in others, had been in an inflationary state; the recapturing was an index of deflation, at least in part. More stable ways of defining the appropriate boundaries may be worked out in the future, accompanied by faculty-administration collaboration.

37. Gerald M. Platt and Talcott Parsons, "Decision-Making in the Academic System: Influence and Power Exchange," in *The State of the University: Authority and Change*, ed. Carlos E. Kruytbosch and Sheldon Messinger (Beverly Hills, Calif., Sage Publications, 1970).

Adaptive upgrading will continue as part of further development of the academic system. This will make for increased efficiency in generating the functionally significant outputs of the system, both to the rest of the society and at the general-action and cultural levels. In terms of the economic model, this depends on maintenance of the demand for these functional outputs, that is, for knowledge, competence, and rational ordering of affect, and for the corresponding social-system outputs bearing on loyalty to cognitively oriented collectivities and roles, as well as value-commitments to cognitive functions.

Adaptive upgrading produces autonomous operation of the academic system, increasing the volume and quality of its outputs. Quality, however, cannot be measured by internal standards only. These standards must be balanced through equilibrated interchanges with those relevant on the demand side, notably their contributions to the performance-capacity of personalities, the solidarity of the societal community, and the social significance of cognitive values at the general-action level; the relevant demand components have to do with loyalty and role-commitment to cognitive enterprises at the social-system level.

The other side of the issue is the development of enhanced capacity to meet such demands. Our previous discussions suggest that a crucial factor in this upgrading for the last generation has been the professionalization of the academic system. In many circles professionalization is a pejorative term, but the question must be faced. The denial of the desirability of professionalization is tantamount to the denial of the desirability of high cognitive achievement at both individual and collective levels. What we may expect is not a reversal of the process of professionalization, but modification in its patterns and forms. To reverse it would lead not to adaptive upgrading but to downgrading.

This brings us to the question of the trend of the process of inclusion. One aspect of it, already discussed at some length, is student membership status in the academic system. The extension of the proportions of the age cohort admitted to institutions of higher education is a new process of inclusion, new relative to the previous history of the system. Another process of inclusion has been the recognition of new fields of intellectual endeavor. New processes of inclusion will probably extend the area of academic acceptability. There will be a variety of experiments in new inclusions, probably not so much in the disciplines as in interdisciplinary combinations and in combinations between academic and nonacademic interests.

In both respects a new phase of inclusion will probably be in the direction of expressive interests. But because of the pluralistic character of American society, with the implications already discussed for the position of the academic system within it, limits exist on the degree to which the university can be moralized, aestheticized, or politicized. Despite these constraints, the boundary with expressive fields is perhaps more open than the others.

This probably provides a special opportunity for the humanities. The demands of secularization of the academic system and of the tradition of scholarship probably have biased the academic humanities in an overrationalistic direction—parallel to some kinds of overtheoretical definition of the sciences compared with empirical components. Expressive concerns may shade into the moral sphere; certainly the humanities, like the social sciences, have much to say about the moral problems of the human condition. If developments in either direction are to integrate with the cognitive components of academia, there must be, however, restraint in both directions.

Thus it would disrupt the academic system if too large a proportion of the energy of academic humanists went into the creative arts in a manner which cuts them loose from the function of criticism or into the cultivation of styles of life (among themselves and their students) too much dominated by expressive needs independent of the disciplines of cognitive control. The balance is subtle and cannot be adequately defined in advance. Trends to include new areas previously considered beyond the pale are to be expected, for example, openness to new content in fields of expressive interest. Thus, permissiveness for the academic use of overtly erotic materials has certainly increased in recent years and will increase further. This permissiveness may spring partly from changes in the structure of the academic community itself, particularly at student levels, as, for example, changes in the relation of the sexes to higher education in the spread of coresidential housing. In this, as in a variety of other respects, stable development of structural change in the academic system will proceed concomitantly with related changes in the society at large.

Recent events suggest increased prominence of expressive interests in American society. We consider this not a reversal of the previous trend of social change but potentially, at least, an extension of the previous trend. The academic system has manifested high sensitivity to this greater emphasis on the expressive. The role of the humanist may prove decisive in a sense parallel to that of the academic critic in the expressive sphere. This is a direction of organization through which there is promise that humanists can span the breach between culture and social structure.[38]

Before commenting about the problem of value-generalization, we wish to make one final point about inclusion. One component of the general ferment that involves expressive and also moral references spills over into the sphere of religion. Probably a genuine current of religious innovation is under way, which will have extracurricular inclusion in the academic system and at least some at curricular levels.[39] In its combination of cultural concern and social organization, the academic system is an appropriate center for innovative movements, especially in their earlier stages; the case of religion may indeed parallel the relation between pure science and technology. Furthermore, insofar as religious innovation finds a place within the academic world, its exposure to cognitive disciplines may mitigate tendencies to get out of control, as, for example, in Anabaptist directions.

Of course, problems are posed by the secularization of the academic system. Religious freedom is supposed to prevail within the university in a sense parallel to that of political and intellectual freedom. This implies resistance against authoritarian control over the university by a single religious movement similar to that against control by a single political movement. Provision for this order of religious freedom within the academic community and a corresponding toleration should prevent the re-establishment of religion in the sense in which it existed in the past, for example, in the New England Protestant colleges and more recently in the Catholic universities. Such re-establishment, even if the religion in question were quite different from the traditional ones, would be incompatible with the main values and functions of the academic system; but this resistance to re-establishment does not preclude academic hospitality to religious concerns.

The processes of inclusion are linked to what we have called value-generalization. A relatively integrated system of common

---

38. In Daniel Bell's sense of the terms. See Daniel Bell, "The Cultural Contradictions of Capitalism," *The Public Interest*, no. 21 (Fall 1970), 16–43.

39. Robert N. Bellah, *Beyond Belief: Essays on Religion in a Post-Traditional World* (New York, Harper and Row, 1970).

values is an essential structural component of a stable social system. The more highly differentiated it has become by internal process and the wider the range of elements which have become part of it from outside through inclusion, the more generalized the value-system must be if commitments to it are to guide implementation in the different parts of a pluralistic system. As part of an evolutionary process, there must be reformulation of the value-system in the direction of higher levels of generalization.

This process has already occurred within the academic complex itself, for example, with respect to the legitimation of the increased differentiation of the curriculum. Thus the steps from the largely classical curriculum to one which includes the natural sciences, the social sciences, and various new disciplines required a conception of cognitive merit not to be taken for granted before.

The legitimacy of the traditional learned professions and the place of training for them in the university had been taken for granted for centuries. In spite of the continuities between the traditional learned professions and the modern arts and science complex, they were differently conceived. One change was that involved in the rise of the conception of scientific medicine—a comparable change occurred in engineering—which introduced the conception of an applied profession as distinguished from one grounded only in clinical experience. The legitimation of this development was possible through conceiving the values of cognitive rationality to cover not only the entire range of intellectual disciplines but also conceptions of relevance for the application of *theoretical* knowledge, as distinguished from only empirical and practical activities.

The corresponding process of generalization with respect to the value-base of the socialization function and the value-base of the cognitive contribution to the role of intellectuals is not yet complete. What is required is a firm and sophisticated cognitive base for the understanding of the student situation and the contribution of general education (in other than strictly curricular respects) to student development. We have attempted to outline the nature of the problems in Chapter 4, relying on various sources from sociology and social psychology, but understanding is only beginning; a substantial intellectual contribution cannot be anticipated for a time yet, though the prospects of improvement seem to be good. It should be kept in mind, however, that the intellectual contribution must be combined with definition of the goals of general education that are not to be derived from the values of cognitive rationality alone; otherwise the undergraduate teacher would be arrogating to himself the role of philosopher-king. It is necessary, though, for such teachers to know what they are doing in their socialization functions at a more sophisticated level than hitherto, and this requires legitimation of the function at the value level.

The problem is even more difficult in the ideological field. We continue to insist that the academic system, including its values, is differentiated from nonacademic concerns, but the older conception of the ivory tower is clearly unacceptable. The patent intellectual vulnerability of most of the ideological doctrines current today is in part to be accounted for by the lack of full legitimation of the broad social philosophy necessary for optimum intellectual contribution to a societal definition of the situation. This is related to such features of the neo-Marxist component of the ideology of the New Left as its neglect of detailed analysis, especially at the level of economic theory, its restriction to certain themes of opposition to the establishment and inherent conflict with it, and a drastically redefined conception of alienation which confers honorific status on processes of social change almost as such.

The proponents of this ideology are understandably defensive about suggestions that, as social theory, Marxism has been intellectually superseded. Because of their association of the intellectual movements in which intellectual progress has occurrred with the reprehensible establishment, they refuse to take seriously the relevant developments in economics, sociology, political science, and psychology. What has resulted is a deflationary dedifferentiation in intellectual content, as well as in value-terms and in affective-solidary contexts, to a more primitive level than the currently available cognitive and value resources can justify. Here the value-component is relevant rather than only intellectual content as such. What is required is *not* a fundamental change of the main pattern of value-orientation, as is so often asserted, but a process of further generalization of the inherited pattern and its integration with the large body of post-Marxian cognitive resources.

Striking as the symbolizations of this new inclusion and value-generalization have been, it is not yet complete, and a corresponding process involving the cognitive complex is still less complete. A symptom of the situation is the coexistence in contemporary radical movements of Marxist-type belief systems which should be in principle atheistic and a high rate of dissidence among the clergy and theological students in all three faiths but without generalized repudiation of religion, as was mandatory for earlier radicals.

Perhaps this curious juxtaposition is itself a symptom of the process of value-generalization. The famous "war between science and religion" marked an acute phase of a conflict in which not only was the intellectual conservatism of religion involved but also the cultural parochialism of science, that is, of the intellectual disciplines. The belief systems of religion in general were widely held to have been "disproved." In this respect Marxism was part of a broader movement. Since the first third of the present century, the cultural climate has changed in this respect. The cultural system has been moving toward higher levels of generality in its organization; and the religion-cognitive conflict has begun to be relativized in the process, as many conflicts have been relativized. Values constitute a link between the cognitive and the constitutive sectors of culture and between culture as a whole and the social system. Such a general process of cultural generalization could not proceed far without involving the value-system.

This process of value-generalization, although authentically a *structural* change, is one of evolutionary advance from previous levels and not a repudiation of the previous main value-pattern of the culture in a sense that would imply that the great traditions of cognitive rationality were fundamentally wrong and must be replaced, for example, by free self-expression. Ideologists often assert such things in their rhetorical pronouncements, but we are not obligated to accept them at face value.

## Conclusion

Our view of the probable modes of change of the academic system should now be clear. We have not presented a survey-type treatment of the academic system as a whole but have concentrated on a particular sector of it, namely, the full universities. Since the emergence of this sector near the turn of the century, it has set the tone for the entire academic system, though not in a sense which would threaten the pluralistic differentiatedness of the larger system. We regard the emergence, development, and institutionalization of the full universities as a culmination of that process of societal change called the educational revolution. Certain features of this sector and its relation to the rest of the system cannot be drastically changed without undoing the effects of that societal process. But this is no more likely than that the postindustrial society will undo the industrial revolution and revert to an agricultural-handicraft economy or that the democratic revolution will be repealed with reversion to absolute monarchy.

The academic system as the culminating focus of the educational revolution is grounded in its status, both at the cultural and the societal levels, as a sector of the modern system, a sector differentiated from others with respect to the relative primacy of cognitive interests and functions. The balances between cognitive and other interests leave room for considerable adjustments in the course of developing processes of social and cultural change, but the radical subordination of these cognitive interests to others would subvert the system. If continued sufficiently long so that other interests become strongly consolidated in the academic system, it would work toward the repeal of the educational revolution, with incalculable consequences for the future of both society and culture. This judgment applies not only to the intellectual disciplines and their fields of application, but to the arts and to religion. In the light of the analyses which have been presented, these points cannot be considered only to be vague manifestations of the sentiments personally held by the authors but to define the broad parameters which apply to the alternatives of further evolution of modern culture and society as distinguished from radical abandonment of the historical trend visible at least since post-Reformation times.

In no way do we contend that the continuation of this main trend is inevitable, though we think that it is probable. There may be a neo-Spenglerian decline of the West, either through nuclear catastrophe or through less dramatic gradual dissolution into chaos. Short of this, there are many possibilities of arrested development with uneasy balances of forces, so that perhaps for centuries there could be in the cognitive complex slow advance but not catastrophic decline.

Even if, to those writing early in the twenty-first century, our relatively optimistic hypothesis of probable continuity turns out to have been correct, we do not expect the coming generation to be a period of simple, smooth, unimpeded progress, in academic or in other spheres. On the contrary, the indications are that it will be a period of turbulence and that, since the academic system has become relatively more important than before, it will be correspondingly involved in the turbulence.

However, periods of what in retrospect were seen to have been those of major social and cultural advance have been turbulent, and the turbulence has been at least as much a symptom of processes of progressive change as it has been one of failure of social and cultural systems to meet their functional exigencies. A pre-eminent example was the seventeenth century, especially in the northwest corner of Europe where, in our opinion, the distinctively modern pattern of society was born.[40] In this, as in a variety of other connections, we repudiate the common sociological view that there is an inherent antithesis between conflict theory and consensus or integration theory and that a sociologist must choose to adhere to one *or* the other.

40. Parsons, *Systems of Modern Societies*, chap. iv.

# 9

## EPILOGUE: SOCIAL-STRUCTURAL
## DIMENSIONS OF HIGHER EDUCATION

When the opportunity to collaborate with Talcott Parsons and Gerald Platt in this theoretical interpretation of the system of American higher education arose, I welcomed it for at least three reasons. First, it provided an opportunity to renew a collaborative relationship with Parsons, which, years ago, produced *Economy and Society*.[1] Parsons and I have maintained a close intellectual and personal relationship during the many years since that book was published, but we have not entered into any collaborative writing projects. Second, the opportunity to collaborate dovetailed with some of my recent research, a study of the processes of growth, structural change, and the vulnerability to conflict in the system of higher education in California during the period between 1950 and 1970.[2] Parsons and Platt in their enterprise and I in mine faced many of the same issues. Third, since in *Economy and Society* I participated in fashioning a part of the intellectual apparatus that informs the present book—namely, the notions of the four functional subsystems of a social system and of the generalized media—collaboration provided an opportunity to return to this apparatus and analyze a system very different from the economy.

Though we agreed to collaborate, the exact pattern of the collaboration was left open. The initial step was for me to review critically an early version of the draft material that now constitutes Chapters 2 and 3. Although I found myslf in sympathy with the lines of argument developed in those early drafts, my work on institutionalization and change in higher education led me

1. Talcott Parsons and Neil J. Smelser, *Economy and Society* (Glencoe, Ill., The Free Press, 1956).

2. A research grant from the Ford Foundation and the American Academy of Arts and Sciences released me from my academic duties at the University of California, Berkeley, for the academic year 1970–71.

to develop a perspective that differed somewhat from the one that Parsons and Platt were building. I responded to the draft material with two long memoranda, in which I indicated not only the ways in which I thought their analysis might be improved but also my own differences in emphasis in approaching the sociology of higher education. In the light of this interchange, it was decided that Parsons and Platt would make whatever use they could of my suggestions and criticisms in revising their material, but that I should prepare a supplementary statement as an epilogue. In this chapter, then, I sketch the rudiments of this supplementary perspective and suggest some lines of interpretation that might flow from that perspective.

### Social Systems, Media of Exchange, and Social Structure

My point of departure is to cite three formulations from Parsons' writings on the theory of action : (1) the complex inter-relations among different functional exigencies that arise in the development of empirical social systems; (2) the development of social structures (and groups) along the lines of the functional dimensions of systems (subsystems) of action; (3) the development of social structures around the processes of the media of exchange among subsystems.

(1) In *Toward a General Theory of Action*[3] and *The Social System*,[4] Parsons and his associates attempted a statement of the relations among three different types of systems—personality, social, and cultural systems. Each system was regarded as defined by an analytic abstraction from concrete social behavior. The personality system was conceived as the organized need-dispositions of the individual actor; the social system was conceived as the organized interactions among two or more actors; and the cultural system was conceived as the organized relations among units of meaning—values, belief-systems, and systems of expressive symbols.[5] Subsequently Parsons identified a fourth major system of action—the behavioral organism—cognate with the other three. In other works and in this book these four systems have been designated as the main subsystems of action.

Empirically, the subsystems of action are regarded as both

---

3. Talcott Parsons and Edward Shils, eds., *Toward a General Theory of Action* (Cambridge, Mass., Harvard University Press, 1951).

4. Talcott Parsons, *The Social System* (Glencoe, Ill., The Free Press, 1951).

5. Parsons and Shils, *Toward a General Theory of Action*, pp. 54–56.

interdependent and interpenetrating. By "interdependent" Parsons means that changes in the character of any system ramify and induce pressures for adjustment or change in other subsystems. No single system, moreover, has causal primacy, as his characterization of a social system indicates:

A social system can be considered as suspended in a web of cultural definitions, whose pressures are by no means uniform or mutually coordinated in different directions. There may be an inherent direction of change in the meaning-premises of the central value-system. The cognitive definitions of the system as object may be subject to many types of change or distortion. Commitments in different classes of personalities are not static. The relations of the society to the skills of the organism and the understanding of the environment are culturally patterned. In each of these contexts there is interaction and not merely a one-way process; and all the relevant factors have complex feedback effects on each other.[6]

By "interpenetrating" Parsons means that the same item may be simultaneously part of several subsystems. A value is a component of the cultural system in the first instance, but through institutionalization it is simultaneously incorporated into the social system; similarly, through internalization it may become an integral part of personality. In this volume the interpenetration between the cultural and social subsystems assumes particular importance, with the moral-evaluative subsystem of the culture interpenetrating with the fiduciary subsystem of the society.[7]

As an empirical entity, a social system emerges as a complicated intermeshing of a variety of systems, each with its own exigencies and each with some requirements for autonomous functioning. Consider a simple social system constituted, for example, by the crew of a ship. Some features of the social organization must be oriented to the needs of the crew's organisms—providing meals and rest periods, for instance. Some must be oriented to the psychological needs of the crew—providing entertainment, expressive activities, and so on. Some must be oriented to coordinating relations among men in different ranks and in specialized service roles. And some must be oriented to establishing and maintaining a system of values and norms in the name of which behavior on the ship is legitimized and regulated.

One implication of this characterization is that cultural patterns can never be institutionalized in pure form. In the process of insti-

6. Talcott Parsons, Edward A. Shils, Kaspar D. Naegele, and Jesse R. Pitts, eds., *Theories of Society* (New York, The Free Press of Glencoe, 1961), p. 979.
7. Chapter 2, p. 36, of this book.

tutionalization—or social-structuring—of cultural patterns, various compromises must be made. This point emerges clearly in Parsons' and Platt's discussion of institutionalization early in Chapter 2. They treat the institutionalization of a cultural pattern as providing normative meaning for social action and socialization. Because their main function is informational, "they do not determine concrete action processes, to say nothing of behavior."[8] To develop an adequate account of this determination, it is necessary to take account of inputs of "energy," which refers to the operation of economic and political interests.[9]

Parsons's and Platt's main mission in Chapters 2 and 3 is to clarify the nature of the cultural aspect of the cognitive complex, its relation to other cultural components, and, in turn, its relation to the social system. This mission takes precedence over the analysis of the shifting interests and tensions generated in the process of institutionalization and, in particular, in processes of institutional change. Toward the end of Chapter 2 Parsons and Platt indicate that their characterization of the norms and values of "the core sector" of the university is an "ideal type" characterization. While asserting that these norms and values influence behavior in the university setting and that the ideal type is an "adequate first approximation" for elite sectors of the system, they also raise the question of the degree to which actual behavior might deviate from the value-normative pattern which has been sketched. While acknowledging that the analysis of such deviance would require "more space than this book can afford,"[10] they nevertheless develop a few lines of argument. For example, given the relatively recent emergence of this "ideal type" of university, it is to be expected that "[the graduate and research complex] stands in some kind of tension with some parts of the matrix from which it has developed," especially undergraduate education.[11] Also, Parsons and Platt argue, the ideal-typical characterization should not obscure the fact that, as a social system, "it is permeated with tensions that have on occasion erupted into open conflict."[12] The major tensions are then characterized in terms of the tension between equality and inequality and between freedom and constraint.

8. Chapter 2, p. 34, of this book.
9. Ibid.
10. Chapter 3, p. 158, of this book.
11. Ibid.
12. Ibid.

In subsequent parts of this epilogue I shall attempt to expand Parsons's and Platt's observations on tension and conflict in the social structure of higher education, and thereby to supplement further the ideal-typical characterization. In particular, I shall argue that various kinds of tensions and conflicts arise both from the institutionalization of a variety of value and normative patterns—some of which are competing—and from recent rapid changes in the social structure of higher education and its environment.

(2) In *Economy and Society*, Parsons and I developed a classification of the four functional subsystems of society—the economy, the polity, the integrative system, and the latent pattern-maintenance and tension-management system. We considered these subsystems to be essential functional foci of organized social activity. We argued, furthermore, that various social structures could be classified in terms of their primary contribution to one of the functional subsystems—industrial firms contribute mainly to the economy, families mainly to the pattern-maintenance and tension-management system, legal institutions to the integrative system, and so on.[13] However, we repeatedly insisted on distinguishing between the analytic character of the functional subsystem and the social structures that specialize primarily in one kind of functional activity.

The polity is related to the government in approximately the same way that the economy is to "business." The analytical system does not coincide with concrete organization but political goals and values tend to have primacy over others in an organ of government, much the same as economic goals and values tend to have primacy in the business organization.[14]

Furthermore, even though a given social organization may give primacy to one type of functional activity, it must also give attention to others as well. A business firm cannot be purely economic in its emphasis. It also has a political dimension, found mainly in its executive and coordinating apparatus; and it must develop some kinds of devices for mediating internal conflicts and tensions. Accordingly, a business firm—like all other types of organizations—tends to develop various kinds of specialized roles and substructures (for example, personnel departments, grievance machinery) that specialize in the nonprimary but still functionally essential activities. Even though these ancillary activities are

13. Parsons and Smelser, *Economy and Society*, chap. ii.
14. Ibid., p. 48.

subordinated to the primary values and goals of the organization, they develop sufficient autonomy so that any organization must be regarded as a multifunctional unit.

Insofar as a social organization develops a number of structurally specialized roles, it also develops bases for the formation of social groups—aggregates of persons who share a common membership and are potentially mobilizable for collective action. Incumbents of common roles have common experiences in relation to the activities, duties, rights, and rewards associated with these roles. On the basis of these experiences they may develop common attitudes, outlooks, and interests. And, sharing these attitudes, outlooks, and interests, they may organize for collective action, including collective conflict. The transition from role membership to group membership, from group membership to common outlook, and from common outlook to common group action is not automatic. These transitions possess a dynamic of their own,[15] and this dynamic can be clearly understood only by supplementing the analysis of the functional specialization of social organization.

In *Economy and Society*, Parsons and I concentrated on the analytic relations among functional subsystems, and we did not analyze extensively either the problems that arise in the concrete social structuring of functional activities or the problems that arise when action-oriented groups are precipitated from the specialized role-structures of social organizations. In this volume on higher education, Parsons' and Platt's analyses reveal a similar concentration. The higher-education system is treated fundamentally as a social structure specializing in implementing the cultural patterns of cognitive rationality. They analyze extensively the differentiation of the university from the rest of the society; it is the main structure specializing in cognitive rationality; they analyze the university's internal differentiation into academic disciplines

15. These observations are scarcely original. They were developed, for example, in the sociology of Karl Marx, who maintained that social groups (classes) crystallize on the basis of common economic positions (bourgeoisie, proletariat, for example), form a common outlook (class-consciousness), and act on the basis of that outlook (revolutionary activity). Tocqueville maintained that the outlook of the major estates in eighteenth-century France depended on the complex patterning of social, economic, and political roles, and that these estates were disposed—for diffrent reasons—to accept reformist or revolutionary outlooks and, given the appropriate historical circumstances, to act upon them. Alexis de Tocqueville, *The Old Regime and the French Revolution* (Garden City, N.Y., Doubleday-Anchor, 1955). The same general logic informs the theoretical work of Ralf Dahrendorf, especially the notion that quasi groups may become interest groups with manifest interests and that these interest groups may become conflict groups. Ralf Dahrendorf, *Class and Class Conflict in Industrial Society* (Stanford, Calif., Stanford University Press, 1959), chap. v.

as well as the combination of the values of rationality with other exigencies in the processes of socialization, the application of knowledge, and the ideological "definition of the situation."

Furthermore, they detail numerous strains associated with the institutionalization and internalization of the values of cognitive rationality. They discuss the hierarchical structuring of groups or "estates," such as tenured faculty, nontenured faculty, graduate students, and undergraduate students. These groups, however, are discussed mainly in terms of their privileges, responsibilities, and freedoms in relation to the values of cognitive rationality. I intend to supplement this discussion by tracing some of the changing social-structural fortunes of these groups in recent times and by analyzing the implications of these changing fortunes for their outlook and behavior.

(3) In *Economy and Society*, Parsons and I developed an extensive discussion of a number of generalized media—especially money and power—that constitute the main basis by which the analytic subsystems of society are interrelated. In particular, we argued that the resources, or "factors of production," for any one subsystem are the outputs of the other subsystems, and that these are exchanged at the boundaries of each subsystem. We warned, however, against identifying the analytic boundary-interchanges between subsystems with any concrete set of relations among organizations or any concrete type of market system. We located the creation of extension of credit, for example, analytically at the major exchange between the polity and the economy. We noted, however, that "credit as a concrete phenomenon extends throughout the economy," and saw this as another instance of the distinction between analytic subsystem and concrete social structure.[16] We treated the flow of capital as a general analytic interchange between polity and economy rather than as a concrete exchange between banks, government lending agencies, and so on, and various kinds of borrowers. We realized, however, that these analytic interchanges are, in fact, structured empirically, though we did not undertake any extensive comparative analysis of these structures.[17] In this volume, too, the generalized media of exchange—intelligence and affect, for example—are treated as integrating mechanisms of the system of action and its various sub-

16. Parsons and Smelser, *Economy and Society*, p. 62.
17. In fact, we specifically noted that we were not undertaking the task of comparative social-structural analysis in that volume. Ibid., p. 84.

systems.[18] Though it is recognized that these generalized media are always structured into concrete interactive relationships, the structure of these relationships is not investigated in any detail in this volume.

By now it should be clear how I wish to supplement Parsons' and Platt's analysis. I am particularly concerned with analyzing the structural—that is, social as contrasted with the cultural—determinants of the recent history of higher education. I shall argue that the structural exigencies associated with the institutionalization of the values of cognitive rationality render higher education especially vulnerable to external and internal conflict. I shall also argue that massive structural changes in American higher education, changes associated mainly with its enormous growth in recent times, have led to other kinds of conflict in and around the university. I shall amplify these arguments in four ways:

(1) While the values of cognitive rationality have been institutionalized in the system of higher education, that system has also been called upon to institutionalize a number of competing value-expectations. By virtue of this development, higher education, particularly the university, has been subject to continuing value-conflicts.

(2) The recent growth of higher education has been so dramatic and so irregular that it has occasioned dislocations in the structural positions of various estates and subestates, which has heightened the sense of relative deprivation among many of these groups. Consider, for example, the kind of differential experience of the various disciplines that arose with the enormous input of research funds into higher education in the late 1950's and the 1960's. The physical and life sciences were by far the largest recipients of these funds; the social sciences were considerably benefited; but the humanities were scarcely touched. Put bluntly, some groups grew fatter from the standpoint of salaries driven up by competition, summer salaries, research assistants, research facilities, and the like, while other groups grew leaner by comparison. The process of growth also created various kinds of ancillary personnel— such as teaching assistants and nonfaculty research personnel— who have taken over some of the functions of faculty but who have not gained access to most of the faculty freedoms and privileges. Although these kinds of changes in structure and group

18. Chapter 1, pp. 24–25, of this book.

relations are acknowledged by Parsons and Platt,[19] their implications are scarcely traced.

(3) Recent structural changes affecting faculty, students, and administrators have created conditions under which Parsons' and Platt's model of studentry and socialization may not apply. I refer particularly to the massive growth of state colleges and junior colleges, which tend to be more "servicing" than "socializing" agencies, and to the changing relations among undergraduates, faculty, and administrators in universities.

(4) In Chapter 7, Parsons and Platt develop a model of a cycle of inflation and deflation as one way of accounting for recent dissidence and conflict in contemporary American higher education. Although extremely suggestive, this model is somewhat limited in accounting for the details of academic protest. I have already indicated that the "investment" phase occasions dislocations among various estates, which in turn generates the potential for divisive conflict among them. In addition, the occurrence of dissidence and conflict itself develops an internal dynamic of its own—with processes of politicization, the responses of authorities to disorder, backlash, and the like—which cannot be derived from the model of inflation-deflation itself, and which should be called upon to supplement this model.

## On the Institutionalization of Competing Principles

One of the structural bases of conflict in the academic system arises from the fact that it is not only an institutionalization of cognitive rationality but it embodies other kinds of value-expectations as well. One reason for this is the fact that, in addition to the primary emphasis on cognitive rationality, subsidiary expectations must be generated for the other functional exigencies in the system.[20] In addition, however, the growth of education has been accompanied by social expectations that will contribute to *other* institutional complexes, which are organized around values other than cognitive rationality.

At the beginning of this book, the authors reiterate their position that the educational revolution is one of three main processes of structural change in modern societies. (The other two are the

19. See, for example, the brief comments on the teaching assistant, Chapter 3, pp. 159–160, and Chapter 7, pp. 334–335, of this book.

20. Chapters 4, 5, and 6 of this book may be regarded as an exploration of these other functional contributions.

industrial revolution and the democratic revolution.)[21] I am in general agreement with the characterization of these processes. However, the three revolutions have developed with different sequential patterns in different societies; often the stimulus to "take-off" in one area was a substantial prior change in another. For example, much of the democratic revolution in Western Europe can be attributed to the appearance of new classes demanding political enfranchisement and influence—classes which emerged as a result of prior commercial and industrial development. The early nineteenth-century burst of educational reform leading to mass public education at the lower levels in America followed the extension of the franchise and was designed in part to "civilize" the electorate into citizenship roles—but before any significant industrial development had taken place. In England, the educational revolution followed considerably behind both extensive industrial development and the extension of the franchise to the new classes. Furthermore, both the need for a skilled labor force and for an educated electorate were strong legitimizing arguments for pressing forward on the educational front. Many of the developing nations, finally, are moving forward rapidly on both the democratic and educational fronts, prior to significant industrial development. In some of these countries, moreover, the production of educated people constitutes a pressure for economic development, so that they can be assimilated into occupational positions commensurate with their level of education. In short, the three revolutions have tended to unfold in different patterns of complex causal interdependence.

Even after all three revolutions have reached an advanced stage —as they have in the United States—the educational system stands in an important servicing relationship to the economy, the polity, and the stratification system. For example, one of the functions of a mass educational system is to meet the need for skills, techniques, and technology required by a highly industrialized economy. This economic service is most visible in various vocational aspects of education, but, in a highly specialized economy like our own, many activities that are carried on in universities can be regarded as occupational training. Another function of an educational system is to train for citizenship in various ways, though this is often much more subtle than the processes of training for occupational roles. Higher education also stands in complex rela-

21. Chapter 1, p. 1, of this book.

tionship to the stratification system. It has come to be one of the major channels for intergenerational mobility, since education is a major factor in recruiting into high-prestige occupational positions. On the other hand, education, once completed, may constitute a considerable barrier to intragenerational mobility: the skill-differentials between the educated and the uneducated adult are the product of so many years' education that it becomes difficult to overcome that differential outside the educational system. In short, education, even if structurally differentiated from other social institutions, maintains a complex network of relations with them.

Since this is the case, the educational system stands continuously in a state of precarious balance and potential conflict over different priorities: to what extent should it be permitted to maximize its own values of cognitive rationality (generating knowledge, searching for truths, teaching and learning in the broadest sense), and to what extent should it be required to "service" the values and needs of other sectors of the society? This question is a subject of continuous uncertainty and conflict. Furthermore, many of the issues affecting higher education, particularly the universities, can be traced to conflicts about its primary mission. The periodic political attacks on the university with respect to "political disloyalty," "corrupting youth," and the like, are conflicts between those who place a premium on the university as a training-ground for responsible and well-behaved citizens and those who press for the freedom of inquiry associated with the values of cognitive rationality, even though such inquiry may be politically unsettling. The conflict between "open admissions" and "the maintenance of standards of quality" is, in part, a conflict between those who regard the university as a facilitator of social mobility and those who place a premium on the university as a safeguard of academic (that is, cognitively rational) traditions. The tension between those who regard higher education as an asset for the state's or the nation's economy and those who regard it as an intrinsically worthy cultural asset reflects the same type of conflict over the central defining value and mission of the university. Since higher education serves many masters, including itself, it is to be expected that it stands on the precipice of value-conflicts at all times.

Aside from potential conflicts between the values of cognitive rationality and other value-expectations, the institutionalization of the values of cognitive rationality alone "build in" potential competition and conflict. I agree that the values of cognitive rationality are at the basis of the main ranking systems that are found in the academic world. Those universities which are ranked "high" are those that have attained excellence in the creation of knowledge and the training of graduate students, many of whom will dedicate their careers to the generation of knowledge. In addition, those institutions—such as state colleges and junior colleges—which do not involve themselves significantly in the core functions of research and graduate training are ranked lower then those who do. Finally, certain professional schools tend to occupy the role of second-class citizens within the university, presumably because they are involved in practical goals and give less weight to the core cognitive values than do the research-oriented academic departments.[22]

One of the consequences of ranking on the basis of achievement in relation to cognitive values—though this consequence is not dwelt on extensively by Parsons and Platt—is that it fosters a spirit of intense competitiveness, status-striving, and conflict among academic organizations and personnel. The widespread struggle for state colleges to become state universities, first in name and subsequently in function, is an obvious example of the struggle to attain renown in the name of goals of academic excellence, which can never be achieved in absolute but only in relative degree. Furthermore, there has been a tendency for "applied" areas such as criminology, social welfare, and education to move in an "academic" direction—to offer Ph.D.'s and to stress research— to such a degree that they come to resemble social-science departments and downplay their traditional professional training functions. And finally, the fact that institutions of lesser rank tend to recruit faculty who have been educated in the graduate schools of universities with higher rank than the recruiting institution probably contributes to the level of relative deprivation experienced in the institutions of lesser rank. Insofar as the recruits have come to identify with the core values of cognitive rationality in the institutions in which they are trained, many necessarily experience their placement in jobs as downward mobility. The typical psychological consequences of such downward mobility, moreover, are disappointment, dissatisfaction, and alienation. Such are some

22. Chapter 5, pp. 230–231, of this book. Another factor influencing the ranking of professional schools in the university is the social status of the practitioners that they train. Thus, the status of law and medical schools tend typically to be higher than the status of schools of criminology and nursing.

of the bases for competition and conflict among different types of educational organizations. They arise, moreover, not from internal contradictions among values, but in the process of structuring social units, social roles, and allocations systems that are necessary if the values of cognitive rationality are to be institutionalized.

The institutionalization of cognitive rationality is also closely associated with the potential for conflict *within* educational institutions. Parsons and Platt note the centrifugal trend in the development of intellectual disciplines—the trend toward specialization in subject matter, which also involves differential achievement in reputation and renown.[23] This tendency would split academic organizations and persons apart from one another in terms of common interest and ranking. Such appears to be one of the inevitable consequences of the institutionalization of the values of universalistic achievement in such a way that absolute attainment of values is in principle impossible because there is no specified upper limit of achievement. I interpret the tendency to organize faculties into large heterogeneous bodies of people who are, in principle, "companies of equals" as one way of contending with the divisiveness, competition, and potential conflict that are built into the institutionalization of the values of cognitive rationality. I would assign the same significance—of contending with competitiveness—to various formal and informal mechanisms that have evolved as part of the traditions of academic life: for instance, the gentleman's agreement in some scholarly circles not to discuss one another's academic work too seriously and critically in general conversation, but to reserve such discussion for highly structured situations such as seminars and panels. Such mechanisms tend to control or limit the competitiveness that arises from the centrifugal tendencies.[24]

Finally, Parsons and Platt argue that the full university is predominantly fiduciary in emphasis. This emphasis "must be grounded in commitment to values—in this case the value of cognitive rationality."[25] Two other features are closely associated with the fiduciary emphasis. The first is the collegial principle of association of faculties, which takes precedence over other organizational principles such as the economic market, the demo-

---

23. Chapter 3, p. 112, of this book.
24. These observations are similar to those ventured by Parsons and Platt in Chapter 3, pp. 160–161, of this book.
25. Chapter 3, p. 123, of this book.

cratic association, and the administrative bureaucracy. The second is the minimization of economic incentives and of authority and power as mechanisms of social control and the predominance of influence and appeal to value-commitments.[26] I agree with these emphases. The academic profession retains to a remarkable degree its fundamental nature of a "calling," which rests on a kind of value-commitment around which the motivation and energy of men and women are organized. In addition, I also agree with the emphasis on the resistance to bureaucratization in the full university. Many of the organizational characteristics of the modern university can be understood as an institutionalized effort to burden the lives of individual scholars as little as possible with bureaucratic obligations. The social organization of the classroom and the academic department is remarkably simple, as organizations go; and the university has proliferated a variety of service occupations—librarians, clerks, research assistants, and so on—many of whose duties are to facilitate the research and teaching by faculty through assuming responsibility for recording, filing, arranging schedules, and the like.

It seems essential, however, to supplement this line of analysis by noting that the relations among the several organizational principles and types of social control are not fixed, but variable. Being variable, they are likely to be in competition as organizing principles. Consider the "collegial" versus the "bureaucratic" principles, for instance. In modern times, as universities have grown in size, they have become increasingly bureaucratized, in the sense that behavior in them is more extensively governed by standardized rules and procedures. Furthermore, growth, specialization, and proliferation of units have moved toward a system of "bureaucratic federation of departments, colleges, schools, business offices, and student personnel establishments,"[27] even though the more informal mechanisms associated with the principle of collegiality retain their vitality in many places. In any case, collegiality and bureaucratic organization should be regarded as a variable mix, and, with respect to the university, the tendency is toward the increasing importance of bureaucratization, which is closely associated with the growth and increasing structural complexity of the universities themselves.

26. Chapter 3, p. 124, of this book.
27. Burton R. Clark, "The Role of Faculty Authority," paper presented at the President's Institute, Harvard Business School, June 20, 1963, *Papers, 1956–1964 of the Center for the Study of Higher Education, University of California, Berkeley*, vol. I.

The salience of the bureaucratic principle is also seen in comparing different kinds of educational institutions. In four-year colleges and in junior colleges, where there is usually less commitment to a calling based on the core value of cognitive rationality, the tendency is to rely more on bureaucratic controls, such as the authority of chairmen, deans, and presidents, and to treat the occupational role more in the nature of a job rather than a calling.

In addition, the salience of bureaucratic controls appears to be related to the type of intensity of conflict in universities. One of the inferences commonly made by boards of trustees and state governments during the years of severe university conflict in America, 1964–1970, was that the universities were not able to govern themselves and that the existing organizational arrangements were not capable of resolving conflict situations. When this kind of inference is made, moreover, the tendency is for administrators and trustees to attempt to restore order by increasing and intensifying bureaucratic controls. One consequence of the heightened politicization of the universities during that period of conflict was that trustees, regents, and legislators tended to intervene directly in the government of the universities, often in the form of passing new regulations relating to conduct, imposing more standardized definitions of the job requirements of faculty, and the like. In short, they superimposed bureaucratic authority on what previously was regulated more by value-commitments and collegial influence.[28]

One consequence of this tendency toward increased bureaucratization arising from attempts to handle conflicts was to place faculty in an increasingly defensive position vis-à-vis administrative authorities, to discourage them from basically collegial types of faculty associations (such as academic senates and assemblies), and to attract them toward more political forms of association, such as a union or some approximation to it. Faculty unionization— and, along with it, arrangements for collective bargaining over remuneration and conditions of work—bureaucratize the academic organization further. Unions, being defensive and protective of their membership, insist on formal safeguards relating to the conditions of work. Traditionally this leads to agreements that are

28. This generalization should be qualified, however, by noting the additional fact that faculties also increase their power vis-à-vis administration during times of crisis. Chapter 3, pp. 136–137, of this book.

put in writing, that is, standardized with respect to the normative regulation of the work role. Such a development also tends to shift the definition of the academic role away from the calling and toward the job and to undercut further collegiality as a form of association.

This reasoning seems to explain differential trends toward unionization in higher education. Traditionally the calling has been more firmly institutionalized in the university complex, whereas the bureaucratic complex characterizes the lower ranks of higher-education institutions. The unionization of college and junior college teachers has proceeded more rapidly and further than that of university faculties, largely because unionization is a collective response to bureaucratic discipline and control. Moreover, the recent move toward unionization of university faculties is associated with the threatened breakdown of the pattern of the package of the calling, tenure, and academic freedom and with the increased tendency for control by bureaucratic rule.

To sum up: While accepting the broad lines of analysis of Parsons and Platt with respect to the primacy of values and organizational principles in higher education, I feel it necessary to supplement that with an analysis of other forces that arise in the institutionalization of those values and organizational principles and in the social processes that accompany that institutionalization.

## Some Recent Structural Changes in Higher Education

In several places Parsons and Platt note the distinctive patterns of structural differentiation associated with the educational revolution. On the one hand, higher education has become differentiated *from* other structures. Academic functions have been differentiated from generalized social-status systems so that, instead of universities being a training ground for a diffuse upper class, they certify professional and intellectual competence. (Needless to say, this competence is often a ticket to high status in the stratification system.) [29] The academic system has also in the process of secularization become more differentiated from the religious system. Finally, as an agency of socialization, formal education has established itself as a structure differentiated from the kinship complex.

American higher education has also experienced a considerable

29. Chapter 1, p. 7, of this book.

level of differentiation *within* the academic system. The differentiation among universities, four-year colleges, and junior colleges is
an example of specialization of functions along structural lines.
Junior colleges offer preparatory work for further academic training, as well as terminal degrees, especially in vocational subjects.
Four-year colleges offer preparatory work for advanced graduate
training, as well as terminal four-year bachelor's degrees and
some professional and advanced degrees. Universities offer both
undergraduate education and advanced training in the professions
and in the intellectual disciplines. The universities also specialize in
academic research. In a number of places, Parsons and Platt comment on the combination of these several functions in the full
university.[30]

Some further inquiry might be made into the consequences that
arise from including all the academic "industries"—general education, advancement of knowledge, graduate and professional training, and contributing to a cultural "definition of the situation"[31]
—into one formal organization, the full university. Historically,
the American university has persistently refused to differentiate
structurally into, for example, upper-division instruction, graduate instruction with no undergraduate instruction, and research
academies with no undergraduate or graduate training. The various functions have continued to be packaged in the full university
form. Parsons and Platt emphasize this lack of separation and tie it
to the delicate balancing of fiduciary responsibilities and the pattern of "marketing" academic goods and services.[32]

My reading of the causes of the resistance to differentiation in
the university would stress factors additional to those singled out
by Parsons and Platt. For example, Harvard might not readily
split into a research academy with graduate training and an
undergraduate college because of the fiduciary factors that Parsons and Platt stress, but it could also be that a major source of
financial support for the graduate school—alumni dollars—would
rapidly decline if Harvard's graduate program were organized on
a completely independent basis. Such a move is almost impossible
politically, given the sources of support for the institution. Political forces also inhibit the separation of undergraduate and graduate-research complexes in public universities. Most of the justifica-

30. Chap. 1, p. 5; Chap. 3, pp. 122–123; Chap. 5, pp. 225–227, above.
31. Chapter 3, pp. 103–107, of this book.
32. Chapter 3, pp. 126–129, of this book.

tion for diverting public money into state institutions rests on an investment—as well as a cognitive-rationality—rationale, namely, that universities are training young men and women for productive employment, are providing opportunities for citizens to move in the stratification system, and are preparing for responsible citizenship. The graduate-research functions are often "tolerated" by the public because the universities continue to fulfill their basic function of educating undegraduates. Political sentiments, in short, are not compatible with public support for structurally differentiated research academies and graduate training centers, with the possible exception of professional schools that meet a felt need, such as schools of law and medicine.

Whatever the various causes of the reluctance of the university to differentiate along functional lines, the continued fusion of functions in a period of extraordinary growth has profound consequences for higher education. The main demand for growth has come from demographic pressures resulting from the cohort born during and after World War II and from an increase in the percentage of the cohort going to college. At the same time the graduate training and research sectors also experienced a boom based both on the need to provide graduate training for college teachers to staff the expanding colleges and on the availability of enormously increased research funds—especially in the late 1950's and 1960's—which went mainly to the universities. Most universities expanded the size of their student bodies, at both the undergraduate and graduate levels; the leading universities, however, expanded faster at the graduate than at the undergraduate level. Many universities have added vast research facilities in the form of laboratories and organized research units. The net effect of this kind of expansion has been to place a greater premium on what Parsons terms the "core of the academic system"—the research and graduate-training complex.

What have been the consequences of this expansion and increase of functions *without* any significant structural differentiation along functional lines? One consequence has been to downgrade the general education functions at the expense of the graduate and professional training and research functions. During the inflationary period, competition for faculty was brisk, and universities held out various inducements for recruitment, such as increased research opportunities and reduced teaching loads, particularly at the undergraduate level. Furthermore, because of the premium on research and graduate training and the increasing preoccupation of faculty with these matters, faculty members began to teach their undergraduate courses more like lower-level graduate courses rather than as media for general intellectual inquiry. At the same time, the high schools, often under competitive pressures themselves, succeeded in upgrading their own curricula, thus taking over some of the functions of introductory freshman courses in college. These combined trends—professionalization in the universities and upgrading of general education in the high schools— meant that universities were beginning to experience a general-education vacuum, particularly at the lower-division level. From a social-psychological point of view, the undergraduate in a large university during the inflationary period was likely to perceive that he was enrolled in a large, elite center that placed a premium on professional training and research and that his need for general education was being served by a faculty whose heart was less in undergraduate teaching than in other activities.

At the same time, faculty members found themselves increasingly involved in their disciplines outside the university—traveling to professional meetings, conferences, and symposia in this country and abroad. In addition, through public service, consulting for government agencies, and so on, academics increased their involvement in the nonacademic sector. As departments grew in numbers of faculty and students, the time required for departmental administration increased accordingly. The academic role moved in the direction of diffusion and fragmentation. The role of the faculty member in the university, like the university itself, resisted differentiation, and as a result became overburdened: spread thinly over a variety of activities. These trends suggest that the faculty member and the university changed in such a way as to reduce the ability of the faculty member to discharge some of his primary fiduciary responsibilities.

While the role of the faculty, the traditional intellectual elite group of the university, was being spread thinner, a number of positions ancillary to faculty activities began to increase in salience—teaching assistants, research assistants, nonfaculty research appointees, research administrators, administrative assistants and clerical personnel in academic departments. All of these are specialized roles in a sense that the faculty member's role is not. The teaching assistant specializes in undergraduate education and is not normally permitted to teach other graduate students; in addition he often occupies a role that is formally and sometimes actually under the control of the faculty member responsible for a course of instruction. The category of "reader," employed in some universities, is even more marginal; a reader does not meet classes, but attends the lectures of the professors, perhaps assists him in preparing examinations, and assists in the grading of papers and examinations. The research assistant specializes only in research and is generally prohibited from formal teaching; he, too, is typically subordinate to a principal research investigator. The research appointee—the postdoctoral fellow, the research associate in an organized research unit—sometimes participates as a peer in research projects, though he normally does not have a faculty appointment, with its various privileges, and normally does not offer formal instruction to either undergraduates or graduates. The departmental administrative assistant and clerical personnel are specialized in that they assist the faculty in matters of administrative routine, but, in practice, some of the faculty's advising functions often fall to these personnel as well.

Thus, in its period of rapid growth, the faculty began to commit more of its talent to the research and graduate-training functions; in order to fill the education gap that resulted, the university expanded the numbers of those in ancillary and subordinate roles removed in various ways from the most prestigious activities of the faculty. As an "estate," the faculty retained control of all the main educational functions—research, graduate training, upperdivision education, and lower-division education—but much of the work in all these categories was actually done by those in roles that were something less than that of faculty member. Even graduate training, that part of the educational process in which the faculty was most directly involved, was shared by the faculty with nonfaculty research appointees in laboratory and other research units. The faculty maintained formal power and responsibility, but the actual performance of many of their duties were slipping away to other nascent "estates."

The fragmentation of the faculty role probably produced a decline in quality in some aspects of faculty performance through overwork and overextension; it also diminished commitment to the teaching enterprise; and increasing involvement with the discipline—with its national and international reference points—may have led to a decrease in relative loyalty to the faculty member's home institution. The growth of ancillary roles created a variety of types of situations in which role-incumbents were asked to perform duties associated with faculty roles but were not given the same degree of formal responsibility or the same kinds of rewards. In those kinds of situations alienation of various sorts is likely to be the social-psychological consequence.

The functional overloading of faculty roles and the partial differentiation of new roles thus created a classical Tocquevillian situation : an elite class retaining its powers and formal responsibilities while allowing the performance of some of its duties to slip into other hands.[33] This state of affairs typically produces an attitude of jealous conservatism on the part of the elite as well as a diminution of loyalty and an increase in resentment and alienation on the part of the emergent estates. These emergent social-psychological postures, moreover, would appear to be among the principal factors that have contributed to the special conflict-proneness of many of these estates during the period of most rapid growth of the higher-education system.

The foregoing sketch of the major lines of structural change and group formation—as well as my other analyses in this chapter—supplements Parsons' and Platt's analysis of the growing importance of the values of cognitive rationality. Their argument is sound; cognitive rationality has attained a victory in the recent history of the academic system. I am also inclined to agree with their prediction that the long-term future is going to bring a new consolidation of the cultural patterns of cognitive rationality and an even more important role for the university. My analysis is what might be called a short-term supplement to their long-term evolutionary diagnosis. It suggests that the processes of structural change that have accompanied these long-term changes have produced a series of irregular structural shifts and dislocations in the system of higher education. Understanding these short-term structural processes, moreover, is essential if we are to generate detailed explanations of the processes of conflict and disturbance that periodically grip that system.

### The Academic System and the Socialization Complex

The structural changes in the system of higher education, such as those analyzed in the preceding section, also carry some implications for the mode of student socialization developed in Chapter 4.

33. Tocqueville, *The Old Regime*, pp. 51, 80–81, 133.

Parsons's and Platt's position is that the educational process of cognitive upgrading—particularly in the undergraduate years—is also a process of socialization analogous to the oedipal transition in early childhood and to the dynamics of psychotherapy. Like the other processes, cognitive upgrading does not occur automatically, but depends on a number of social and psychological conditions. For example, this kind of socialization occurs under a condition of "the relative insulation of the individuals being socialized from systems external to the socializing unit."[34] A second condition is the "relatively undifferentiated character of the individual being socialized," which, in the college situation, is created by "breaks with family and community ties."[35] On more than one occasion Parsons and Platt stress the relatively "total" environment of the university.[36] In addition, undergraduate socialization calls for the existence of a kind of "moral authority" represented by the socializing agents. The motivational leverage to draw the student toward a higher level of cognitive functioning is found in his identification with a community which includes faculty members; and the same time, there is a strong, undifferentiated identification with the peer collectivity. The leverage exercised by faculty members is manifested in their insistence that behavior and performance be judged in terms of cognitive standards of validity. The result of the socializing process is a more differentiated personality, with an upgraded cognitive component, new levels of cognitive understanding of values, and a new sense of identity, which implies "identification in a differentiated plurality of values, interests, goals, and memberships which are integrated with each other so that the personality is not torn by unresolvable conflicts."[37] Student socialization, in short, equips the individual with a new level of personality functioning that permits him to cope more effectively with the complexities of role demands and social involvements that adult life brings.

This process of socialization is not without strain and tension. The individual ultimately must discard older and simpler patterns in favor of new, more complicated ones. Many disturbances accompany the process, such as regressions to earlier modes of functioning, expressions of hostility, and expressions of fantastic or

34. Chapter 4, pp. 167–168, of this book.
35. Chapter 4, p. 168, of this book.
36. Chapter 4, pp. 175, 211–212, of this book.
37. Chapter 4, p. 171, of this book.

utopian thinking. These disturbances are, however, tolerated to a greater degree in the permissive and supportive collegiate atmosphere than they would be under other circumstances. In the context of the strains of socialization—as well as the environment within which these strains develop—Parsons and Platt interpret some of the themes of recent student protest: the condemnation of university faculty and administration for complicity in the sins of society; the charge that the academic community is competitive and divisive; the charge that students are powerless and that the system is undemocratic; and the charge that the system is repressive in various ways. They regard the expression of these disturbances as an integral part of the socialization process in the undergraduate years.[38] In addition to this factor of "affective frustration resulting from college socialization," Parsons and Platt attribute the expression of these critical themes to "tensions in the wider society" and "displaced personal problems."[39]

Parsons and Platt supplement this model of socialization with an analysis of recent changes in higher education which have intensified some of the features associated with the model. They mention the change in the faculty's role—in the direction of greater involvement in graduate teaching and research—which means both an upgrading of the capacities of the faculty and the devotion of less exclusive attention to the undergraduate; this change parallels the changing role of the father in the early phases of the industrial revolution. They also mention several ways in which the autonomy of students has been increased—with respect to extracurricular activities, participation in the design of the curriculum, and so on—thereby reinforcing "the permissive and supportive aspects of the socialization environment" and accentuating "the dedifferentiations and resistances to socialization."[40] Such changes presumably help account for why the strains and disturbances in the socialization process have become so much more intensive in recent years.

I agree that the phase of socialization in the undergraduate years bears resemblances to other prototypical episodes of socialization in the life-cycle of the individual; I also think that the socialization aspect has been seriously neglected in most recent discussions of the disturbances that higher education has experi-

---

38. Chapter 4, pp. 217–218, of this book.
39. Chapter 4, p. 218, of this book.
40. Chapter 4, pp. 186–187, of this book.

enced. I would like to suggest, however, that the factors stressed by Parsons and Platt—affective frustration associated with college socialization, tensions in the wider society, and displaced personal problems—should be supplemented by analyzing the impact of a number of processes of growth and structural change not stressed by them. The net impact of these processes of growth and change, which I shall identify presently, is that the condition under which that model of socialization is fully applicable may be diminishing in its relative importance in the system of higher education as a whole.

Let me begin this supplementary line of reasoning by pointing to Parsons's and Platt's contrast between the college and the high school as settings for socialization. College education means longer and more intensive exposure to the values of cognitive rationality, even though those values permeate both systems. High school is less "total" an experience because the student is more dependent financially and emotionally on his family than in college. In high school the student role is more compulsory and less autonomous. And the high school is less diversified, less pluralistic, more bureaucratic, and more hierarchical than the college. The college experience, in short, "extends the socialization process, developing the individual so that his personality can articulate with a differentiating, rationalizing, and changing society. Intelligence, universalistic standards of evaluation, autonomy, flexibility, and rationally oriented legitimate achievement are features of this extended socialization."[41]

I agree with this characterization. I should also like to suggest, however, that the same kinds of contrasts may be observed, though not so strikingly, *within* the higher education system, and that, correspondingly, the Parsons-Platt model of "collegiate" socialization applies more fully to certain elite sectors of higher education than to other sectors. (If this is so, it should not be surprising, since their volume self-consciously focuses on the elite sectors.) The model seems most relevant to small, liberal-arts colleges with high academic standards and a tradition of diffuse faculty involvement in the lives of students (colleges such as Swarthmore and Oberlin) ; and distinguished private institutions with substantial emphasis on graduate training and research, but also with a tradition of involvement in undergraduate teaching (universities such as Harvard, Princeton, and Stanford) ; and, perhaps to a lesser extent, older and

41. Chapter 4, pp. 211–215, of this book.

higher-prestige public state universities (such as Wisconsin, Michigan, and Berkeley). These kinds of institutions have a tradition of relative insulation from the wider society; and, although not total institutions, they do have many of the characteristics of a diffuse moral community. They have traditions of moral dedication on the part of faculty to their work and their students. They have institutionalized arrangements—deans, tutors, housemasters, as well as informal expectations regarding faculty-student relations —that bring faculty and administration into more general relations with students than are found in the classroom alone. They are built on the assumption of continuity of student attendance from freshman through senior year, so that their involvement in the institution is fairly long-term. Traditionally, these institutions have involved themselves in a wide range of items of students' behavior—living and eating arrangements, drinking habits, sexual activity, and general conduct considered proper in that institution. These institutions, in short, have had the kind of setting in which the diffuse identifications germane to the Parsons-Platt model of socialization have ample opportunity to develop.

Parsons and Platt argue that much of the strain in the socialization process in higher education can be understood as resulting from the fact that these kinds of institutions have "moved away" from the diffuse community model through a process of upgrading and increasing student autonomy. Their case is compelling. However, if we consider the pattern of changes in the system of higher education as a whole, particularly in the public sector and in the nonelite sectors, we may discover the emergence of structural settings that differ in significant—though certainly not in all—respects from the setting assumed in the Parsons-Platt model of socialization.

The first change to be noted is the growth of educational institutions whose services to students are more functionally specific than the kinds envisioned in the model presented in Chapter 4. I refer here to the expansion, both in size of institution and number of institutions, of the state colleges and the junior or community colleges. Such institutions have experienced a growth rate greater than the universities in general and much greater than that of the private universities. State colleges are, like the universities, institutions that specialize in socialization in the context of standards of cognitive rationality; in this respect they resemble universities much more than they resemble other types of organizations, such as business firms or hospitals. Nevertheless, there are differences as well. Most state colleges and community colleges lack the sense of a special culture or mystique and the sense of community associated with private institutions with centuries of educational tradition. Seldom are these institutions residential; most students live either at home or in private housing. They also have much higher drop-out and transfer rates than private colleges and universities. In these kinds of institutions, furthermore, the administration takes little interest in the conduct of students beyond their academic performance and general conduct on campus. It is assumed, though not always made explicit, that the institutions of the family and civil authority will be responsible for imposing the more diffuse moral controls on conduct. Furthermore, it is assumed that students are interested in exposing themselves to the kind of knowledge that teachers have to offer—in this sense the experience *is* one of socialization—but the relationship between students and faculty is more instrumental than in the ideal-type college based on diffuse community ties.

The implication of these structural features of the specific-service institutions of higher education is that many of the processes predicated in the Parsons-Platt model may not be so salient. They should certainly be present in *some* degree, since going to almost any college marks some extension and intensification of the socialization processes associated with high schools. But many of the state colleges and community colleges do not meet the conditions of being insulated from the institutions of the surrounding community. Furthermore, the ties between students and faculty and administrators are sufficiently fleeting that those processes of diffuse identification, fundamental in the Parsons-Platt model, are weaker in this setting. On the basis of this reasoning, I would conclude that whatever dissatisfaction, alienation, and disturbances are experienced by students in specific-service institutions of higher education rest on a different mix of determinants—some in common with, but some different from, those found in the university setting. In particular, students enrolled in these more functionally-specific, more bureaucratic, and lower-prestige institutions may be more likely to experience a somewhat different sort of relative deprivation from that experienced by students in elite institutions—namely, that although in a formal sense they have been admitted into an institution of higher education, yet they are being treated too much like high school students and are *not* being presented with the conditions and opportunities present in other sectors of higher education.[42]

Many four-year colleges and community colleges, then, possess characteristics that lead one to doubt whether they meet fully the assumptions of a diffuse moral community essential to the Parsons-Platt model of socialization. Still other institutions—such as the large public universities—historically have had those more diffuse characteristics, though not to the same degree as the ancient private colleges and universities. Yet in the inflationary period, these large public universities underwent dramatic demographic and structural changes in addition to experiencing the effects of upgrading and increasing autonomy of students; these changes may have also created fragmentation, disintegration, and anomie.

The first type of pressure on the community mechanisms in these large public institutions was the phenomenal growth in the size of their student bodies and faculties. Given the increase in size of classes, numbers of undergraduate majors in some departments, as well as the tendency for the faculty to move in the direction of graduate teaching and research, it became more difficult for faculty members to remain in diffuse contact with very many undergraduates. Advising and counselling tended to become more perfunctory for the same reasons. In addition, it became more difficult to maintain a paternalistic relationship between administrators (for instance, deans of students) and the individual students that composed the swollen ranks of undergraduate student bodies. Simple limitations of time and emotional energy imposed by the numbers made for relatively greater impersonality.

To these demographic trends must be added the fact that practices such as admissions and grading were becoming more standardized. And finally, the growth of junior colleges and state colleges alongside the universities, as well as the increasing tendency for students to interrupt voluntarily their studies in the 1960's, meant an increase in the transfer and drop-out rates. Between 1960 and

42. Certainly this sort of relative deprivation is experienced by the faculties of such institutions. Early in the 1960's a poll of faculty sentiment by the California Coordinating Council for Higher Education indicated that junior college faculty members wished to have a system of academic rank established and that they desired that junior colleges presently within high school districts or unified school districts be given separate districts. Many respondents indicated that "since there is no academic rank, and since some Junior Colleges are within unified school districts, the atmosphere of a 'glorified high school' prevails." Coordinating Council of Higher Education, *Faculty Opinion toward Salary, Fringe Benefits, and Working Conditions*, Report No. 1007 (Sacramento and San Francisco, Calif., August 1963), p. 36.

1970, for example, for the University of California system as a whole, between 35 and 45 percent of the undergraduate students in attendance at a given year were not in attendance there during the previous year. This fact demands that we re-examine the assumption that a large public university with these characteristics could be considered a community in any real sense; the relations between faculty members and students, on the one hand, and administrators and students, on the other, were becoming relatively unenduring. Such changes suggest that the structural bases for the process of affective attachment and identification implied in the model of socialization developed by Parsons and Platt may have been in the process of erosion.

True, many of the public universities experienced a process of upgrading in the 1950's and 1960's. This is illustrated not only in the involvement of faculty competence in more graduate training and research but also in the increasing curricular demands on undergraduate students—demands associated with the post-Sputnik response in the educational system. But this upgrading was taking place in the context of the diminishing presence of the agents of socialization. These processes are similar to the dynamics outlined by Parsons and Platt; but one wonders whether or not the processes were carried so far in some institutions that the process tipped over the fine line between increasing autonomy and increasing neglect.

The fact that universities were failing to change as rapidly in some respects as in others suggests another source of relative deprivation. In many cases, administrative rules and procedures remained relatively unchanged, although students were expected to be more independent and responsible with respect to their academic experiences. Although the 1950's and early 1960's showed some liberalization of rules, the controls associated with the principle of in loco parentis were slower to erode than the traditional faculty-student and administration-student relations on which this principle was built and could function viably. The administrative rules and regulations came to correspond less with the realities of the social relationships in the system. Students tended to receive the message that they were expected to perform at high levels of competence in the context of educational arrangements which were moving in the direction of a more specific-service model, but they found themselves still exposed to a variety of rules relating to political activity, visiting hours in dormitories, and the like.

Recent changes in living arrangements, disciplinary rules, and student participation have tended to reduce this discrepancy.

The main line of my argument is this: Although the themes of student protest of the 1960's were much the same in the large public universities as they were in the private liberal arts colleges and distinguished private universities, the mix of determinants was probably different in the two sets of cases.[43] Parsons and Platt tend to interpret the symbolism of protest as symptomatic of a phase of socialization in a particular structural setting. They see protest emanating from a combination of the pressures, identifications, and movement toward a higher cognitive capacity. Though those factors are certainly not absent in the cases I have singled out for analysis, a rather different, though overlapping, package of structural changes and processes contributed to alienation and its manifestation in protest. The changes I have mentioned suggest that the protest carried with it a complaint against a situation in which greater expectations were being generated among students, but in which the agencies of socialization were so weak that the process of socialization in the name of these expectations could not be carried out effectively.

To conclude this section, I shall explore further the parallel between the oedipal transition, the psychotherapeutic situation, and the socialization process in undergraduate education—in particular, the potentiality of seduction of the parental figure (or parental-surrogate). Parsons and Platt note the parallel explicitly:

Contexts where expressive and affective components are particularly important offer various seductive possibilities. The therapeutic situation gives rise to the problem of countertransference; familial socialization gives rise to erotic fantasies on the part of children as well as parents. . . .

Some of these reactions occur in the college-student socialization phase . . .[44]

The resistances to seduction are, in the original case, institutionalized in the incest taboo. This taboo contributes to an affective alliance between the father and mother, which is utilized as a lever in the socialization process. Parsons and Robert F. Bales described the significance of the incest taboo for socialization as follows:

43. Like Parsons and Platt, I am limiting my observations to the determinants associated with the higher-education system. Like them, I consider extra-academic sources of the protest, such as the civil rights movement and the existence of an unpopular war, highly important.
44. Chapter 4, pp. 179–180, of this book.

[The incest taboo] tends to concentrate the erotic attachment of the marital pair on each other, to preserve their support of each other, though their roles are different and complementary, and to keep the access of power and authority within the family coincident with the generation difference. It allows the mother to serve as the symbolic focus of love and gratification to the child, and still to make her love conditional as necessary for his socialization. It allows the father to serve as a symbolic focus of negative affect without destroying his authority. Or the symbolic significance may be reversed, particularly perhaps for the female child. Usually, probably, both parents are to some degree symbols of both love and hate, according to context.[45]

From the standpoint of effectiveness of socialization, one parental figure must not be seduced into erotic alliance with the oedipal child. This is disruptive to the personality development of the child; it arouses the anxiety associated with the oedipal wishes that he is struggling to repress and invites and legitimizes expression of the destructive impulses toward the other parent. The incest taboo, in short, is a social arrangement that allies the parents with one another in a solidary relationship, provides a complicated set of levers for exerting pressures on the child to develop, and gives him a complicated set of objects of identification. In so far as this solidary relationship is broken, it encourages the child to form an alliance against the other parent. In any socialization process, the degree to which incestuous tendencies—or their affective equivalent in nonfamilial situations—will be manifested is problematical. Parsons and Platt note occasions on which students perceive positive countertransference on the part of faculty and occasions on which faculties have interceded on behalf of students against administrators and civil authorities in situations of conflict.[46] By the same token, the degree to which acting-out of regressive impulses will be permitted is also problematical and variable.[47]

In this connection, let us consider the implications of some of the structural changes I noted above[48] for the probability of the encouragement of acting-out on the part of dissident students. In particular, some structural developments tended to identify the faculty member more with the discipline than with his home institution; and some persons enjoyed less than full membership in the

45. Talcott Parsons, Robert F. Bales, et al., *Family, Socialization, and Interaction Process* (Glencoe, Ill., The Free Press, 1955), p. 306.
46. Chapter 4, p. 181, of this book.
47. Chapter 4, p. 178, of this book.
48. Pp. 404–409.

academy, such as teaching assistants and research personnel. Even though these categories of persons were cast in the role of second-class citizens in relation to the faculty, however, they retained some measure of authority in the educational and research processes. Earlier I developed arguments that suggested a high level of relative deprivation and disaffection on the part of these groups.

Because faculty authority was fragmented to a considerable degree during the inflationary period, a social situation was created that increased the probability of seduction of persons in positions of some authority to join students in attacks on other authorities, whether these be faculty, administrators, or law-enforcement officials. It increased the probabilities that some categories of "nonstudent" authorities would cross the sharp boundary that usually exists between students and various categories of authority.[49] The fragmentation of roles created opportunities for the formation of nascent oedipal triangles and coalitions. Furthermore, insofar as dissident students were joined by faculty members, teaching assistants, or graduate students, this constituted in some degree an oedipal invitation to express previously repressed hostile feelings.[50] In my observation of conflict situations, in a variety of university settings in the 1960's, I gained the impression that a conflict situation between students and administration was typically magnified and electrified when the dissident students were joined by faculty or teaching assistants.

To conclude: My impressions of Parsons' and Platt's treatment of the socialization process is that they have concentrated on the internal psychological dynamics of the socializee and on the interactive relationship between socializer and socializee in the higher-education setting. In doing this they have produced a novel contribution to our understanding of the socialization process during the collegiate years. They have emphasized less, however, the structural changes in higher education that have tended to produce variations—including breakdowns—in this process of socialization. In this section I have attempted to point out a number of structural developments that suggest the necessity of developing a more diverse array of models of undergraduate socialization.

49. Chapter 4, p. 175, of this book.
50. I leave aside the question of whether these hostile feelings are realistically based. I assume that all conflicts between authorities and subordinates display a mixture of feelings based on current realities and regressive feelings.

## The Dynamics of Inflation and Deflation

My remarks on the model of inflation and deflation developed in Chapter 7 can be brief because in the main I find the account of the recent dynamics affecting the elite sector of higher education to be a sound one. It is particularly helpful to distinguish the multiple levels of interchange—cultural, general action, and social-system—at which the cycle of overinvestment followed by withdrawal has occurred. Only by so doing can we understand the extraordinarily complex symbolism of the crisis that higher education has witnessed in the past decade.

Accurate and subtle as the account generated by Parsons and Platt is, it could well be supplemented by a more precise analysis of the mechanisms by which inflation developed and subsequently reversed itself. The logic of Parsons' and Platt's model is that the heavy investments of various media have been accompanied by the very high expectations for performance on the part of the university system in particular—which in the nature of the case could not be fulfilled; this being so, it is followed by a phase of "holding back" the various media, which took the form of a withdrawal of trust and manifested itself in belief systems that downgrade the cognitive emphasis. To account for the extremity of the reversal phase of the cycle, however, it is necessary to go beyond this rather general, overall analysis and inquire into some of the more microscopic processes that accompany processes of overinvestment and withdrawal—structural dislocations that are occasioned by heavy investment, the formation of groups that crystallize around these structural dislocations, the relative deprivation experienced by the various groups, and the political processes that emerge from conflicts among these groups. Since I have stressed these kinds of variables throughout this essay, I shall conclude with two brief illustrations of how they can throw additional light on the dynamics of inflation and deflation as described in Chapter 7.

The process of overinvestment reflects, as Parsons and Platt argue, the heightened expectations for performance on the part of the academic system. For this reason alone we would expect an increased influx of various kinds of generalized media. But, in addition, that process of investment triggers certain processes of conflict and competition *within* the academic system that further exaggerated the demand for inputs of resources and thus aggravated the "overinvestment" phenomenon. Let me illustrate. Parsons and Platt regard the key to the inflationary process to be both "the enhanced prestige of the academic system in society" and "the enhanced position of the elite institutions" within the academic system.[51] Concretely this meant a qualitative upgrading of elite institutions by the input of resources dedicated to graduate training and research. Because these resources were channeled disproportionately to high-quality universities, this created a sense of relative deprivation on the part of lower-prestige institutions granting the doctorate, as well as various kinds of four-year colleges. This relative deprivation, combined with the sense of increased opportunity, intensified the competition among educational institutions. Lesser institutions scrambled to participate in the growth and upgrading—by increasing their enrollments, by developing programs for advanced degrees, by beginning research programs, by changing their name to "university" rather than "college." At the same time, elite institutions joined in the competitive struggle for resources to preserve or even enhance their privileged status. The process of investment generated a new political demand for inputs of resources—a demand stimulated by internal competition and status-striving among colleges and universities—and further augmented inflationary pressures. Many governing boards and state legislatures in the 1960's found themselves wondering how they could control the competitive scramble for resources by different colleges and universities. This mechanism of internal competition compounded the effects created by the investment process and exaggerated the inflationary effects.

A second illustration: Parsons and Platt argue correctly that the "suddenness with which a critical situation developed at Berkeley in 1964 and then spread to other institutions" cannot be understood without taking into consideration the inflationary character of the period leading up to that time.[52] In the first instance the crisis in the elite institutions between 1964 and 1970 marked a withdrawal of influence and intelligence from the academic "bank" out of a loss of confidence, which was in turn related to the "bank's" relative failure to perform in the light of heightened expectations. I am basically in accord with this diagnosis. Yet this was only one aspect of the withdrawl of media. It was followed by

51. Chapter 7, p. 323, of this book.
52. Chapter 7, pp. 312–313, of this book.

a very complicated backlash, which amounted, in effect, to an additional withdrawal of influence on the part of many of the sectors of support other than students (alumni, legislators, the general public). The mechanisms of this further withdrawal, however, were somewhat different from those leading to the initial student-administration confrontations. They resulted as much from the fact that *a crisis had occurred* as it did from a simple withdrawal of overinvested resources. After all, most of the critical confrontations between students and administrators on these campuses involved a direct challenge to authority, considerable violence, and extensive violations of the law. When this kind of crisis occurs, a general alarm spreads throughout the society, whether or not the institution in question has experienced an "overinvestment" of confidence in the recent past. The alarm spreads because authority has been challenged and because the functioning of an institution has been thrown into doubt.[53] Of course, if high hopes and abundant resources have been invested in this institution in the recent past, the reaction to a failure of authority in a conflict situation is likely to be all the more intense. But whatever the mix of determinants, it is apparent that *both* the dynamics of long-term investment *and* the dynamics of crisis, reaction to crisis, and management of crisis must be brought to bear on explaining the drama and intensity of the turning point between inflation and deflation.

53. This phenomenon, that the eruption of conflict is itself the occasion for the genesis of further conflict, is quite general. Cf. Neil J. Smelser, *Theory of Collective Behavior* (New York, The Free Press of Glencoe, 1962), pp. 257–259, 356–358.

# TECHNICAL APPENDIX: SOME GENERAL THEORETICAL PARADIGMS

## Historical Antecedents

This book has attempted not only to mobilize pertinent information about American universities in a relevant way but to pose problems in terms of a technical analytical scheme, the theory of action. In particular we have endeavored to interweave analysis at the level of the general system of action with analysis on the level of the social system, a functional subsystem of the general action system.

In our theoretical judgments, we have been guided by paradigms at both levels. Those dealing with the general action system have changed most since previous publication,[1] but we are presenting here all of our formalizations to date. After outlining them, we shall say something about the theoretical gaps still existing.

The starting point is the four-function paradigm explicated in Chapter 1. Although this was originally conceived as general to action,[2] the first detailed exposition of its implications occurred at the social-system level, specifically in the work done by Smelser and the senior author in *Economy and Society*.[3] That book produced the insights (1) that the economy could be treated, in terms of the four-function paradigm, as the adaptive subsystem of a society and (2) that the input-output categories traditionally treated in economic theory as the factors of production and the shares of income were categories of *relation* between the adaptive subsystem and the other functional systems of the society. This was how the format of the societal interchange system of Figure A.1 emerged—as did the tabular view of the structure of the social system (formulated in Figure A.2) and of its interchange processes (formulated in Figure A.3).

These two insights were only a beginning. Assuming the existence of an interchange paradigm, we had two further problems. The first was that

---

1. Cf. Talcott Parsons, "Some Problems of General Theory in Sociology," in *Theoretical Sociology: Perspectives and Developments*, ed. John C. McKinney and Edward A. Tiryakian (New York, Appleton-Century-Crofts, 1970).
2. Cf. Talcott Parsons, Robert F. Bales, and Edward A. Shils, *Working Papers in the Theory of Action* (New York, The Free Press, 1953).
3. Talcott Parsons and Neil J. Smelser, *Economy and Society* (London, Routledge and Kegan Paul; and New York, The Free Press, 1956).

of locating the sources and destinations of categories of input and output. We decided that the family household, traditionally regarded by economists as the unit of consumption and the source of the input of labor as a factor of production to the economy; should be located—as a matter of primacy—in the *pattern-maintenance subsystem* of the society. Resolving this question tentatively with the idea that a pair of inputs and outputs had a common source and destination left two further logical possibilities. Next we had to locate the source of the factor input of capital to the economy. We decided to locate it in the political subsystem. The only remaining open possibility, the interchange with the still unexplored integrative system, was assigned to the factor postclassically introduced into economic analysis by Marshall and Schumpeter; we adopted Marshall's term "organization."[4]

The second problem resulted from the circumstance that we were thinking in terms of four functional categories and indeed that, since Marshall, economists dealt with four factors of production and shares of income, but that, internal to any four-unit set, were only *three* interchanging pairs. Even if we properly located three of our input-output pairs from the point of view of the economy as adaptive subsystem, what about the fourth?

On both sides of the relation, clues existed to a possible solution of this problem. Economic theory traditionally regarded one of the factors of production, land, as occupying a special place. In our functional analysis of action systems and specifically at the social level, the pattern-maintenance function also occupied a special place. Perhaps the specialness of pattern-maintenance lay in the fact that this subsystem was not engaged in the same *order* of interchanges with the other subsystems, just as the specialness of the total quantity of land in an economy (as distinguished from the allocation of parcels) is not a function of its price.

One final assumption-decision remains to be mentioned. We tied together the input and output categories relative to a single pair of subsystems into a double-interchange bundle. In making this assumption, we were following the precedent of economic theory. The standard formula concerned the interchange between producing firms and consuming households. The source of control over consumers' goods for households lay in the productive output of firms in a sufficiently differentiated economy. The relation, however, was established through effective demand, by which economists meant the actual capacity to offer money payment for the transfer of rights of possession in consumers goods. These transfers of rights were satisfactory to firms in the sense of ultimately leading back to their profitability in particular lines of production. At the same time the consuming household was the source of the labor supply on which the processes of economic production were dependent. Through various stages of conceptual refinement, members of the household entered the labor force, became involved in em-

4. Alfred Marshall, *Principles of Economics* (London, Macmillan, 1925). Also, Joseph A. Schumpeter, *The Theory of Economic Development*, trans. Redvers Opie (Cambridge, Mass., Harvard University Press, 1934).

ployment, and were the earners of money incomes and the like. The money income from the output of labor then became the source of "effective demand"—in the sense of the household's capacity to make money offers for the purchase of goods. The justification of putting these components together in a single bundle lies in the development of the structure of societies in the course of the development of the division of labor in the sociological sense used by Durkheim.[5] If for a "firm" in the economic sense is substituted "employing organization" as a source of money income to the household, a transition from the economic to the more general social level can be worked out.

These theoretical developments brought the focus of attention to the role of a generalized medium of exchange, in the economic case—money. The consumption-labor supply bundle could only constitute a unitary bundle if it were held together by monetary evaluations and transactions. It, therefore, became imperative to investigate the nature of money as a generalized symbolic medium of interchange—a term we have adopted to avoid the strictly economic connotations of the word "exchange." By this path we arrived at treating the relations among functional subsystems of an action system in terms of interchanges involving generalized media of interchange. The underlying conception has been that the functional paradigm not only defined tangible structural units like business firms, particular households, industries, residential aggregates of households, and the like but that it also gave the rationale for treating together a variety of the bundles of oriented and meaningful dynamic process. This could be worked out paradigmatically in terms of the relation of the economy to consuming households and the economy's relation to the sources of the other factors of production.

Such a line of theoretical development could have constituted no more than a refinement of economic sociology. However, we were theoretically more ambitious than this. Having worked out the paradigm which has been sketched in terms of its circumstantial concrete developmental situation, we wanted to generalize it to the structure and functioning of a social system at the differentiated societal level taken as a whole. The first step, documented in the paper "On the Concept of Political Power," was to use the economic model as a basis for reformulating political thinking about power; specifically, we treated power as a generalized symbolic medium in interchange not completely parallel to money, but as belonging in the same category as money.[6] This involved reconsideration of many controversial theoretical problems involved in the political field. The process of theoretical development was then further pursued into the other two functional subsystems of a society, namely, the integrative subsystem (now called the

5. Emile Durkheim, *The Division of Labor in Society*, trans. George Simpson (New York, The Free Press, 1969).

6. Talcott Parsons, "On the Concept of Political Power," in *Politics and Social Structure* (New York, The Free Press, 1969), chap. xiv, pp. 352–404 (reprinted from *Proceedings of the American Philosophical Society*, 107 [June 1963], 232–262).

"societal community") and the pattern-maintenance subsystem (now called the fiduciary subsystem).

## The Paradigms of the Social System

Figure A.1 presents a schematic format of the social system, locating both structural subsystems and interchange connections. The *structure* of the social system is presented diagramatically in Figure A.2 broken down to the sixteen-cell level. This is to say, the four larger boxes represent the primary functional subsystems of a society or another type of social system that has become sufficiently differentiated to make the distinctions meaningful. These are (in the society) the economy as the adaptive subsystem, the polity as the goal-attainment subsystem, the societal community as the integrative subsystem, and the fiduciary system as the subsystem with the pattern-maintenance responsibility. These four subsystems are then shown as linked with each other in pairs, themselves interpreted to have functional significance.

Each of the four subsystems is then broken down again by the same functional logic into four subsystems, and each of these is given a designation. Since the present book has been particularly concerned with the fiduciary system, we undertook in Chapter 1 to outline the rationale of the four-system breakdown of the fiduciary system.

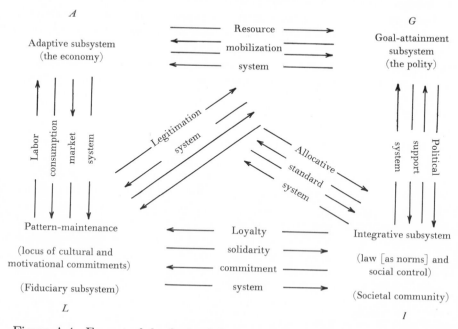

Figure A.1. Format of the Societal System: Structure and Interchange Sets

*Note:* Figure A.1 from Talcott Parsons, *Politics and Social Structure,* copyright © 1969, p. 398. By permission of The Macmillan Co. and The Free Press, New York, N.Y.

# TECHNICAL APPENDIX

The four functional subsystems constitute a cybernetic hierarchy in the order L-I-G-A. In the discussion of substantive problems throughout the book we tried to give the reader an adequate understanding of our view that the cybernetic control which we attribute to a superordinate system in this hierarchy does not imply domination in every respect. Control is compatible with fundamental autonomy and two-way interchange. We tried to make this point clear with reference to the concept of institutionalized individualism where, although cultural and social systems are cybernetically superordinate to the personality of the individual, the autonomy of that personality is a primary feature of an individualistic action system. Cybernetic hierarchy is at the same time linked to feedback relationships, which underlines the reciprocal character of the interchanges.

The reader familiar with the history of this scheme will note several differences from the arrangement of the subsystems in Figure A.2 in previous publications, notably, the one presented in the technical note appended to the paper, "On the Concept of Political Power."[7] First, the subsystems are arranged so that the cybernetic hierarchy runs clockwise, starting at the upper left and running around to the lower left. There is a certain arbitrariness in the diagramming of this structure in only two dimensions; a three-dimension model which treated these as steps in a spiral staircase would be more accurate. However, it is not worthwhile for present purposes to pursue technicalities this far.

Second, we have placed the pattern-maintenance subsystem of each primary unit on the outside corner. If the basic pattern of ordering is not to be altered, this has the effect of placing the four integrative subsystem units on the upper and lower edges of the diagram, but on the inner corners of each subsystem; the four adaptive subsystem units are on the outer edges, both left and right, but also on the two inside corners. This leaves the four units classified as having goal-attainment functions on the inside corners of the total paradigm.

This rearrangement was first worked out for what we will present as Figure A.6, the paradigm of the "Structure of the General Action System." There, it has been justified in terms of a theme emphasized throughout this book, namely, the importance of the internal environments of the system of action as seen from the perspective of the individual person as actor. This theme first became evident to us in social science perspective from reconsideration of Durkheim's work in the light of biological thought. If this rearrangement were appropriate at the level of the general system of action, it should also be appropriate at the social system level. For example, two important fields of application are to be found (labeled with the small letter "g") in interchanges internal to the social system between functional subsystems. One of them is between the economy and the fiduciary subsystem, in relation to which the consumer's interest in economic goods is shaped by

7. Ibid.

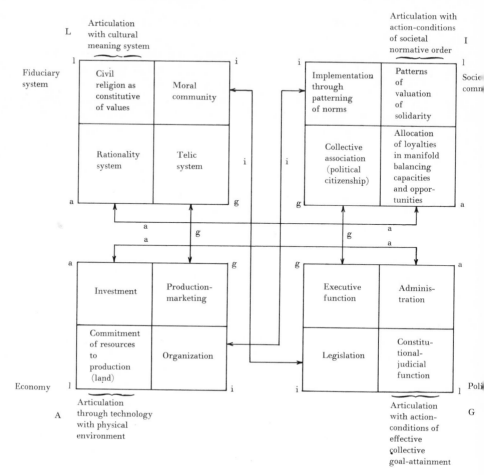

Figure A.2. Structure of the Social System

standards of taste, that is, on the background of expressive symbolism. This connection provides an opportunity for developing the theory of consumption farther. The second context is the problem of the relation of political leadership to constituency support, a problem of the relation of the polity to the integrative system.

The labelings of the six interchange pairs with the small letters "a," "g," and "i" are meant to call attention to a relationship which holds between this way of looking at the structural system paradigm and the two primary axes of the action system outlined in Chapter 1, namely, the external-internal and the instrumental-consummatory. The process which by this particular set of diagramming conventions comes to focus in the horizontal dimension has to do with adaptive function. The distinction around which the instrumental-consummatory dichotomy is built concerns what some economists used to call "time preference." This is to say, it has to do with the problem of relative immediacy of the enjoyment of benefits from resources and the delay of that enjoyment in favor of the function of increase of the resource base.

However, we do not in the present presentation associate the external-internal distinction with the vertical dimension. Our new arrangement shifts the emphasis and holds that the pattern-maintenance function is especially concerned with the maintenance of the boundaries between a system of reference and its environment. This is justification for placing the L cells at the most isolated positions of all, namely, at the corners of the paradigm. This placement symbolizes their insulation from direct interchanges with other subsystems. Reinforcement in this set of judgments has come from the apparent parallels with biological theory both at the level of genetics and that of population and species biology.[8] In relation to what is nonsystem, the adaptive and the pattern-maintenance functions strike us as the primary foci of definition of the status of the system.

The integrative functions, on the other hand, are concerned with the internal environment of the system. They define the ways in which the action-situations of units and subsystems come to be a function of structures that transcend the particular subsystem itself, but which at the same time are characteristic of the larger system. Durkheim was the action-level theorist whose two axes of solidarity, mechanical and organic, delineated the two integrative axes of the action system and, at a lower level of generality, that of society.[9]

Finally, the g or vertical interchange pairs, though external from the point of view of the interchanging subsystems, are internal from the point of view of the larger system of which they are both parts. Relative to the adaptive function, g is concentrated on short-run interests; relative to the integrative function, it is concentrated on particularistic as distinguished from systemic interest. In terms of biological parallels, g comes closer to physiological levels as distinguished from those with more of either a developmental significance for the individual organism or an evolutionary one for the species.

Contrary to our previous views, we do not lay special stress on the *subsystems* of the source and destination systems of these interchanges, a question which has aroused disagreement among some of those involved in these theoretical problems.[10]

8. Cf. *Daedalus* material in Gerald Holton, ed., *The Twentieth Century Sciences: Studies in the Biographies of Ideas* (New York, Norton, 1972); and Ernst Mayr, *Populations, Species, and Evolution* (Cambridge, Mass., Belknap Press of Harvard University Press, 1970).

9. Talcott Parsons, "Durkheim on Religion Revisited: Another Look at *The Elementary Forms of the Religious Life*," in *The Scientific Study of Religion: Beyond the Classics*, ed. Charles Y. Glock and Phillip E. Hammond (New York, Harper and Row, 1973).

10. See Johannes J. Loubser, Rainer Baum, Andrew Effrat, and Victor Lidz, eds., *Explorations in General Theory in Social Science* (New York, The Free Press, 1973).

As in Figure A.6, the paradigm for the structure of the General Action System corresponding to Figure A.2 for the social system, we have inserted suggestions in brackets at each of the four pattern-maintenance corners of the paradigm of foci of articulation of the integrative system—at the general action level—with the other action systems. The adaptive articulation (related to land in economic theory) is the only one that reaches outside the general system of action. Land mediates the relationship between the social system and the physical environment. The functional reference is primarily adaptive. Physical resources have to be made socially meaningful through the process of economic production, but so far as physical components are involved, "natural" resources have to be processed by technological procedures, the goals of which are prescribed by application of the economic value-category of utility (see Figure A.4 below).

The other three articulations are with the relevant aspects of the general system of action. The G-subsystem of a society, the *polity*, articulates with the physical environment, especially through the territorial reference of its sphere of control, which includes the territorial jurisdictions of governments but also control of the physical premises in which organizational activities are carried on, for example, university buildings. The main emphasis, however, is to the action-conditions of effective goal-attainment, including the availability of the relevant human resources at the level of participating personalities and the general-action grounding of the normative order of the society, coming to focus in its *legitimacy*—especially that of authority—in Max Weber's sense.[11] The I subsystem of a society articulates with those aspects of the general action system important for grounding normative order at the societal level. At one level this is grounding in the moral-evaluative commitments of the culture, the source of what Durkheim called its moral authority. Its effectiveness in controlling action, however, is also a function of the economy of affect, that is, predominantly social-affective relations at the general action level. The L subsystem of a society relates to the aspect of the cultural system which articulates meanings that define the situation as a generalized medium of interchange. Bellah's concept of the civil religion[12] is such a focus of mediation to the social system. The cultural system in turn is the focus of the legitimation, not of authority but of the institutionalized values underlying the moral authority of the more substantive normative order of a society.

Figure A.3 attempts to spell out the four-fold interchange paradigm between all four functional subsystems of the society. This is virtually unchanged from the version published in the technical note to the paper "On the Concept of Political Power."[13] Only one change of terminology is

11. Max Weber, *The Theory of Social and Economic Organization*, trans. A. M. Henderson and Talcott Parsons (New York, The Free Press, 1969).
12. Robert N. Bellah, "Civil Religion in America," *Daedalus* (Winter 1967), pp. 1–21.
13. Parsons, "On the Concept of Political Power."

introduced, namely, putting "legitimation of claims to loyalties" in the place of "value-based claims of loyalties" in the L-I interchange. The paradigm does, however, need elucidation, couched as it is in terms of the four generalized symbolic media of interchange of the society as a system: money anchored in the economy, power anchored in the polity, influence anchored in the societal community, and value-commitments anchored in the fiduciary system. We have generalized the classical paradigm of economic theory to the social system as a whole by treating each of the six as consisting of a double interchange; but we have self-consciously moved to a higher level of abstraction from that employed by economists. For example, in the prototypical A-L relation, the economist's formula consisted of exchange of money for goods and services on the one side, labor on the other. Subject to the imperatives of theoretical generalization, however, the latter categories are dealt with at the level not of concrete control of particulars but of value-commitments on the part of the putative providers of such control. The problem of the relation of these two levels has come up several times in the course of the book where we have tried to relate the generalized medium to the particularized valuables for which they may be exchanged. The students of this appendix should be aware that Figure A.3 is couched at the level of generalized media throughout and that for certain applications a shift of level is required. The details for that shift probably can be worked out ultimately in formal paradigms. Many of the terms employed to designate the twenty-four different categories are terms which to some degree compromise between these two levels. The use of the term "goods" and "labor" are examples, but there are others. Care is necessary in use of the paradigm.

At several points in the book we have brought up another consideration about generalized media, namely, that externally to the primary anchorage of a medium (such as the anchorage for money in the economy) the medium functions to acquire control of resources through interchange. Thus the firm which sells consumer goods acquires the money income which can be used to acquire control of factors of production. Internally, however, the same medium functions as an agency of cost control. This is the basis of the relation between the two left-hand vertical columns in Figure A.4. The coordination standard—an example of "norms" as distinguished from "values" —is the standard specifically revelant to the cost-control function. In the economy the coordination standard is that of solvency. We have introduced one terminological change here by using the term "compliance" in the G box of the coordination standard column in place of "success," a term which never seemed appropriate.

The A and G columns of Figure A.4 designate contexts of operation of each of the four media as sanctions, arranged not by interchange system as in Figure A.3 but by control of factor inputs and product outputs respectively. Thus money, though not itself a factor of production, controls (buys)

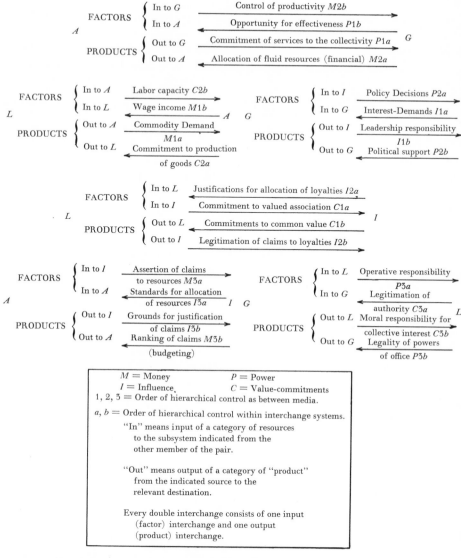

Figure A.3. The Categories of Societal Interchange

*Note:* Figure A.3 from Talcott Parsons, *Politics and Social Structure*, copyright © 1969, p. 399. By permission of The Macmillan Co. and The Free Press, New York, N.Y.

labor and capital as the primary factors, in the A-L and the A-G interchange systems respectively, whereas for consuming systems money buys outputs of the economy, namely goods (in A-L) and services (in A-G).

The involvement of power is parallel. On the one hand, it commands the two primary mobile factors of effectiveness, namely control of productivity (in G-A) and interest-demands (in G-I) (as justified in terms of appeal to norms). On the other hand, the consumers or beneficiaries of the outputs from the process can use power to command these outputs in the form of fluid resources (for example, through budget allocation in G-A) and of leadership responsibility for valued goals (in G-I).

In Figure A.4, negative and positive sanction types alternate in the hierarchy of control. Power, as the medium depending on negative-situational sanctions, is sandwiched between money (below it) with its positive-situational sanctions and influence (above it) with its positive-intentional sanctions.

Returning to Figure A.3, power is also involved in the legitimation system (L-G), but this time as code, as an aspect of authority. This may be conceived as a mechanism for linking the principles and standards in the L and G rows. What is called the assumption of operative responsibility (P3a), which is treated as a factor of integrity, is responsibility for *success* —as internally indexed by compliance—in the implementation of the value-principles, not only of collective effectiveness but of integrity of the paramount societal value-commitments. The legitimation of authority (C3a) imposes the responsibility to attempt such success. Legality of the powers of office on the other hand (P3c), as a category of output to the polity, is an application of the standard of pattern-consistency. At the various relevant levels action may and should be taken consistent with the value-commitments. In exchange for legal authorization to take such action, the responsible officeholder must accept moral responsibility for his use of power and his decisions of interpretation (C3b).

In a sense not clear when Figure A.4 was first formulated, the L and I vertical columns, that is, the farthest left and the one next to it, correspond to the analytical distinction between values and norms. To be sure, this is explicit in the designation *value-principle* for the left-hand column but not in the designation *coordination standard* for the column next to it. An example of the latter is solvency as a standard for the business firm. This means that the *primary* norms governing decision-making for the firm as a unit in the economy should concern the balance of monetary receipts and monetary costs. This (rather than any psychological generalization) is the core of the "profit motive." The profit motive is not so much a specific norm as a standard which ties together a ramified set of more particular norms to which business decision-makers may reasonably be held to be bound. Stress on the word primary is necessary. No concrete collectivity can be exclusively ordered by the norms governed by one particular standard. Business firms are bound by norms expressing the other three standards as well as solvency, but this fact does not eliminate the primacy of the standard of solvency.

The two coordination standards of greatest significance for the subject matter in this book are consensus and pattern-consistency. By consensus, in the context of this book we mean essentially the voluntary status of ordered participation in the collective life of academic communities. In this

| Components of media and interchange reciprocals | CODES | | MESSAGES (sanctions) | | Types of sanction and of effect |
|---|---|---|---|---|---|
| Media in hierarchy of control | Value-principle | Coordination standard | Factors controlled | Products controlled | |
| | | | **Source** | **Destination** | |
| **L** Value-commitments | Integrity | Pattern-consistency | Wages $A$ / Justification of loyalties $I$ | Consumers' demand $A$ / Claims to loyalties $I$ | Negative-intentional (activation of commitments) |
| **I** Influence | Solidarity | Consensus | Commitments to valued association $L$ / Policy decisions $G$ | Commitment to common values $L$ / Political support $G$ | Positive-intentional (persuasion) |
| **G** Power | Effectiveness | Compliance | Interest-demands $I$ / Control of productivity $A$ | Leadership responsibility $I$ / Control of fluid resources' $A$ | Negative-situational (securing compliance) |
| **A** Money | Utility | Solvency | Capital $G$ / Labor $L$ | Commitment of services $G$ / Expectation of goods $L$ | Positive-situational (inducement) |
| | $L$ | $I$ | $G$ | $A$ | |

Figure A.4. The Social-System Media as Sanctions

*Note:* Figure A.4 from Talcott Parsons, *Politics and Social Structure*, copyright © 1969, p. 403. By permission of The Macmillan Co. and The Free Press, New York, N.Y.

context the affective balances of academic communities are of great significance. Because of their academic functions, it is imperative that these should be integrated with the relevant parts of the cognitive complex, but serious deficits in the affective sphere have the same order of negative significance that financial deficits would have for firms. Pattern-consistency is revelant with reference to the values of cognitive rationality. The essential point is the maintenance of the primacy of the standard defined in terms of those values at the core of the academic system, even though this standard has to be combined with others in a number of interpenetrating boundary relationships.

# TECHNICAL APPENDIX

## *Paradigm of the General Action System*

Figure A.5 sets forth the main components of the general action paradigm, components extensively treated in this book. In the order of cybernetic hierarchy L-I-G-A, the functional subsystems are the cultural system, the social system, the psychological (or personality) system, and the behavioral organism. Each of these is the focus of a generalized symbolic medium of interchange, namely, definition of the situation, affect, performance capacity, and intelligence in the same L-I-G-A order. As with the social system in Figure A.1, all of the six internal double-interchange systems in which the media are involved are given designations.

Figure A.6 spells out this paradigm on the structural side. It is constructed on the same basis as Figure A.2 was for the social system, but with differing content references because of the different system reference levels. The articulation between the two is made explicit in that the I subsystem of Figure A.6 is subdivided into the same four general subsystems of the social system which appeared as the main boxes in Figure A.2.

The ideas for the rearrangement of the ordering of the subsystems compared to earlier forms of presentation of a structural paradigm for an action

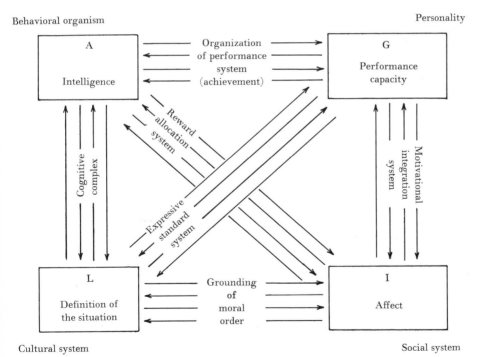

Figure A.5. Format of the General Action System

system originated at the general action level and were then applied to that of the social system. One advantage of this reorganization is diagrammed in terms of the references placed in brackets in relation to each of the four pattern-maintenance corners. Thus, we can speak of the behavioral organism and its genetic component as the main locus of integration of action in the biosphere and, through that, in the physical environment. The corresponding category for the personality system is the meaning of problems for the individual life, that is, what biologically is the phenotype and its passage through the life course from birth to death. In connection with the social system, the meanings in the course of human history grow out of collective life that transcends the time span of the individual and are not reducible to meanings at the organic level of analysis of biological systems. Finally, the cultural system is the point of articulation of human action

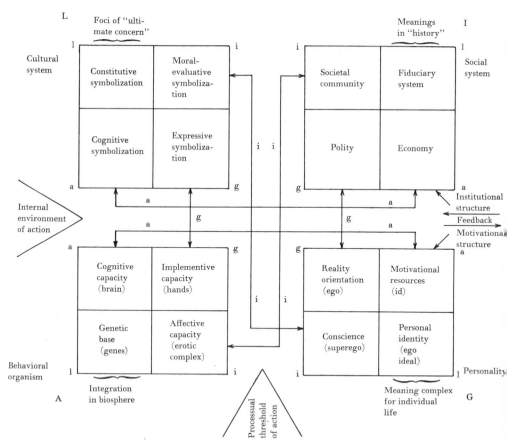

Figure A.6. Structure of the General Action System

systems with the foci of what Tillich called "ultimate concern"[14] or Weber the "problems of meaning" in the primarily religious sense.[15] This is a way of lending significance to the corners of the structural paradigm, that is, to the pattern-maintenance subsystems of each of the four functional subsystems. It helps to highlight the significance of the general rearrangements commented on for the social-system case in the section above, The Paradigms of the Social System. It highlights the significance of the conception of the internal environment of the action system which defines the relations between individuals as the operating units of action formulated structurally in the combined behavioral organism and the personality and, on the other hand, the milieu social formulated in terms of the combination of social and cultural systems, namely, the I and L subsystems. This conception of the relation of individual actors to an internal environment has been used discursively throughout the analysis; it has provided a key to our conception of the cognitive complex. It is our view that the cognitive complex has to be spelled out at all four levels in the structure of the general system of action: the cultural level in the category of knowledge as a type of cultural object; the personality level in the category of competence; the societal level in the category of rationality; and the level of the behavioral organism through the overall operation of intelligence as a generalized symbolic medium. Parallel considerations with reference to the expressive complex led us, in the introductory portion of Chapter 6, to a revision of our previous account of the relations between personality, the expressive aspects of culture, and the phenomena of symbolization at ideological levels.

In the personality subsystems we have adopted essentially a Freudian categorization of structure, although in that of the behavioral organism we do not stand far from the main traditions of behavioral psychology.

The present mode of structural diagramming highlights the significance of the two axes of the general functional paradigm discussed in Chapter 1. Our treatment of articulation of the pattern-maintenance subsystems highlights the conception of the *definition* of a system of action as distinguished from its environment. In particular the concepts of ultimate concern and of history define boundaries of *meaning* at the macro level of the action system, whereas those of the biosphere and the individual life course define them for the individual *organism-personality*. In addition to the conception of the internal environment, we point to a processual threshold of action which is related to the conception variously formulated as "delayed gratification," "time preference," and in other ways. The essence is the alternative of selection; in Kluckhohn's analysis of values, it is the distinction

---

14. Paul Tillich, *The Courage to Be* (New Haven, Conn., Yale University Press, 1952).
15. Weber, *Theory of Social and Economic Organization*.

between relatively immediate interests and longer-run interests.[16] The alternative of selection is related to that between unit interests and collective interests.

Figure A.7 parallels Figure A.3; it is an attempt to categorize the six double-interchange subsystems at the level of the general system of action. Although the general format remains unchanged, the categorization has been substantially revised since the last published version.[17] The revisions were largely a consequence of struggling with the analytical problems of defining the cognitive complex and the various input-output relations in which it was involved among the different subsystems at the general action level. The orienting change was to introduce the two categories of knowledge and competence in the A-L and A-G interchanges as product outputs of the behavioral organism—or "intelligence-cognitive" system—conceived as a subsystem with cognitive primacy. Much has been made of the parallel between knowledge and competence at the general action level and goods and services as corresponding outputs of the process of economic production. Once this identification of output categories had been worked out, three of the six interchanges fell into a pattern of order, namely, the three involving the A subsystem: A-L, A-G, and A-I. The other reordering developed from consideration of the L-I interchange. This involved the considerations that Durkheim raised about the internal environment of action and about the relation between the sense in which the acting participant in society was faced with that environment as a set of social facts[18] and as a normative structure which imposed its imperative by moral authority. Our view increasingly became that the L-I interchange was the focus of this syndrome; an implication of this then was that the moral problem involved the social level and therefore that our previous views about moral involvement in the L-G interchange had to be revised. This revision was formulated in the introductory section of Chapter 6. The G-I interchange system, which has remained stable through these processes of revision, formulates the context which Freud called the "object relations" of the individual personality.[19]

A few words should be said about the problem of affect, a difficult theoretical problem which has aroused controversy among members of the inner circle of action-theory people. Despite these controversies the authors of this book conclude that the conceptualization of affect as the medium anchored in the social system is correct. The reconsideration of the inter-

16. Clyde Kluckhohn, "Values and Value-Orientations in the Theory of Action: An Explanation in Definition and Classification," in *Toward a General Theory of Action*, ed. Talcott Parsons and Edward A. Shils (Cambridge, Mass., Harvard University Press, 1951).

17. John C. McKinney and Edward A. Tiryakian, ed., *Theoretical Sociology: Perspectives and Developments* (New York, Appleton-Century-Crofts, 1970).

18. Durkheim, *The Division of Labor*.

19. Talcott Parsons, "Freud's Theory of Object Relations," in *Social Structure and Personality* (New York, The Free Press, 1964), chap. iv.

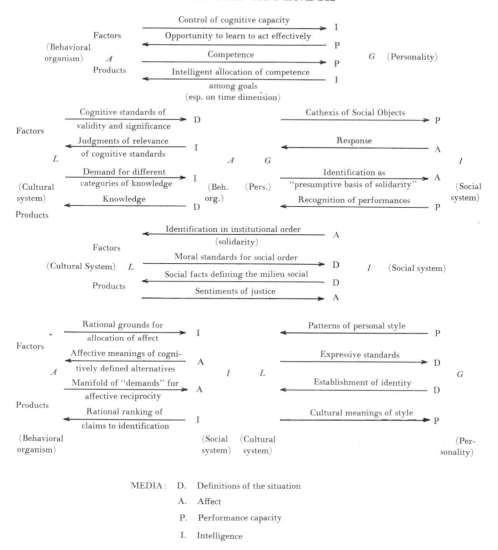

MEDIA: D. Definitions of the situation

A. Affect

P. Performance capacity

I. Intelligence

Figure A.7. General Action-Level Interchanges

change system at the general action level has confirmed our original allocation and has clarified the grounds of its theoretical legitimacy. If the G-I interchange were considered by itself, it might be thought a toss-up in which direction the affect-performance-capacity exchanges went. The theoretical question involves the involvement of affect in the two other interchange systems: the L-I and A-I interchanges. In L-I, affect involves the institutionalization of solidarity in relation to the moral standards of a cultural order and regulates the acceptance of involvement in solidarity reinforced by sentiments of justice. The A-I interchange system underlies our

439

analysis of the relations between the cognitive complex and affective engagement in cognitive pursuits in the setting of social community. Integration of affective concerns with the cognitive bases of the allocation of affect and loyalties is the key area in this respect.[20]

The media at the general action level are not entirely homologous with media at the social-system level. As J. G. Loubser has suggested, since the social system is treated as a subsystem of the general action system, certain constraints which operate at the social-system level should not be operative at the level of general action. This has proved to be a most fruitful suggestion.[21] We first worked with it in the attempt to take advantage of the parallels between money and intelligence as well as to take cognizance of the differences between them. Money as a medium of economic exchange is in the first instance used to acquire or transfer to others property rights in commodities. In a sense these are rights of exclusive possession at various levels. Knowledge, however, as an object of interchange in the cognitive system, is not in the same sense bought and sold though it is produced and transmitted through the teaching-learning relationship. The acquisition of knowledge from others does not require the abandonment of possession by the original possessor. A teacher can transmit knowledge to his students, but he does not thereby cease to *know* what he was talking about. We were careful to distinguish this higher degree of freedom at the general action level from any lifting of the constraint of scarcity with respect to intelligence as a medium. Scarcity in the intelligence case concerns the fact that problem-solving is an action process and, as such, takes time and consumes other resources. Instant problem-solving is not possible; wishing to know everything desirable to know without effort and without expenditure of resources does not produce results.

This principle of relation between the social-system level and that of general action has proved generalizable. Late in Chapter 2 we applied it to the relation between solidarity and influence on the one hand and identification and affect on the other. Solidarity is the constraint of integration at the societal level which does not operate at the level of general action. One can become identified with other persons at the general action level without undertaking the mutuality of obligation which solidarity entails. However, without that mutuality of obligation, one cannot speak of institutionalization, and such relations would, therefore, be inherently unstable.

When and if media for the other three subsystems of the general action system have been defined and analyzed, their operation will probably turn out to involve constraints of the same order relative to the general action media which have been found at the social-system level.

---

20. The theoretical problem is not yet resolved, but it may be possible to help by shifting the definition of affect more in the normative direction and that of performance-capacity in a direction emphasizing "motivation."

21. It has already been made use of in Chapters 2 and 6 of this book.

# TECHNICAL APPENDIX

## Intrasystem Exchanges and Temporal Changes of the Inflationary and Deflationary Trends, Post-World War II, 1964 and 1968–1970 (as analyzed in Chapter 7)

The following diagrams can only be appreciated in concert with other media exchanges illustrated in the technical appendix. We focus in this section on the exchanges of intelligence as anchored in the behavioral organism. Such a focus means that the adaptive subsystem at the general action level (the behavior organism) constitutes the point of reference of the analysis; in anthropological kinship terms the point of reference is "ego."

If the ego is anchored in the organism and its medium of interchange is intelligence, ego spends intelligence not only for cultural products and factors but also for personality and social-system products and factors. The organism exchanges intelligence with these other subsectors for performance-capacities and affect, the media anchored in these other subsystems, and for the particulars they control.

In an ideally balanced era (noninflated), the organism[22] expends intelligence proportionally for factors and outputs from all three subsystems: cultural, social, and personality. A cognitively inflated condition produces disproportionate expenditures. The organism exchanges intelligence in larger proportion for knowledge and for cognitive standards of validity and significance to the cultural system than for affective meaning of cognitively defined alternatives from the social system, for instance.

This picture of exchange internal to the general action level between the organism and the other three subsystems, complex as it is, does not exhaust inflationary distortions in the cognitive cultural direction. Simultaneously the cultural system invests intelligence inputs into cognitve symbolization, such as long-range knowledge production, rather than in expressive, moral, or constitutive symbolization. Since no one set of illustrations can portray the simultaneity of the qualitative exchanges and the relative quantitative changes at different times, we must simplify a complex story.

The Western tradition has experienced a mild but increasing inflationary cognitive trend: a creeping intelligence inflation for almost three hundred years. The rapid growth of higher education, the large number of participants, and the demands for knowledge production on the cultural system since World War II intensified this cognitive inflationary trend. The demands for intelligence inputs between World War II and 1964 increased the scarcity and thus raised prices for intelligence inputs into the personality and social systems. The growing need of the cultural system for intelligence was the straw that broke the camel's back. However, the events over the

22. The relation between the "behavioral organism" as formally presented in Figure A.6 above and the functional category "cognitive" is not yet fully worked out. The concept "intellect" seems to be important, perhaps as a zone of interpenetration between organism and personality.

last decade or so began to redress the inflationary process both among systems at the general action level and internal to the cultural system by a deflationary countermovement, as we have stated in Chapters 7 and 8.

Following World War II the exchange between the cultural system and the organism was only mildly inflationary. The lines between the systems indicate a normal balance of exchange between the culture and the organism.

Coincidentally, the interchanges of intelligence for affect between the organism and the social system were also relatively normal as were those between the organism and the personality. That is, the balance of exchange was at about the same intensity (see this appendix, Figure A.7, the A-I and A-G interchanges at the general action level).

By 1964, and despite the countermovement, inflation of cognitive culture had proceeded quite far, as is illustrated by the double black lines in Figure A.9 between the cultural system and the organism, suggesting the inflated character of the exchange.

Of major importance here are the exchanges between the social system and organism and between the personality and organism. In the latter exchange, for example, for large segments of the personality population, the personality was investing in a narrow range of goals ("intelligent allocation of competence among goals," in Figure A.7, G-A interchange) over a long period of time, thus delaying gratification in order to maximize particular types of competences (especially cognitive competences). This is illustrated below. (For the total interchange, see Figure A.7, G-A interchanges at the general action level.)

Between the social system and the organism, "rational ranking of claims to identification" and "rational grounds for allocation of affect" expenditures of intelligence were being sacrificed as were affective returns from the social system. (For diagramatic portrayal of the A-I interchange, see Figure A.7.)

By 1968–1970 the deflationary trend had become evident. The culture-organism interchange had either returned to the post–World War II level or had been even more deflated. (The post–World War II level of intelligence

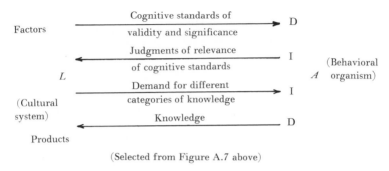

(Selected from Figure A.7 above)

Figure A.8. Post–World War II

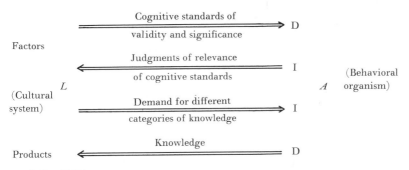

Figure A.9. 1964

*Note:* The four double black lines are meant to indicate a feature of an inflationary state of the system where orderly directionality of the movement of interchange components has broken down.

expenditure is being used as the standard by which to gauge monetary inflation.) The deflated situation is represented by the broken lines.

The demand for intelligence expenditure was shifted to those of community (I) and personality (G) as sources. Simultaneously, many of those attacking the culture were suggesting that intelligence inputs be shifted to noncognitive symbolizations.

Figure A.12, the equivalent at the general action level of A.4 at the social-system level, has had to be revised in two respects from the version presented in the McKinney and Tiryakian article.[23] In the first place, the two right-hand columns have been revised in the light of the revisions in Figure A.7; they do not require further comment because the principles on which the categories have been placed in the various boxes are exactly the same as were used in Figure A.4, and all of them will be found in the appropriate places in Figure A.7.

In the two left-hand columns, which deal with the code level, a further revision has taken place. As has been noted earlier, the term "code" is not meant in the technical sense in which that term is used in the expression "the genetic code." It follows the usage of Roman Jacobson and Morris Halle and other linguistic scientists in using "code" as distinguished from "message."[24] Code is a categorical framework at levels of vocabulary, grammar, and syntax which provides the frame of reference for the formulation of particular messages. As such, a code communicates nothing.

The problem which has to be faced was where to place subcategories of rationality, including cognitive rationality. In the earlier McKinney-Tiryakian version, subcategories of rationality had been placed in the L column.[25] This seems to have been erroneous. They should, we now think,

23. McKinney and Tiryakian, *Theoretical Sociology.*
24. Roman Jacobson and Morris Halle, *Fundamentals of Language* (The Hague, Mouton, 1956).
25. McKinney and Tiryakian, *Theoretical Sociology.*

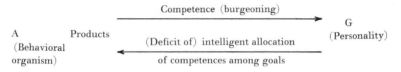

Figure A.10. The 1968–69 Turning Point

be regarded as *value* standards, and value standards at the general action level should be regarded as equivalent to coordinative standards at the level of the social system. Therefore, they should be placed in the integrative column. On this basis, it seems plausible to introduce Weber's two categories of *Zweckrationalität* and *Wertrationalität*.[26] The term rationality could also have been used in the integrative cell, but something like harmonization seemed mor appropriate. However, harmonization comes close to a synonym of integration. Its focus lies in the social system as part of general action; it has integrative functions for the general action system and not only internally to itself. This column, in the A cell, was the appropriate place to put the category, *cognitive rationality*.

The pattern-maintenance column, then, essentially takes up the category of meaning and attempts to subdivide it according to the four functional references of the action system. Appropriately, the category of cognitive validity and significance, so important to us throughout the book, falls neatly into the classification of meaning types in the A cell. A category of meaning is not only one of mode of orientation but it has normative significance. We would like to relate this placing to the problem of objectivity and the relation of cognitive objectivity to values in the last section of Chapter 2.

## Unresolved Problem Areas

The formalized materials reviewed in this appendix and diagrammatically presented in Figures A.1 through A.8 are incomplete compared with what a complete paradigmatic formalization of the action system would require. Several gaps need to be filled in order to approach a higher level of completeness. One gap is that the level of formalization presented here is worked out only for two out of the five action systems which figure prominently in our analysis, namely, the general system of action and the social system. For the other three, the cultural system, the personality system, and the behavioral organism, the structural paradigm has not been carried beyond the first level of breakdown, that is, into four subsystems. This should be attempted at the next level down, that is, into a sixteen-cell structural table. The difficulties which have been encountered, however, in carrying the structural analysis as far as we have, even for two systems of

26. Weber, *Theory of Social and Economic Organization*, chap. i, sec. 2, pp. 115–118.

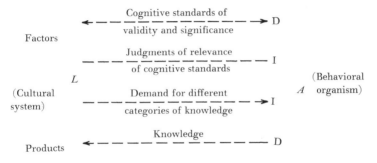

Figure A.11. 1968–1970

action, warn us that this task should not be undertaken lightly, but will require much hard analytical work.

This is still more the case for the dynamic aspect of the paradigm. Ideally, there should be complete identification of symbolic media and characterization of interchange sets for each of these other three subsystems of the general action system. The amount of work that went into the revision of the version of the interchange paradigm for the general action system between the form presented in the McKinney-Tiryakian volume[27] and that presented in the present version is another index of the magnitude of the task. This revision would have to be worked out for three analytically distinct systems in such a way as to link adequately with the state of knowledge in three not closely integrated fields, namely, a boundary zone of anthropology and of culturally oriented disciplines, of the psychology of personality, and, finally, of certain aspects of psychology and human biology. The three resulting paradigms must then be related with each other and with the two already worked out, especially that of general action. This is a formidable task; a level of formalization comparable to the one presented here for two subsystems could not be accomplished without a great deal of work.

A second problem area still imperfectly worked out concerns the setting of action in its environment. The relation to the physical environment, for example, in ecological fields, involves the relations of action to the biosphere. We have stressed the continuity of the characteristics of living systems throughout organic and sociocultural evolution. An assertion of such continuity is somewhat less programmatic today than it used to be because some important connections can now be established. Nevertheless, this is still an incomplete field. The progress of the theory of action depends on the adequacy with which these articulations can be worked out with aspects of the organization of subsymbolic behavior and on the relation of the behavioral reference to both genetic and physiological references in organic biology. The present book has not been concerned with these problems except peripherally, but the theoretical framework with which it operates articulates with these problem areas. The articulation which we anticipate

27. McKinney and Tiryakian, *Theoretical Sociology*.

| Media in hierarchy of control \ Components of media and interchange reciprocals | Code level — L Patterns of meaning | Code level — I Value standards | Message level — Factors controlled A (sources) | Message level — Products controlled G (destination) |
|---|---|---|---|---|
| **L** Definition of the situation | Constitutive grounds of meaning of human condition | *Wertrationalität* grounded in moral authority | Judgments of relevance of cognitive standards [A] — Identification in institutional order [I] | Demand for (different categories of) knowledge [A] — Sentiments of justice [I] |
| **I** Affect | Institutionalization of meaning relevant to society | Harmonization of identities grounded in social imperatives | Moral standards for social order [L] — Cathexis of social objects [G] | Social Facts— the milieu social [L] — Recognition of performance [G] |
| **G** Performance-capacity | Internalization of meaning relevant to personality | *Zweckrationalität* grounded in practicality | Response [I] — Control of cognitive capacity [A] | Identification [I] — Allocation of competence [A] |
| **A** Intelligence | Grounds of cognitive validity and significance | Cognitive rationality grounded in cognitive standards | Opportunity to learn [G] — Cognitive standards [L] | Competence [G] — Knowledge [L] |

Figure A.12. General Action Media as Sanctions

should be achieved in a nonreductionist way. The key to an understanding of the future of the university cannot be located in the neurophysiology of the human central nervous system without reference to psychological, sociological, and cultural considerations.

At the other end of the scale of evolutionary emergence lies the problem of adequate theoretical analysis of the boundary problems of action in the direction of what in Figure A.6 is called the area of "ultimate concern." Such scholars as Robert Bellah, with conceptions like symbolic realism,[28] are performing work that promises clarification in these areas relative to the older philosophical traditions of Western society. However, this clarification will also prove to be a complicated task; codifiable results will probably not be forthcoming for a considerable period.

A similar set of problems arises from the attempt to diagram the relation-

---

28. Robert N. Bellah, "Religion and Social Science," in *The Culture of Unbelief*, ed. R. Caporale and A. Grumelli (Berkeley, Calif., University of California Press, 1971), chap. xiv.

ships we are dealing with on two dimensions only. These problems involve the fact that cybernetic hierarchy is not a simple system of absolute domination of the higher-order elements over the lower but of certain kinds of control intricately interwoven with bases of autonomy of the cybernetically lower-order components and subsystems. We illustrated this with institutionalized individualism, a concept prominent in this book. The cybernetic control-condition distinction relates to the information-energy distinction; its further refinement and clarification will be necessary. The cybernetic-control distinction relates also to the system of cultural meanings and the code framework within which meanings are organized and to the genetic component in the determination of the characteristics of species and individual organisms at the organic level. Genetic patterning is fundamentally related to cultural patterning, which in turn is fundamentally related to the cybernetic idea. Still, much remains to be done in this area.

Finally, this problem area is related to our concern with the process of institutionalization, that is, to the way in which the cultural components of the cognitive complex are organized as integral parts of going social systems and become relatively stabilized. Further clarification in this area will help in resolving problems of the modes of integration of action systems and, relative to general action, of social systems. One consideration is the sense in which a society like that of the contemporary United States can or cannot be characterized as having a common value-system. In the sense that we discussed it in Chapter 2, it can. However, such a society is not characterized by flat uniformity of shared values; variability is of substantial significance. This significance is connected with our views about the pluralistic structure of the society. Pluralism in turn relates to the problems of cybernetic control and of the ranges of autonomy relative to it as well as to the forces making for structural change at several different levels.[29]

The above is not an exhaustive catalogue of areas in which the paradigm of the theory of action is incomplete. We are aware of this incompleteness and indeed of other inadequacies, as, for example, possible bias. However, improvement of the state of knowledge in this, as in other areas, depends on adequate communication among the groups with the interest and competence to deal seriously with such problems. Therefore, incomplete as our theory is, we are laying our conceptual cards on the table in order to promote further thought and work.

29. See Robin Williams, "Change and Stability in Values and Value Systems," in *Stability and Social Change*, ed. Bernard Barber and Alex Inkeles (Boston, Mass., Little, Brown and Co., 1971), pp. 123–159. Also, Edward A. Shils, "Centre and Periphery," in *The Logic of Personal Knowledge: Essays Presented to Michael Polanyi* (London, Routledge and Kegan Paul, 1961), pp. 117–131.

# INDEX

# INDEX

Academic community: place of in societal community, 203–209; suggested changes in, 347–348

Academic freedom, 123, 128; and opportunity for achievement, 148–149; and core sector, 153–157; and tolerance of diversity, 199; and rights for individual political opinion, 293; as framework for influence, 309; essentiality of, 364–365. *See also* Tenure

Academic professionalism: and the cognitive complex, 109–110; components of, 141

Academic system: output categories of, 260–262, 361, 381; societal inputs in, 262–265; more than a power system, 305n; internal and external outputs of, 361; adaptive upgrading of, 381; culmination of educational revolution, 387; and socialization complex, 409–419. *See also* Higher education; University, modern

Academics: professionalization of, 123–124; stress on cognitive primacy by, 230. *See also* Faculty members; Intellectuals

Access, presumptive right of, 358–359

Accounting, profession of, 100, 248

Achievement: academic freedom as opportunity for, 148–149; rewards for, 157; differential, 177

Action: defined, 8; internal environment of, 83; Smelser on theory of, 390. *See also* Action systems

Action systems, 8–26; cultural system, 8, 15; social system, 9, 15; personality system, 9, 15; behavioral organism, 9, 15; structure of, 15; environments of, 22–23, 30–31; place of integration in, 23–24; symbolic media of, 24–25, 267; Smelser on, 390–391

Activism, student, 215–224. *See also* Conflict

Adams, Brooks, 120n

Adams, Henry, 120n

Adams, John, 120n

Adaptation, 13–14

Administration, profession of, 100, 248–249, 255

Administration, university: stratification of, 135–136; power of, 136–137; increased differentiation in, 380

Administrative assistants, 407–408

Adolescence, and studentry, 164

Adorno, T. W., 179n, 210n

Affect, 83–86; as symbolic medium, 24, 84, 267; as mode of integration, 83–84; as medium of interchange, 305, 310, 395–396; relation of intelligence to, 326, 330; and alienation, 331–332; anchorage of in social system, 332n; and frustration, related to socialization, 412

Affective banking, 195–196

Affective complex, complement to cognitive complex, 190, 195

Age, of university students, 376. *See also* Studentry

Agnew, Spiro, 280n

Alienation, 167; defined, 331; symptom of inflation of affect, 331–332; new conception of, 385; and fragmentation of faculty role, 408–409

Allen, John William, 277n

Amnesty, student, 343n

Application of knowledge, training in, 6

American Academy of Arts and Sciences, 120n

American Philosophical Society, 120n

Amherst College, 353

Anthropology: rise of, 287; broadening of issues in, 296

Applied case, 117–118

Applied professions, 104; function of in university, 94; divisions of, 97–98; training for, 97–100; structure of world of, 231; engineering, 233–234; architecture, 234–235; medicine, 235–236, 239–241; law, 236–238, 241–246; primary and secondary education, 246–247; social work, 247–248; administration, 248–249; clinical priorities of, 249–256; and the

# INDEX

# INDEX

University, public: growth in size of, 415; transfer and drop-out rates of, 415–416

University system: development of, 4–6; graduate and undergraduate training in, 5; crisis of, 27

Utilitarianism, 284

Value-commitment, 268–270; as medium of interchange, 305; inflation-deflation of, 320, 326; and fiduciary subsystem, 332

Value-generalization, 383–384

Value-pattern, 38; and anthropology, 296–297

Value-system, 38

Values: internalization of, 216, 410; conflicts in, 396

Veysey, Laurance R., 353n

Viet Nam War, 340n, 344n

Wage income as societal input, 262–263

Wald, George, 201n

Warren, Bruce L., 214n

Warren, Earl, 245n, 253

Watson, James D., 138n

Weber, Max, 139n, 215, 275; on Protestantism and industry, 43, 44, 120; on the ideal type, 59, 158; on nonempirical belief systems, 62; on rationalization, 63, 190, 320; on rationality, 81–82, 96, 117; on value-neutrality of science, 86–88; on value relevance of knowledge, 104; on meaning of the human experience, 253–254; on legitimation of authority, 261; on bureaucracy, 284n

Weinstein, Fred, 164n, 167n, 181n, 331n; on change in society, 346n

Welfare professions, 100, 247–248, 255. *See also* Social work

*Wertrationalität*, 190

White, Winston, 38n, 189n

Whitehead, Alfred N., 63n, 64n

Whyte, William Foote, 213n

Williams, Robin M., 34n

Williams College, 353

Wilson, Robert C., 180n, 201n

Wisconsin, University of, 5, 413

Women, inclusion of, 376

Wright, Charles R., 170n, 213n

Yale University, 5

Zloczower, Abraham, 172n

*Zweckrationalität*, 190

463